INUYASH

VOL. 45

Shonen Sunday

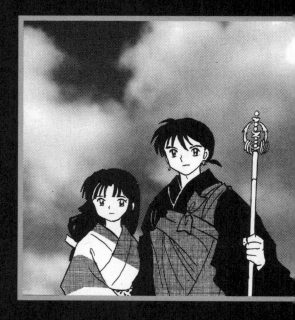

STORY AND ART BY
RUMIKO TAKAHA

CONTENTS

THE STORY THUS FAR

Long ago, in the "Warring States" era of Japan's Muromachi period, dog-like half demon Inuyasha attempted to steal the Shikon Jewel—or "Jewel of Four Souls"—from a village. The village priestess, Kikyo, put a stop to his thievery with an enchanted arrow. Pinned to a tree, Inuyasha fell into a deep sleep, while mortally wounded Kikyo took the jewel with her into her funeral pyre. Years passed...

In the present day, Kagome, a Japanese high school girl, is pulled down into a well and transported into the past. There she discovers trapped Inuyasha—and frees him.

When the Shikon Jewel mysteriously reappears, demons attack. In the ensuing battle, the jewel *shatters*!

Now Inuyasha is bound to Kagome with a powerful spell, and the grudging companions must battle to reclaim the shattered shards of the Shikon Jewel to keep them out of evil hands...

LAST VOLUME The battle rages on against Inuyasha's archenemy Naraku, who covets the shards of the Shikon Jewel... A mysterious demon attacks a pack of wolf demons related to Inuyasha's rival, Koga. In the ensuing battle, Moryomaru enters the fray, young wolf demon Shinta is taken hostage, and Koga ends up at a terrible disadvantage. Inuyasha and the others rescue their friends, but at the price of Moryomaru obtaining the Shikon shard given to Kai! Is this what Naraku intended all along...?

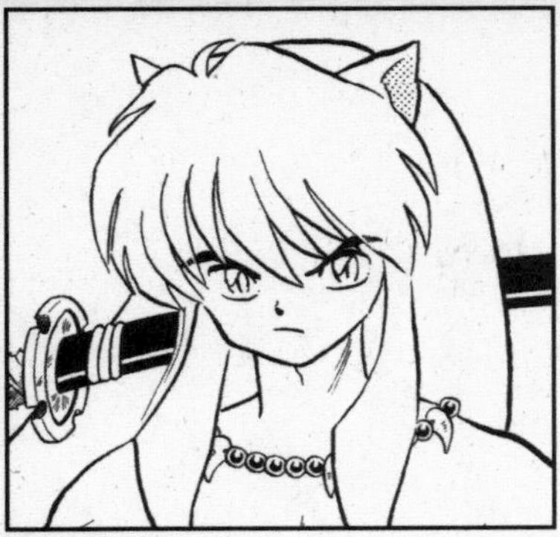

INUYASHA
Half-demon hybrid, son of a human mother and demon father. His necklace is enchanted, allowing Kagome to control him with a word.

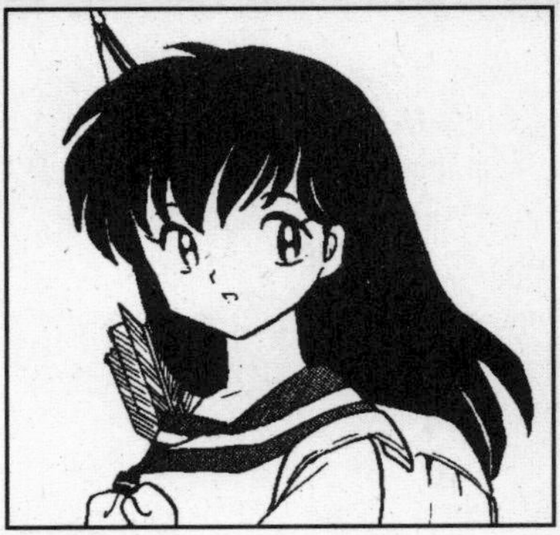

KAGOME
Modern-day Japanese schoolgirl who can travel back and forth between the past and present through an enchanted well.

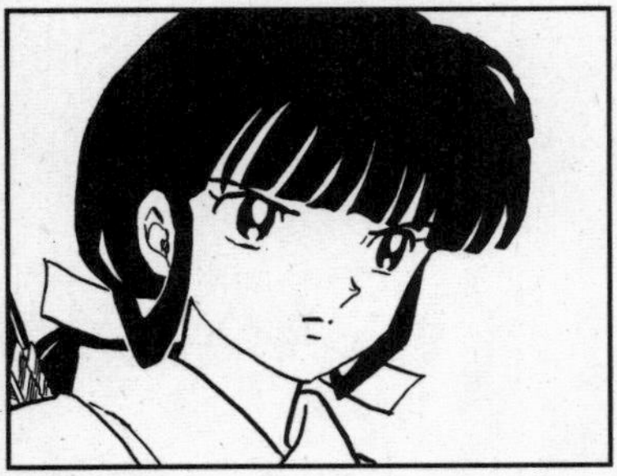

KIKYO
A powerful priestess once in charge of protecting the Shikon Jewel who has been brought back to life. Kagome is her reincarnation. Naraku, disguised as Inuyasha, killed her, and she seeks revenge.

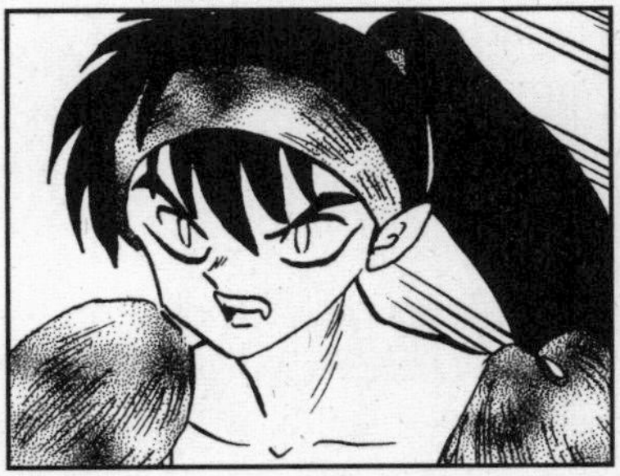

KOGA
Leader of the Wolf Clan, Koga is himself a wolf demon and, because of Shikon shards in each of his legs, possesses super speed. Enamored of Kagome, he quarrels with Inuyasha frequently.

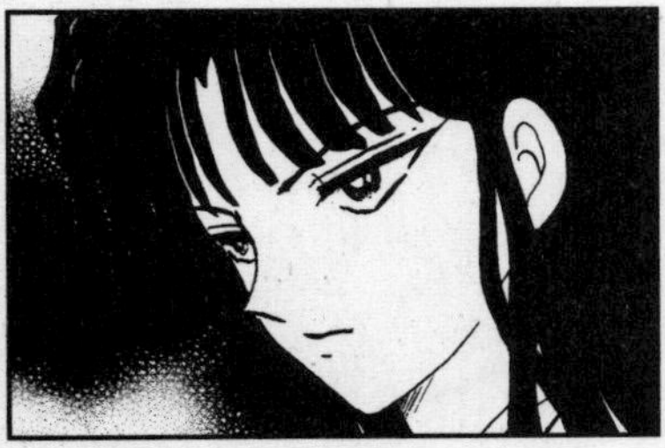

NARAKU
Enigmatic demon mastermind behind the miseries of nearly everyone in the story. He has the power to create multiple incarnations of himself from his body.

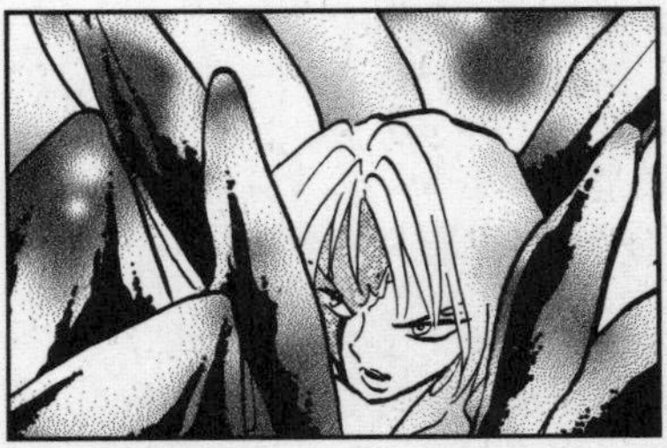

MORYOMARU
Has a deformed arm he got from protecting a shrine. In cahoots with Naraku. Immune to energy-based attacks.

SCROLL 1
YOMEIJU

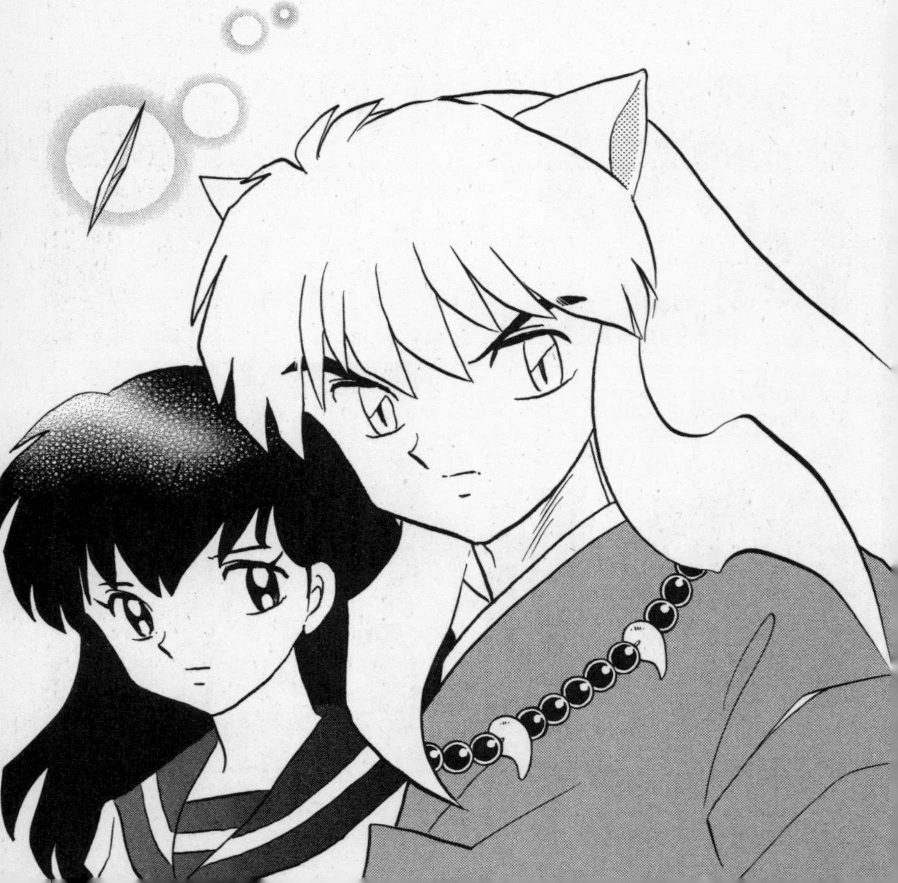

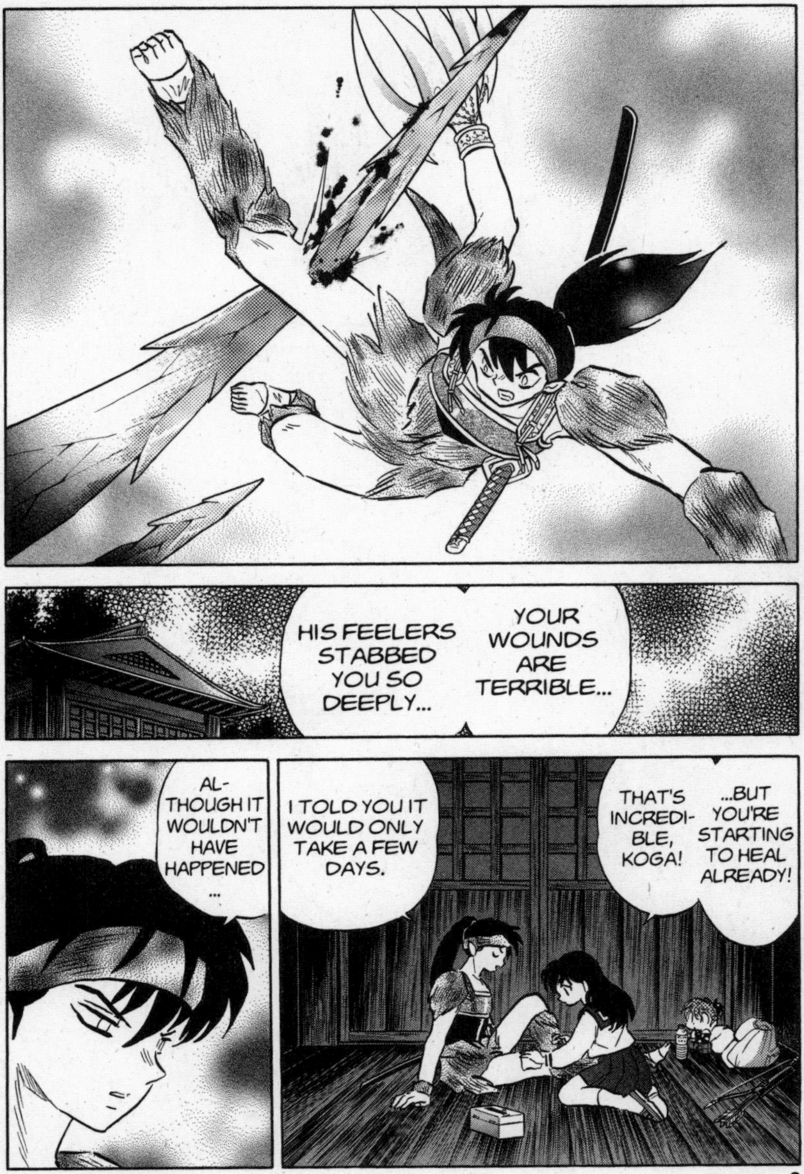
YOUR WOUNDS ARE TERRIBLE...
HIS FEELERS STABBED YOU SO DEEPLY...
...BUT YOU'RE STARTING TO HEAL ALREADY!
THAT'S INCREDI-BLE, KOGA!
I TOLD YOU IT WOULD ONLY TAKE A FEW DAYS.
AL-THOUGH IT WOULDN'T HAVE HAPPENED ...

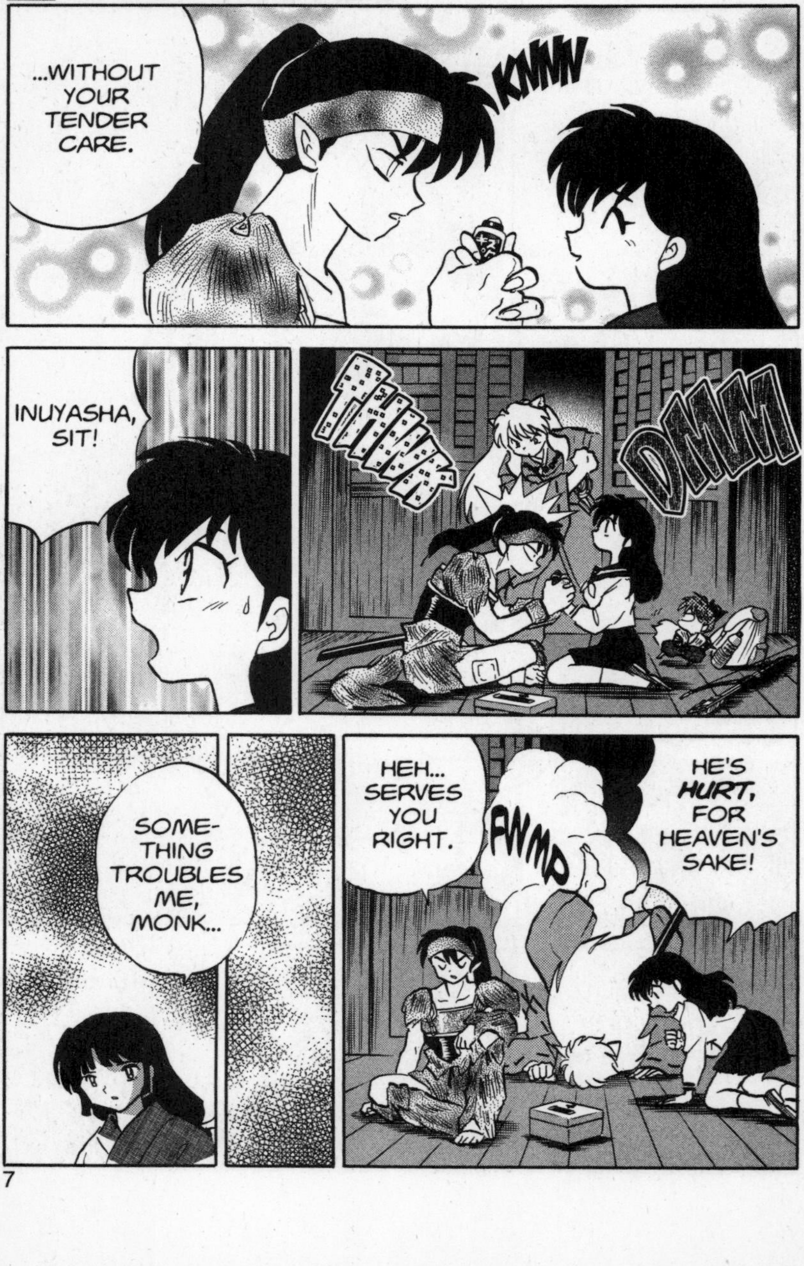
...WITHOUT YOUR TENDER CARE.
KNMN
DMMM
THWAK
INUYASHA, SIT!
HE'S ***HURT,*** FOR HEAVEN'S SAKE!
FWMP
HEH... SERVES YOU RIGHT.
SOME-THING TROUBLES ME, MONK...

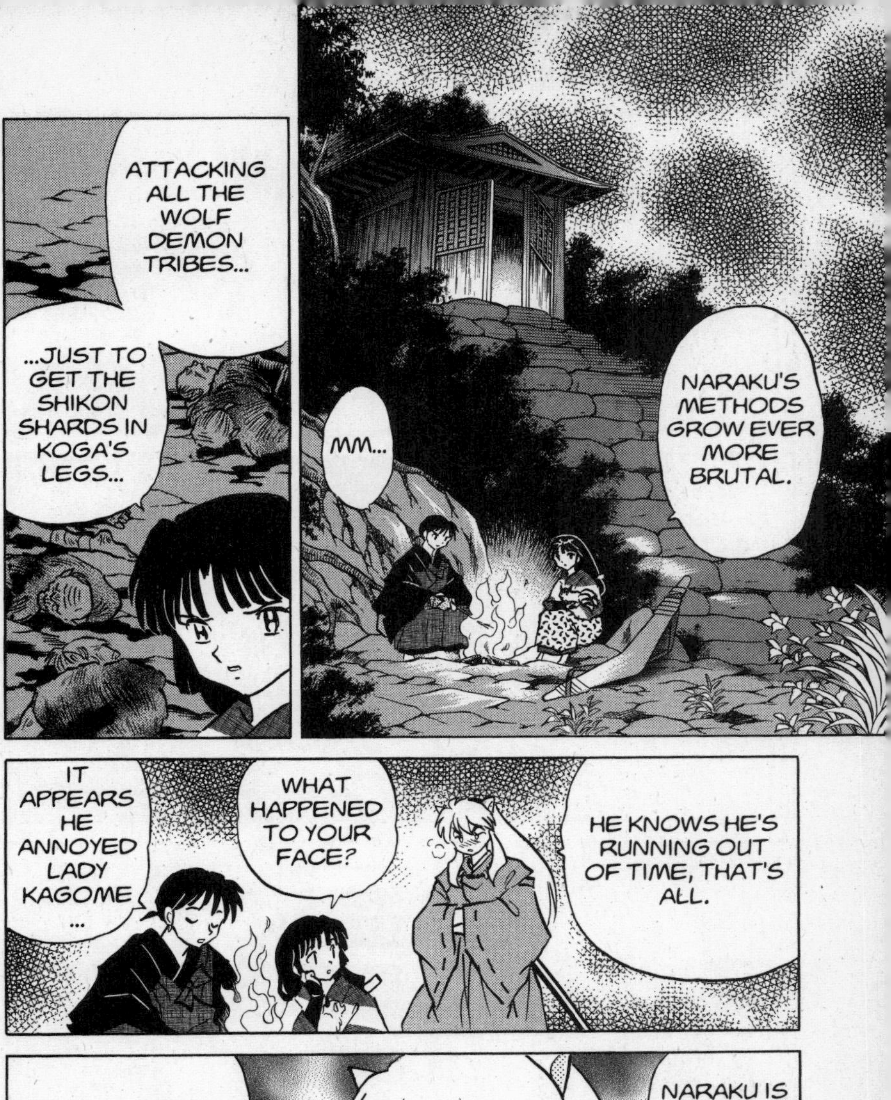
NARAKU'S METHODS GROW EVER MORE BRUTAL.
MM...
ATTACKING ALL THE WOLF DEMON TRIBES...
...JUST TO GET THE SHIKON SHARDS IN KOGA'S LEGS...
HE KNOWS HE'S RUNNING OUT OF TIME, THAT'S ALL.
WHAT HAPPENED TO YOUR FACE?
IT APPEARS HE ANNOYED LADY KAGOME ...
NARAKU IS GETTING FRANTIC.
I MEAN, HE SICS MORYOMARU ON ME...

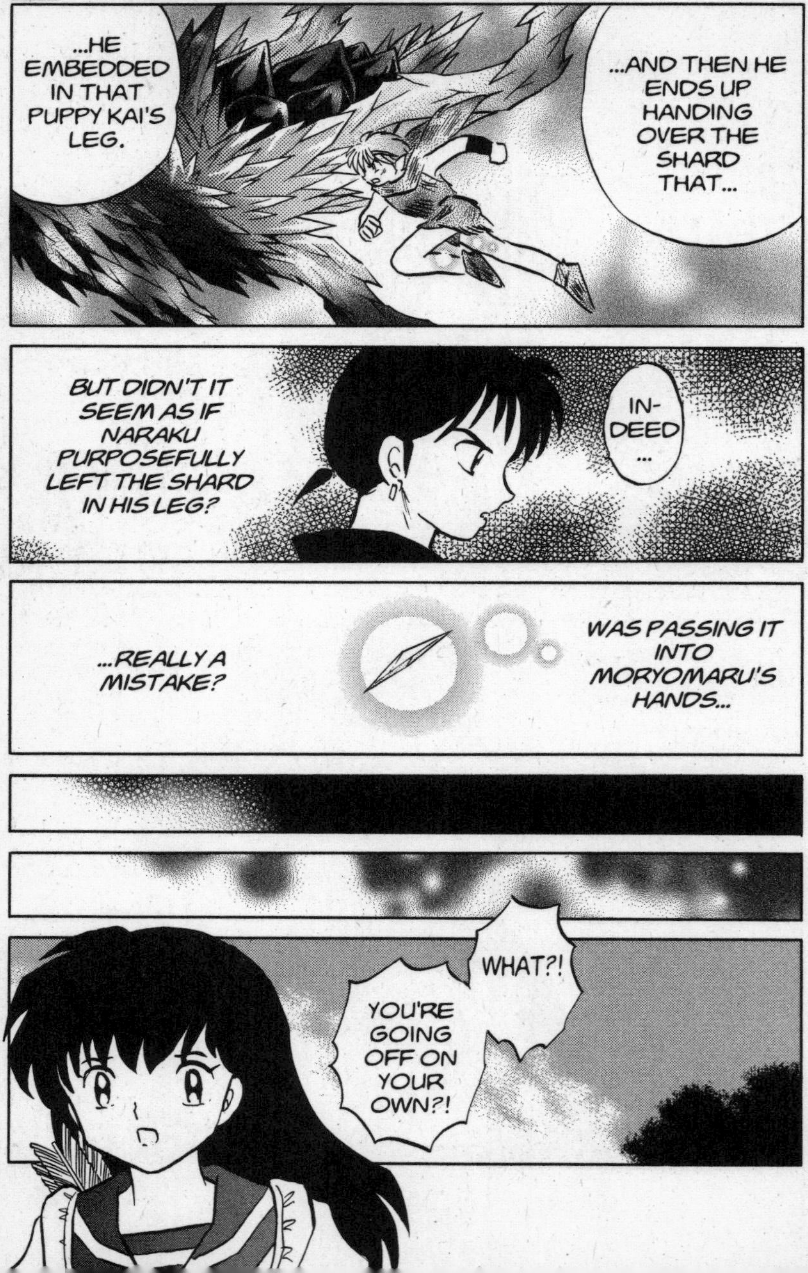
...AND THEN HE ENDS UP HANDING OVER THE SHARD THAT...
...HE EMBEDDED IN THAT PUPPY KAI'S LEG.
IN-DEED...
BUT DIDN'T IT SEEM AS IF NARAKU PURPOSEFULLY LEFT THE SHARD IN HIS LEG?
WAS PASSING IT INTO MORYOMARU'S HANDS...
...REALLY A MISTAKE?
WHAT?!
YOU'RE GOING OFF ON YOUR OWN?!

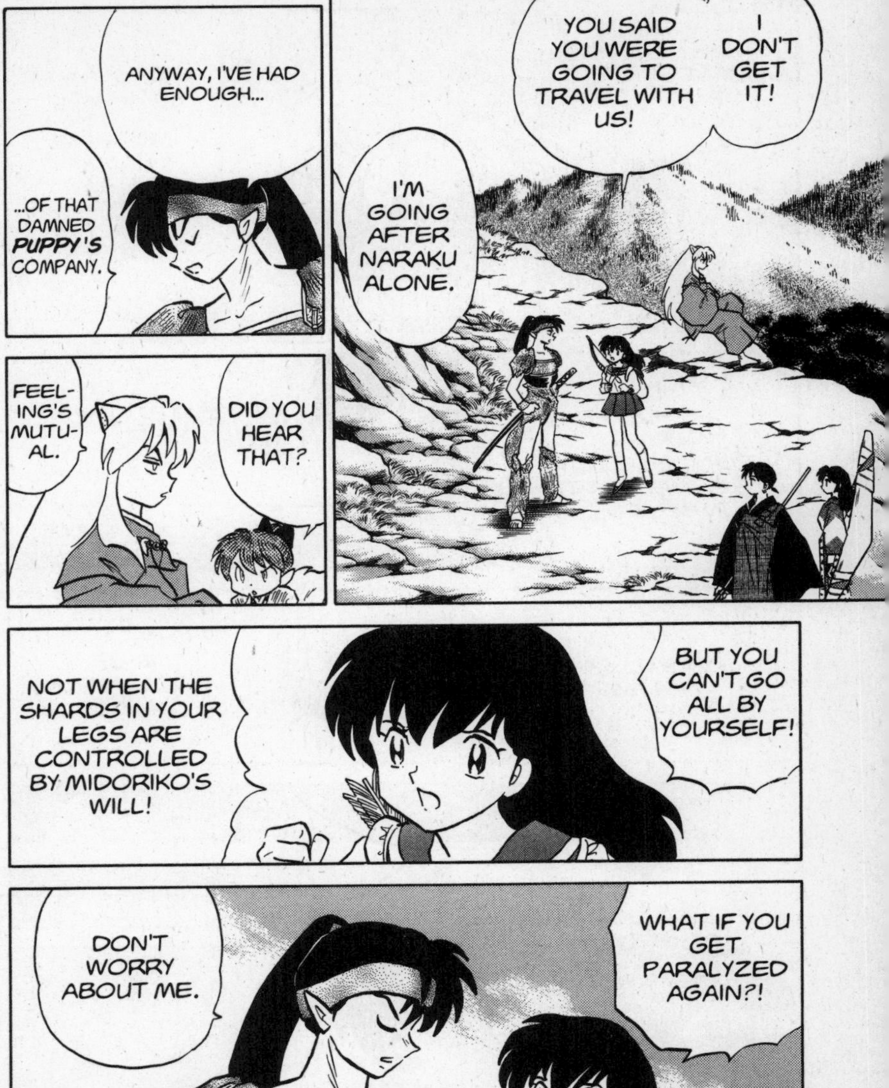
I DON'T GET IT!
YOU SAID YOU WERE GOING TO TRAVEL WITH US!
I'M GOING AFTER NARAKU ALONE.
ANYWAY, I'VE HAD ENOUGH...
...OF THAT DAMNED **PUPPY'S** COMPANY.
DID YOU HEAR THAT?
FEEL-ING'S MUTU-AL.
BUT YOU CAN'T GO ALL BY YOURSELF!
NOT WHEN THE SHARDS IN YOUR LEGS ARE CONTROLLED BY MIDORIKO'S WILL!
WHAT IF YOU GET PARALYZED AGAIN?!
DON'T WORRY ABOUT ME.

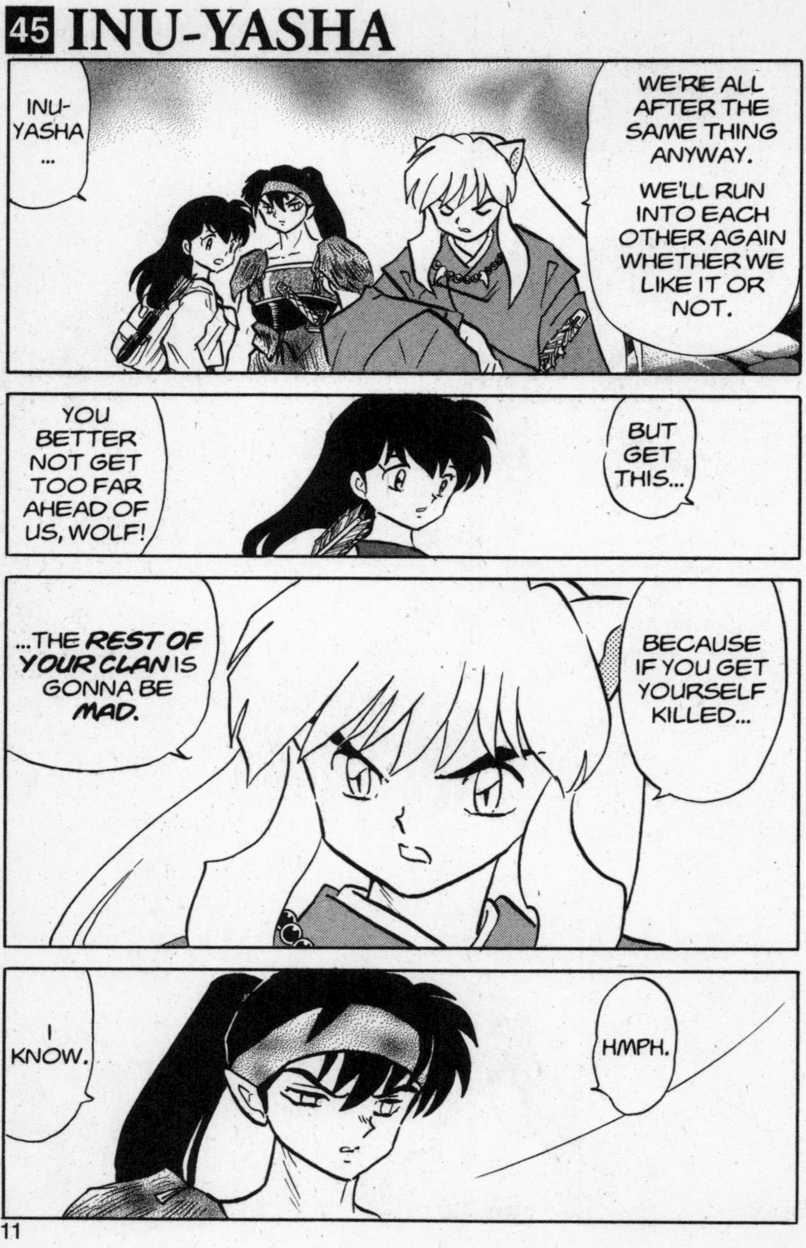
WE'RE ALL AFTER THE SAME THING ANYWAY.
WE'LL RUN INTO EACH OTHER AGAIN WHETHER WE LIKE IT OR NOT.
INU-YASHA ...
BUT GET THIS...
YOU BETTER NOT GET TOO FAR AHEAD OF US, WOLF!
BECAUSE IF YOU GET YOURSELF KILLED...
...THE **REST OF YOUR CLAN** IS GONNA BE **MAD**.
HMPH.
I KNOW.

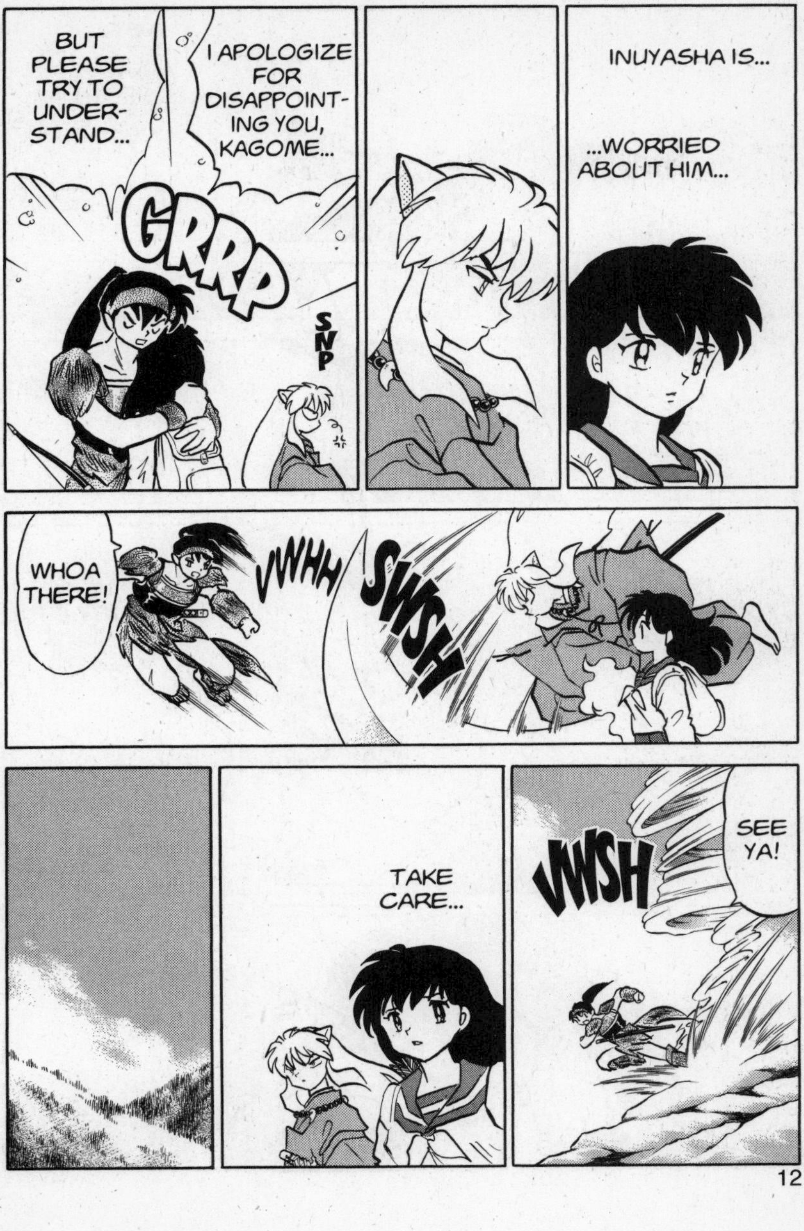
INUYASHA IS...
...WORRIED ABOUT HIM...
I APOLOGIZE FOR DISAPPOINT-ING YOU, KAGOME...
BUT PLEASE TRY TO UNDER-STAND...
GRRP
SNP
SWSH
VWHH
WHOA THERE!
SEE YA!
VWSH
TAKE CARE...

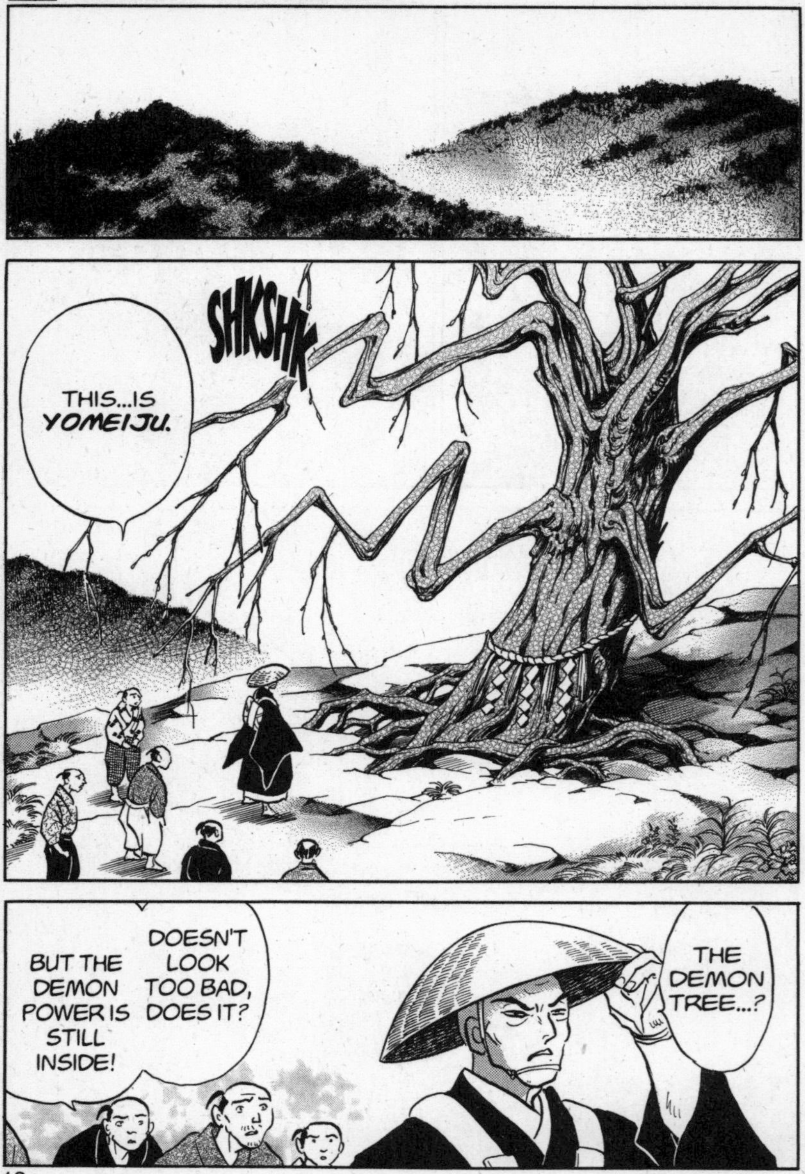
SHKSHIK
THIS...IS *YOMEIJU.*
THE DEMON TREE...?
DOESN'T LOOK TOO BAD, DOES IT?
BUT THE DEMON POWER IS STILL INSIDE!

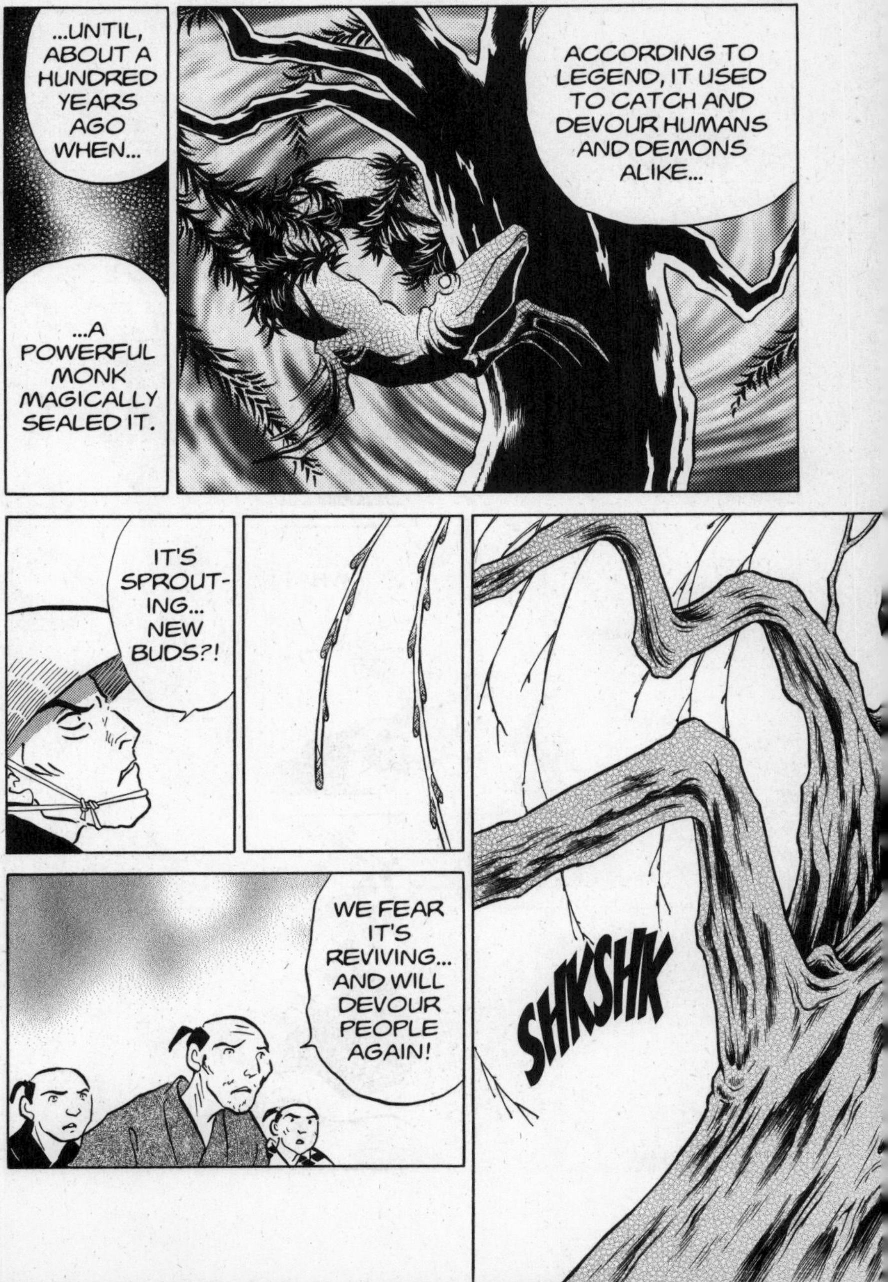
ACCORDING TO LEGEND, IT USED TO CATCH AND DEVOUR HUMANS AND DEMONS ALIKE...
...UNTIL, ABOUT A HUNDRED YEARS AGO WHEN...
...A POWERFUL MONK MAGICALLY SEALED IT.
SHKSHK
IT'S SPROUT-ING... NEW BUDS?!
WE FEAR IT'S REVIVING... AND WILL DEVOUR PEOPLE AGAIN!

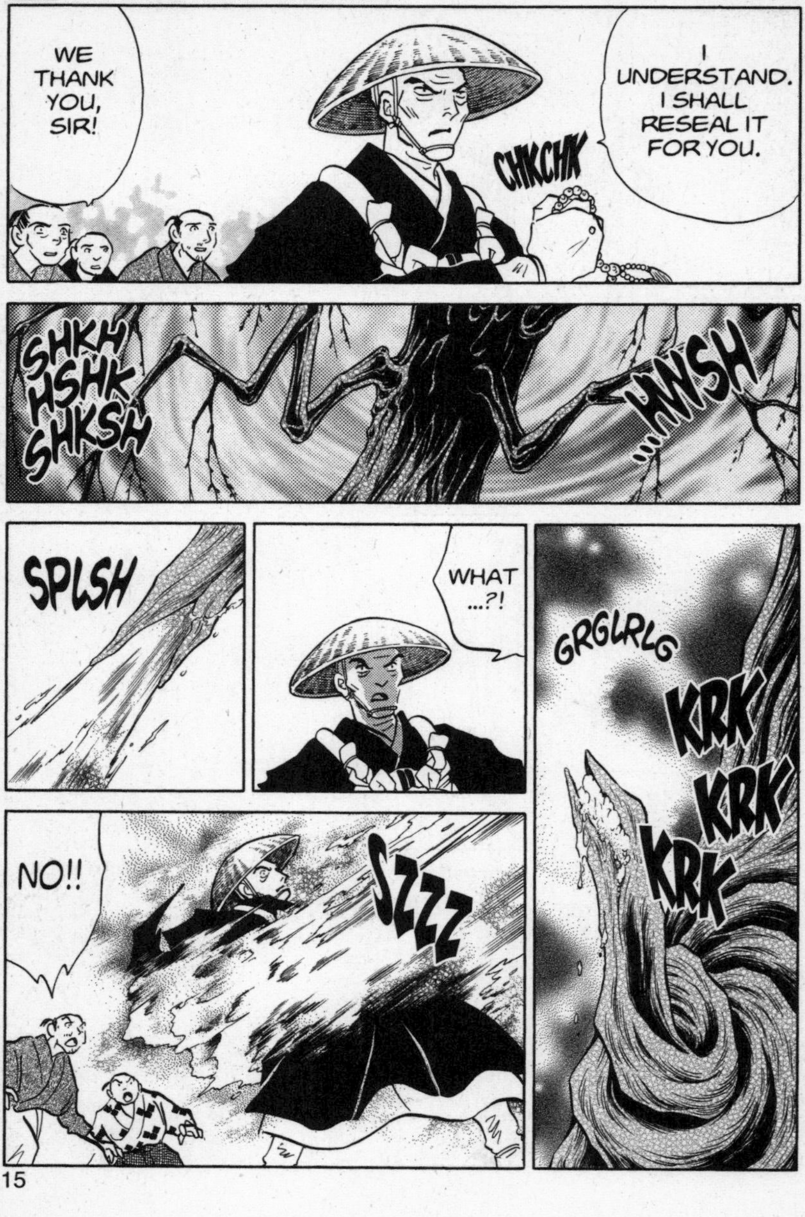
I UNDERSTAND. I SHALL RESEAL IT FOR YOU.
CHKCHK
WE THANK YOU, SIR!
...WHSH
SHKH HSHK SHKSH
GRGLRLG
KRK KRK KRK
WHAT ...?!
SPLSH
SZZZ
NO!!

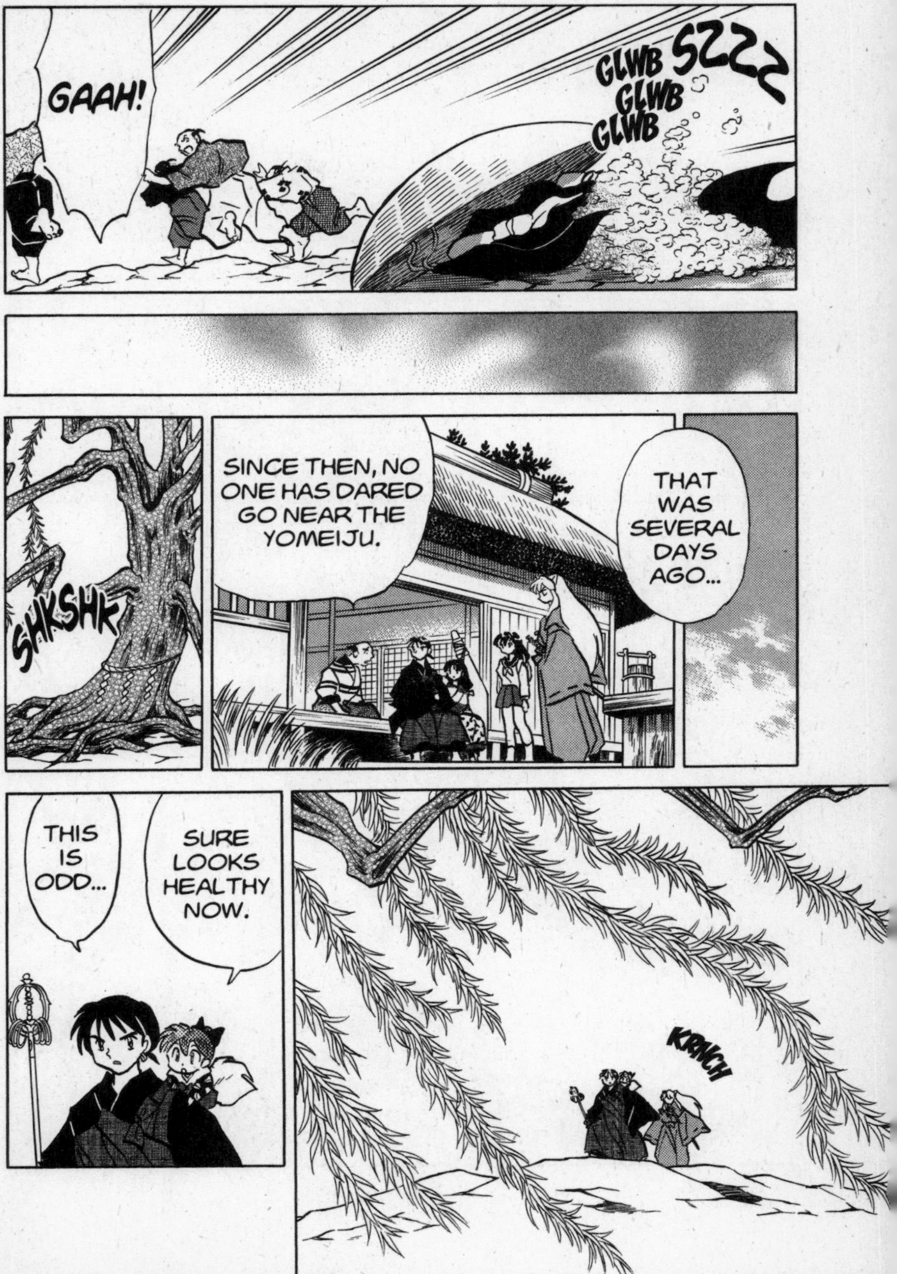
SZZZ
GLWB GLWB GLWB
GAAH!
THAT WAS SEVERAL DAYS AGO...
SINCE THEN, NO ONE HAS DARED GO NEAR THE YOMEIJU.
SHKSHK
KRNCH
SURE LOOKS HEALTHY NOW.
THIS IS ODD...

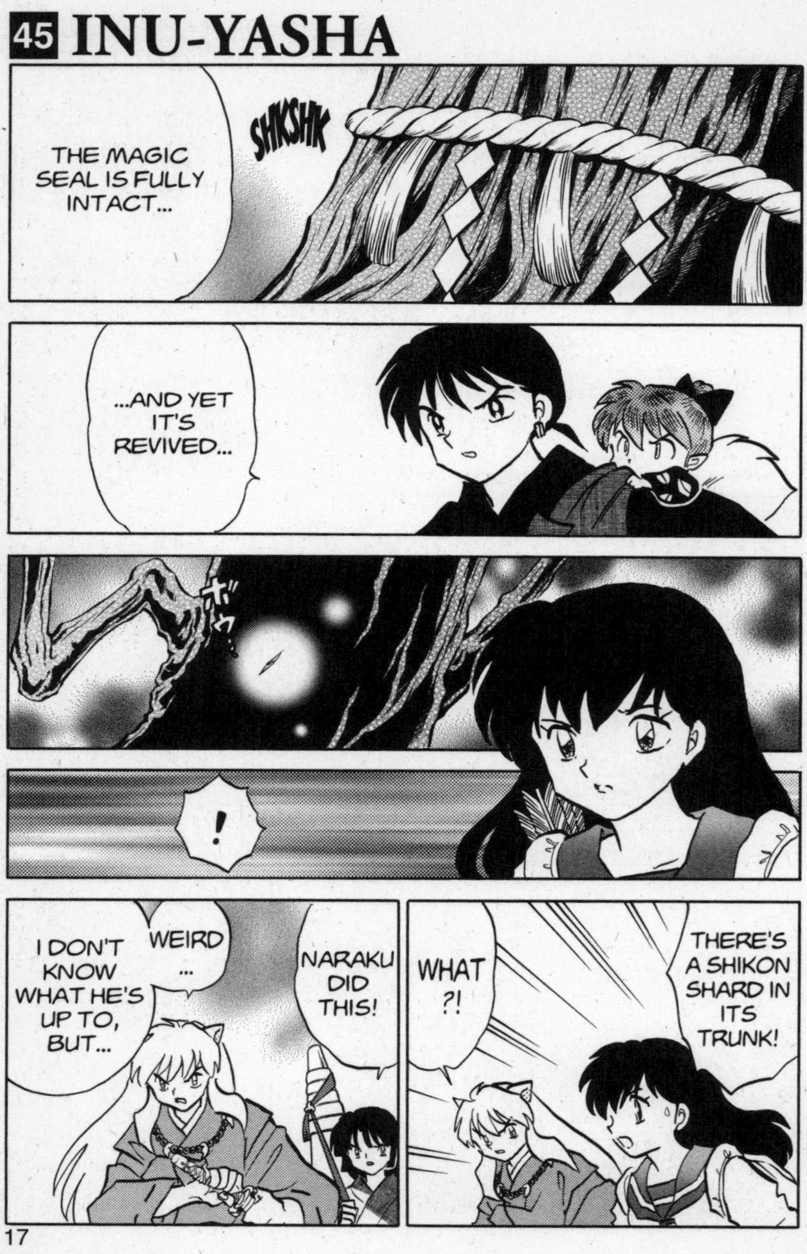
SHKSHK
THE MAGIC SEAL IS FULLY INTACT...
...AND YET IT'S REVIVED...
ボゥ
!
THERE'S A SHIKON SHARD IN ITS TRUNK!
WHAT ?!
NARAKU DID THIS!
WEIRD ...
I DON'T KNOW WHAT HE'S UP TO, BUT...

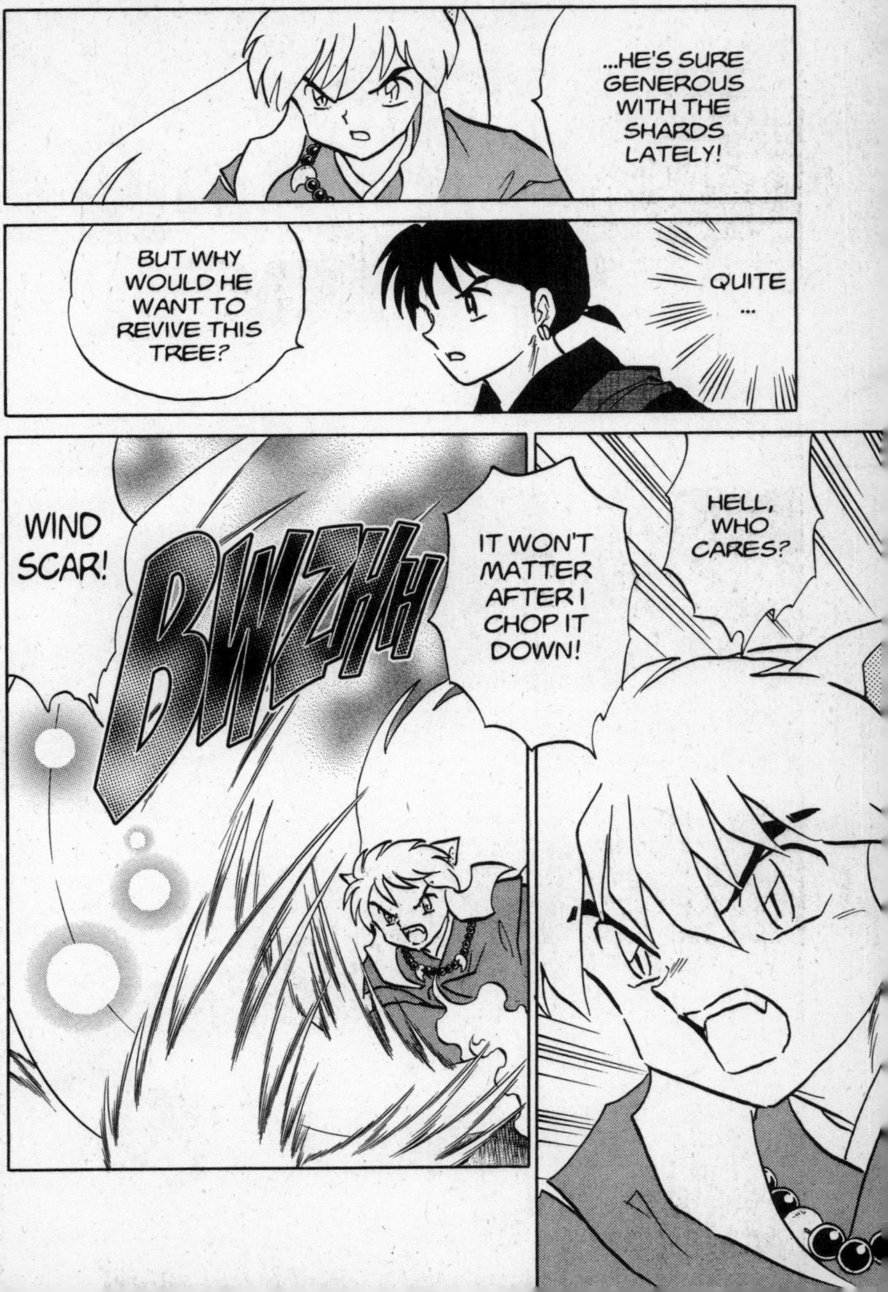
...HE'S SURE GENEROUS WITH THE SHARDS LATELY!
QUITE ...
BUT WHY WOULD HE WANT TO REVIVE THIS TREE?
HELL, WHO CARES?
IT WON'T MATTER AFTER I CHOP IT DOWN!
BWZHHH
WIND SCAR!

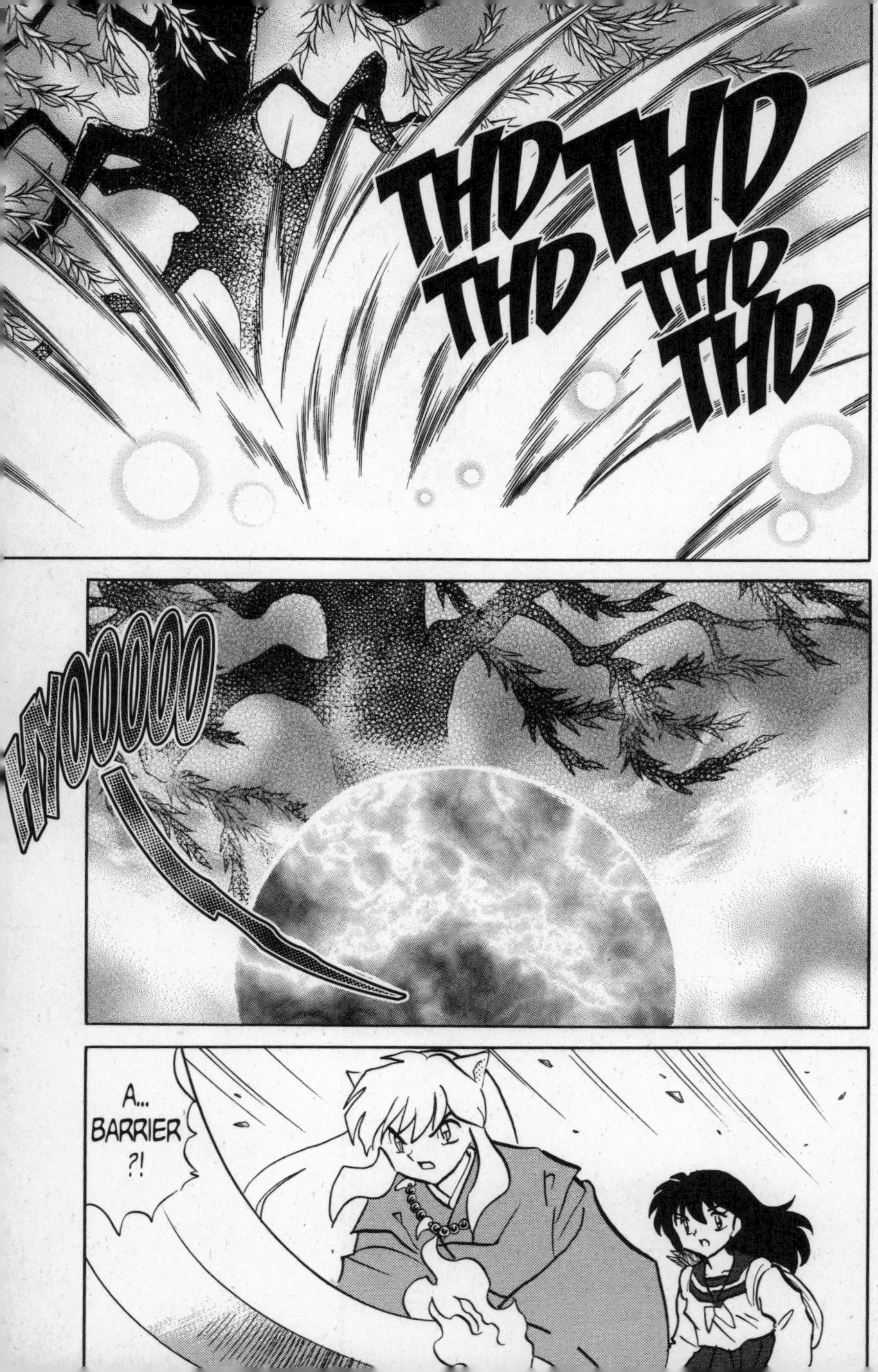
THD THD
THD THD
THD
HYOOOOO
A... BARRIER ?!

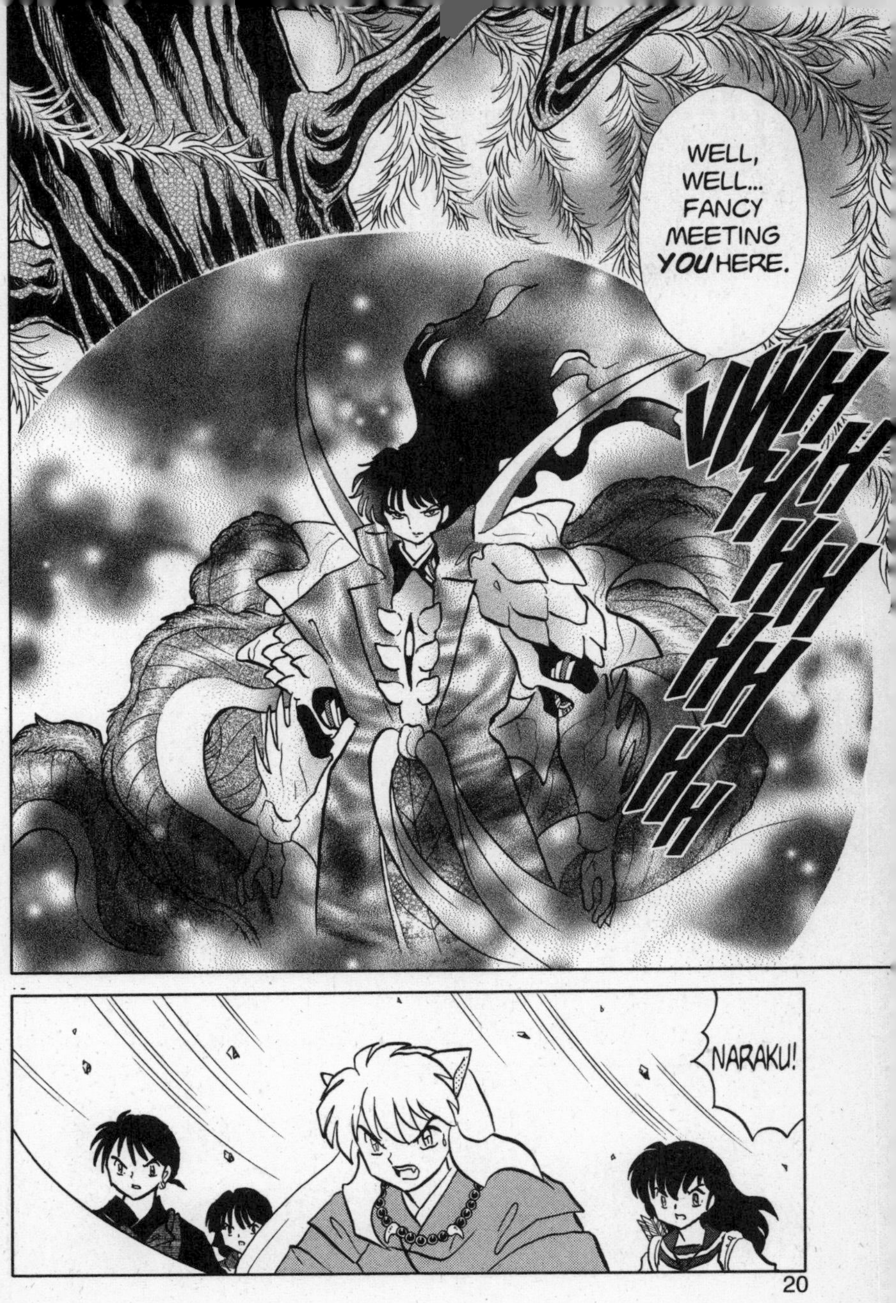
WELL, WELL... FANCY MEETING YOU HERE.
VWHHHHHHH
NARAKU!

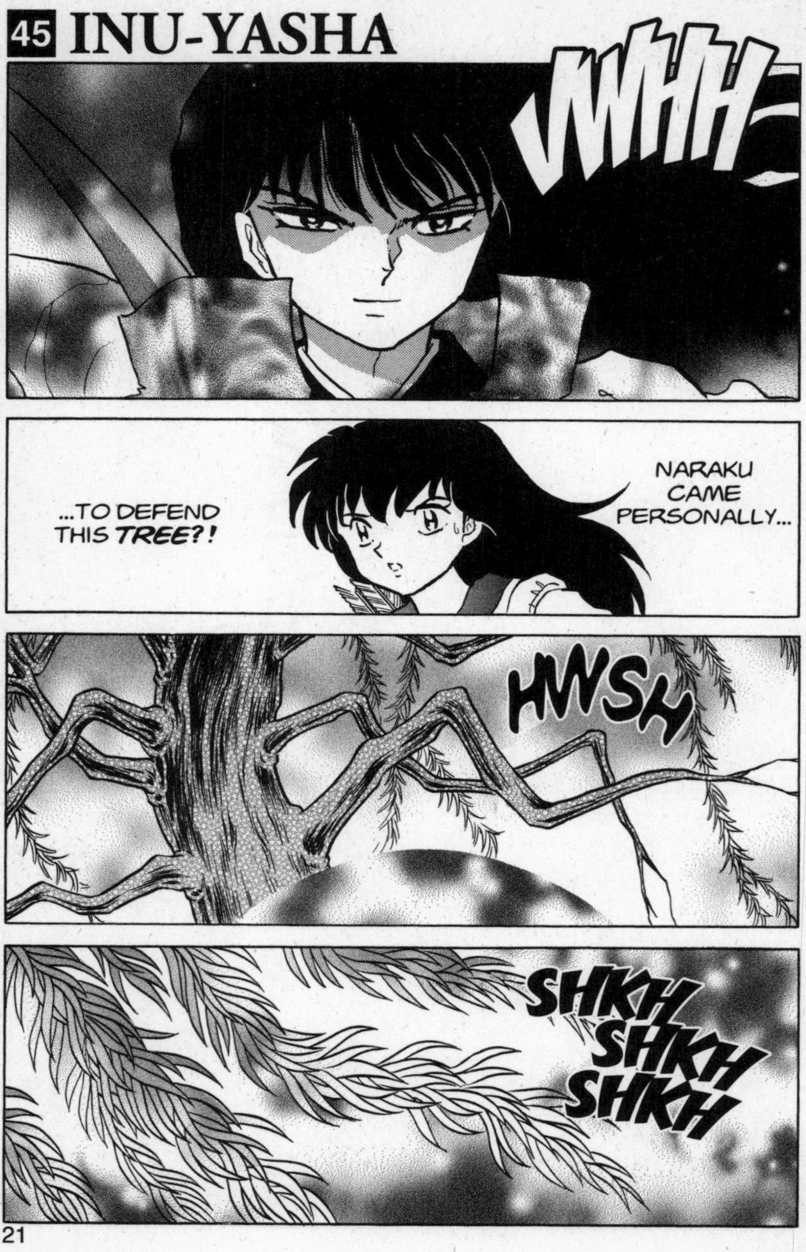
VWHH
NARAKU CAME PERSONALLY...
...TO DEFEND THIS TREE?!
HWSH
SHKH SHKH SHKH

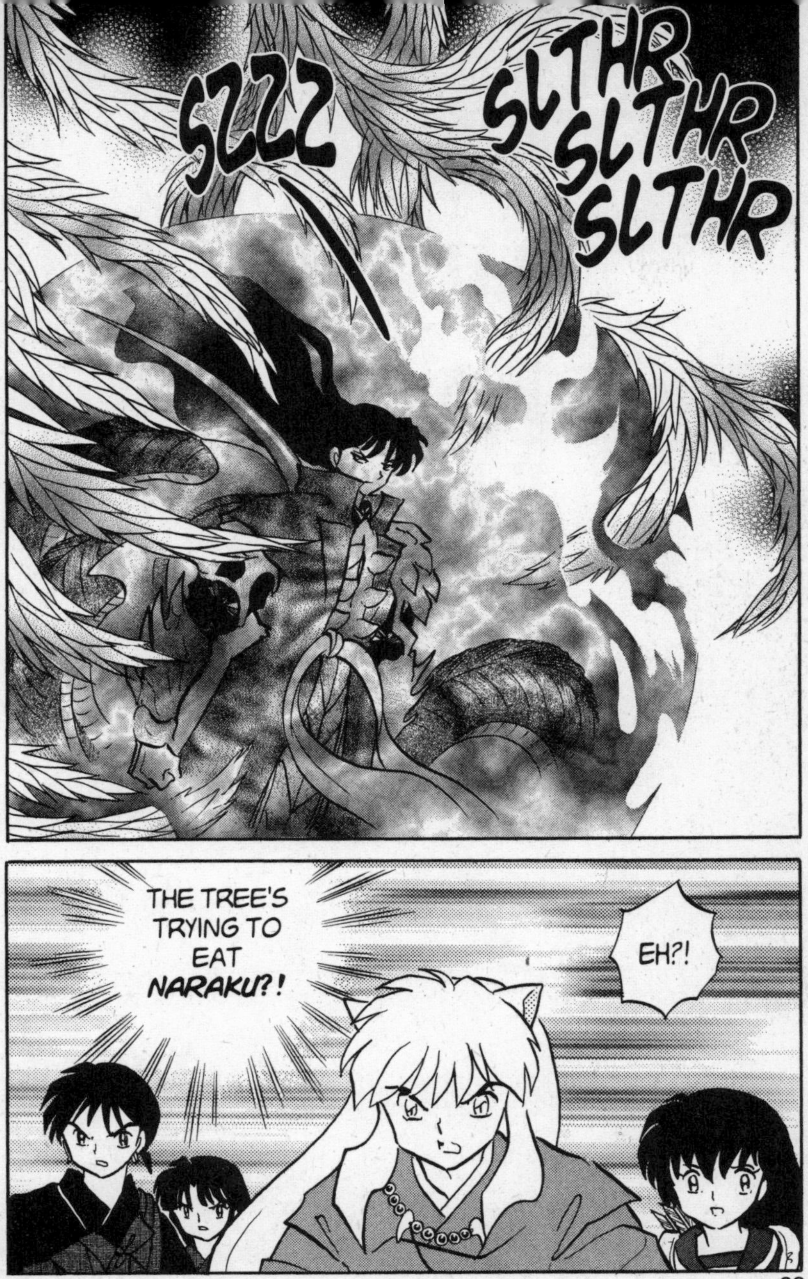
SLTHR SLTHR SLTHR
SZZZ
EH?!
THE TREE'S TRYING TO EAT NARAKU?!

SCROLL 2
YOMEIJU'S POWER

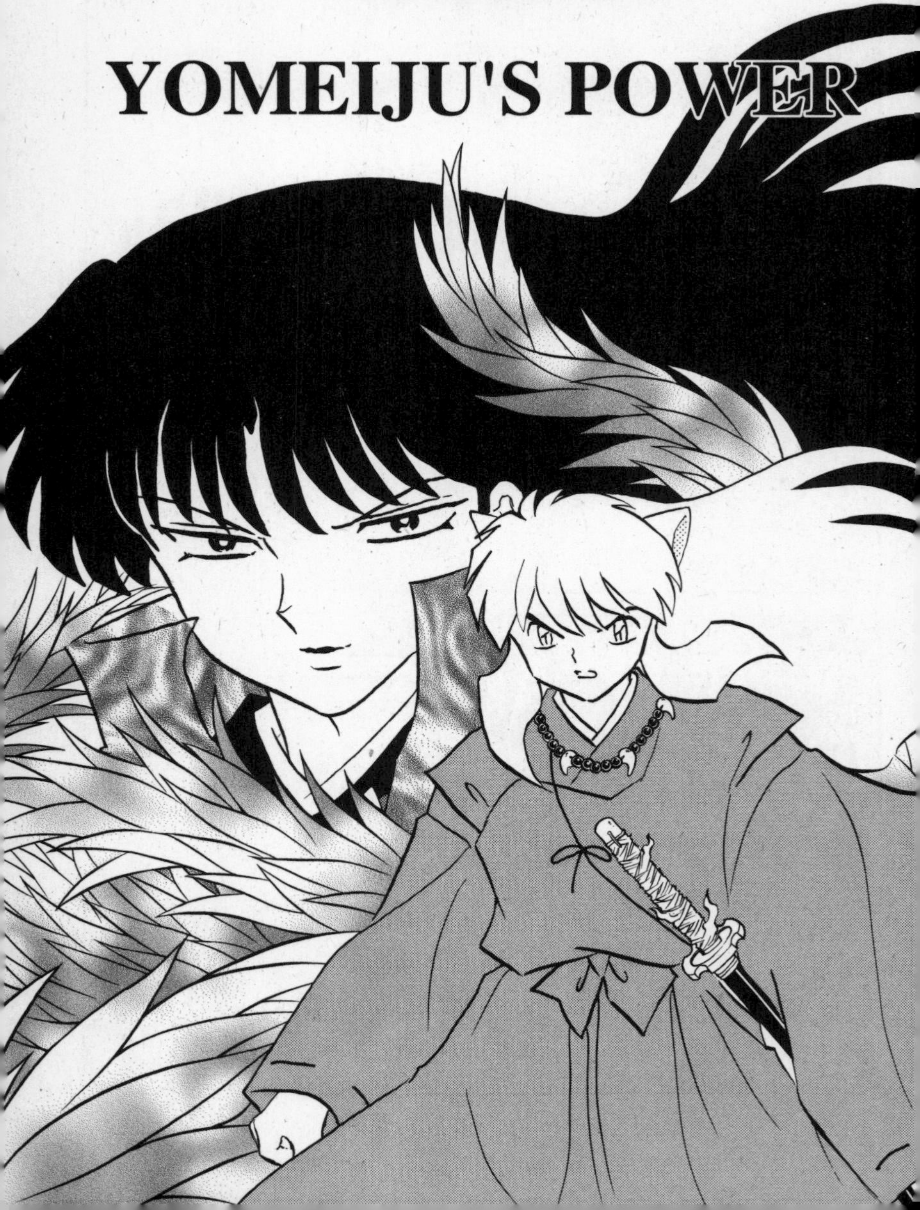

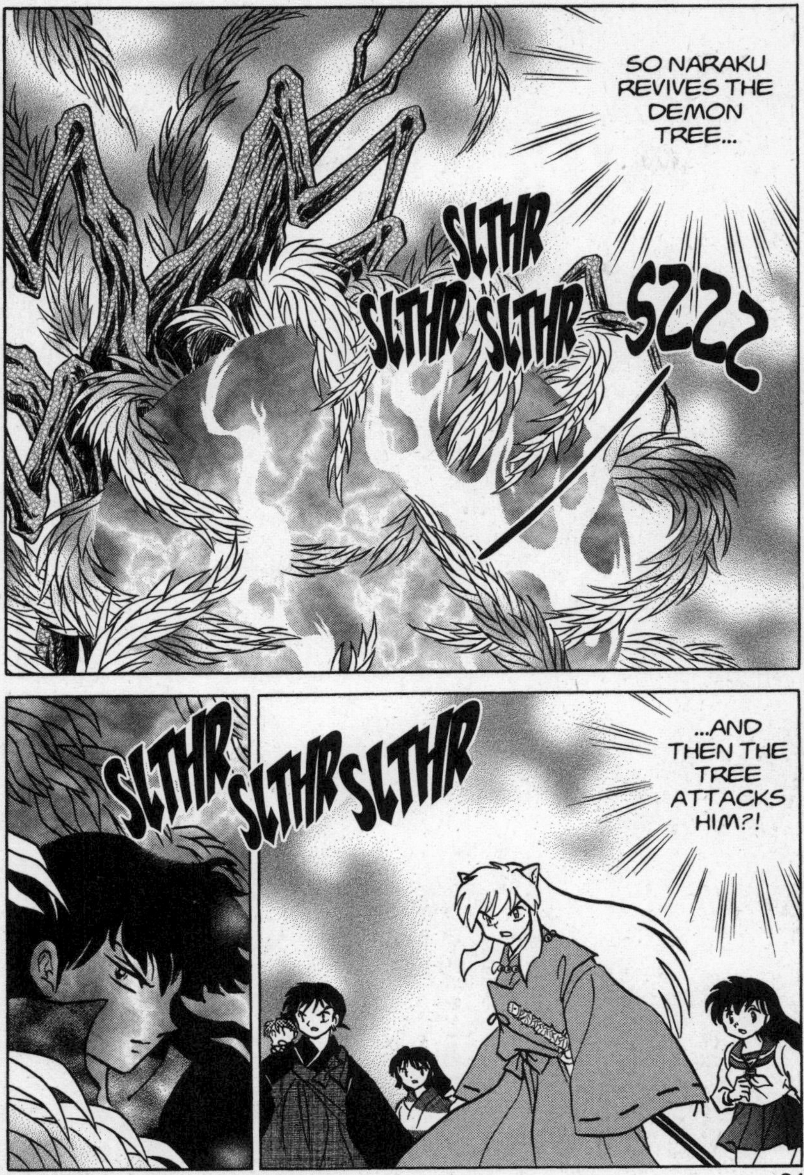
SO NARAKU REVIVES THE DEMON TREE...
SZZZ
SLTHR
SLTHR SLTHR
...AND THEN THE TREE ATTACKS HIM?!
SLTHR SLTHR SLTHR

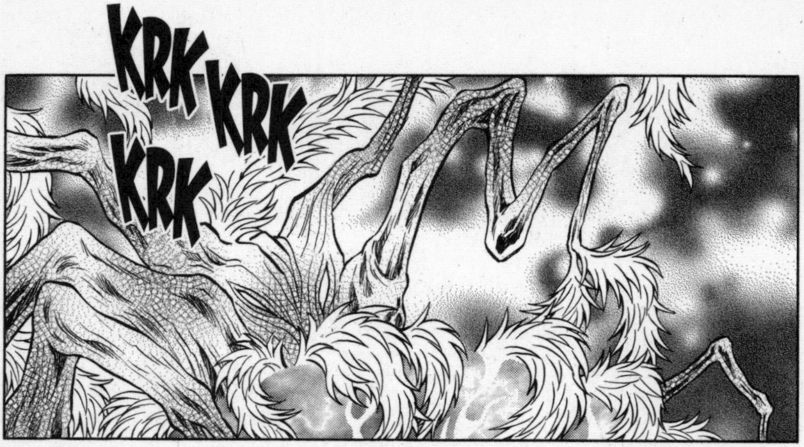
KRK KRK
KRK

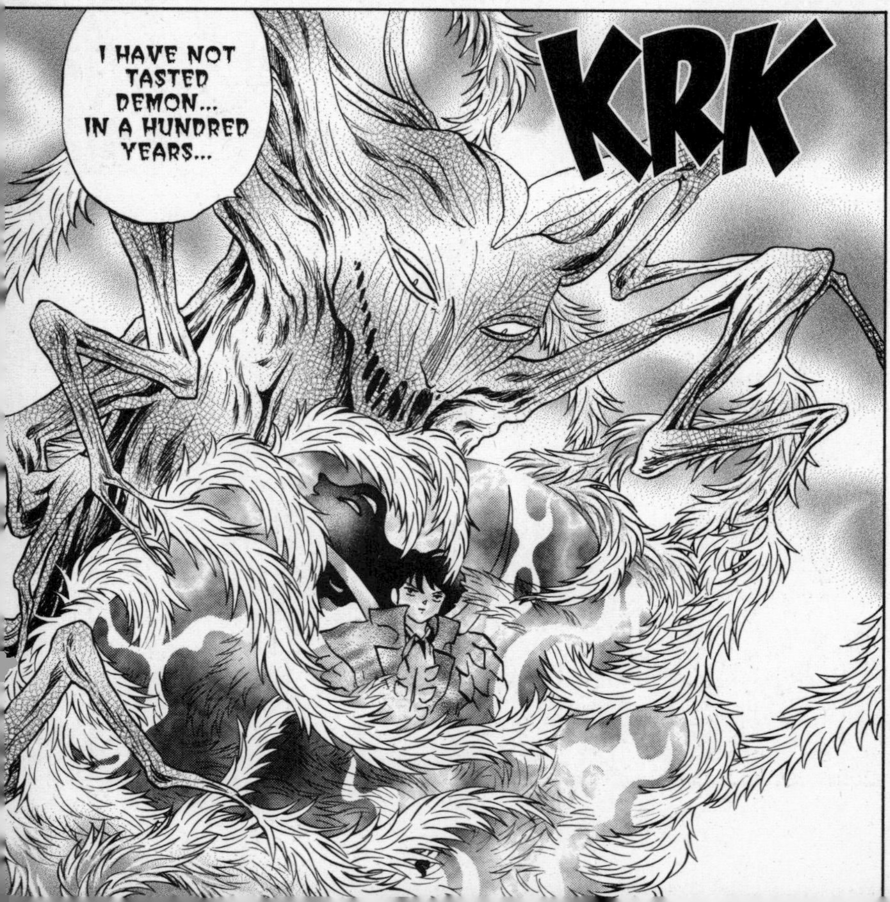
KRK
I HAVE NOT TASTED DEMON... IN A HUNDRED YEARS...

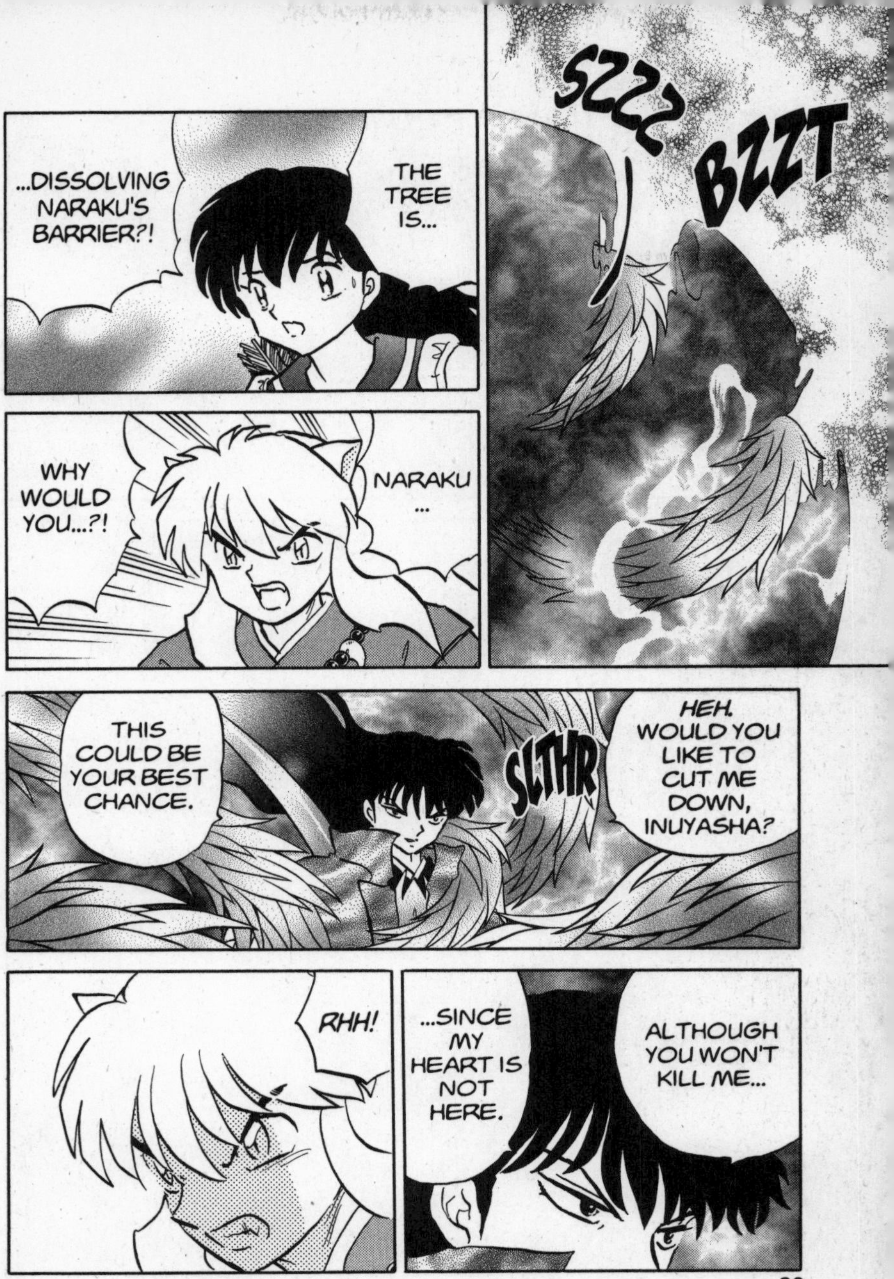
SZZZ
BZZT
THE TREE IS...
...DISSOLVING NARAKU'S BARRIER?!
NARAKU...
WHY WOULD YOU...?!
HEH. WOULD YOU LIKE TO CUT ME DOWN, INUYASHA?
SLTHR
THIS COULD BE YOUR BEST CHANCE.
ALTHOUGH YOU WON'T KILL ME...
...SINCE MY HEART IS NOT HERE.
RHH!

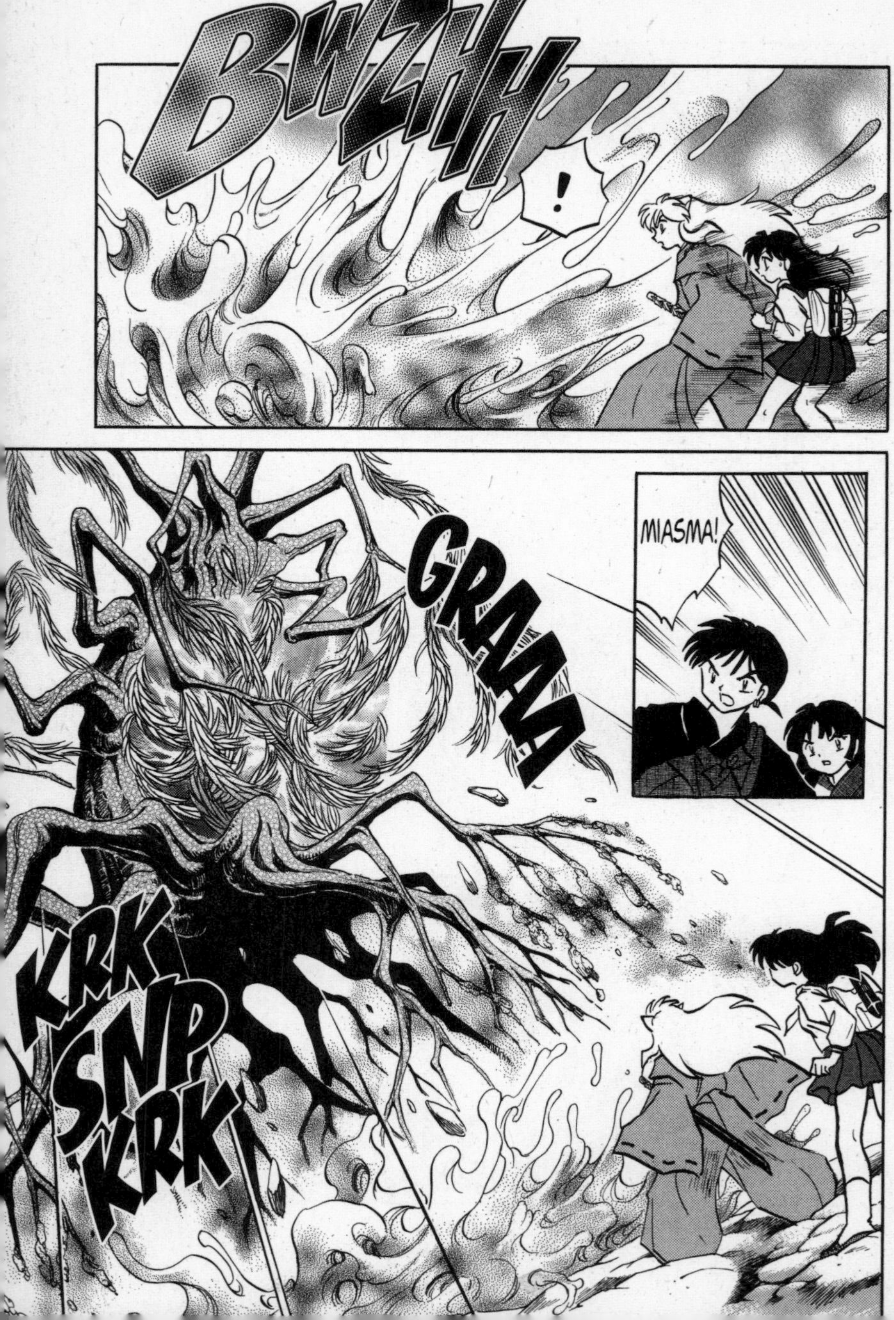
BWZHH
!
MIASMA!
GRAAA
KRK
SNP
KRK

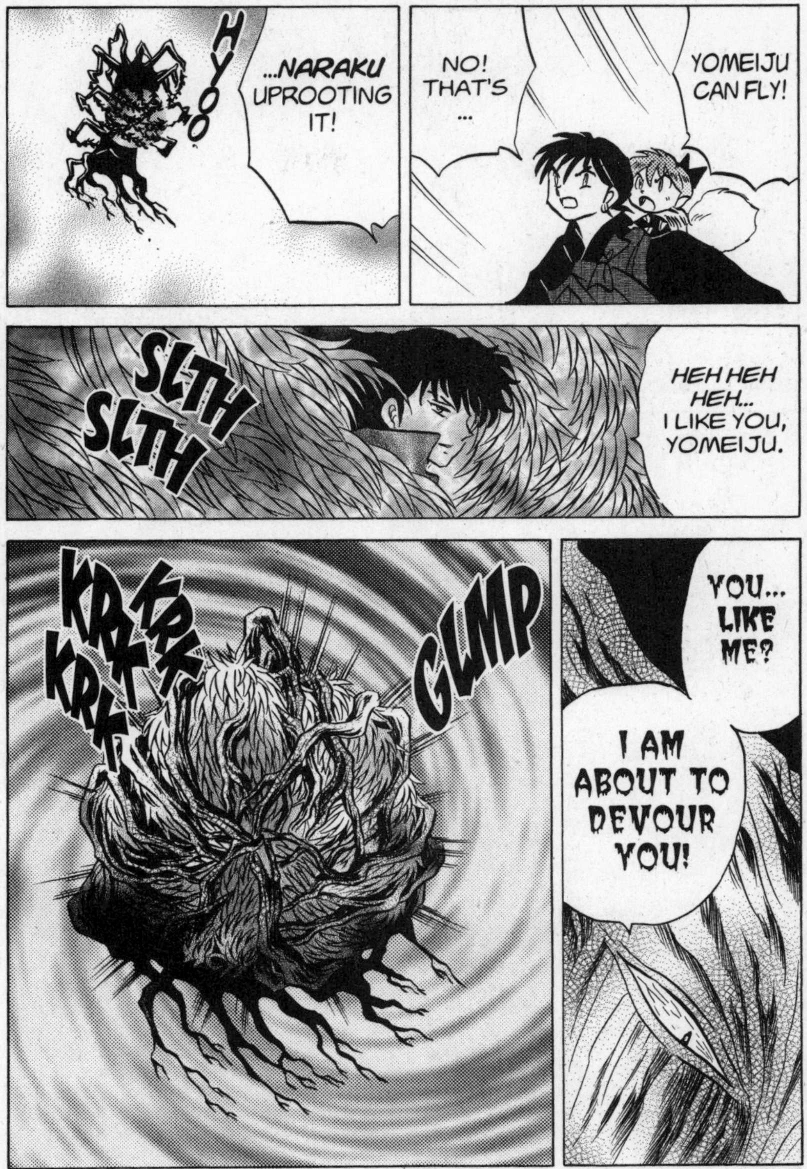
YOMEIJU CAN FLY!
NO! THAT'S ...
...NARAKU UPROOTING IT!
HYOOO
HEH HEH HEH... I LIKE YOU, YOMEIJU.
SLTH SLTH
YOU... LIKE ME?
I AM ABOUT TO DEVOUR YOU!
GLMP
KRK KRK KRK KRK

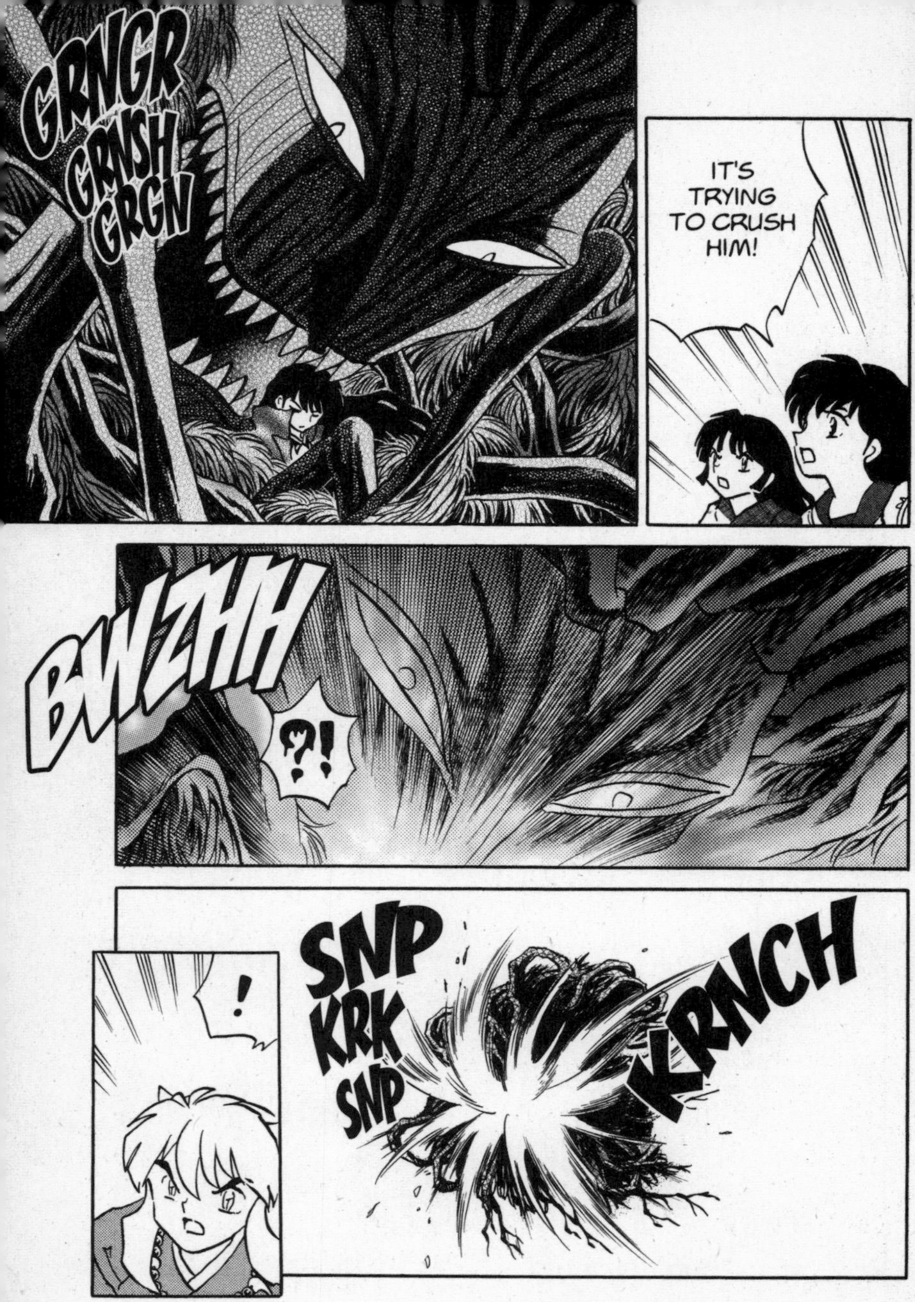
IT'S TRYING TO CRUSH HIM!
GRNGR GRNSH GRGN
BWZHH
?!
KRNCH
SNP KRK SNP
!

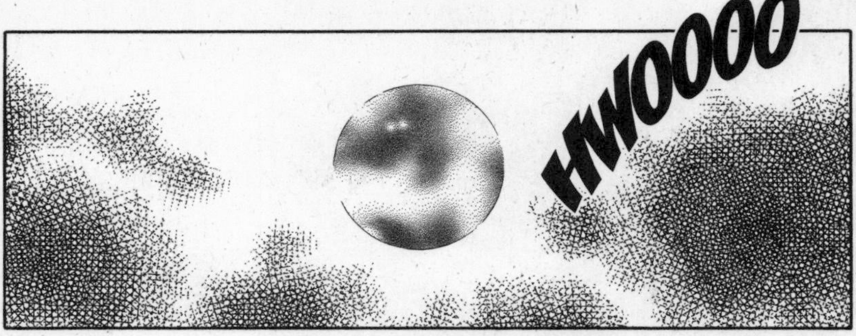
HWOOOO
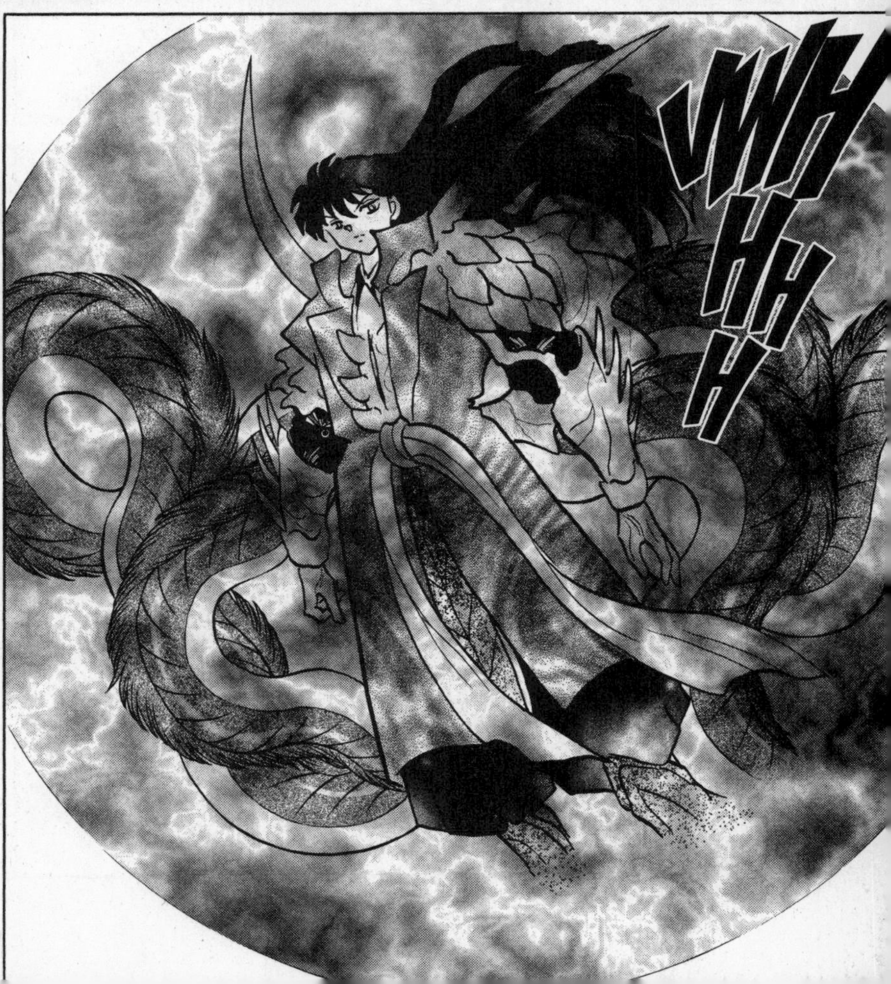
VMMHHHHH

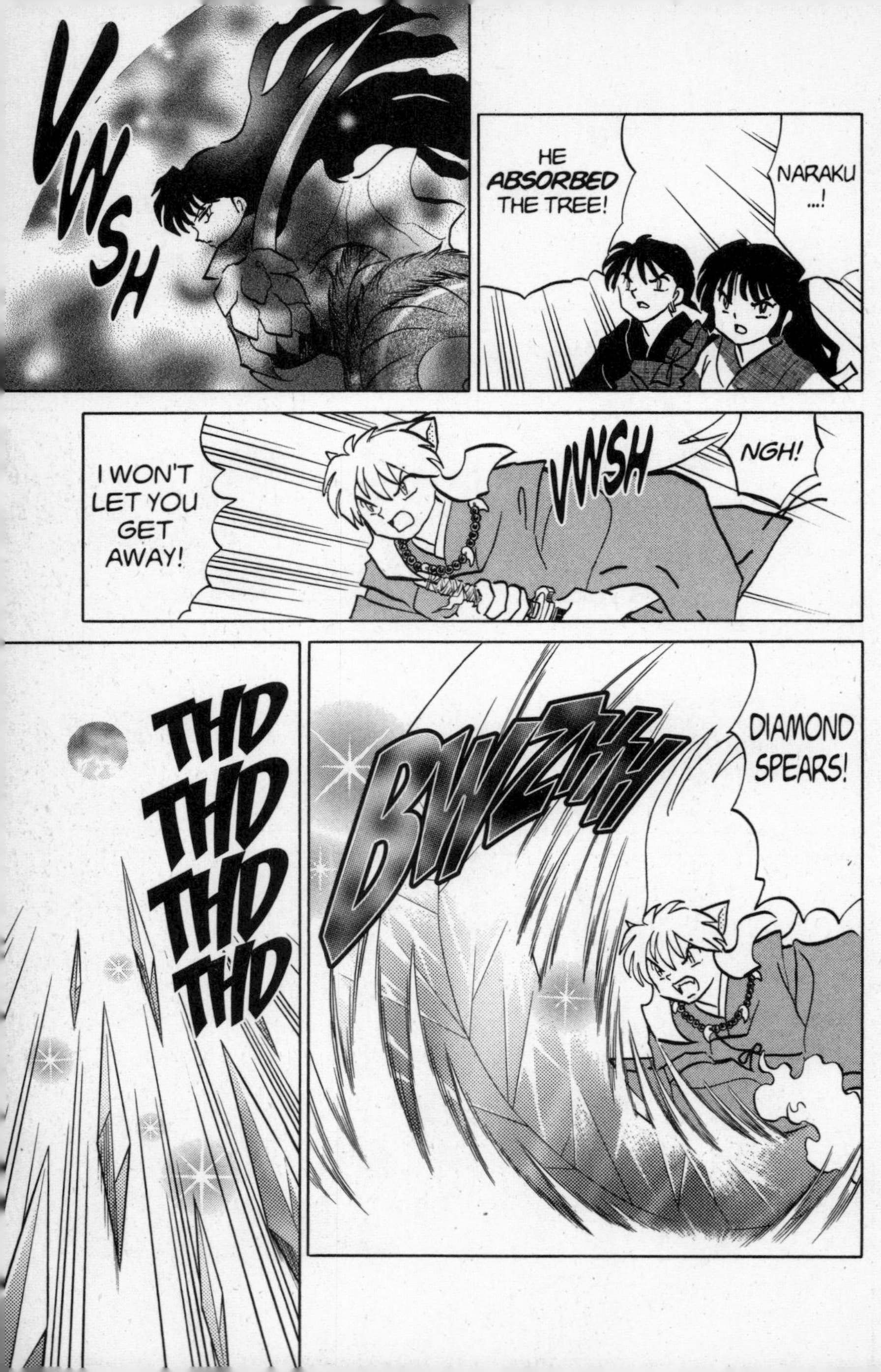
NARAKU ...!
HE ABSORBED THE TREE!
VWSH
NGH!
VWSH
I WON'T LET YOU GET AWAY!
DIAMOND SPEARS!
THD THD THD THD

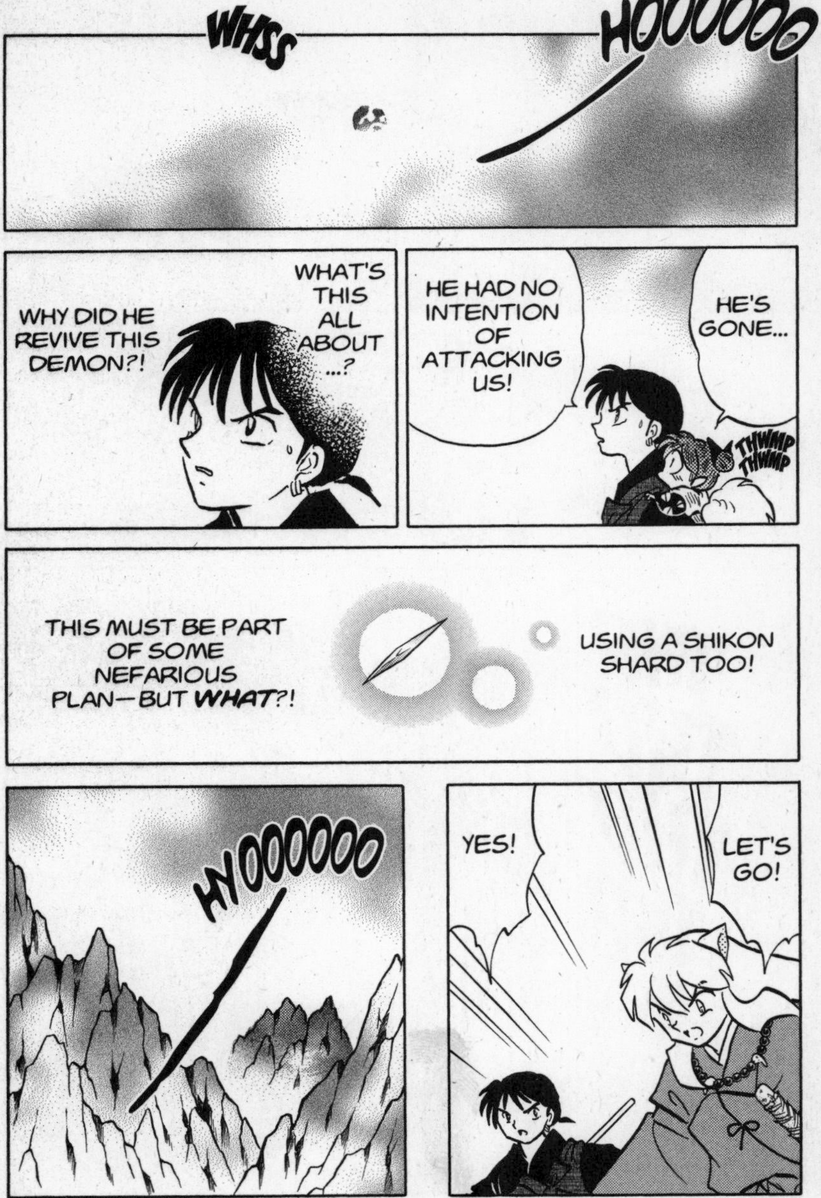
HOOOOOO
WHSS
HE'S GONE...
HE HAD NO INTENTION OF ATTACKING US!
THWMP THWMP
WHAT'S THIS ALL ABOUT ...?
WHY DID HE REVIVE THIS DEMON?!
USING A SHIKON SHARD TOO!
THIS MUST BE PART OF SOME NEFARIOUS PLAN—BUT WHAT?!
LET'S GO!
YES!
HYOOOOOO

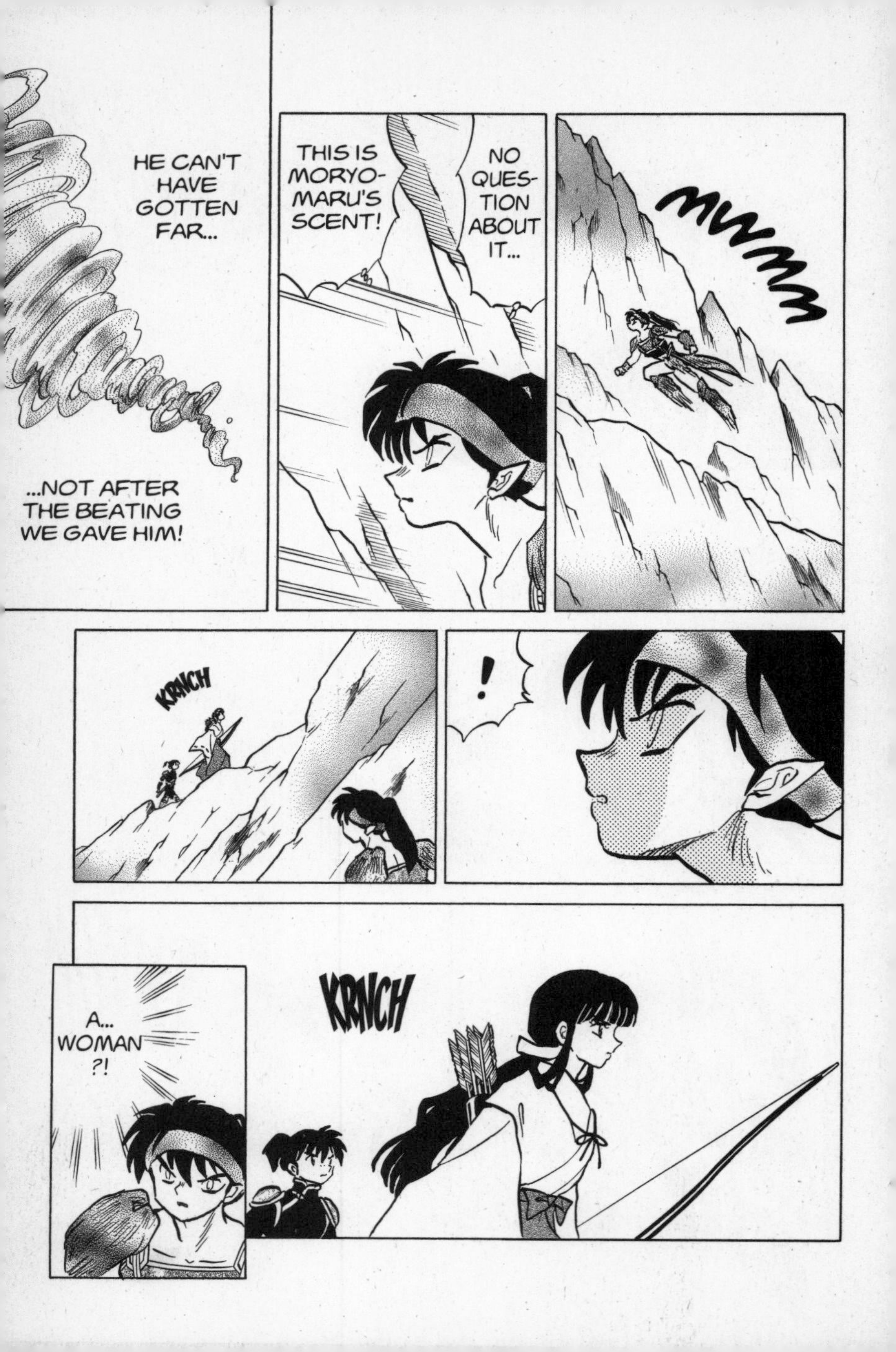
MWMM
THIS IS MORYO-MARU'S SCENT!
NO QUES-TION ABOUT IT...
HE CAN'T HAVE GOTTEN FAR...
...NOT AFTER THE BEATING WE GAVE HIM!
!
KRNCH
KRNCH
A... WOMAN ?!

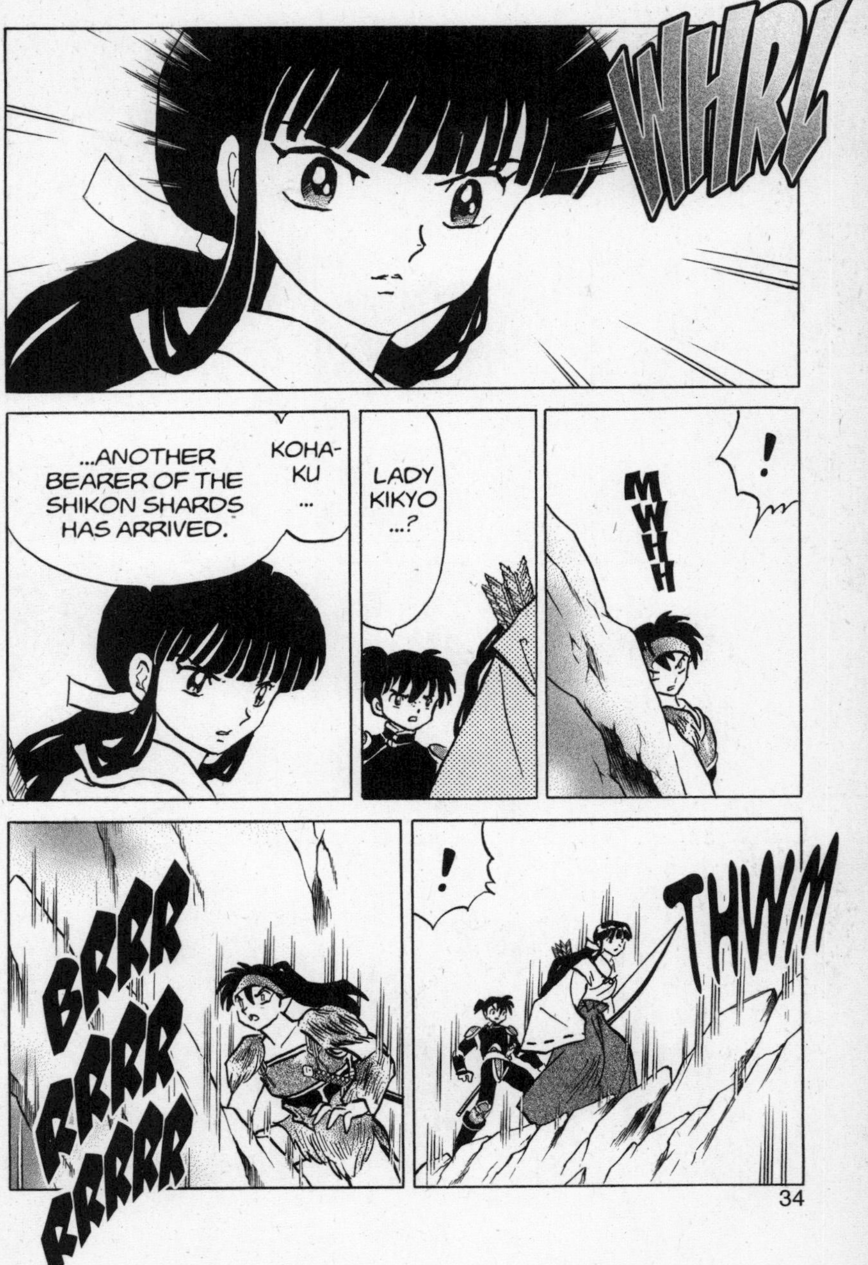
WHRL
!
MWHH
LADY KIKYO ...?
KOHA-KU ...
...ANOTHER BEARER OF THE SHIKON SHARDS HAS ARRIVED.
!
THWM
BRRR RRRR RRRR RRRRR

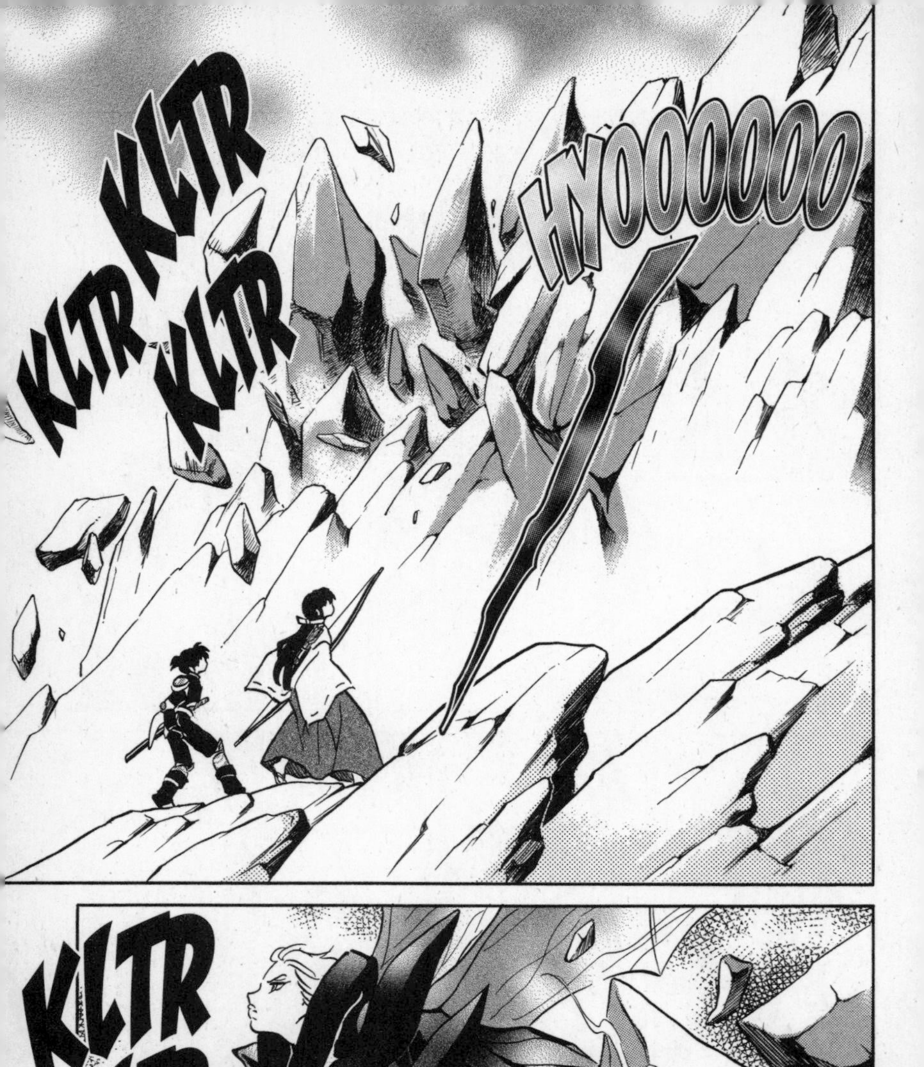
HYOOOOOO
KLTR KLTR
KLTR KLTR

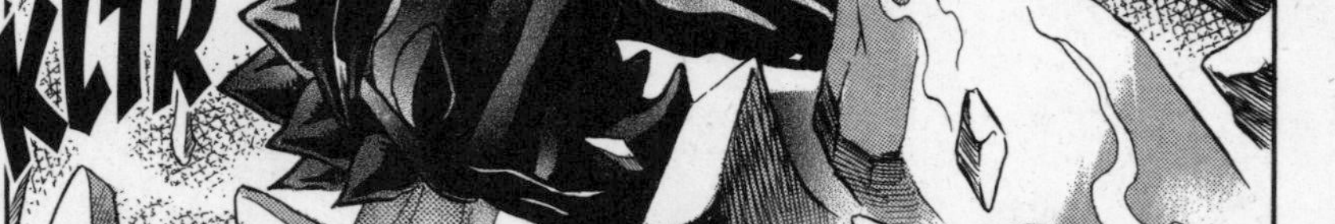
KLTR KLTR

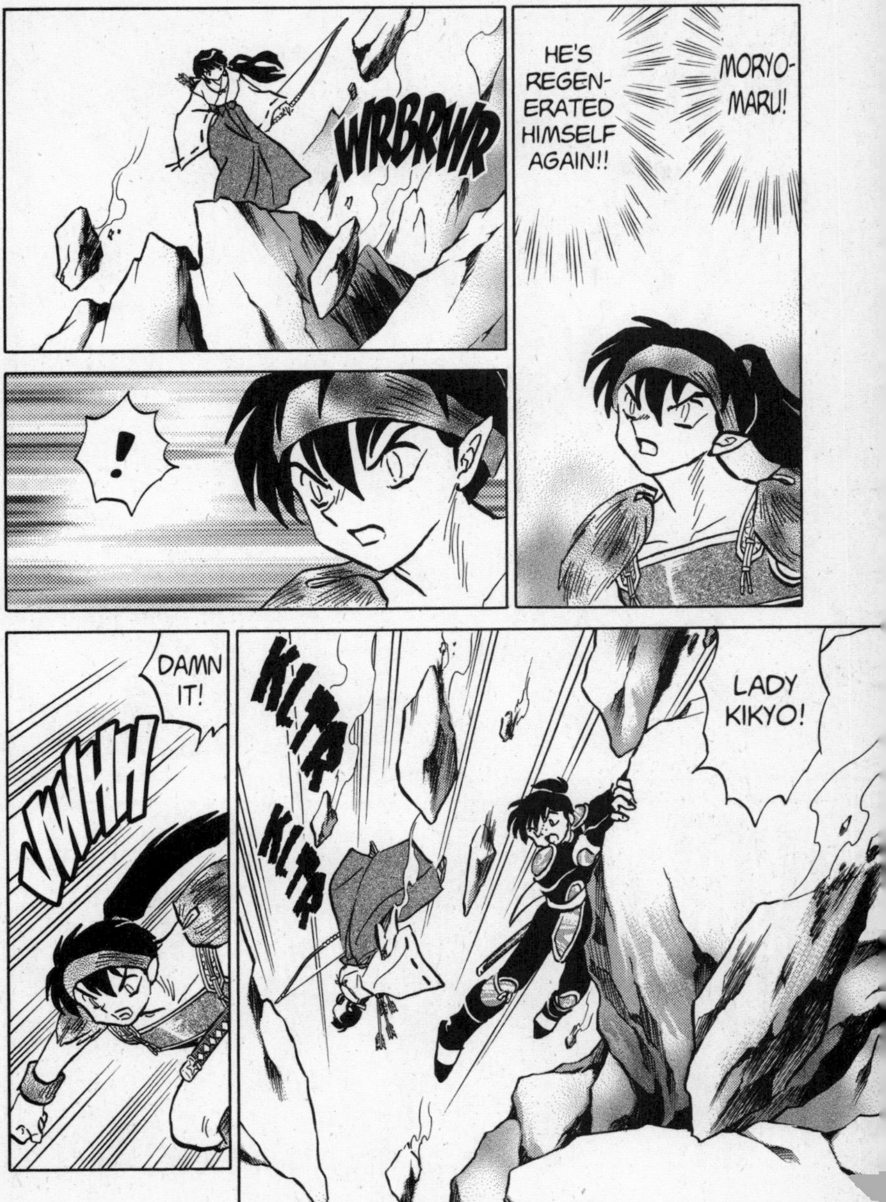
MORYO-MARU!
HE'S REGEN-ERATED HIMSELF AGAIN!!
WRBRWR
!
LADY KIKYO!
KLTR KLTR
DAMN IT!
JWHH

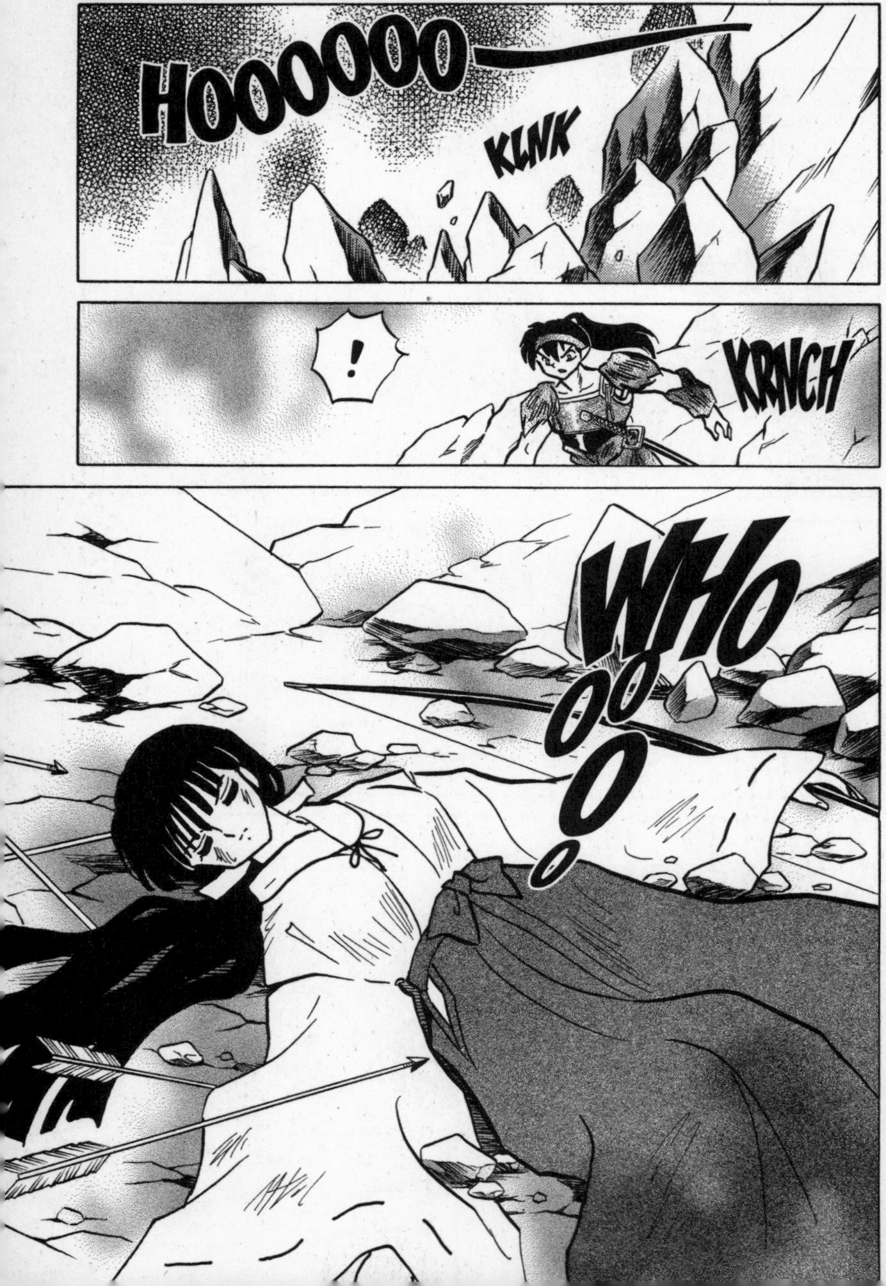
HOOOOOO
KLNK
KRNCH
!
WHOOOOOO

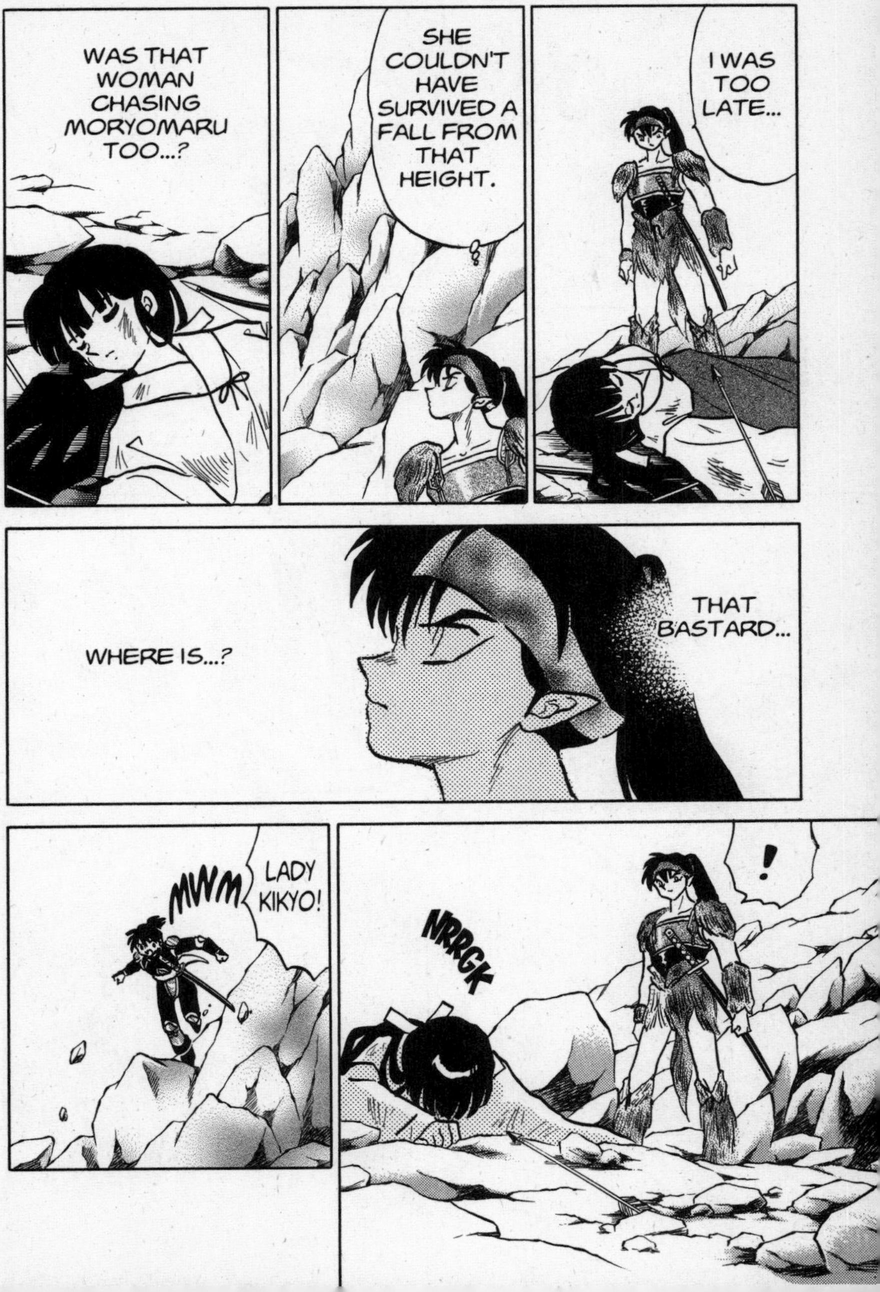
I WAS TOO LATE...
SHE COULDN'T HAVE SURVIVED A FALL FROM THAT HEIGHT.
WAS THAT WOMAN CHASING MORYOMARU TOO...?
THAT BASTARD...
WHERE IS...?
!
NRRGK
LADY KIKYO!
MWM

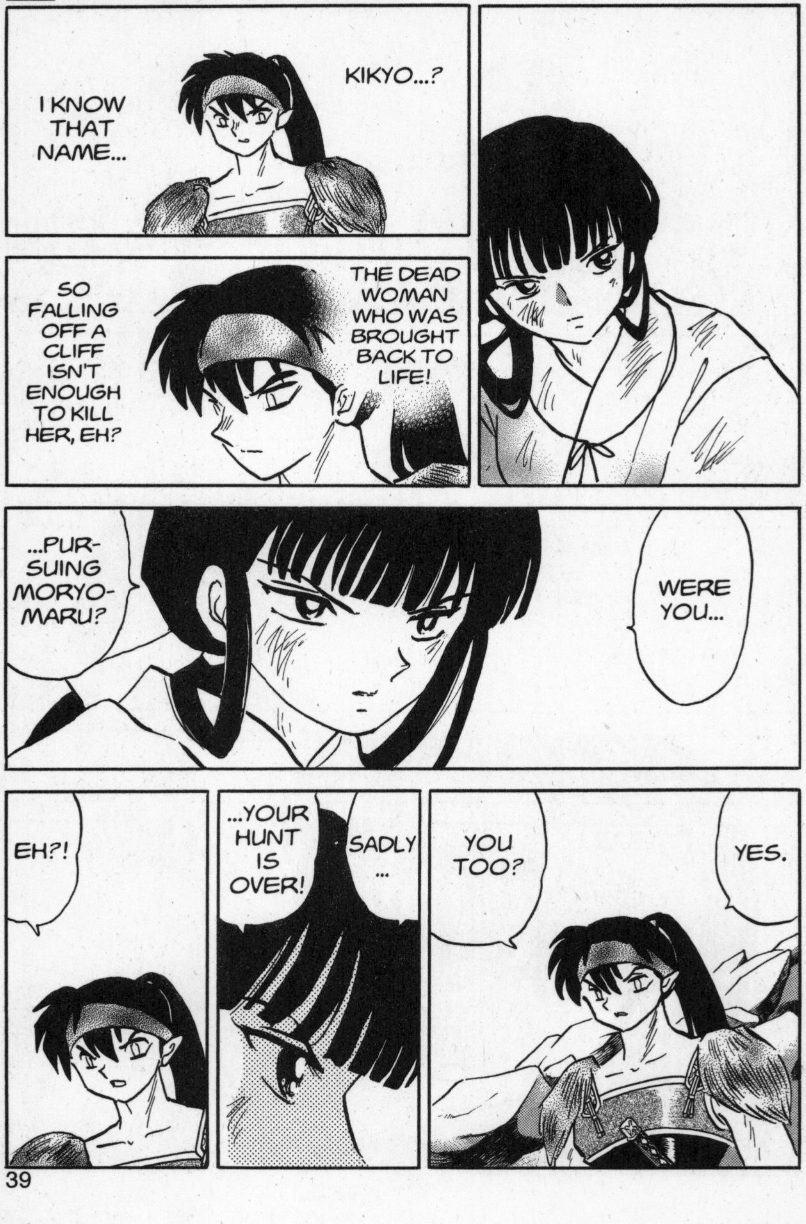
KIKYO...?
I KNOW THAT NAME...
THE DEAD WOMAN WHO WAS BROUGHT BACK TO LIFE!
SO FALLING OFF A CLIFF ISN'T ENOUGH TO KILL HER, EH?
WERE YOU...
...PURSUING MORYOMARU?
YES.
YOU TOO?
SADLY...
...YOUR HUNT IS OVER!
EH?!

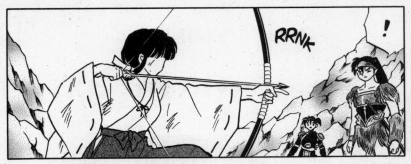

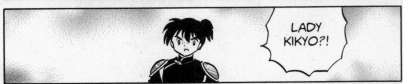

LADY KIKYO?!

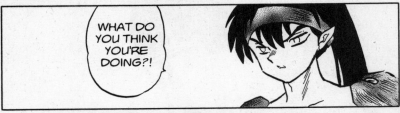

WHAT DO YOU THINK YOU'RE DOING?!

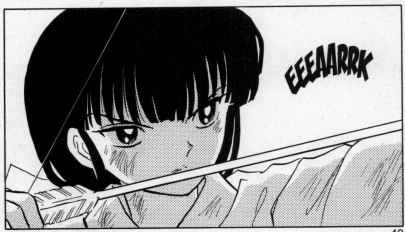

40

SCROLL 3

CONFRONTATION

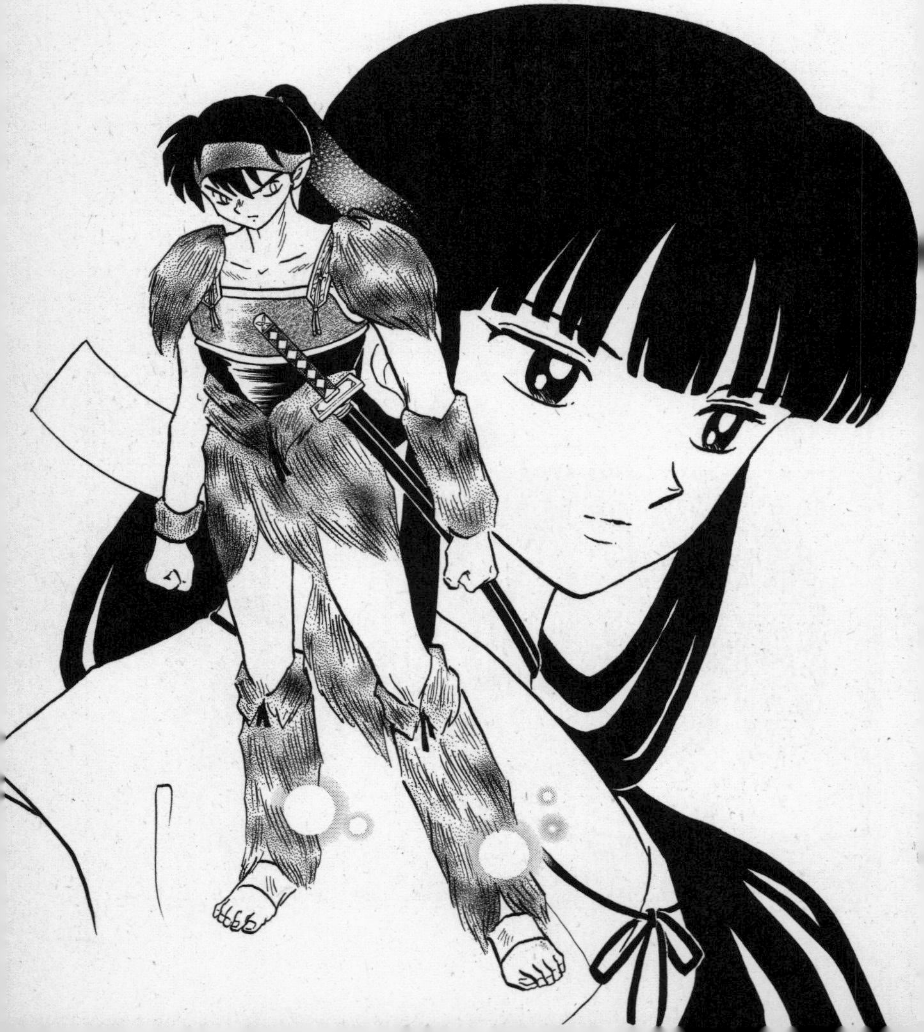

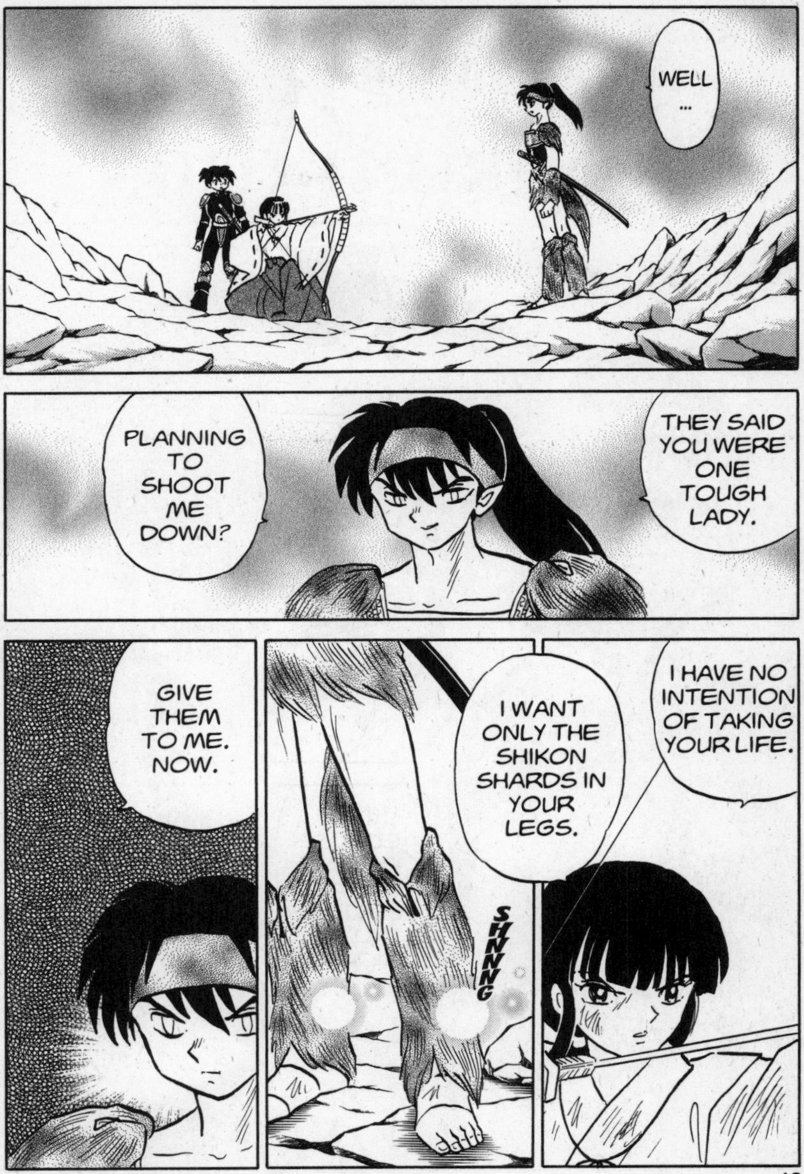
WELL ...
THEY SAID YOU WERE ONE TOUGH LADY.
PLANNING TO SHOOT ME DOWN?
I HAVE NO INTENTION OF TAKING YOUR LIFE.
I WANT ONLY THE SHIKON SHARDS IN YOUR LEGS.
SHNNNG
GIVE THEM TO ME. NOW.

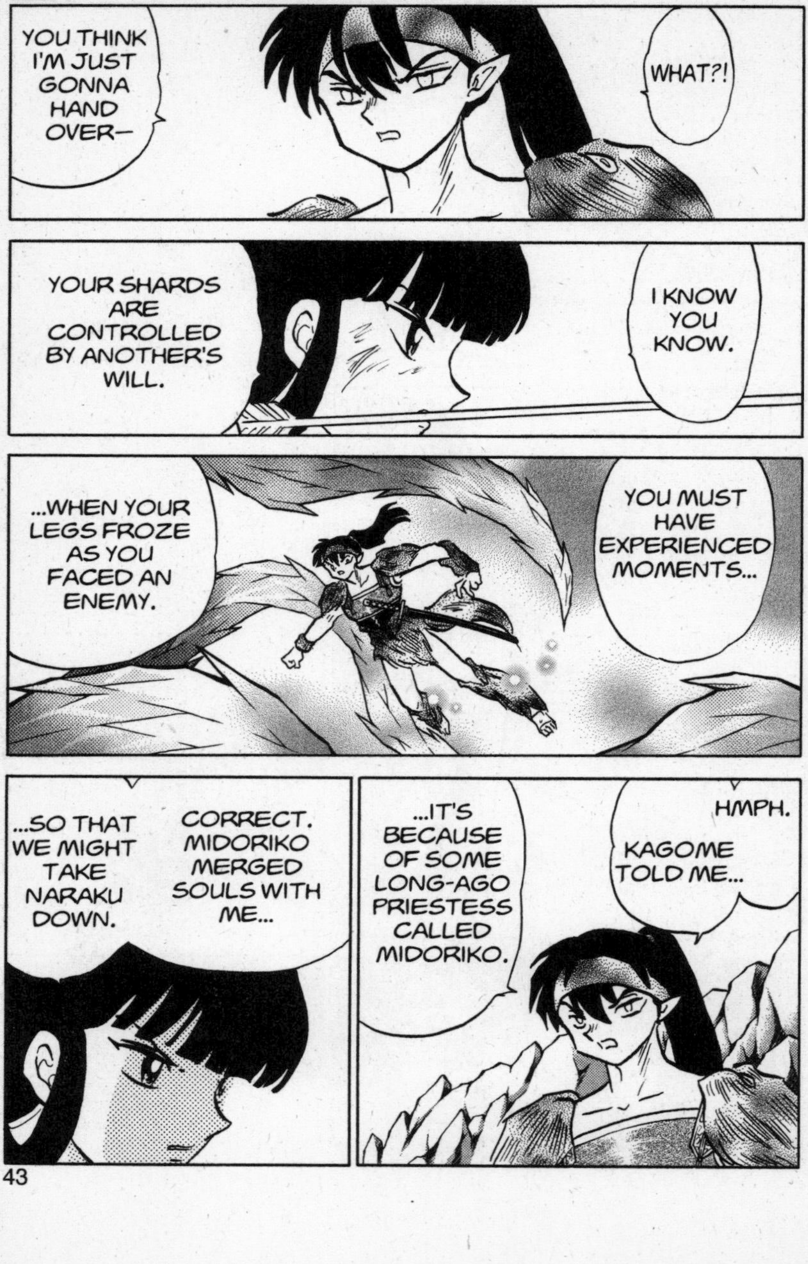
WHAT?!
YOU THINK I'M JUST GONNA HAND OVER—
I KNOW YOU KNOW.
YOUR SHARDS ARE CONTROLLED BY ANOTHER'S WILL.
YOU MUST HAVE EXPERIENCED MOMENTS...
...WHEN YOUR LEGS FROZE AS YOU FACED AN ENEMY.
HMPH.
KAGOME TOLD ME...
...IT'S BECAUSE OF SOME LONG-AGO PRIESTESS CALLED MIDORIKO.
CORRECT. MIDORIKO MERGED SOULS WITH ME...
...SO THAT WE MIGHT TAKE NARAKU DOWN.

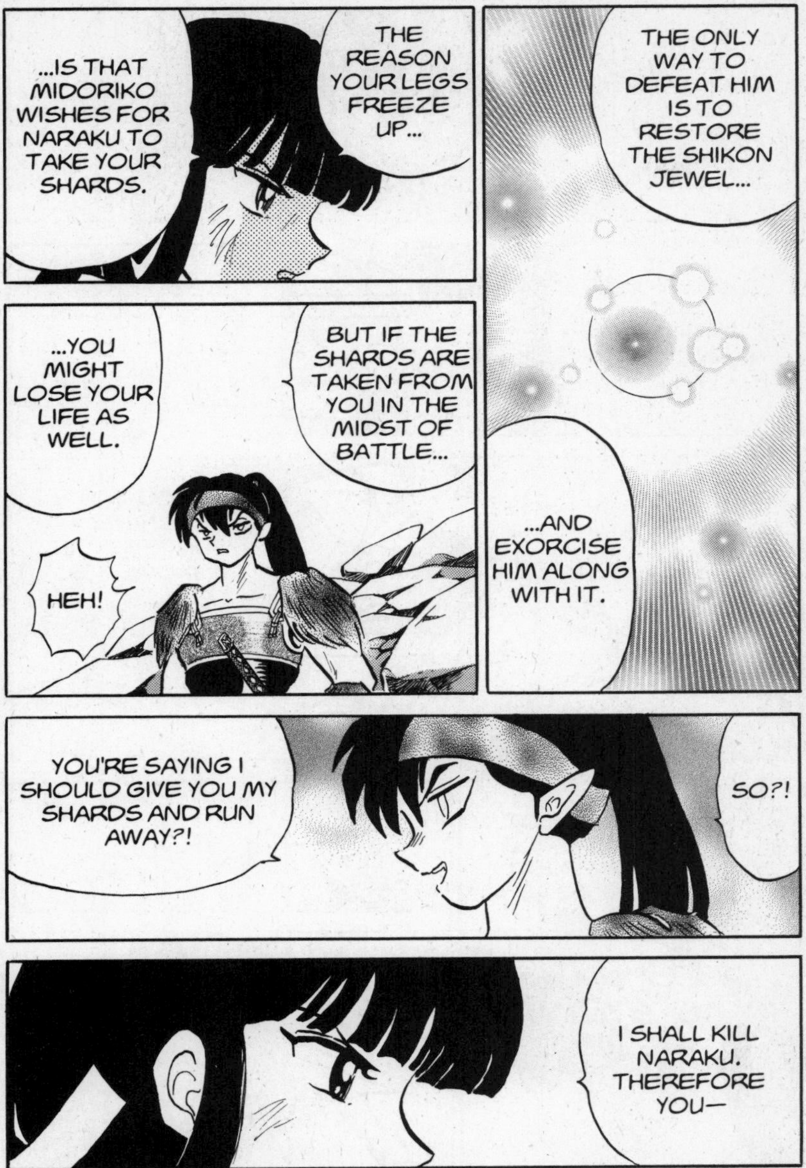
THE ONLY WAY TO DEFEAT HIM IS TO RESTORE THE SHIKON JEWEL...
...AND EXORCISE HIM ALONG WITH IT.
THE REASON YOUR LEGS FREEZE UP...
...IS THAT MIDORIKO WISHES FOR NARAKU TO TAKE YOUR SHARDS.
BUT IF THE SHARDS ARE TAKEN FROM YOU IN THE MIDST OF BATTLE...
...YOU MIGHT LOSE YOUR LIFE AS WELL.
HEH!
SO?!
YOU'RE SAYING I SHOULD GIVE YOU MY SHARDS AND RUN AWAY?!
I SHALL KILL NARAKU. THEREFORE YOU—

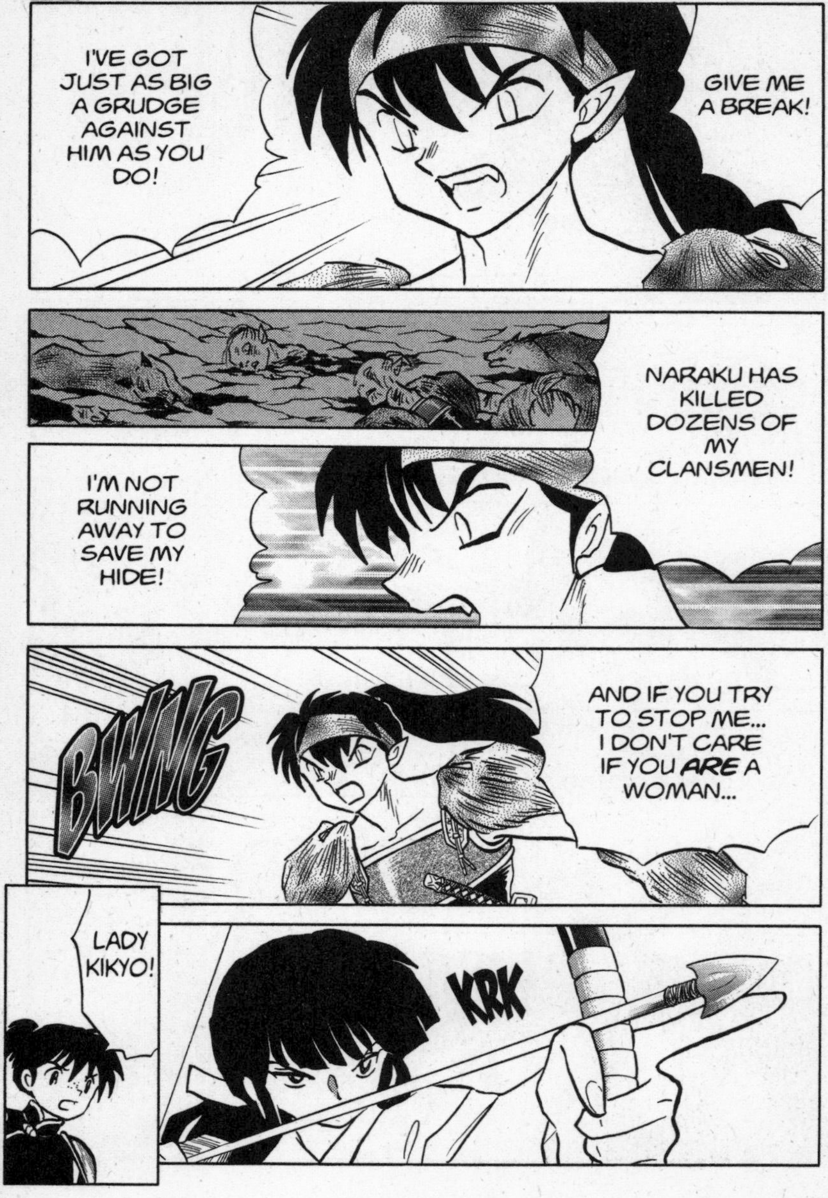
GIVE ME A BREAK!
I'VE GOT JUST AS BIG A GRUDGE AGAINST HIM AS YOU DO!
NARAKU HAS KILLED DOZENS OF MY CLANSMEN!
I'M NOT RUNNING AWAY TO SAVE MY HIDE!
AND IF YOU TRY TO STOP ME... I DON'T CARE IF YOU *ARE* A WOMAN...
BWING
KRK
LADY KIKYO!

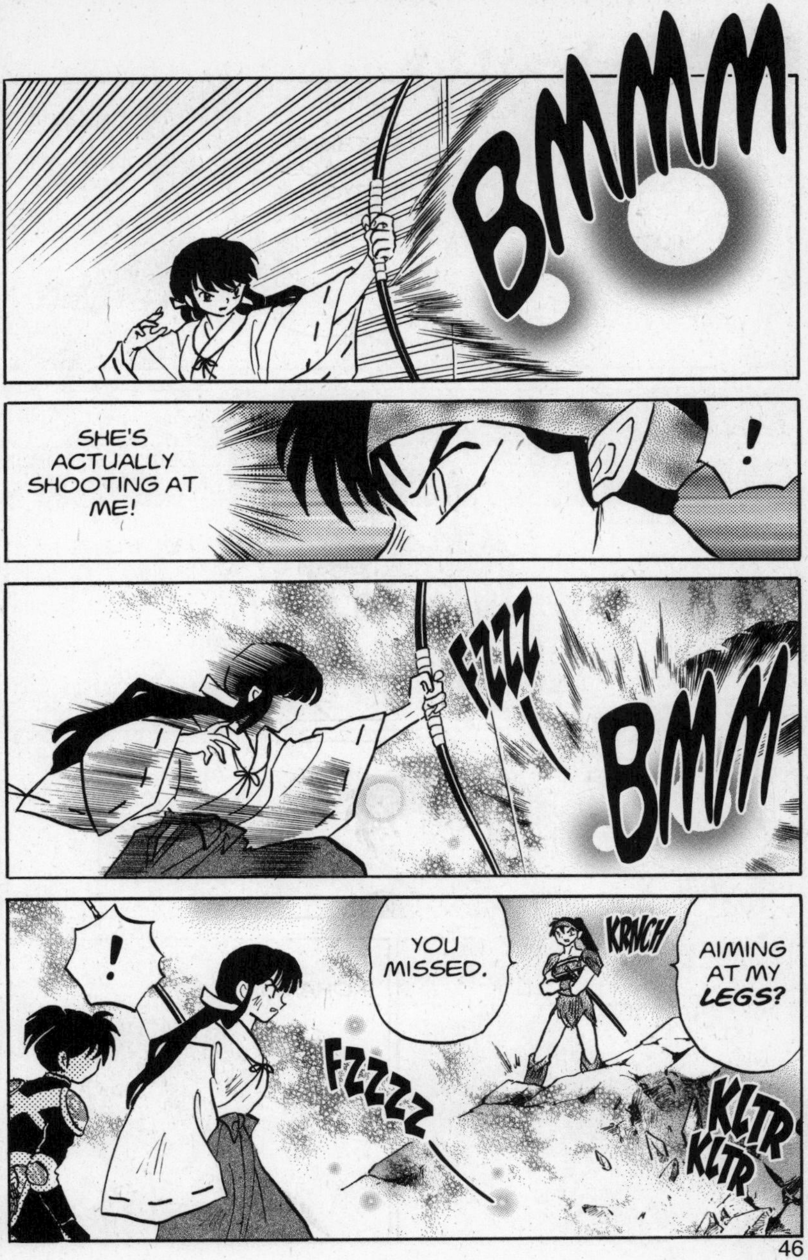
BMMM
!
SHE'S ACTUALLY SHOOTING AT ME!
FZZZ
BMM
AIMING AT MY *LEGS?*
KRNCH
YOU MISSED.
KLTR KLTR
FZZZZ
!

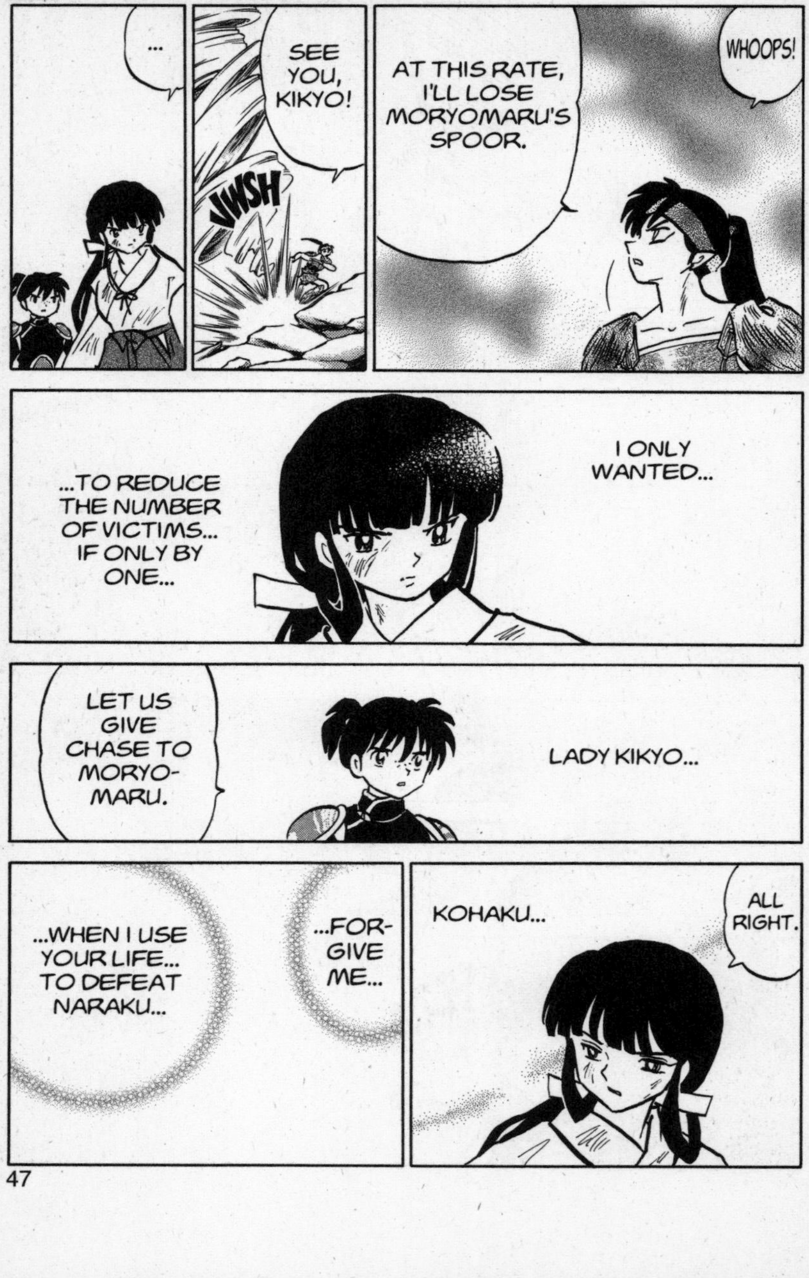
WHOOPS!
AT THIS RATE, I'LL LOSE MORYOMARU'S SPOOR.
SEE YOU, KIKYO!
VWSH
...
I ONLY WANTED...
...TO REDUCE THE NUMBER OF VICTIMS... IF ONLY BY ONE...
LADY KIKYO...
LET US GIVE CHASE TO MORYO-MARU.
ALL RIGHT.
KOHAKU...
...FOR-GIVE ME...
...WHEN I USE YOUR LIFE... TO DEFEAT NARAKU...

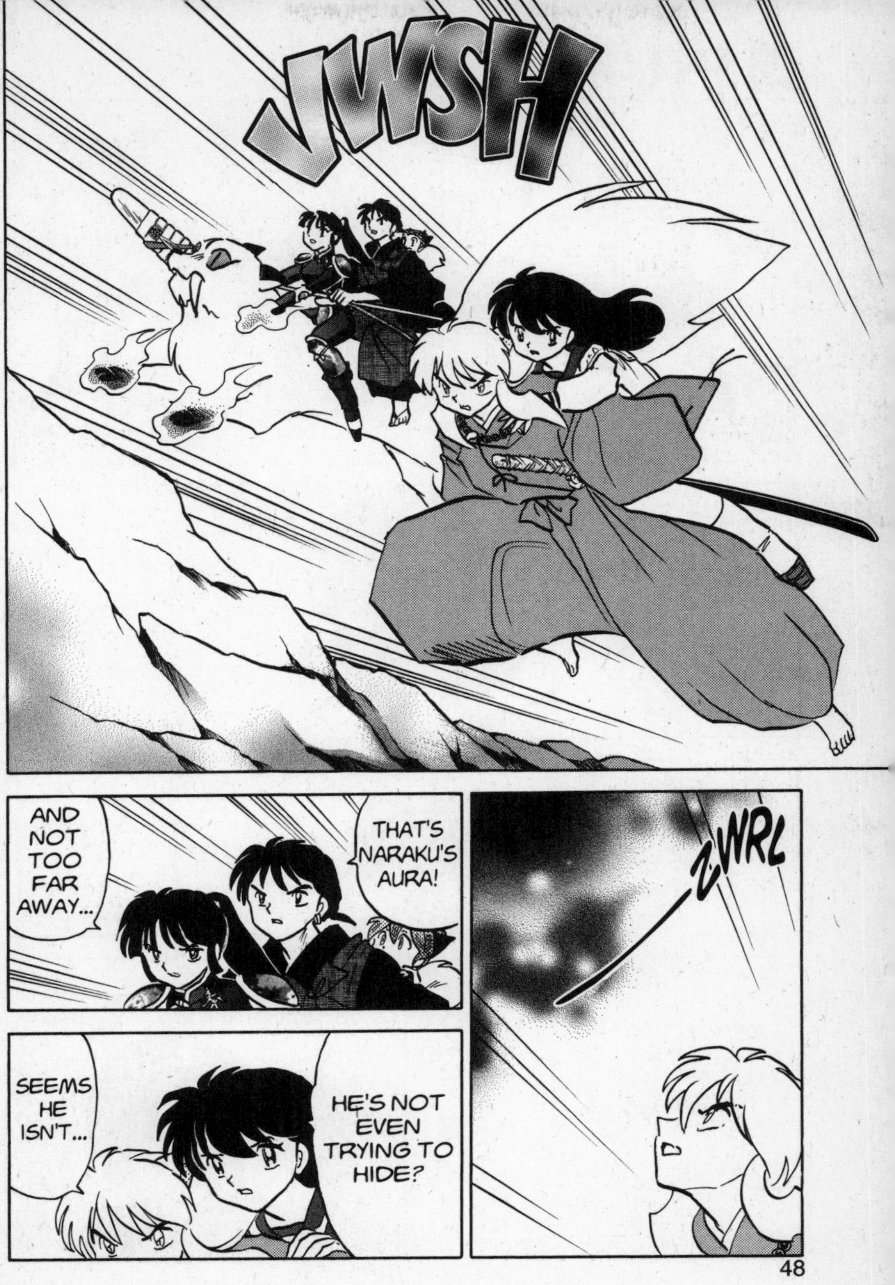
JWSH
ZWRL
THAT'S NARAKU'S AURA!
AND NOT TOO FAR AWAY...
HE'S NOT EVEN TRYING TO HIDE?
SEEMS HE ISN'T...

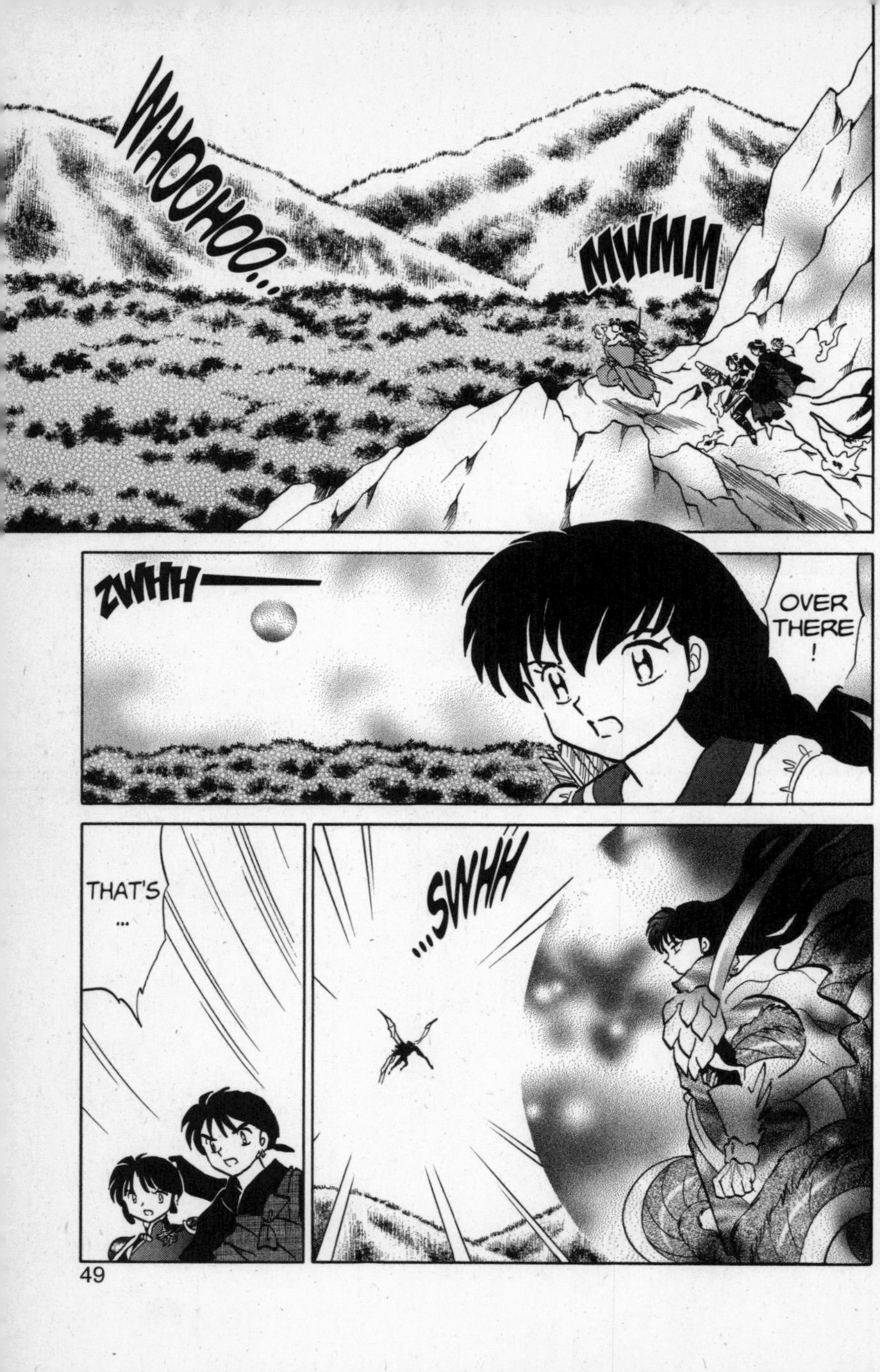
MWMM
WHOOHOO...
OVER THERE!
ZWHH
...SWHH
THAT'S...

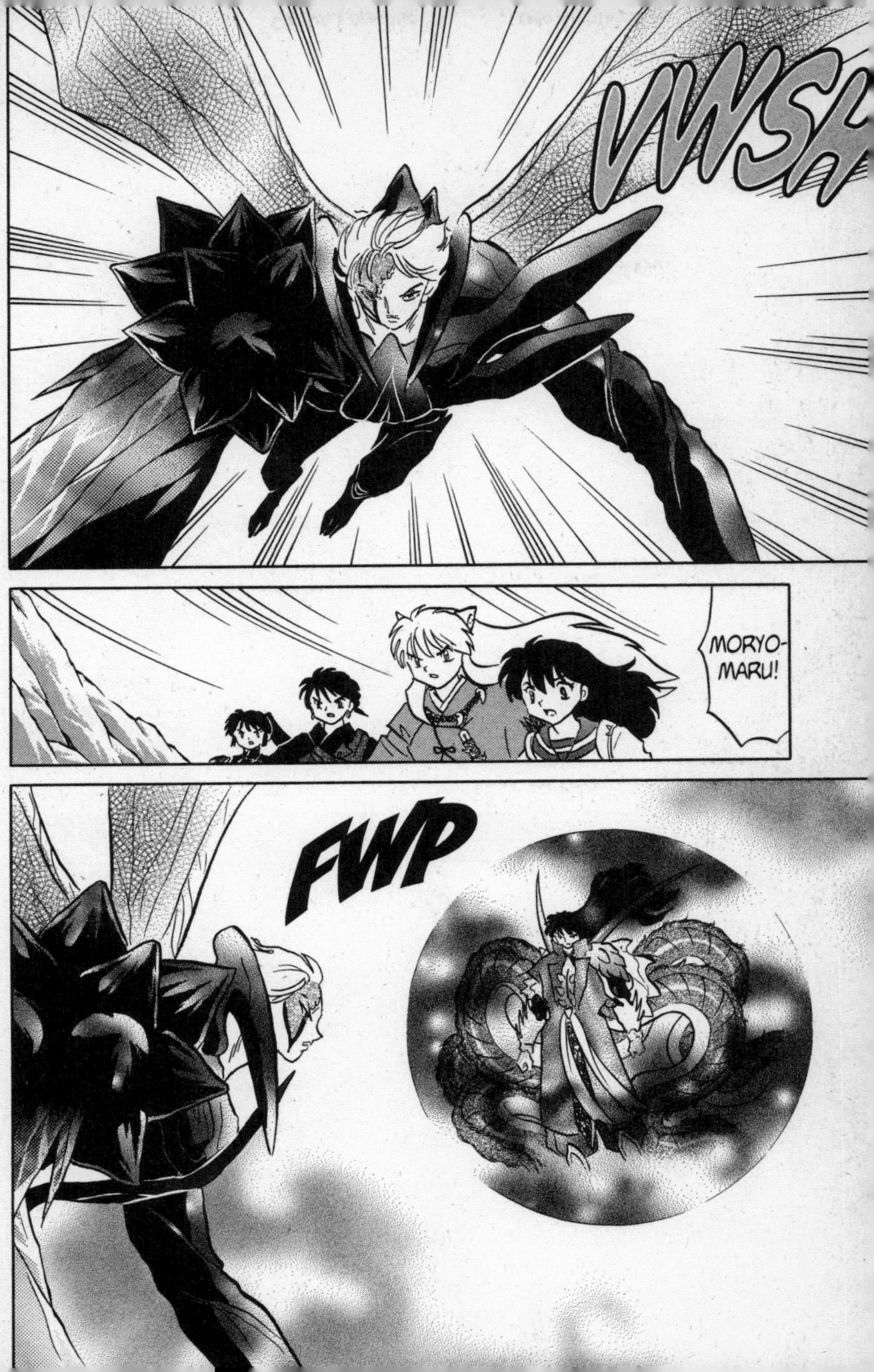
VWSH
MORYO-
MARU!
FWP

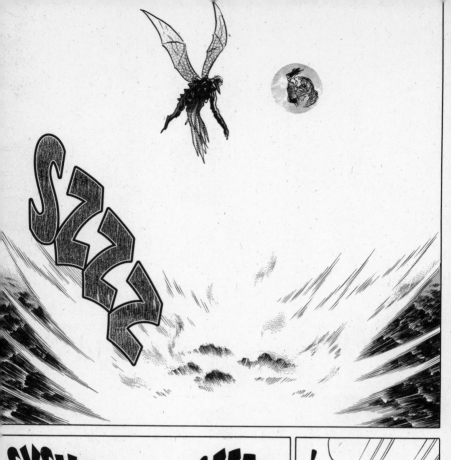

SZZZ

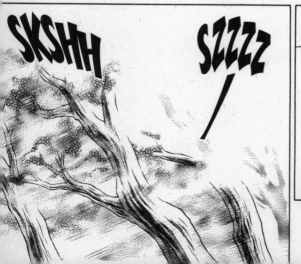

SKSHH

SZZZZ

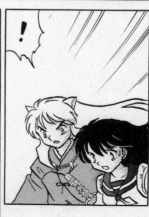

!

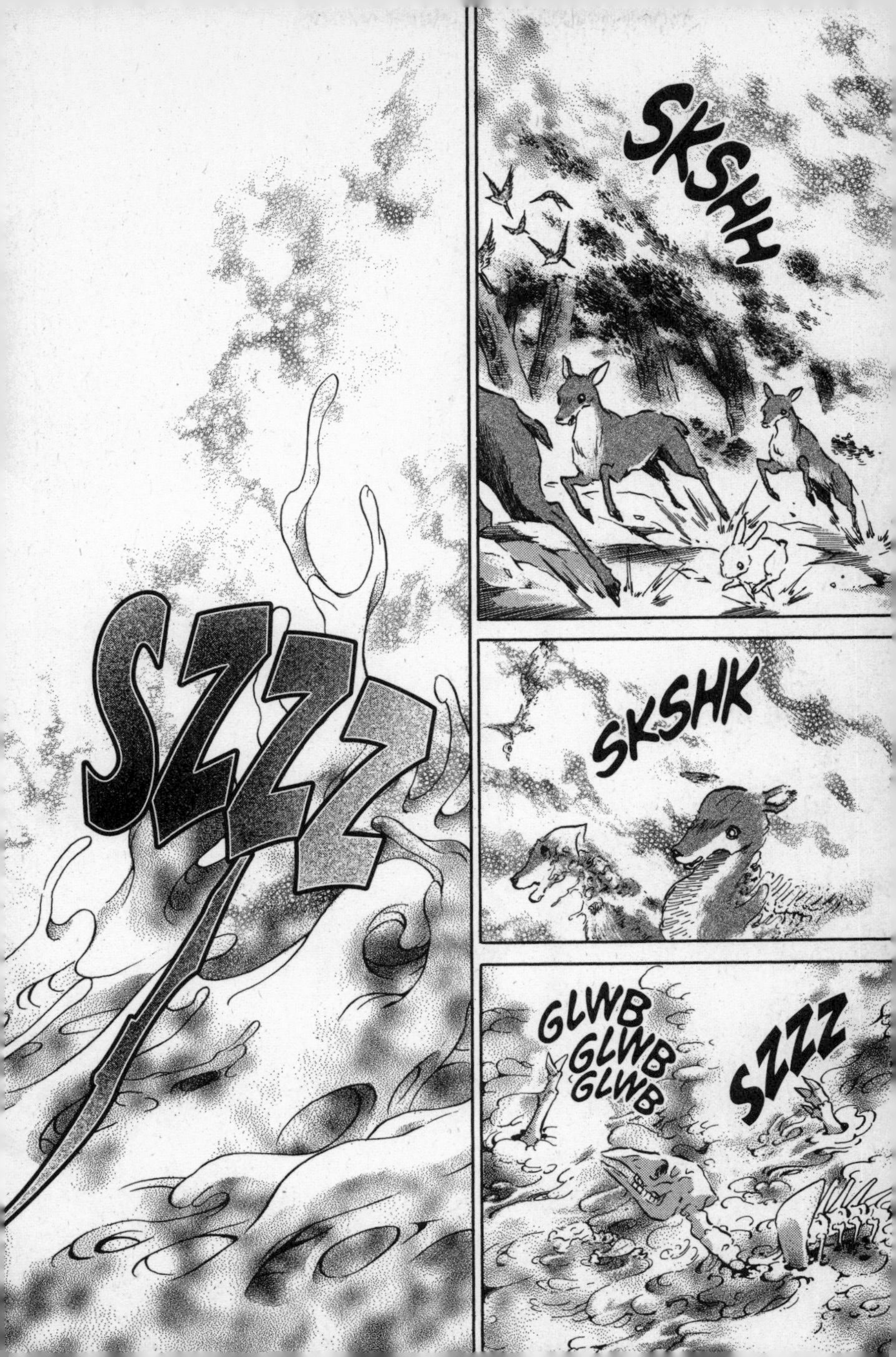
SKSHH
SKSHK
SZZZ
GLWB GLWB GLWB
SZZZ

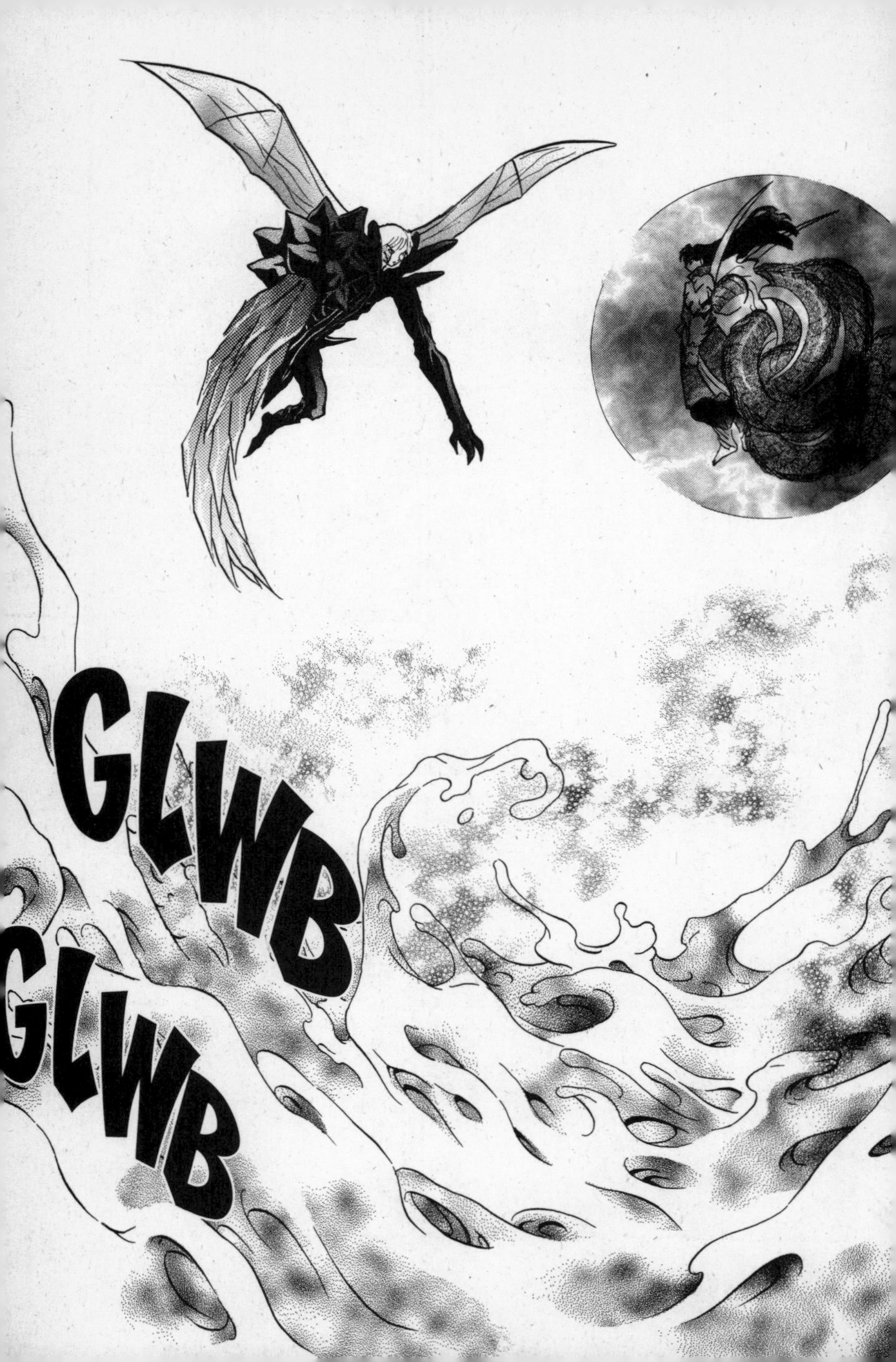
GLWB
GLWB

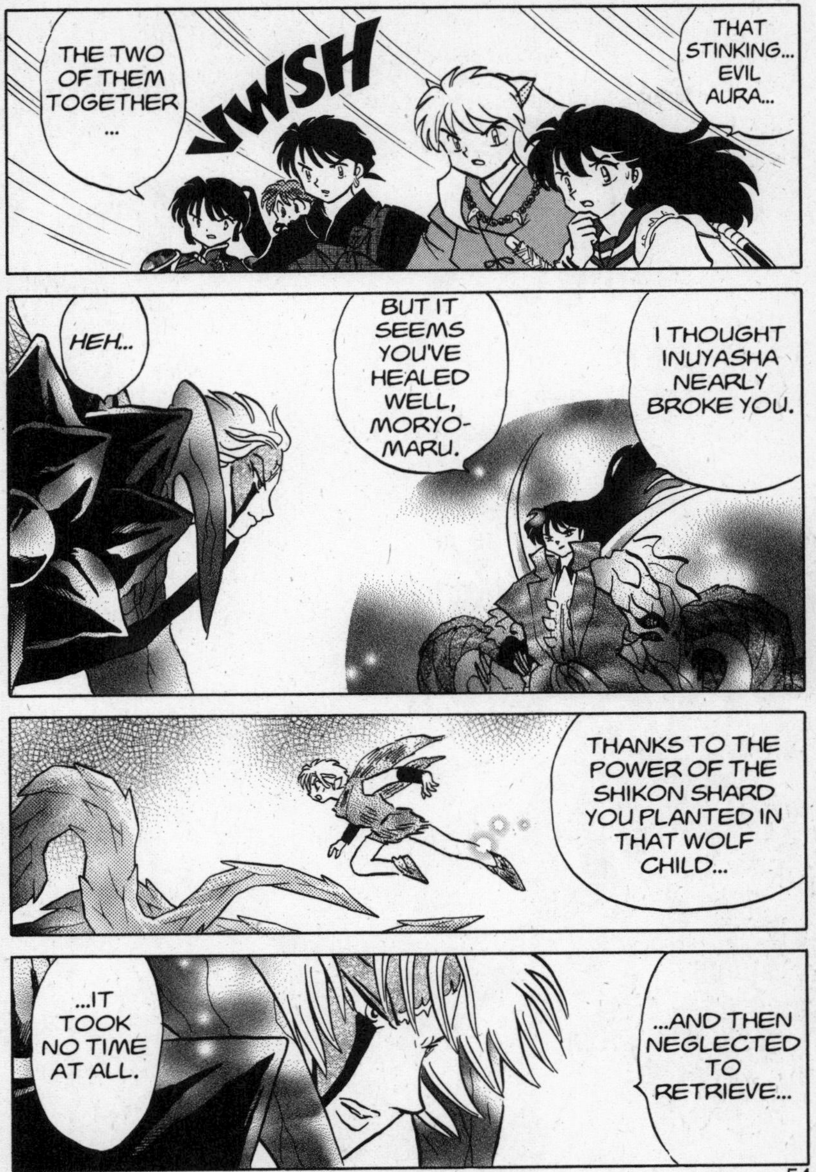
THAT STINKING... EVIL AURA...
VWSH
THE TWO OF THEM TOGETHER ...
I THOUGHT INUYASHA NEARLY BROKE YOU.
BUT IT SEEMS YOU'VE HEALED WELL, MORYO-MARU.
HEH...
THANKS TO THE POWER OF THE SHIKON SHARD YOU PLANTED IN THAT WOLF CHILD...
...AND THEN NEGLECTED TO RETRIEVE...
...IT TOOK NO TIME AT ALL.

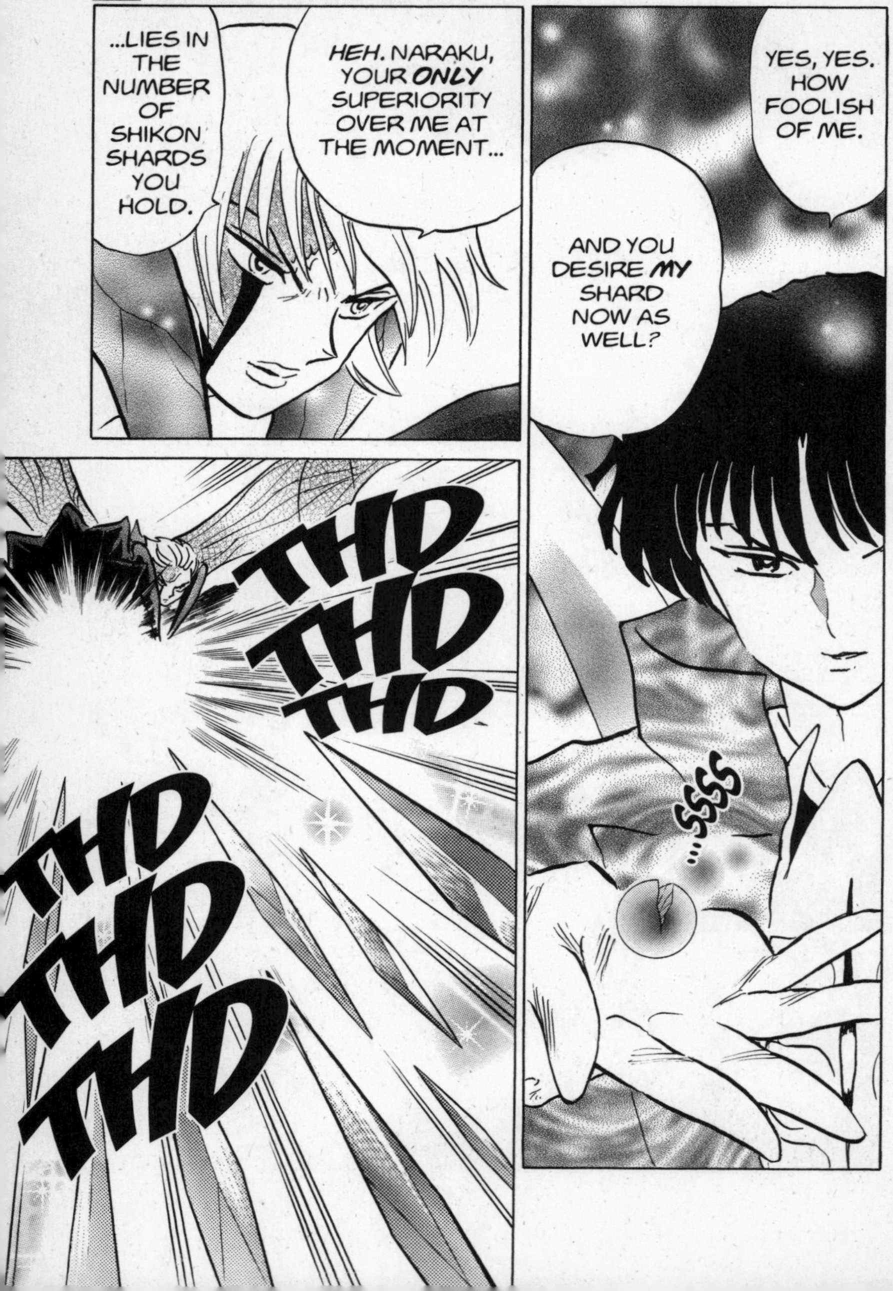
YES, YES. HOW FOOLISH OF ME.
AND YOU DESIRE MY SHARD NOW AS WELL?
...SSSS
HEH. NARAKU, YOUR ONLY SUPERIORITY OVER ME AT THE MOMENT...
...LIES IN THE NUMBER OF SHIKON SHARDS YOU HOLD.
THD THD THD
THD THD THD

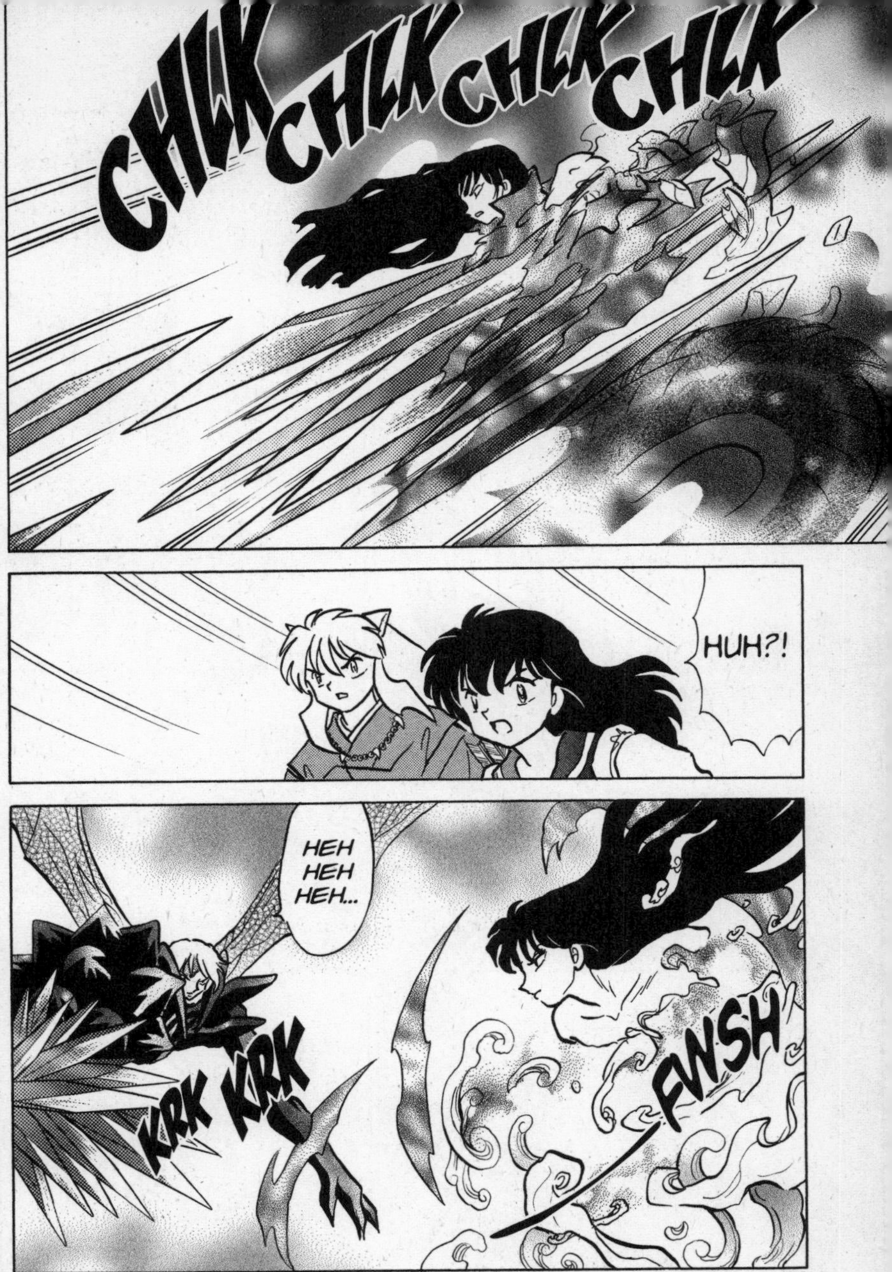
CHLK CHLK CHLK CHLK
HUH?!
HEH HEH HEH...
FWSH
KRK KRK

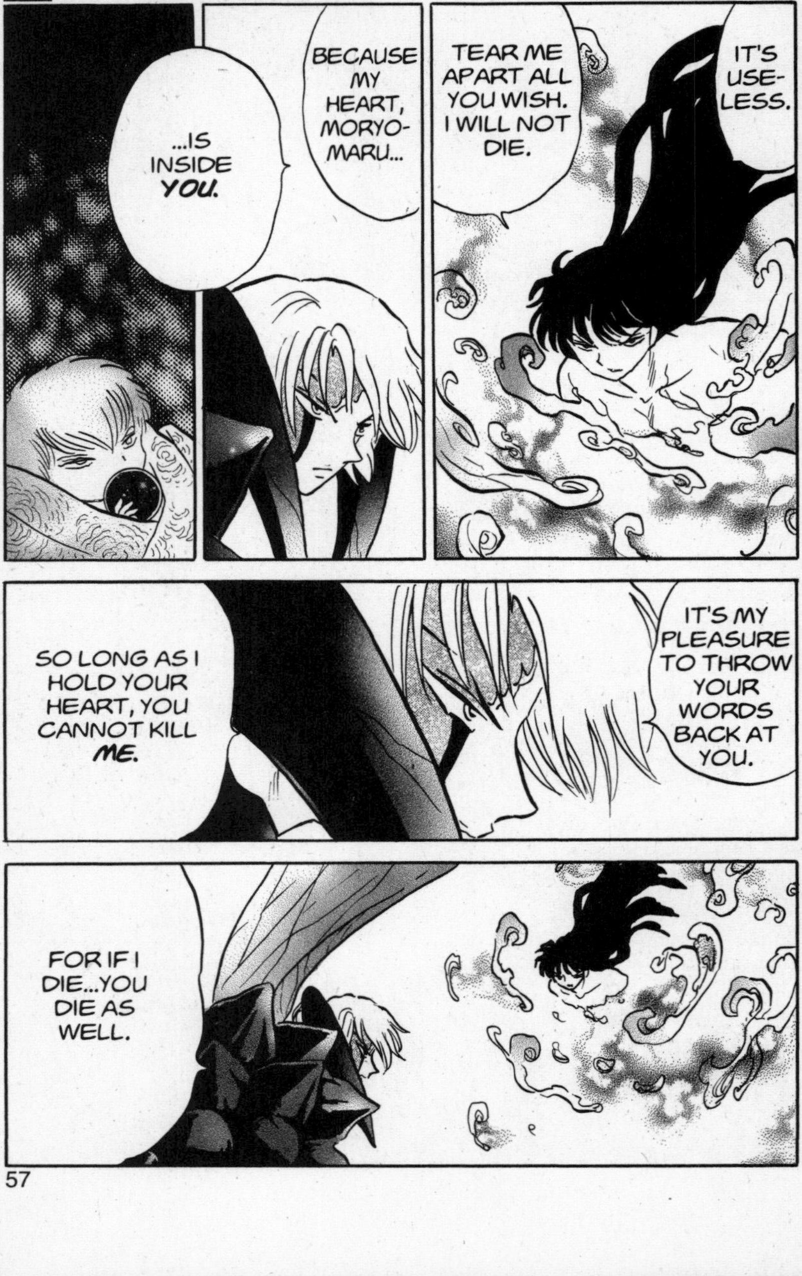
IT'S USE-LESS.
TEAR ME APART ALL YOU WISH. I WILL NOT DIE.
BECAUSE MY HEART, MORYO-MARU...
...IS INSIDE YOU.
IT'S MY PLEASURE TO THROW YOUR WORDS BACK AT YOU.
SO LONG AS I HOLD YOUR HEART, YOU CANNOT KILL ME.
FOR IF I DIE...YOU DIE AS WELL.

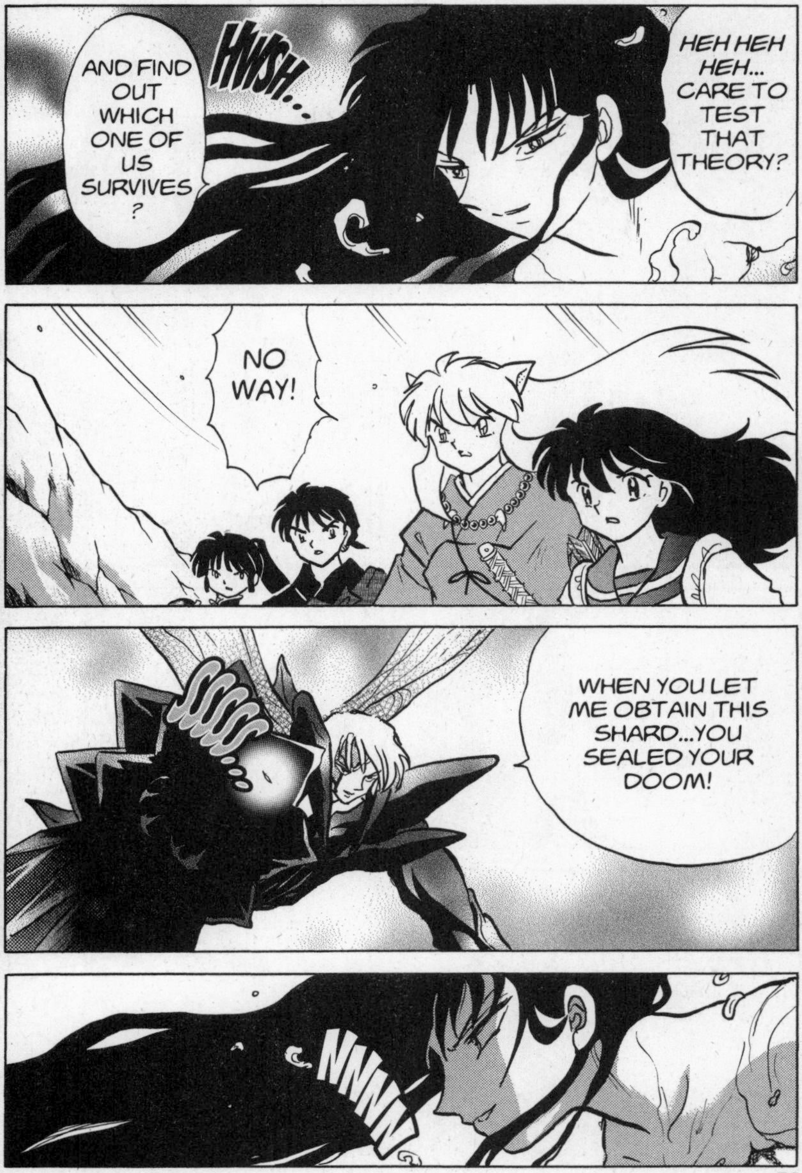
HEH HEH HEH... CARE TO TEST THAT THEORY?
HWSH...
AND FIND OUT WHICH ONE OF US SURVIVES?
NO WAY!
WHEN YOU LET ME OBTAIN THIS SHARD...YOU SEALED YOUR DOOM!
SSSSS...
NNNN

SCROLL 4
ABSORPTION

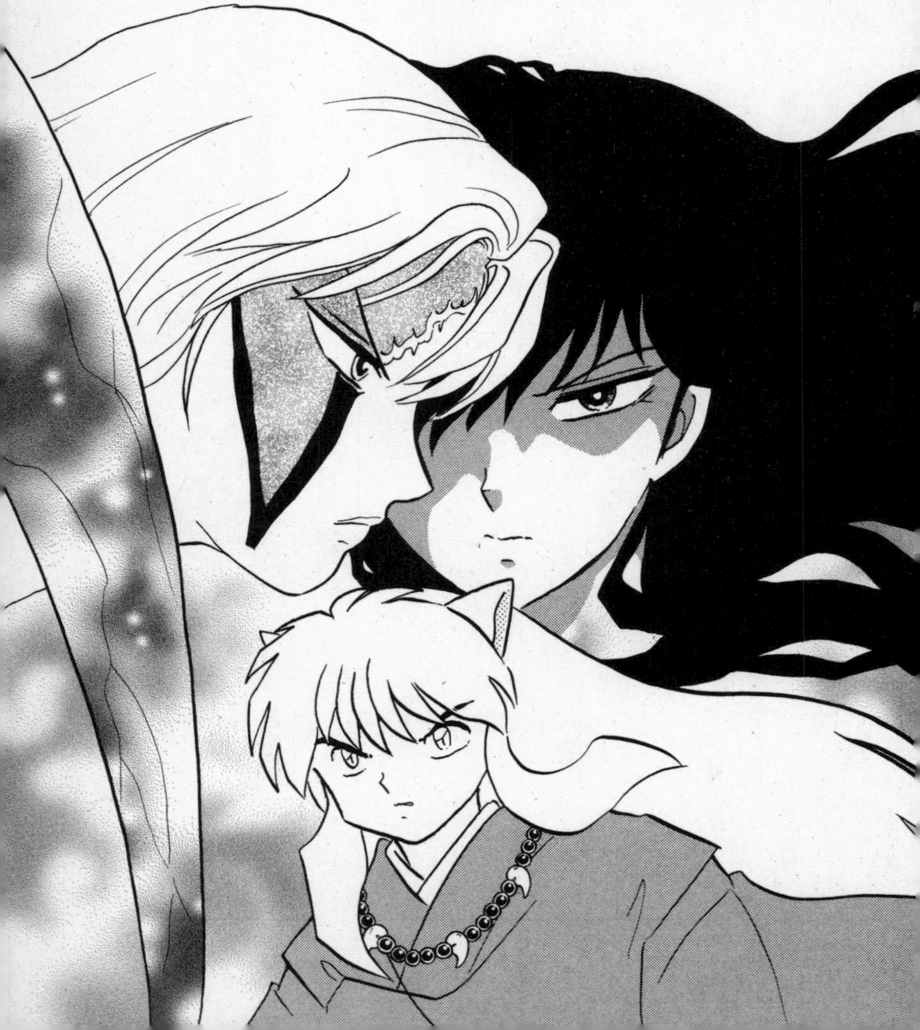

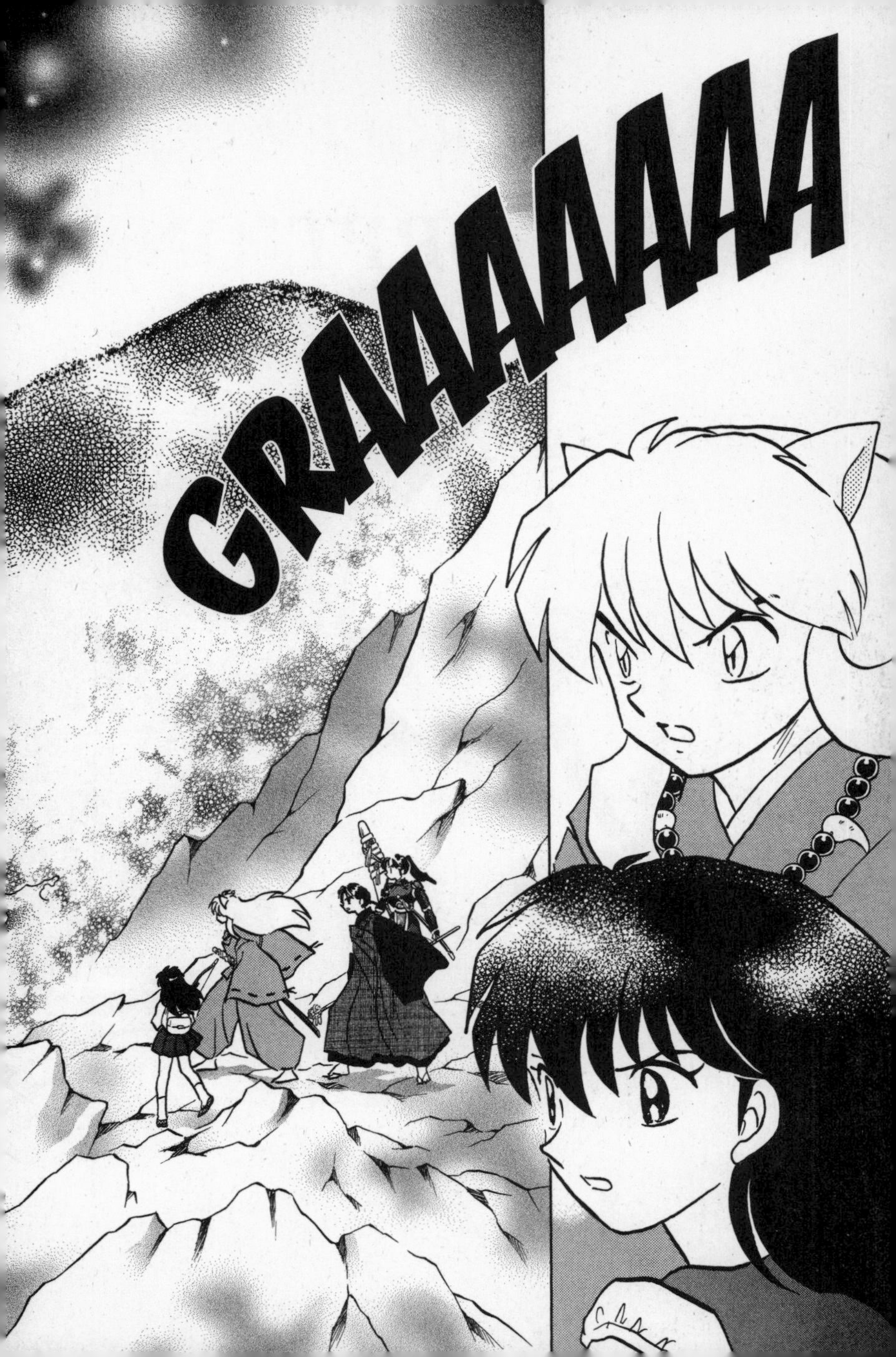
GRAAAAAAA

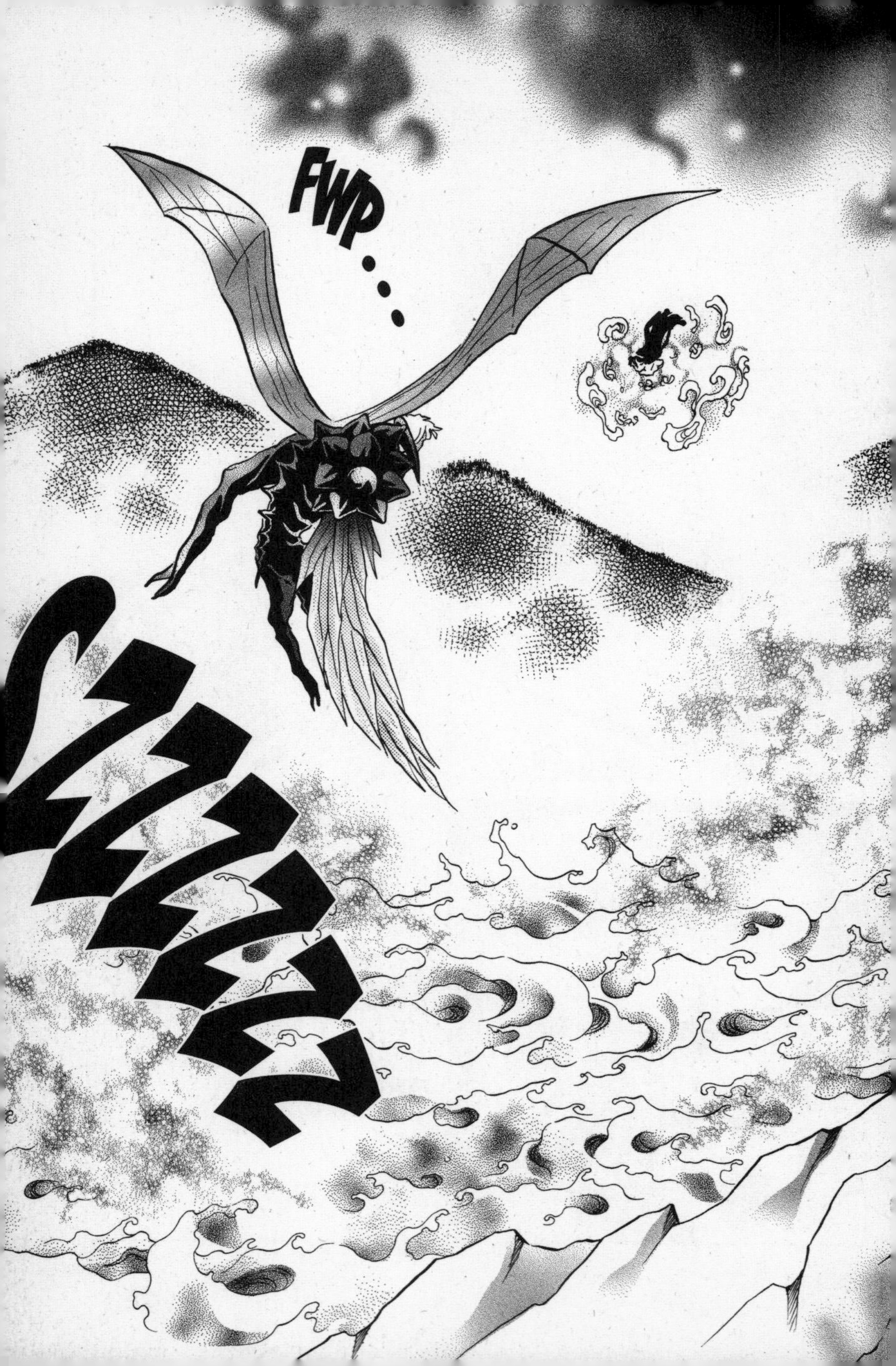
FWP...
CHZZZZZZ

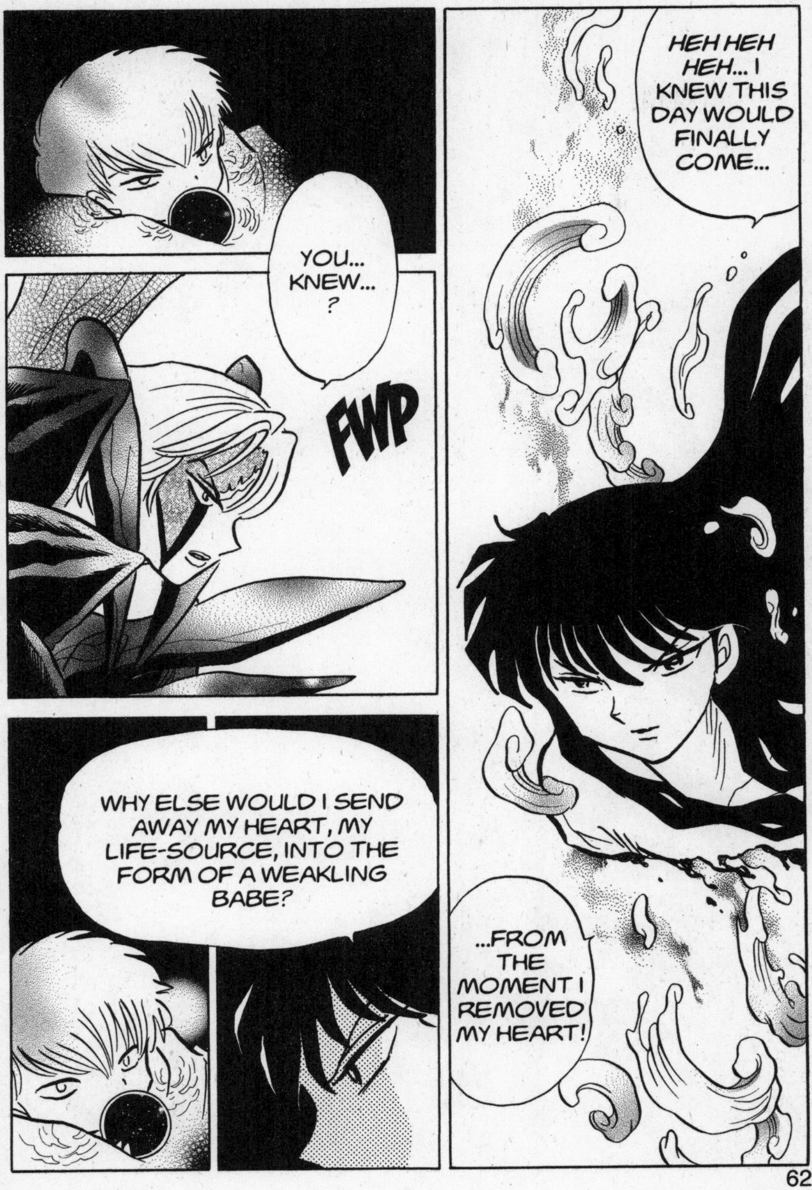
HEH HEH HEH... I KNEW THIS DAY WOULD FINALLY COME...
...FROM THE MOMENT I REMOVED MY HEART!
YOU... KNEW... ?
FWP
WHY ELSE WOULD I SEND AWAY MY HEART, MY LIFE-SOURCE, INTO THE FORM OF A WEAKLING BABE?

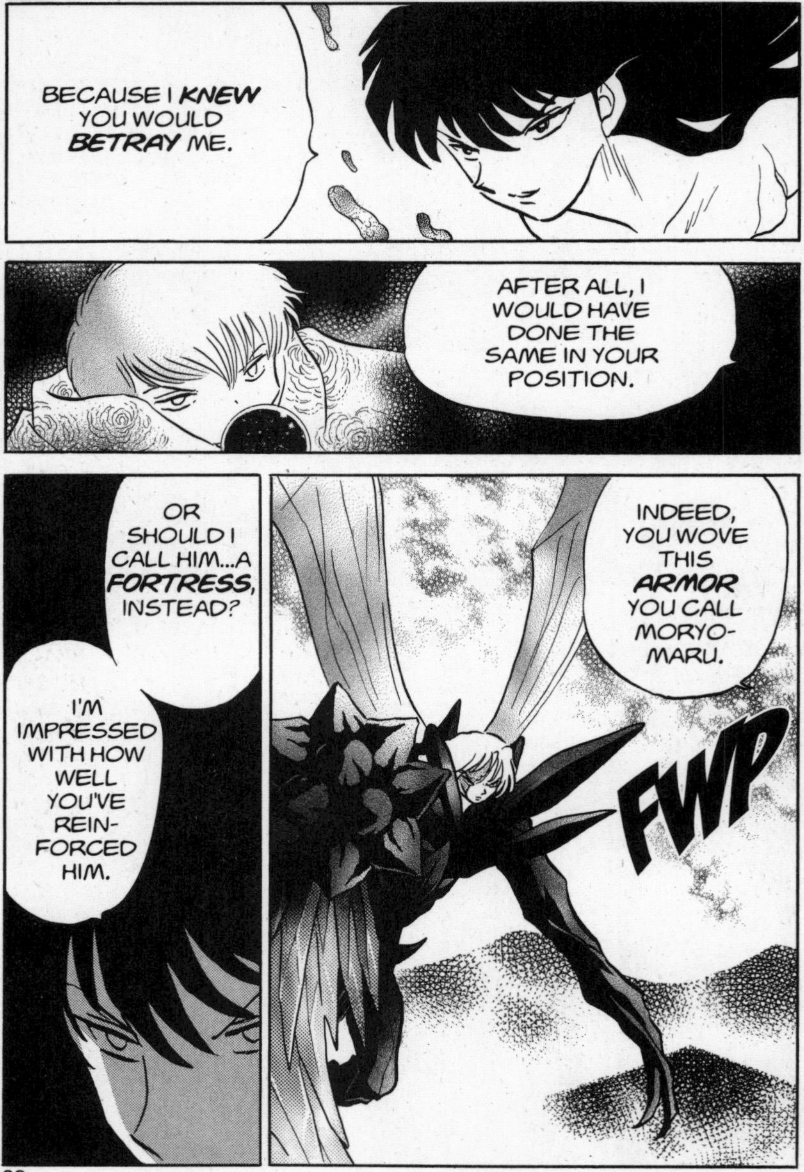
BECAUSE I **KNEW** YOU WOULD **BETRAY** ME.
AFTER ALL, I WOULD HAVE DONE THE SAME IN YOUR POSITION.
INDEED, YOU WOVE THIS **ARMOR** YOU CALL MORYO-MARU.
FWP
OR SHOULD I CALL HIM...A **FORTRESS**, INSTEAD?
I'M IMPRESSED WITH HOW WELL YOU'VE REIN-FORCED HIM.

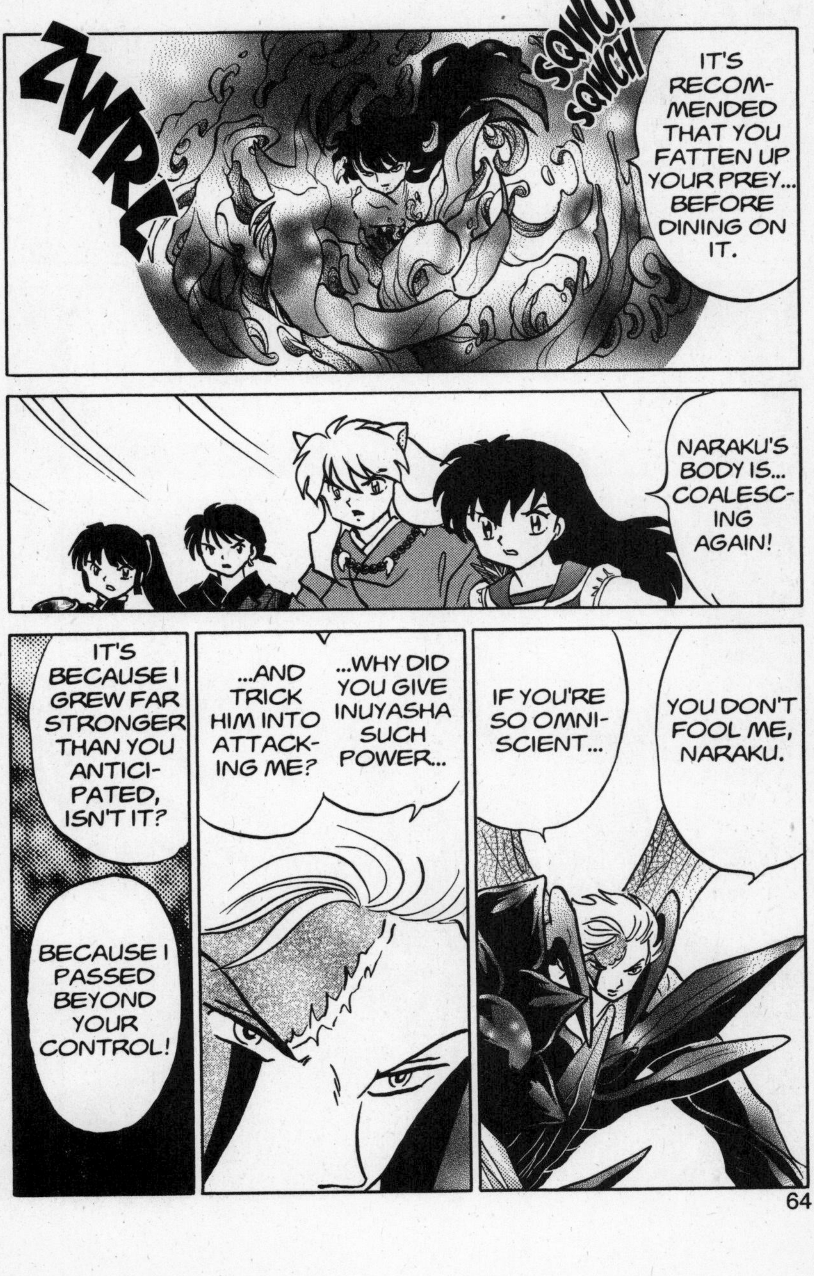
IT'S RECOMMENDED THAT YOU FATTEN UP YOUR PREY... BEFORE DINING ON IT.
SQWCH SQWCH
ZWRL
NARAKU'S BODY IS... COALESCING AGAIN!
YOU DON'T FOOL ME, NARAKU.
IF YOU'RE SO OMNISCIENT...
...WHY DID YOU GIVE INUYASHA SUCH POWER...
...AND TRICK HIM INTO ATTACKING ME?
IT'S BECAUSE I GREW FAR STRONGER THAN YOU ANTICIPATED, ISN'T IT?
BECAUSE I PASSED BEYOND YOUR CONTROL!

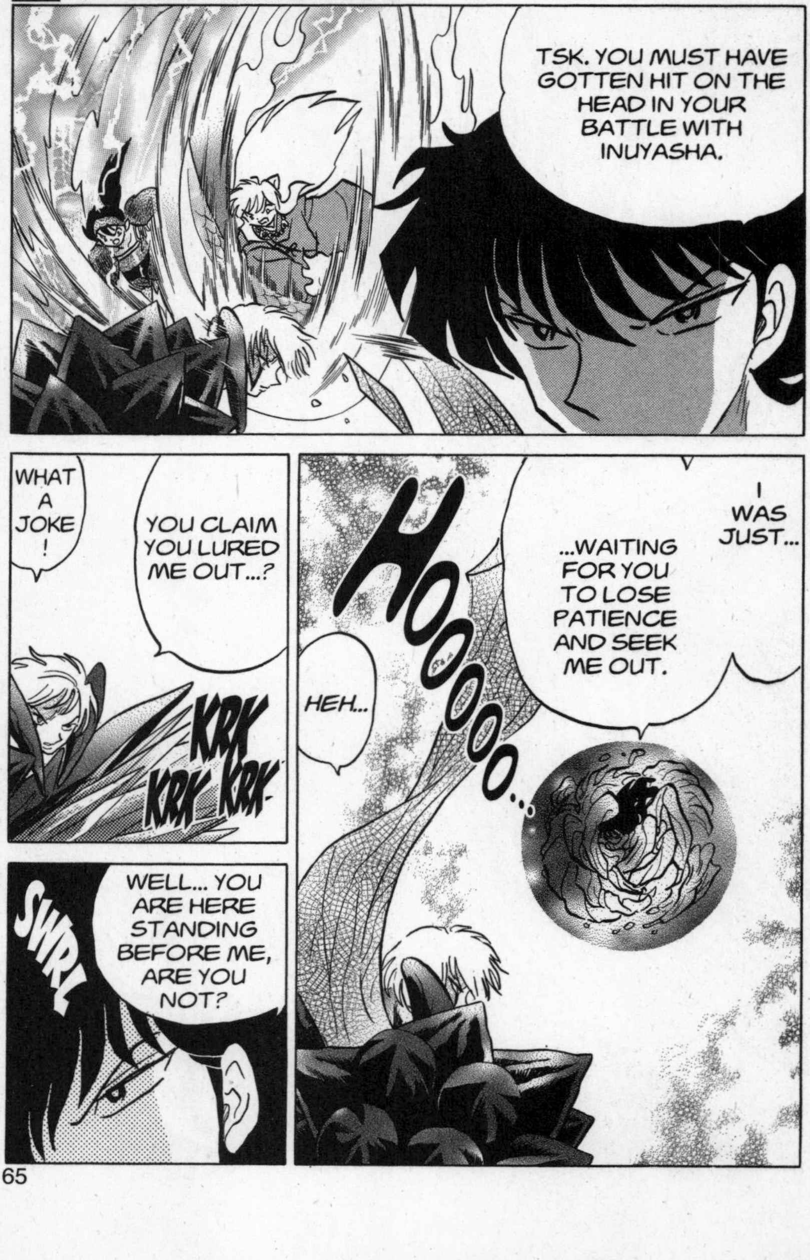
TSK. YOU MUST HAVE GOTTEN HIT ON THE HEAD IN YOUR BATTLE WITH INUYASHA.
I WAS JUST...
...WAITING FOR YOU TO LOSE PATIENCE AND SEEK ME OUT.
HOOOOOO...
HEH...
YOU CLAIM YOU LURED ME OUT...?
WHAT A JOKE!
KRK KRK KRK KRK
SWRL
WELL... YOU ARE HERE STANDING BEFORE ME, ARE YOU NOT?

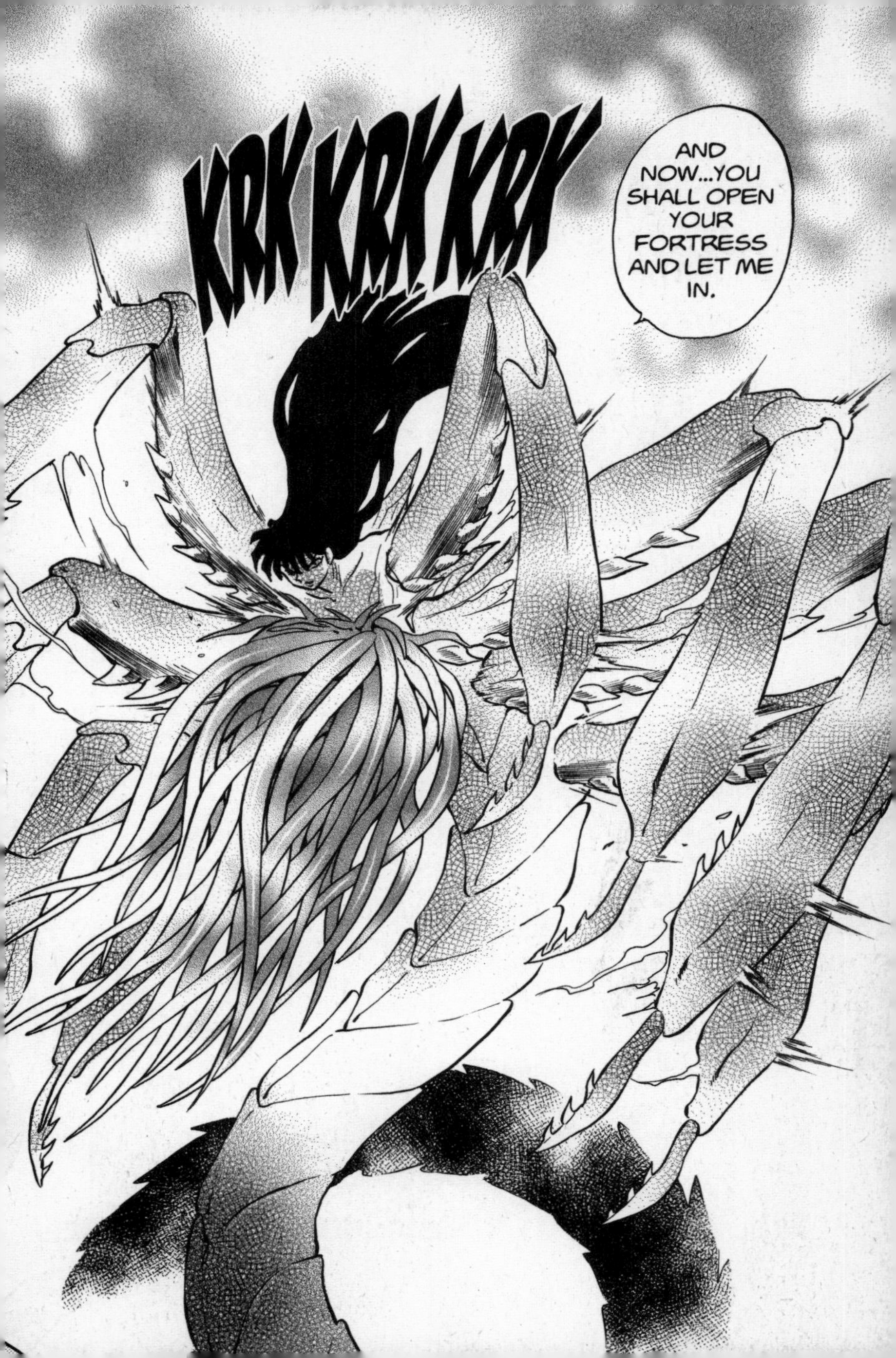
AND NOW...YOU SHALL OPEN YOUR FORTRESS AND LET ME IN.
KRK KRK KRK

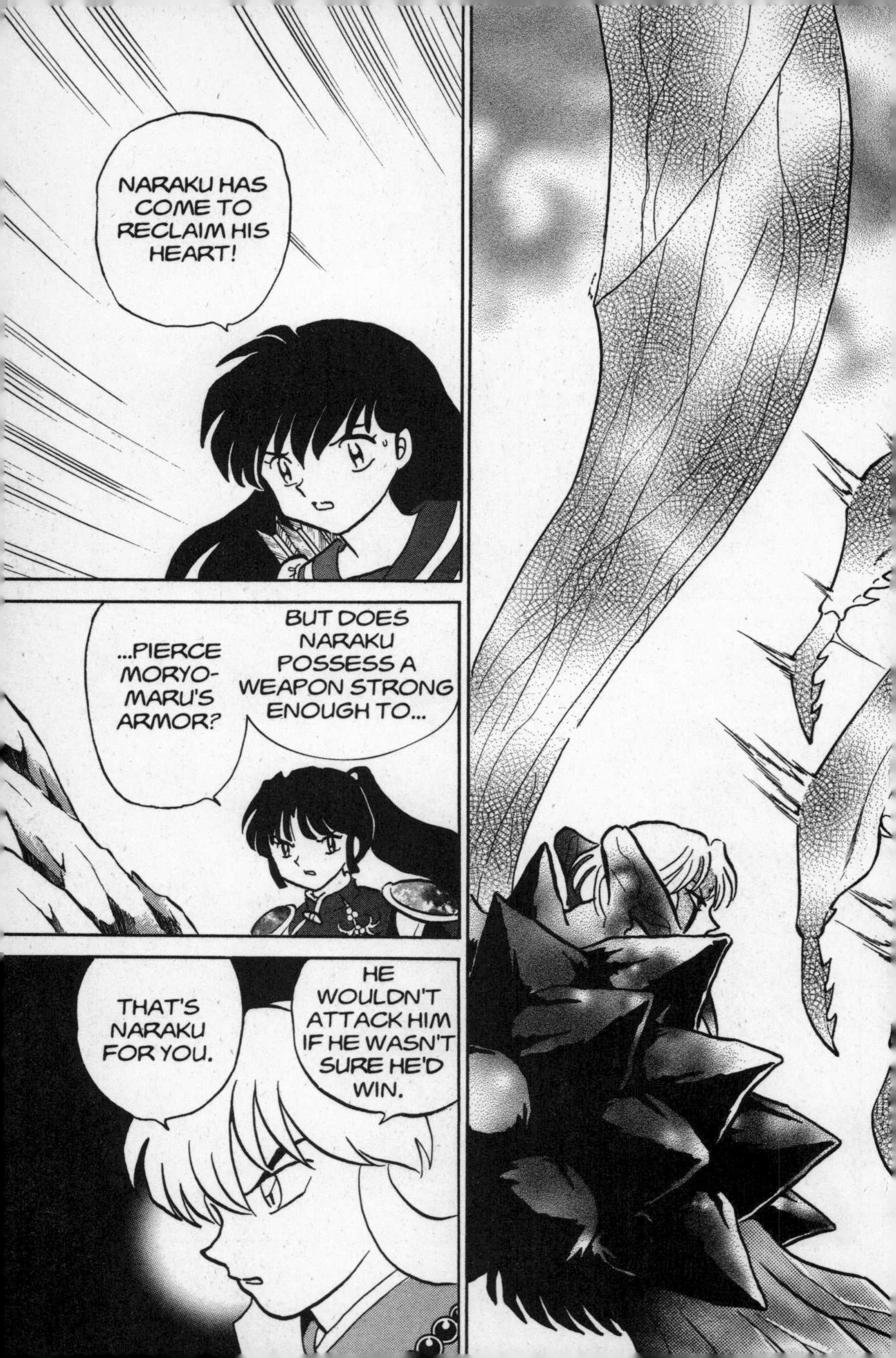
NARAKU HAS COME TO RECLAIM HIS HEART!
BUT DOES NARAKU POSSESS A WEAPON STRONG ENOUGH TO...
...PIERCE MORYO-MARU'S ARMOR?
HE WOULDN'T ATTACK HIM IF HE WASN'T SURE HE'D WIN.
THAT'S NARAKU FOR YOU.

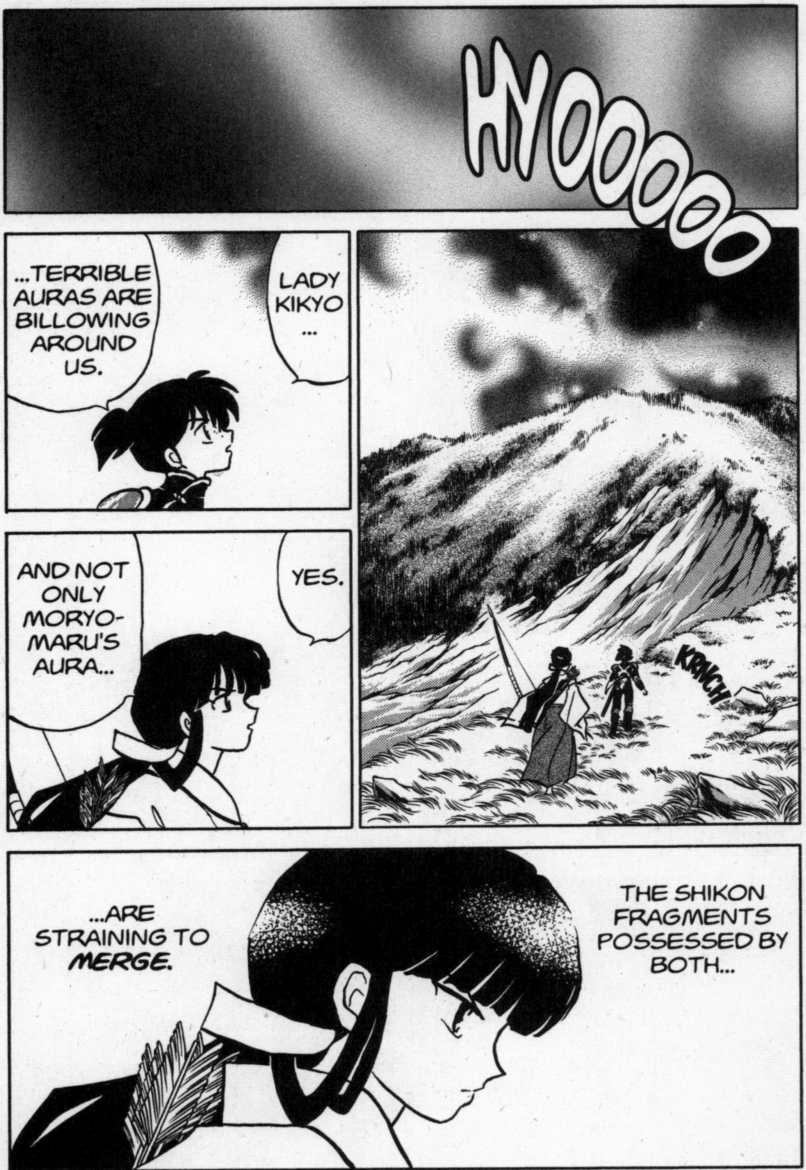
HYOOOOOO
KRANCH
LADY KIKYO...
...TERRIBLE AURAS ARE BILLOWING AROUND US.
YES.
AND NOT ONLY MORYO-MARU'S AURA...
THE SHIKON FRAGMENTS POSSESSED BY BOTH...
...ARE STRAINING TO *MERGE*.

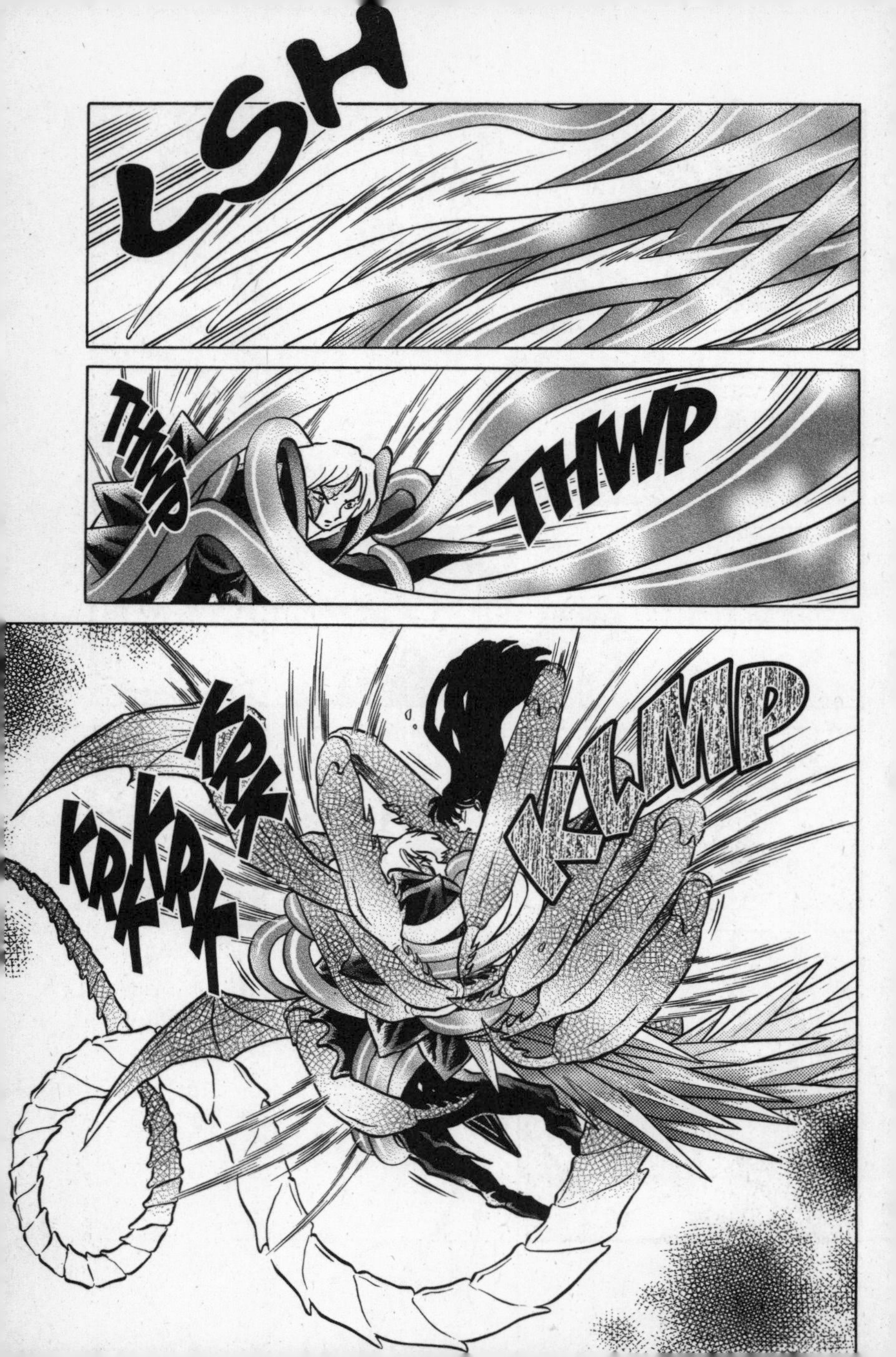
LSH
THWP
THWP
KLUMP
KRK
KRK
KRK

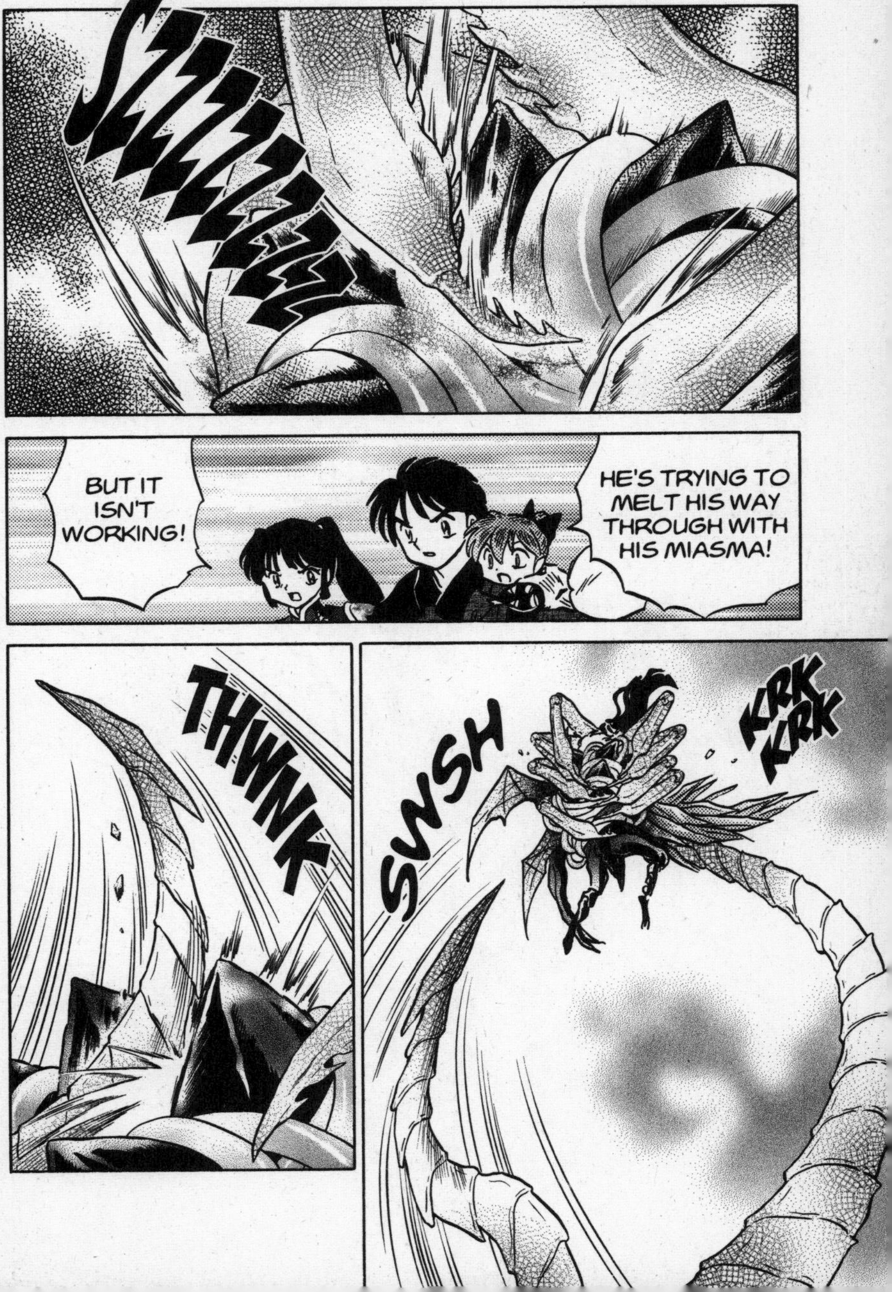
SZZZZZZZZ
HE'S TRYING TO MELT HIS WAY THROUGH WITH HIS MIASMA!
BUT IT ISN'T WORKING!
KRK KRK
SWSH
THWNK

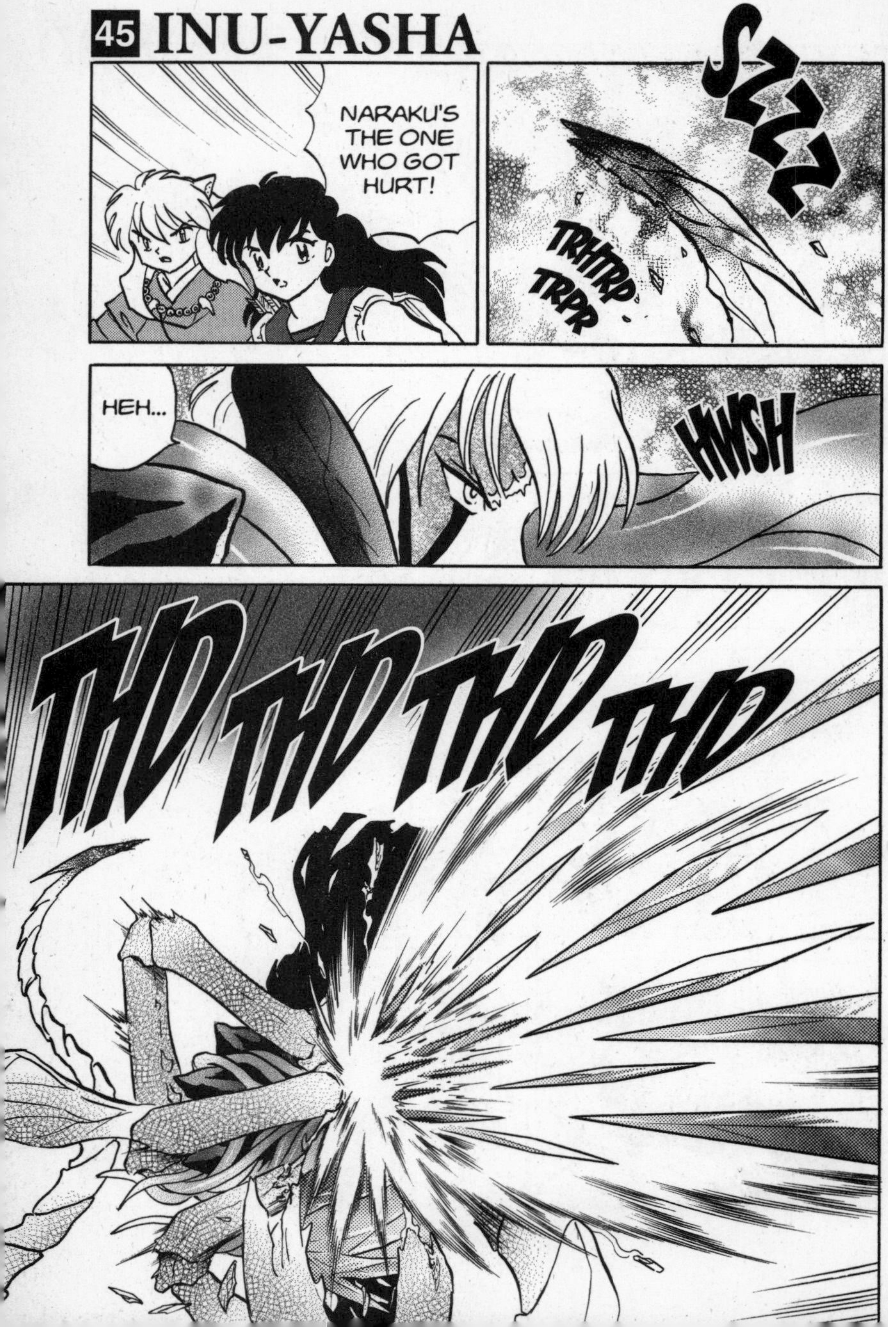
SZZZ
TRHTRP TRPR
NARAKU'S THE ONE WHO GOT HURT!
HWSH
HEH...
THD THD THD THD

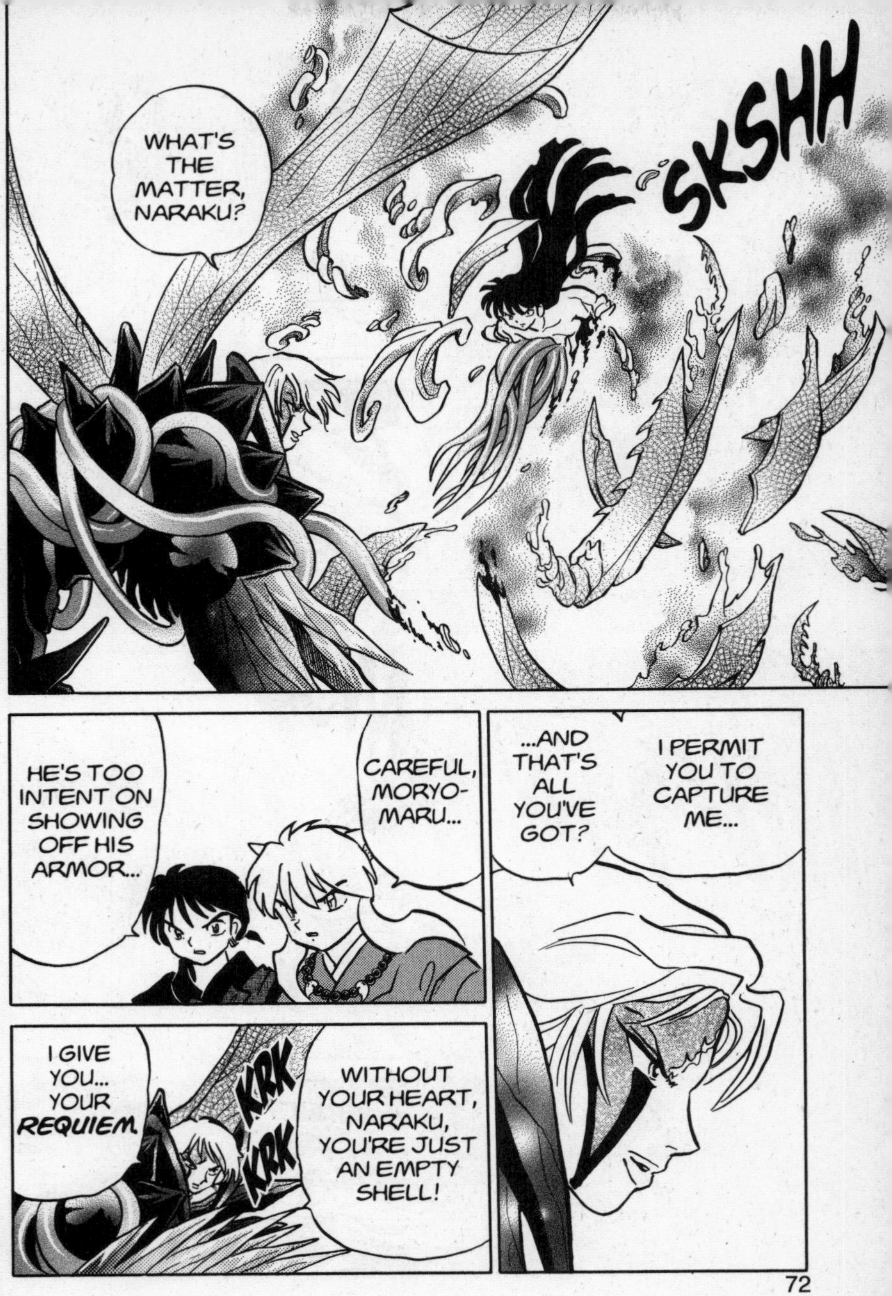
SKSHH
WHAT'S THE MATTER, NARAKU?
I PERMIT YOU TO CAPTURE ME...
...AND THAT'S ALL YOU'VE GOT?
CAREFUL, MORYO-MARU...
HE'S TOO INTENT ON SHOWING OFF HIS ARMOR...
WITHOUT YOUR HEART, NARAKU, YOU'RE JUST AN EMPTY SHELL!
KRK KRK
I GIVE YOU... YOUR *REQUIEM.*

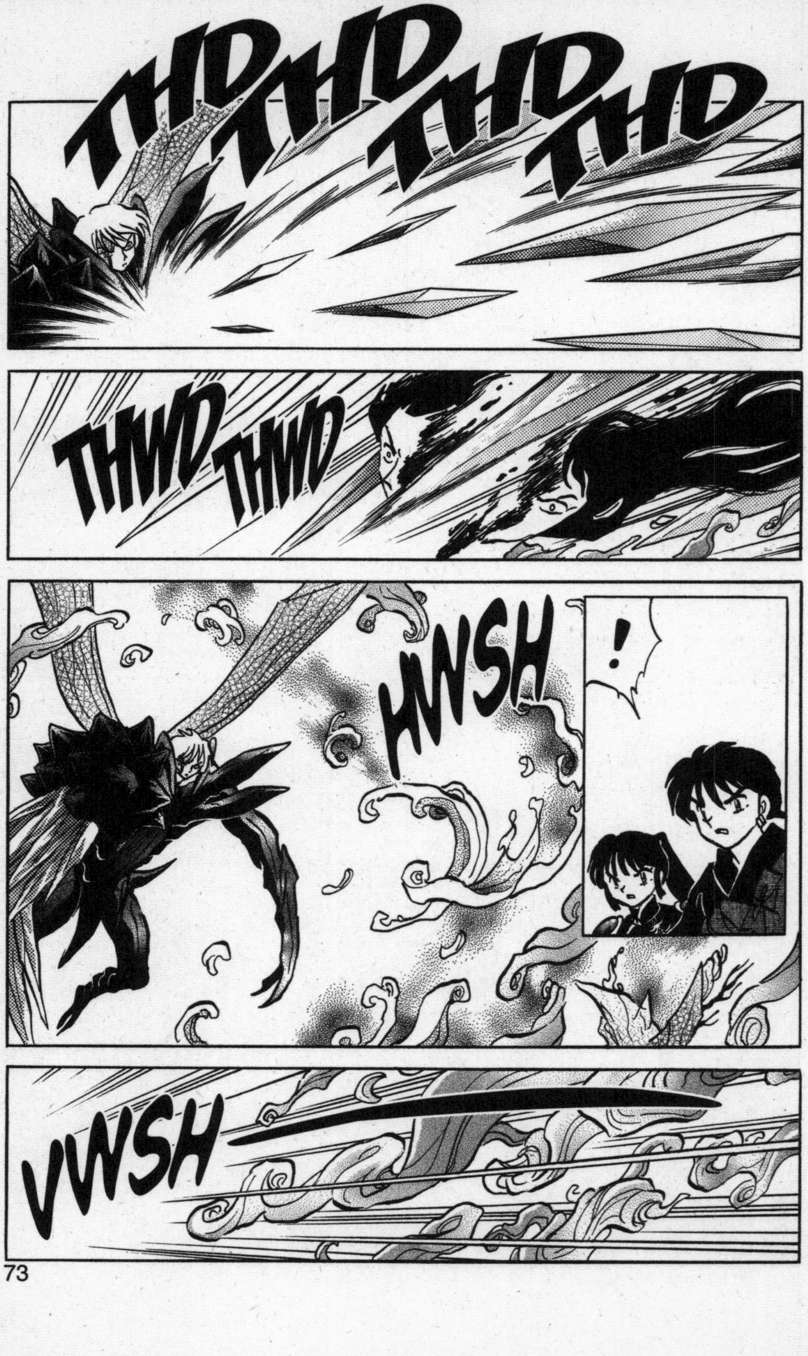
THD THD THD THD
THWD THWD
!
HWSH
VWSH

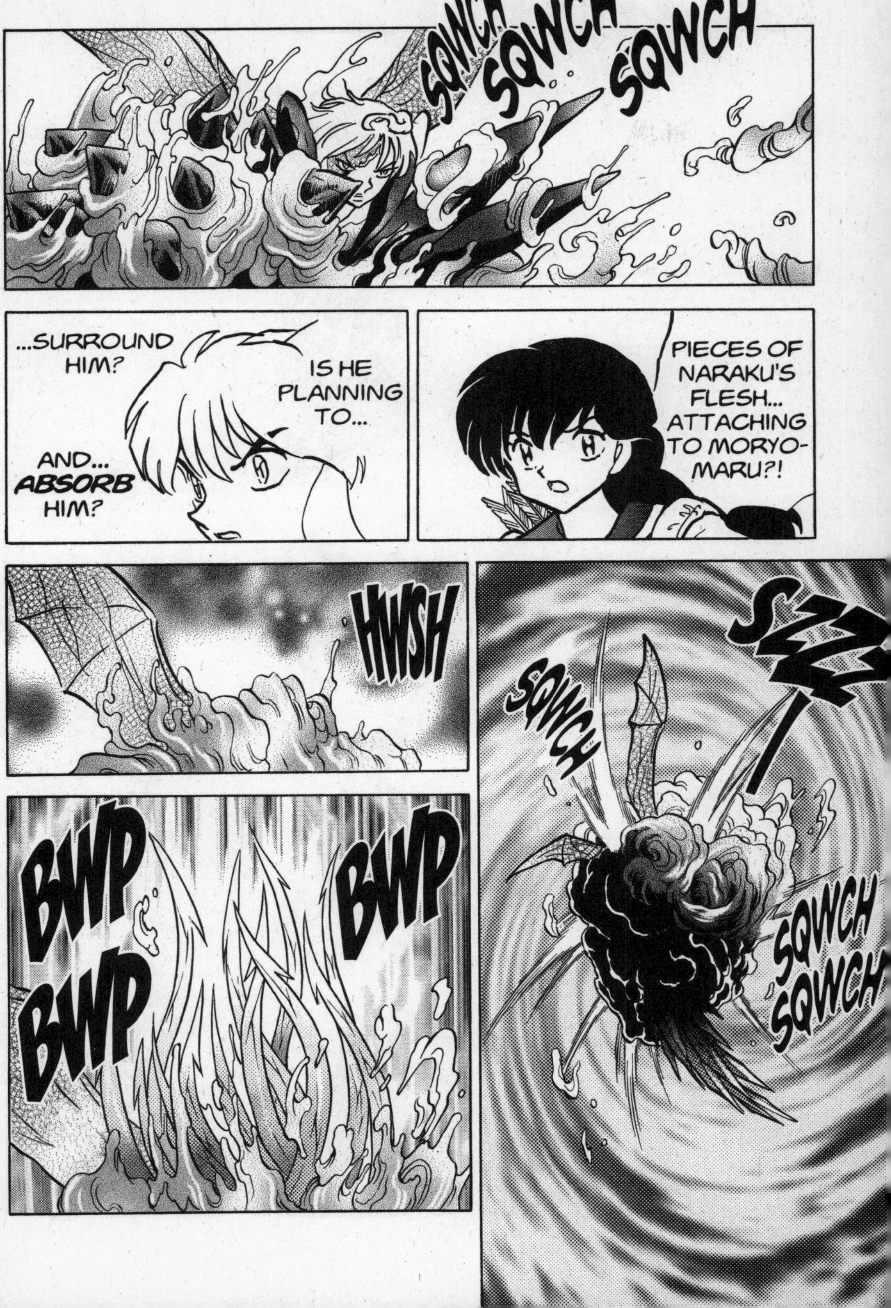
SQWCH
SQWCH
SQWCH
PIECES OF NARAKU'S FLESH... ATTACHING TO MORYO-MARU?!
IS HE PLANNING TO...
...SURROUND HIM?
AND... ABSORB HIM?
SQWCH
SQWCH SQWCH
HWSH
BWP
BWP
BWP

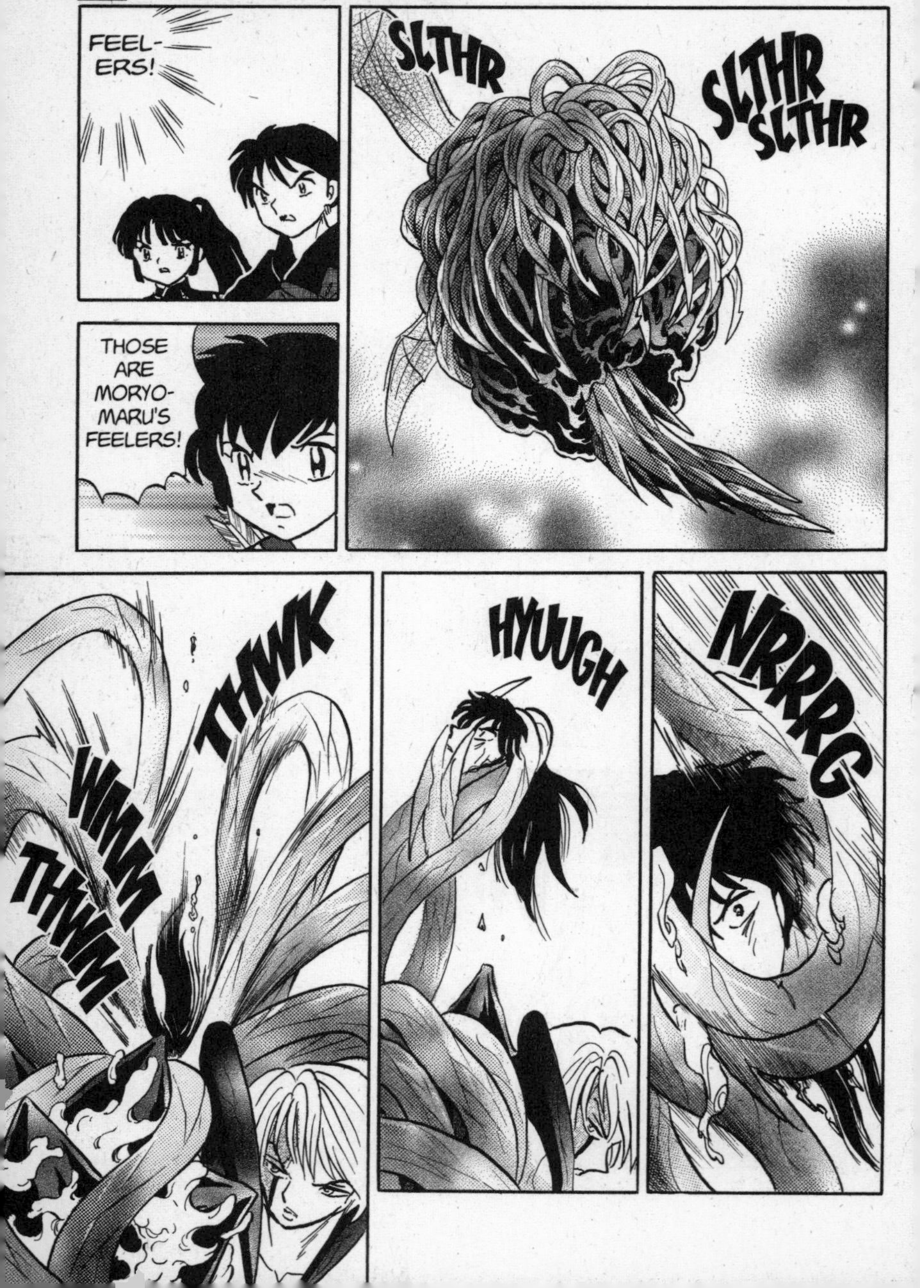
SLTHR
SLTHR SLTHR
FEEL-ERS!
THOSE ARE MORYO-MARU'S FEELERS!
NRRRG
HYUUGH
THWK
WMM THWM

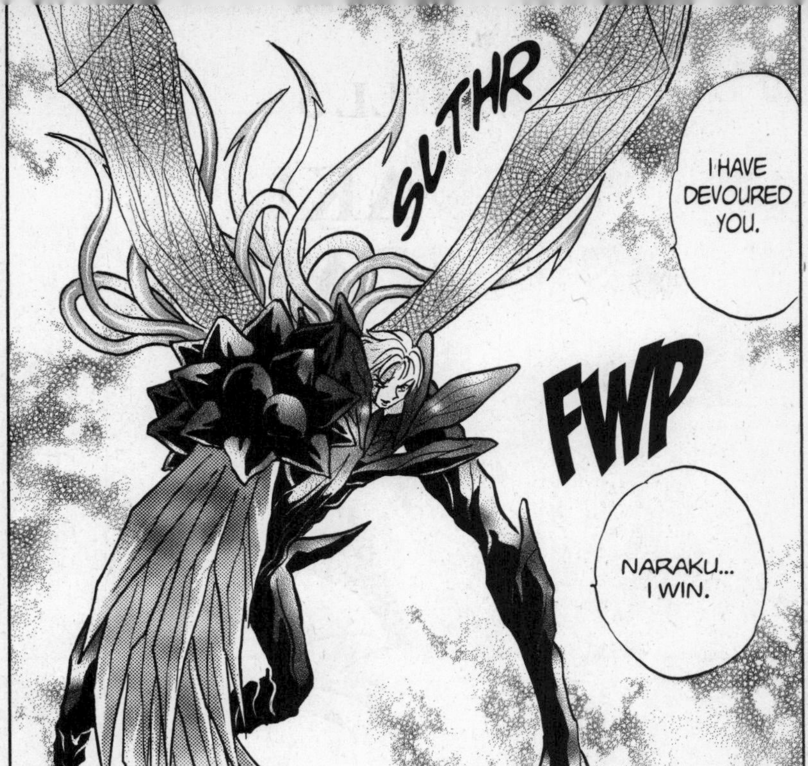
I HAVE DEVOURED YOU.
SLTHR
FWP
NARAKU... I WIN.

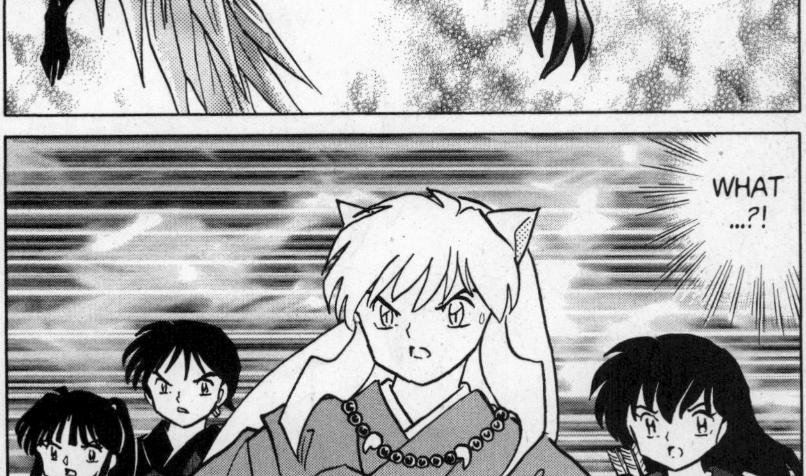
WHAT ...?!

SCROLL 5

NARAKU ERADICATED

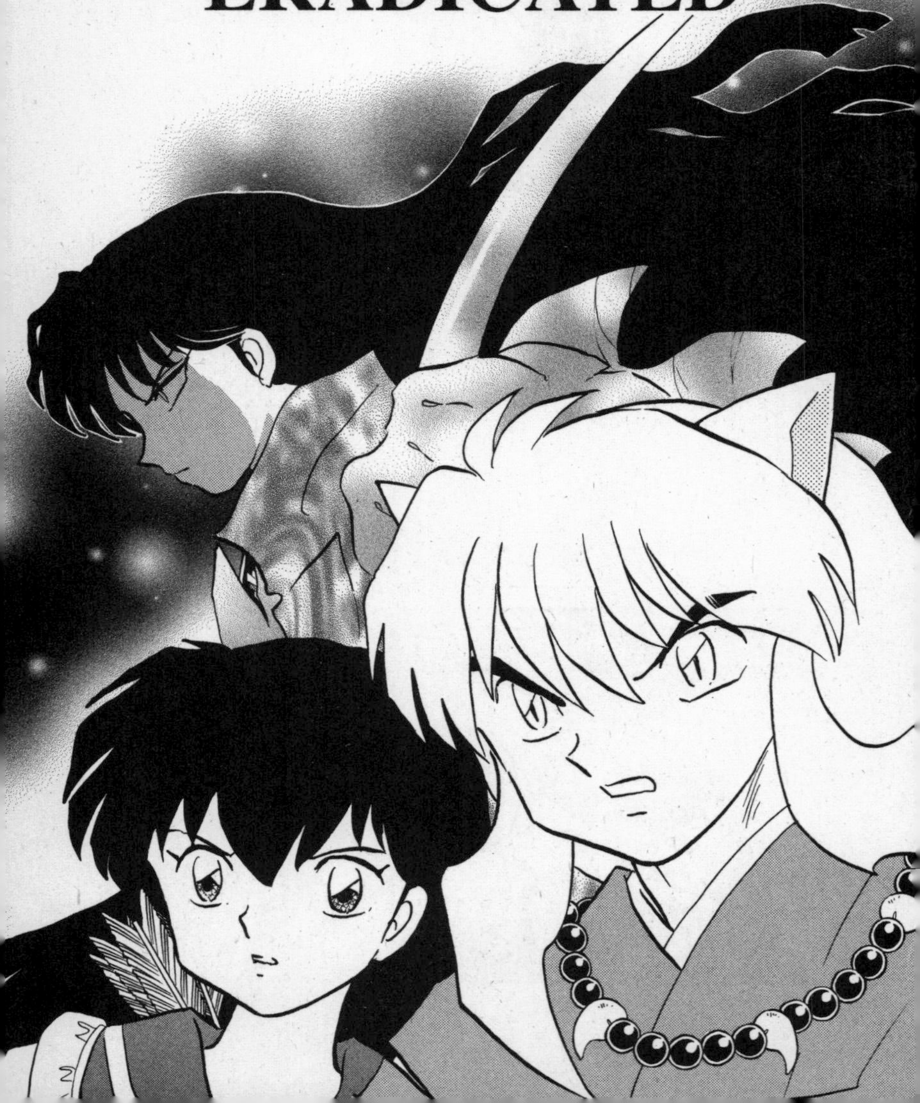

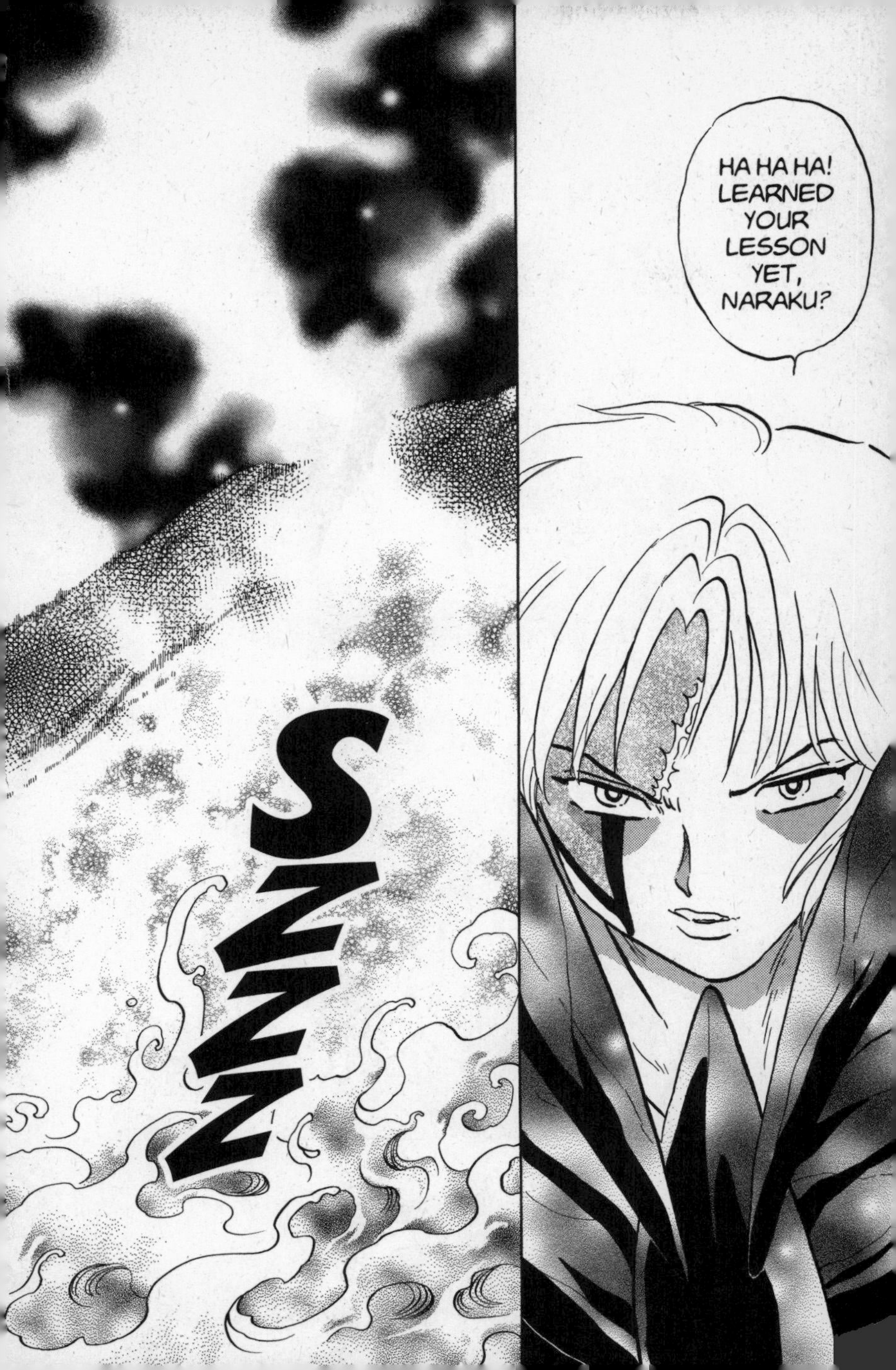
HA HA HA! LEARNED YOUR LESSON YET, NARAKU?

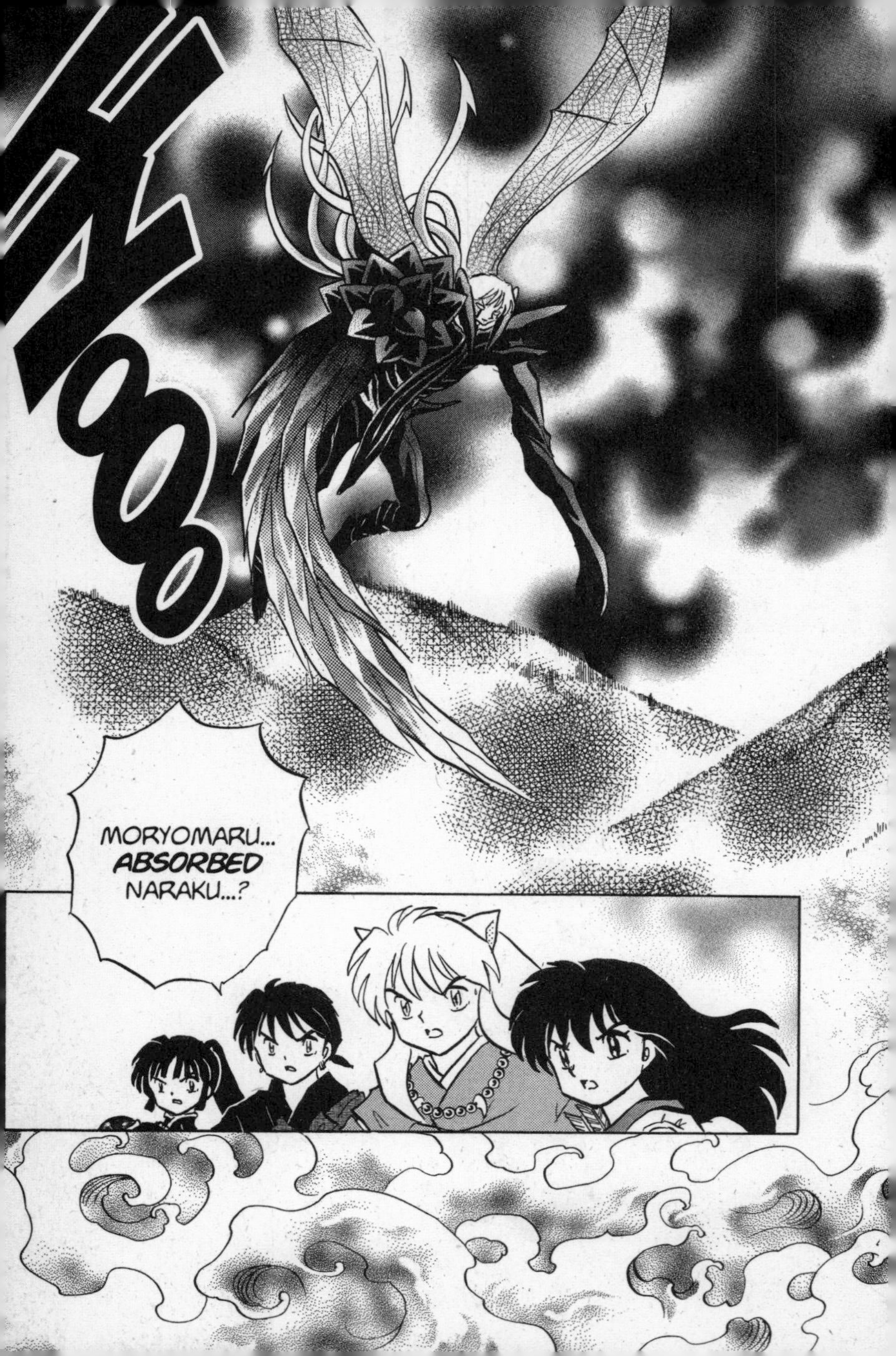
DOOO
MORYOMARU... **ABSORBED** NARAKU...?

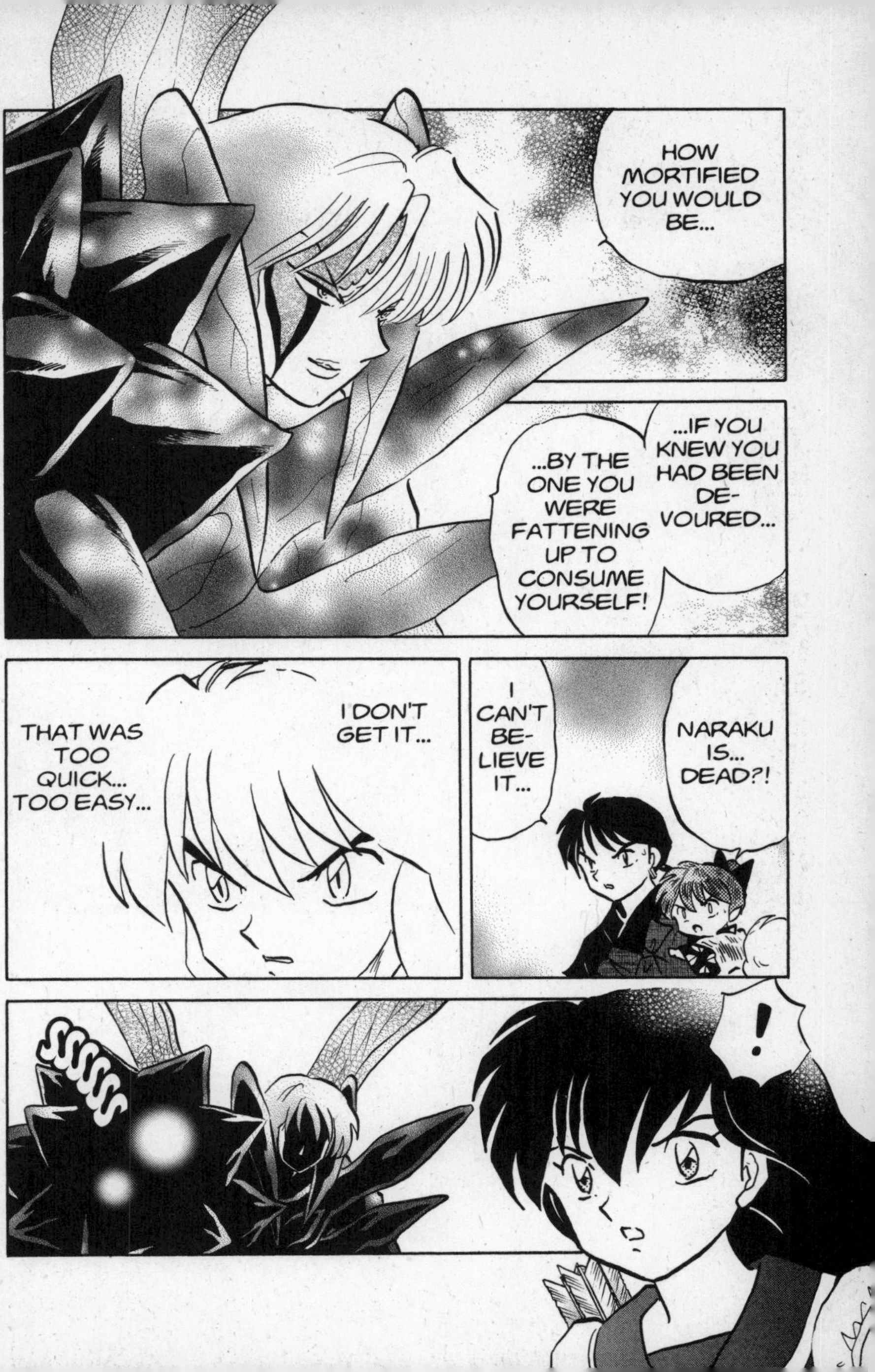
HOW MORTIFIED YOU WOULD BE...
...IF YOU KNEW YOU HAD BEEN DE- VOURED...
...BY THE ONE YOU WERE FATTENING UP TO CONSUME YOURSELF!
NARAKU IS... DEAD?!
I CAN'T BE- LIEVE IT...
I DON'T GET IT...
THAT WAS TOO QUICK... TOO EASY...
!
SSSSS

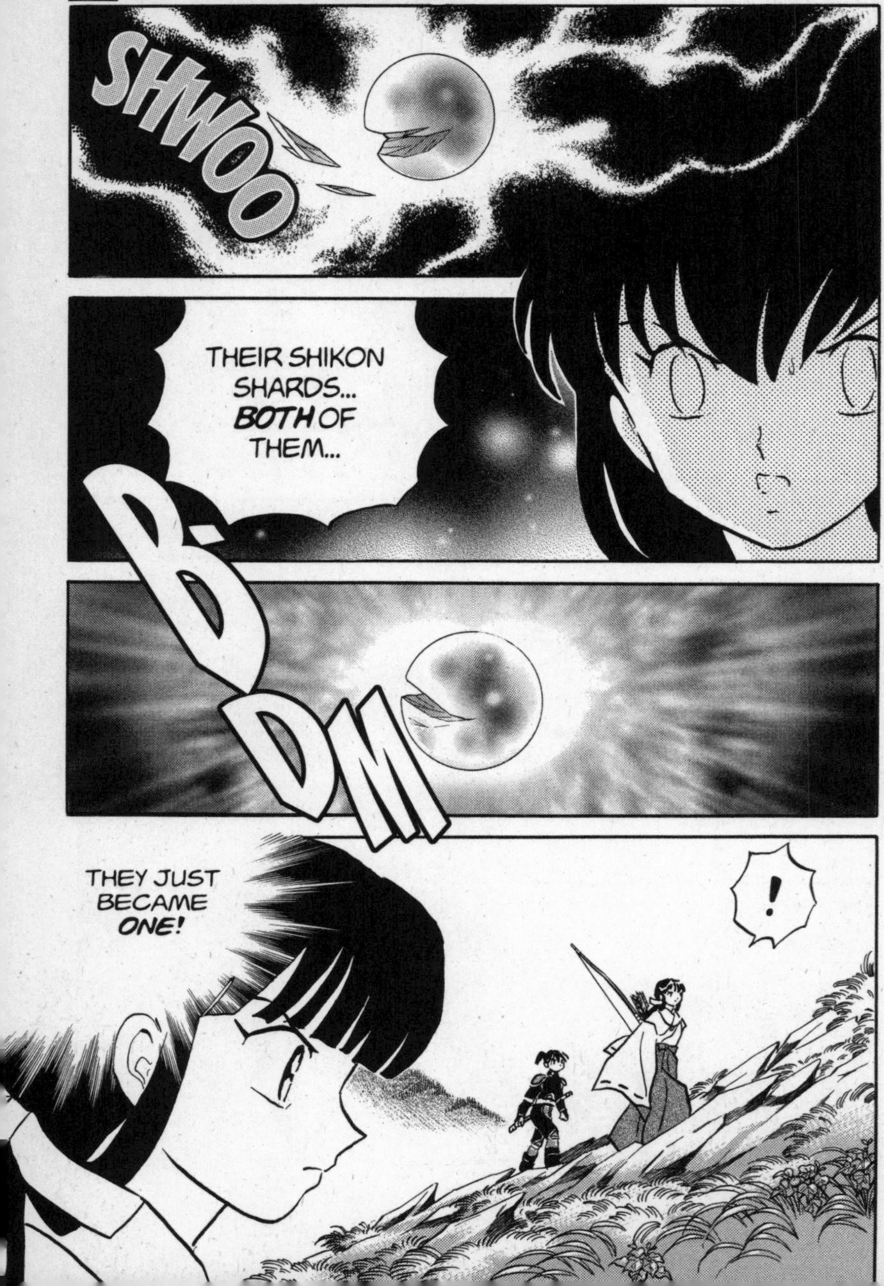
SHWOO
THEIR SHIKON SHARDS... BOTH OF THEM...
BDDM
THEY JUST BECAME ONE!
!

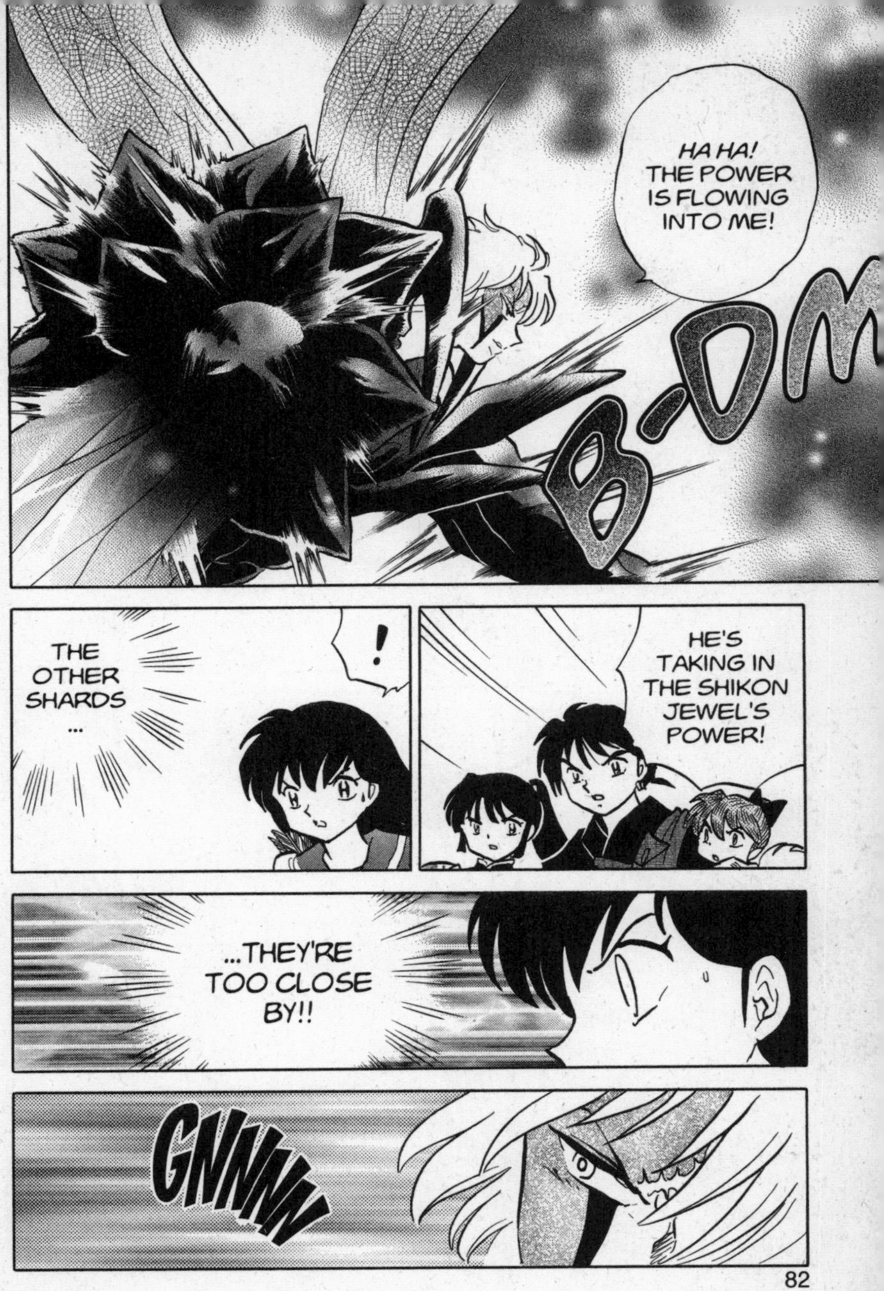
HA HA! THE POWER IS FLOWING INTO ME!
B-DOM
HE'S TAKING IN THE SHIKON JEWEL'S POWER!
!
THE OTHER SHARDS ...
...THEY'RE TOO CLOSE BY!!
GNNNN

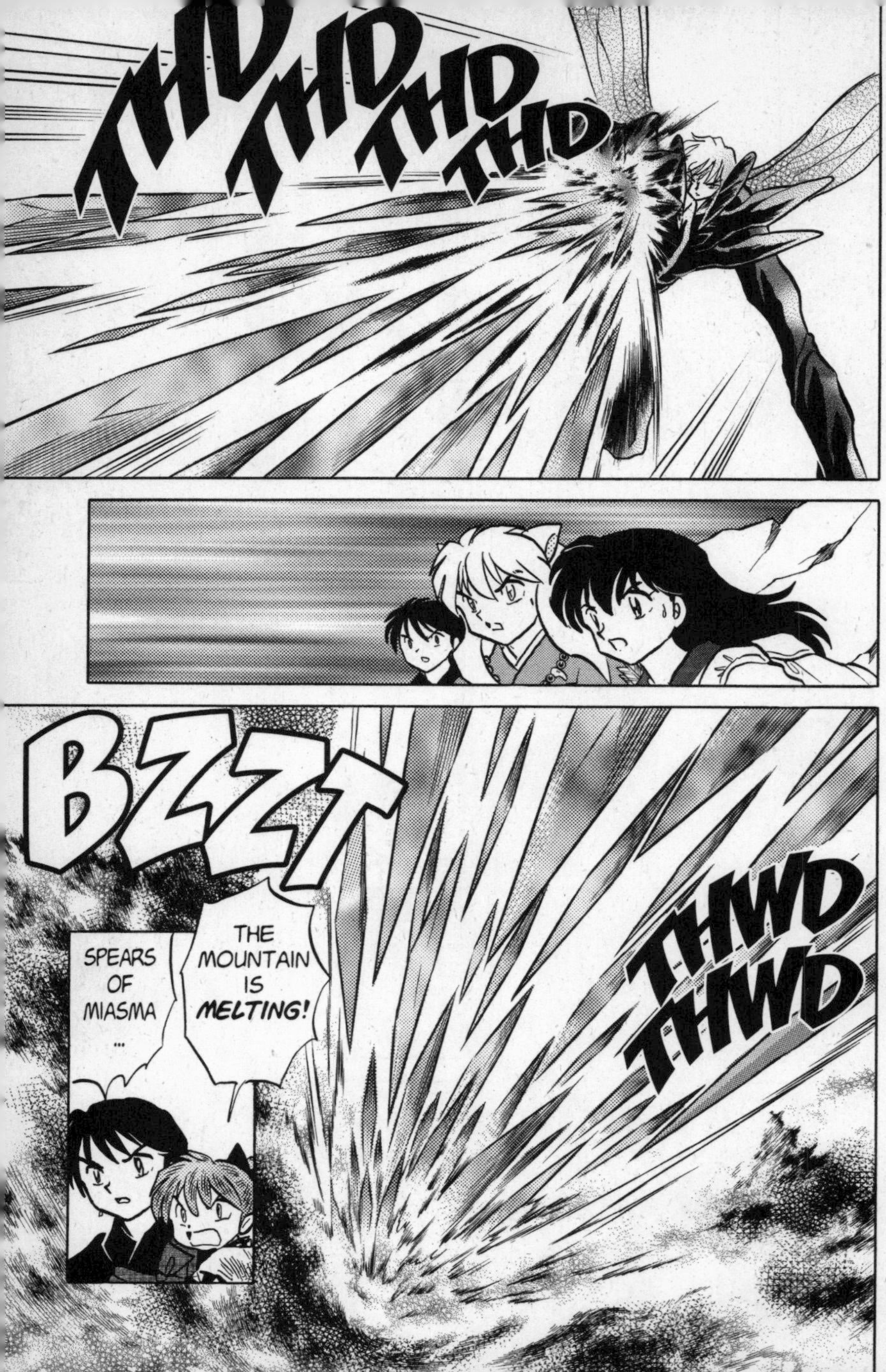
THD THD THD THD
BZZT
THWD THWD
THE MOUNTAIN IS *MELTING!*
SPEARS OF MIASMA ...

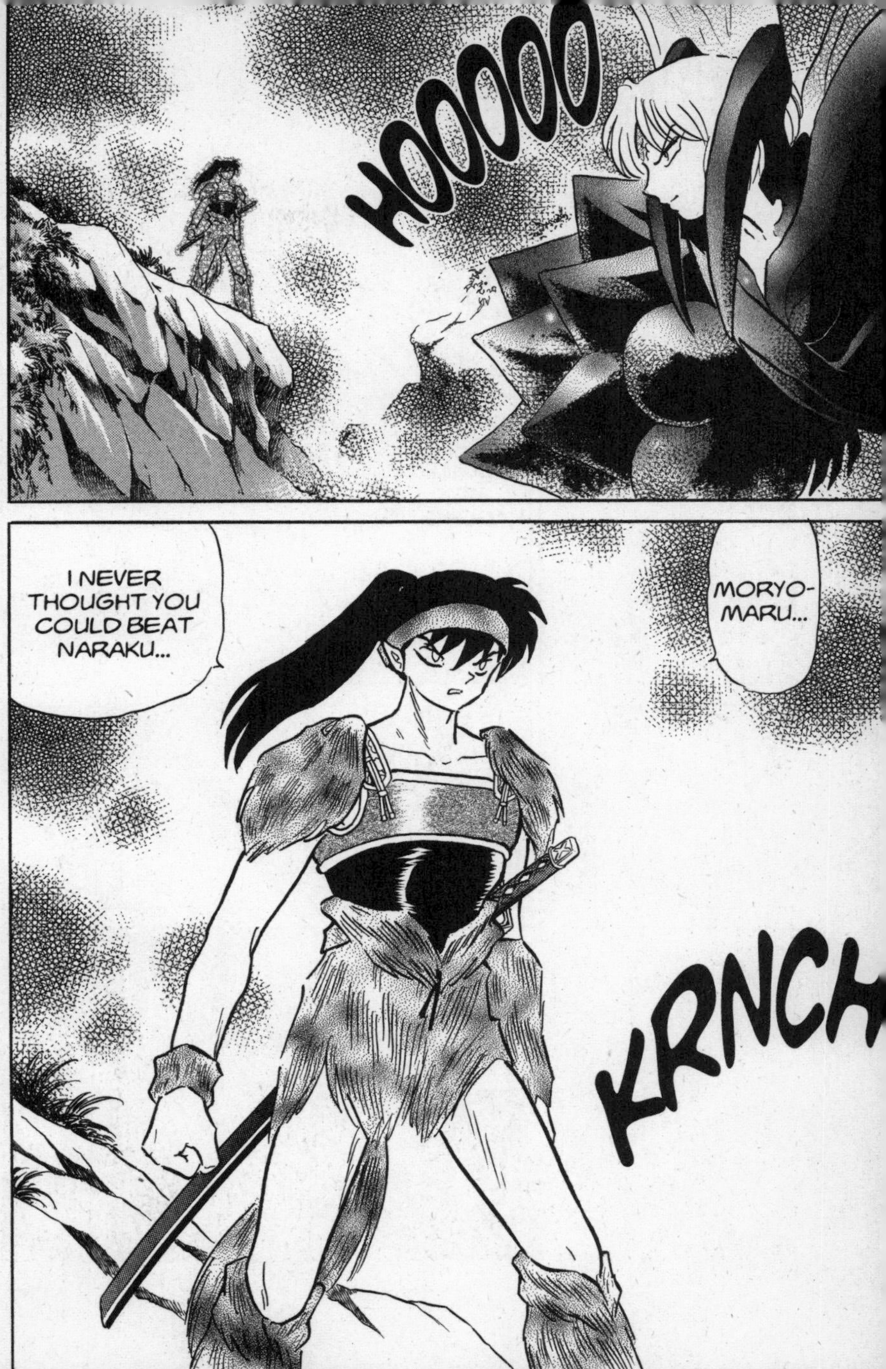
HOOOOO
MORYO-MARU...
I NEVER THOUGHT YOU COULD BEAT NARAKU...
KRNCH

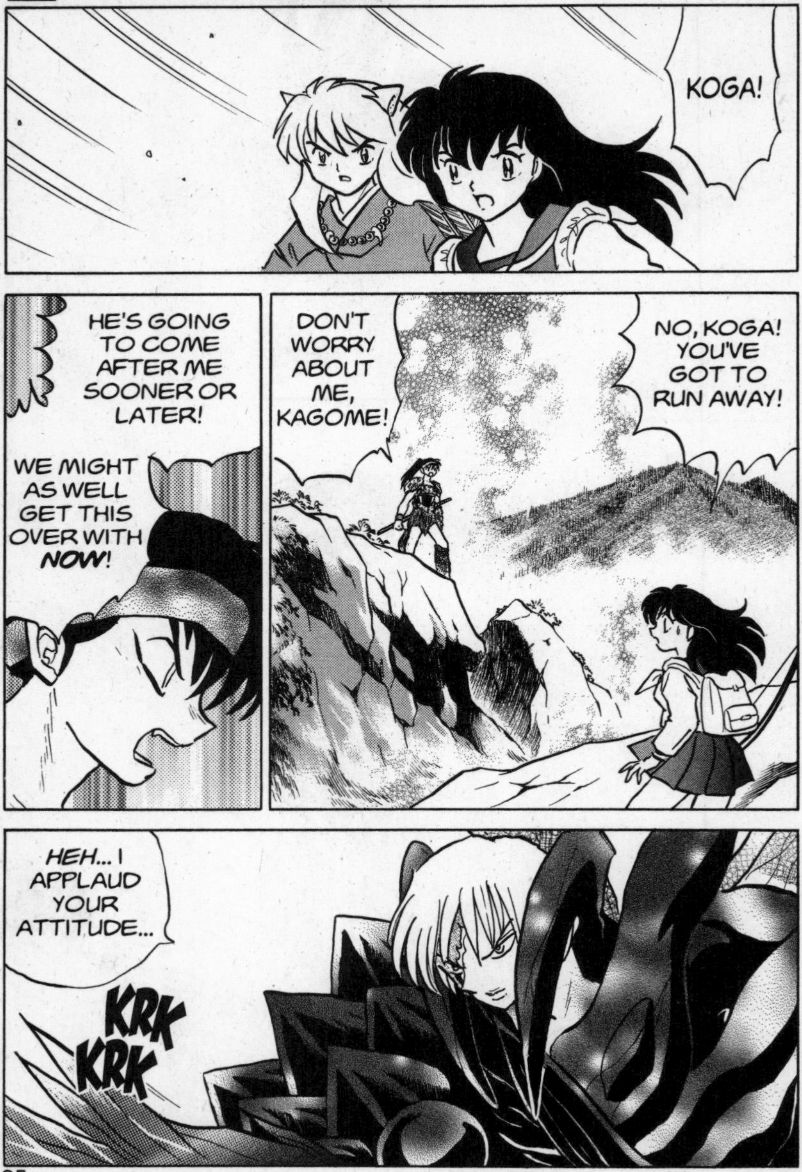
KOGA!
NO, KOGA! YOU'VE GOT TO RUN AWAY!
DON'T WORRY ABOUT ME, KAGOME!
HE'S GOING TO COME AFTER ME SOONER OR LATER!
WE MIGHT AS WELL GET THIS OVER WITH *NOW*!
HEH... I APPLAUD YOUR ATTITUDE...
KRK KRK

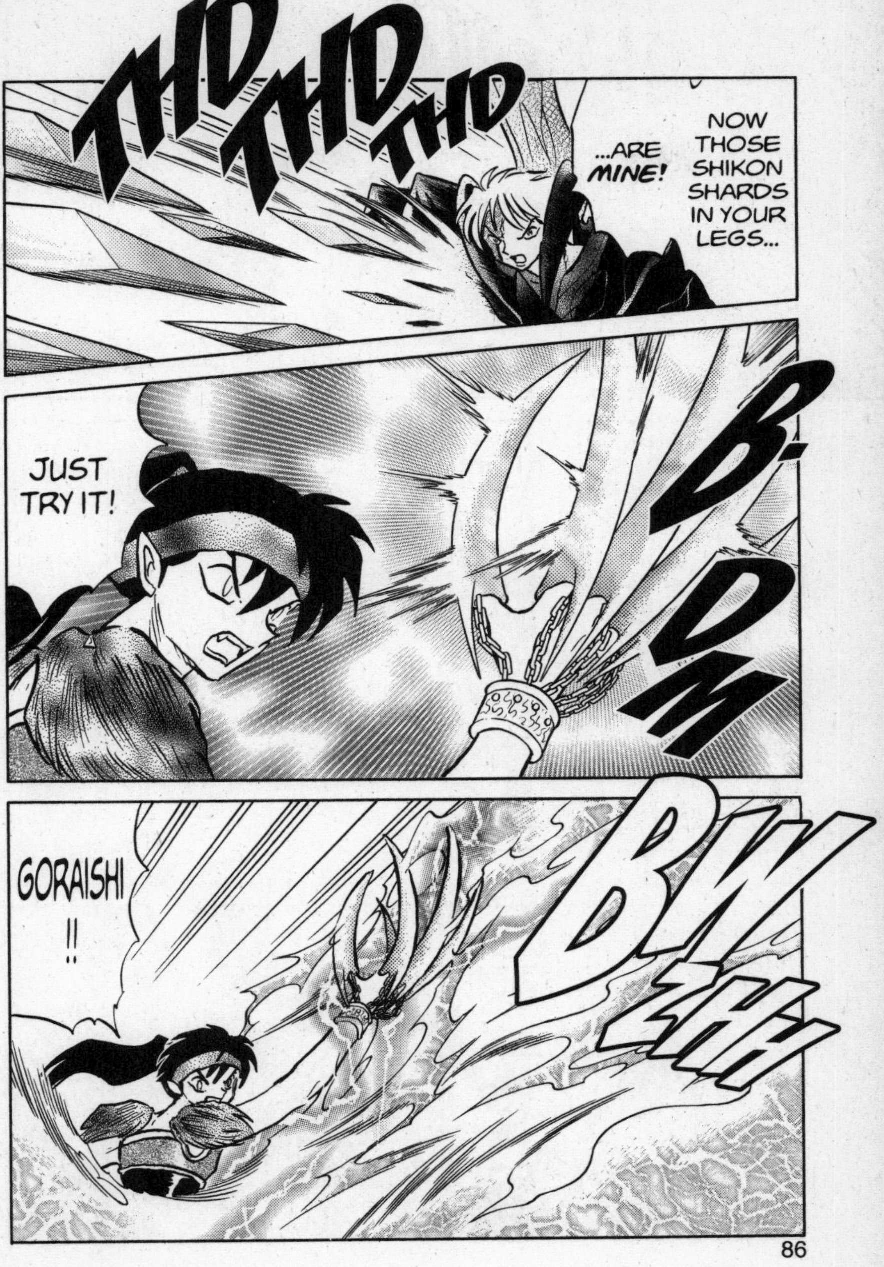
NOW THOSE SHIKON SHARDS IN YOUR LEGS...
...ARE MINE!
THD THD THD
B-DM
JUST TRY IT!
BWZHH
GORAISHI !!

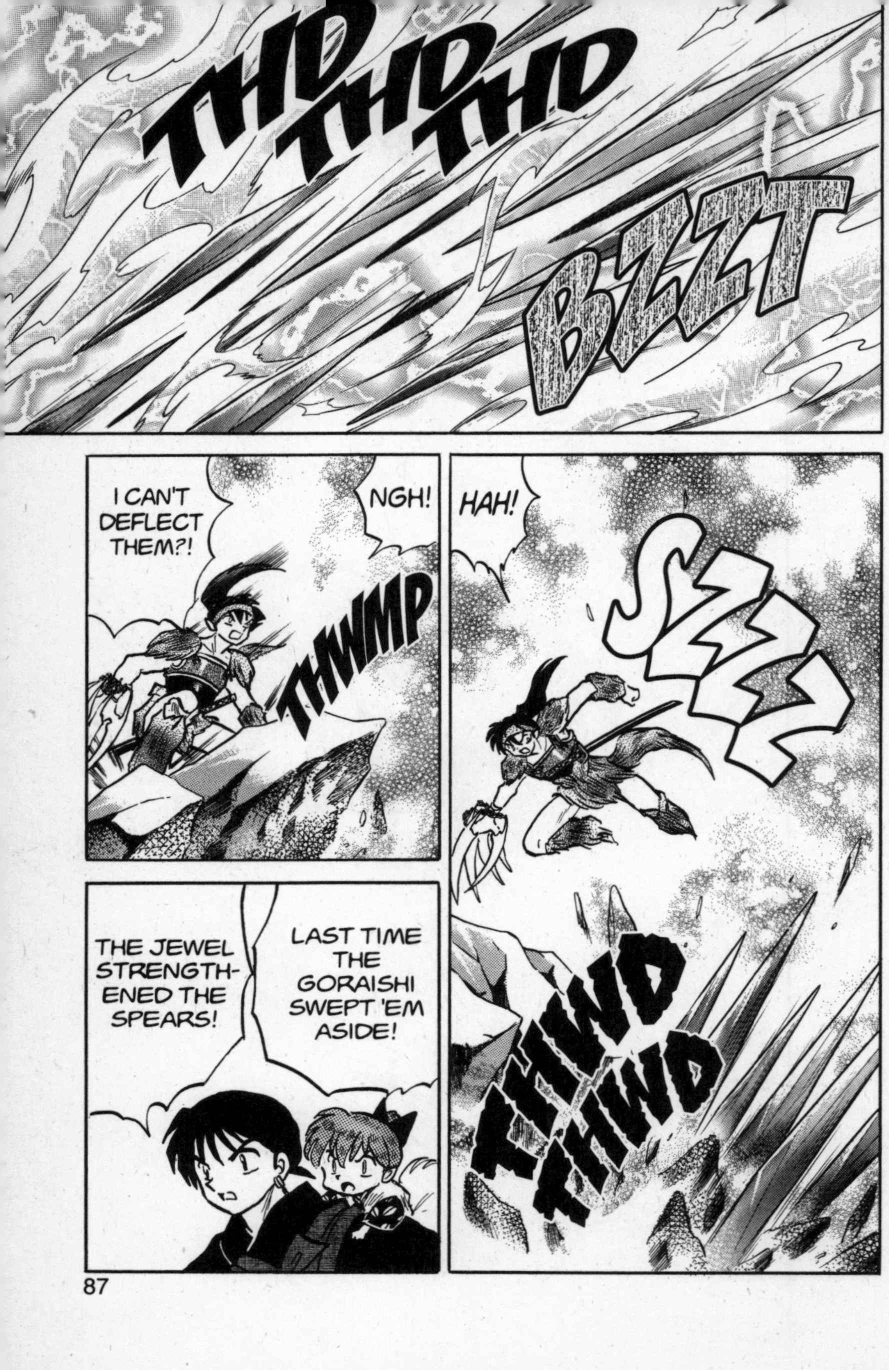
THD THD THD
BZZT
HAH!
SZZZ
THWD THWD
NGH!
I CAN'T DEFLECT THEM?!
THWMP
LAST TIME THE GORAISHI SWEPT 'EM ASIDE!
THE JEWEL STRENGTH-ENED THE SPEARS!

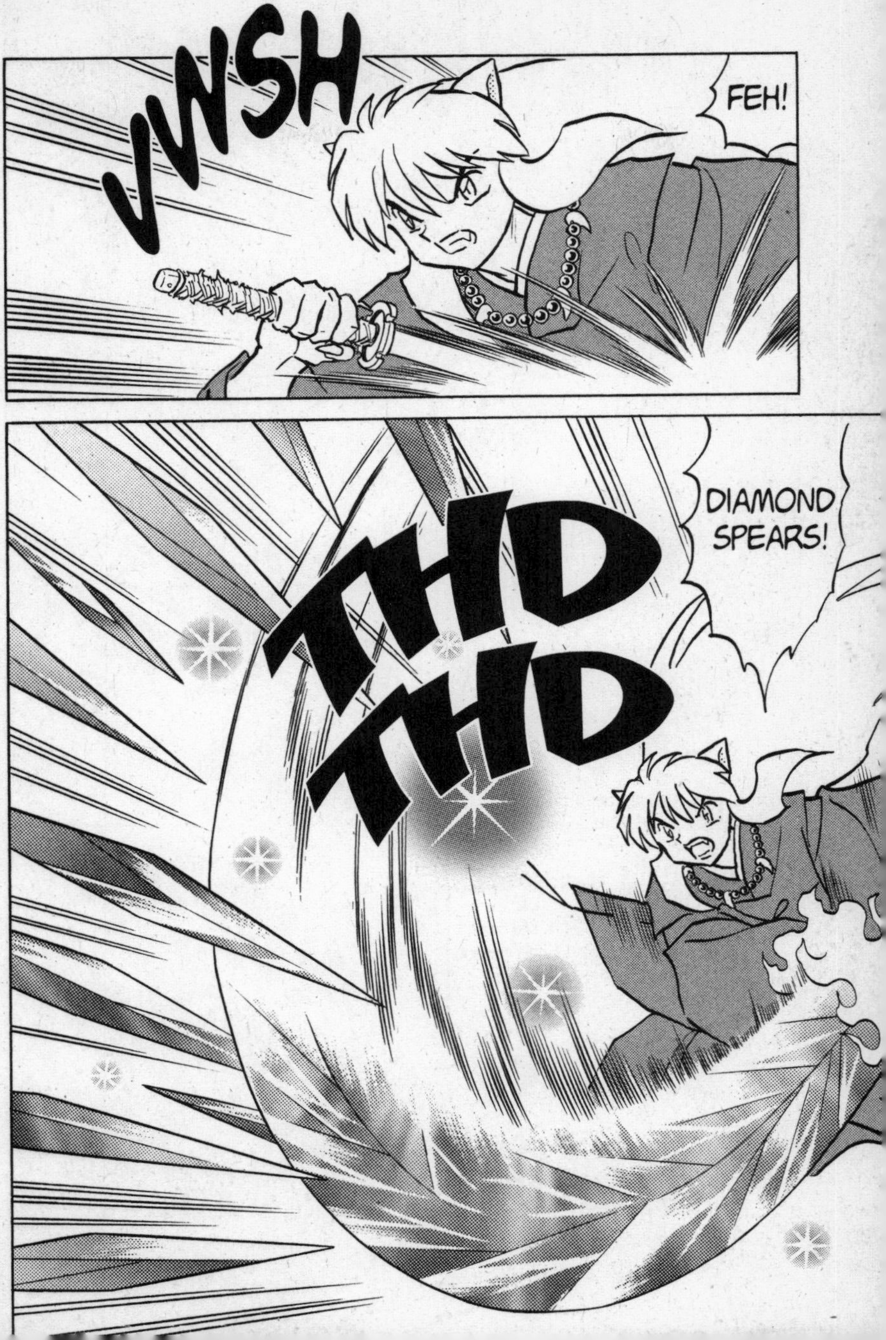
FEH!
VWSH
DIAMOND SPEARS!
THD THD

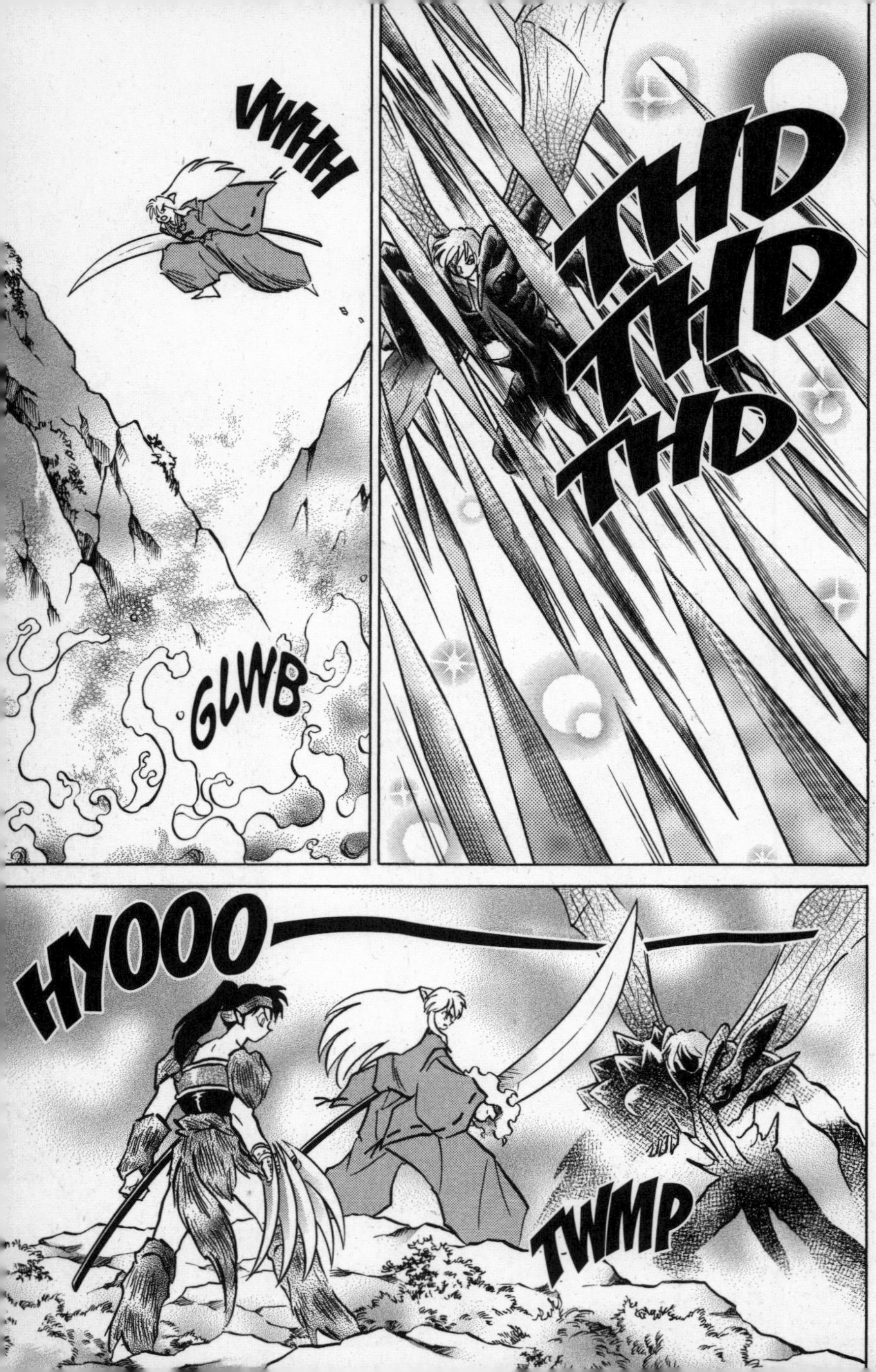
THD THD THD
VWHH
GLWB
HYOOO
TWMP

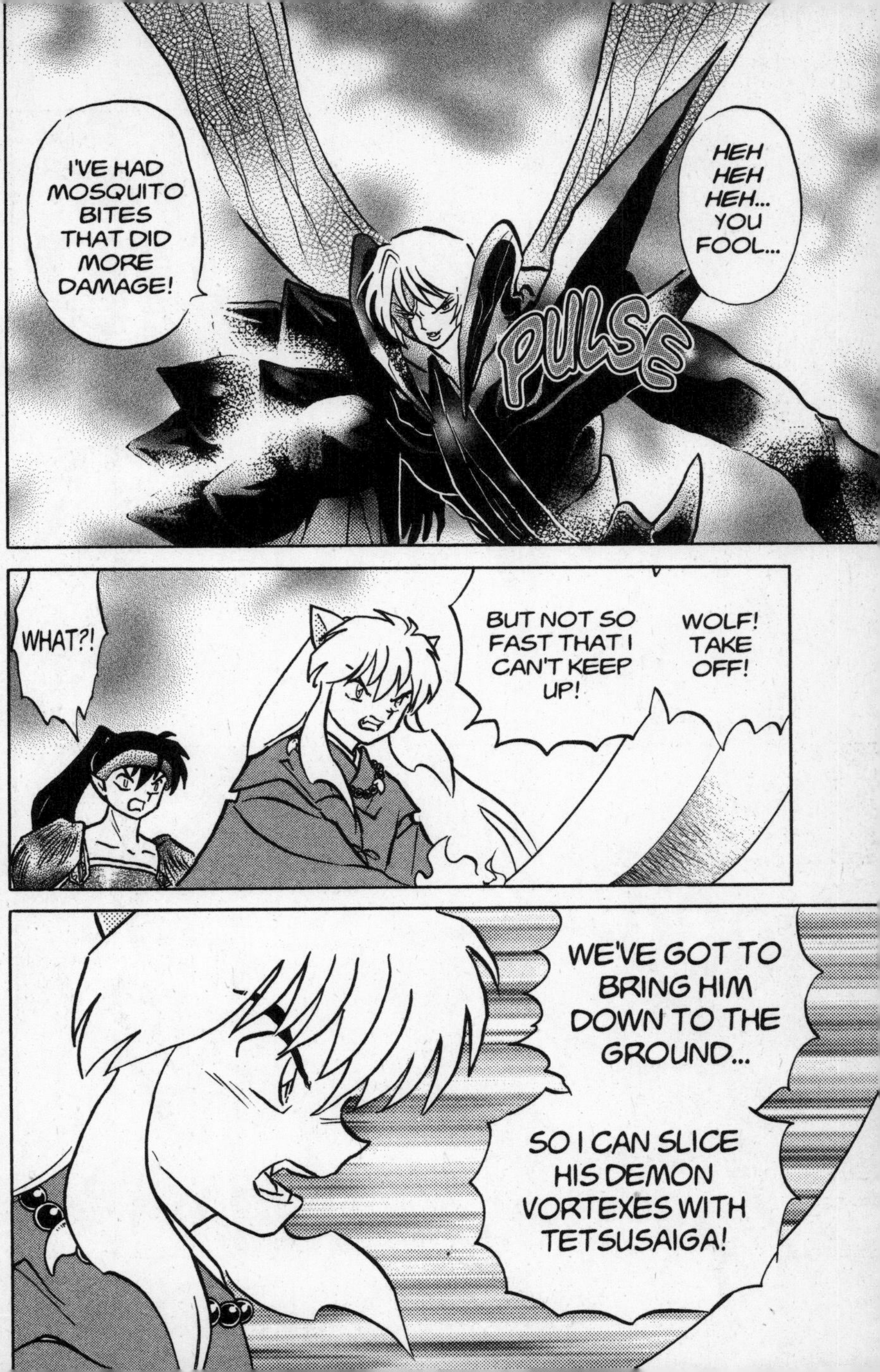
HEH HEH HEH... YOU FOOL...
PULSE
I'VE HAD MOSQUITO BITES THAT DID MORE DAMAGE!
BUT NOT SO FAST THAT I CAN'T KEEP UP!
WOLF! TAKE OFF!
WHAT?!
WE'VE GOT TO BRING HIM DOWN TO THE GROUND...
SO I CAN SLICE HIS DEMON VORTEXES WITH TETSUSAIGA!

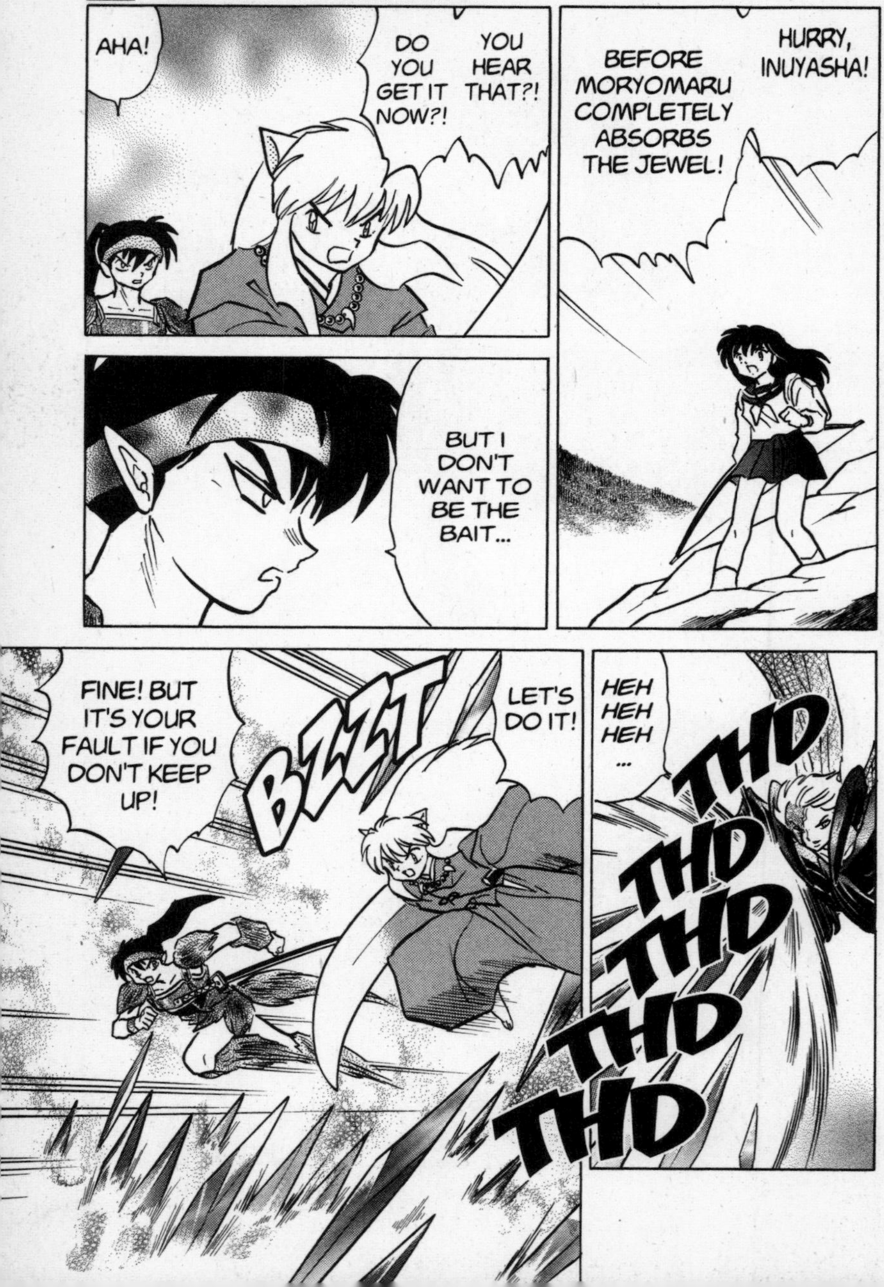
HURRY, INUYASHA!
BEFORE MORYOMARU COMPLETELY ABSORBS THE JEWEL!
YOU HEAR THAT?!
DO YOU GET IT NOW?!
AHA!
BUT I DON'T WANT TO BE THE BAIT...
HEH HEH HEH ...
THD THD THD THD THD
LET'S DO IT!
BZZZT
FINE! BUT IT'S YOUR FAULT IF YOU DON'T KEEP UP!

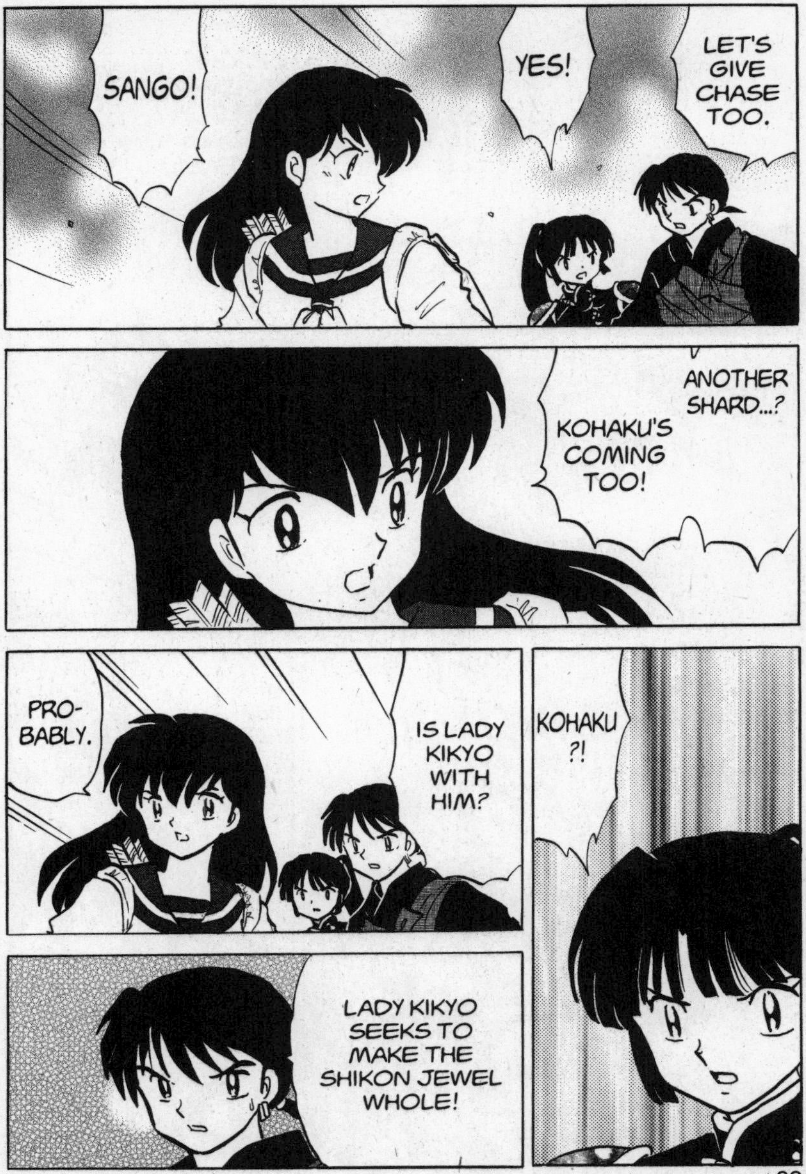
LET'S GIVE CHASE TOO.
YES!
SANGO!
ANOTHER SHARD...?
KOHAKU'S COMING TOO!
KOHAKU ?!
IS LADY KIKYO WITH HIM?
PRO-BABLY.
LADY KIKYO SEEKS TO MAKE THE SHIKON JEWEL WHOLE!

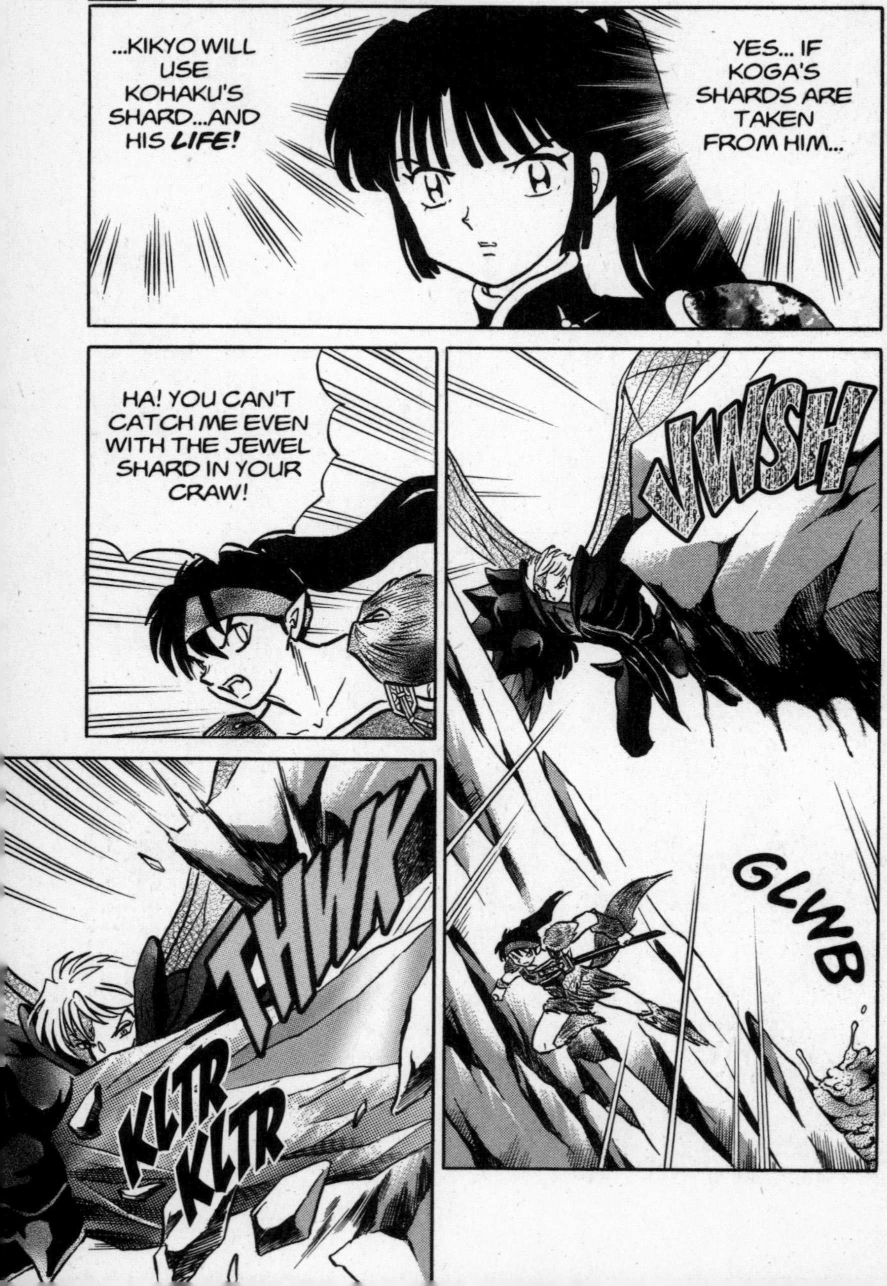
YES... IF KOGA'S SHARDS ARE TAKEN FROM HIM...
...KIKYO WILL USE KOHAKU'S SHARD...AND HIS *LIFE!*
JWSH
GLWB
HA! YOU CAN'T CATCH ME EVEN WITH THE JEWEL SHARD IN YOUR CRAW!
THWK
KLTR KLTR

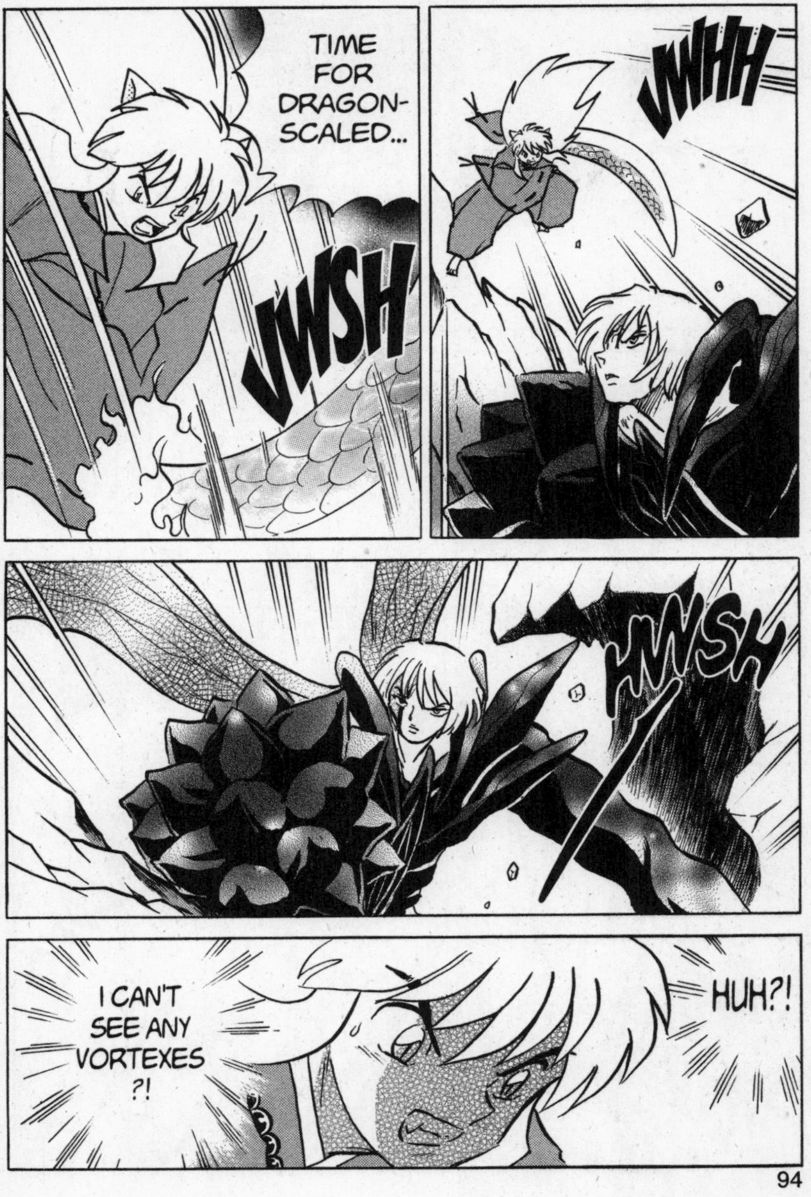
VWHH
TIME FOR DRAGON-SCALED...
VWSH
HWSH
HUH?!
I CAN'T SEE ANY VORTEXES ?!

SCROLL 6

HEATED BATTLE

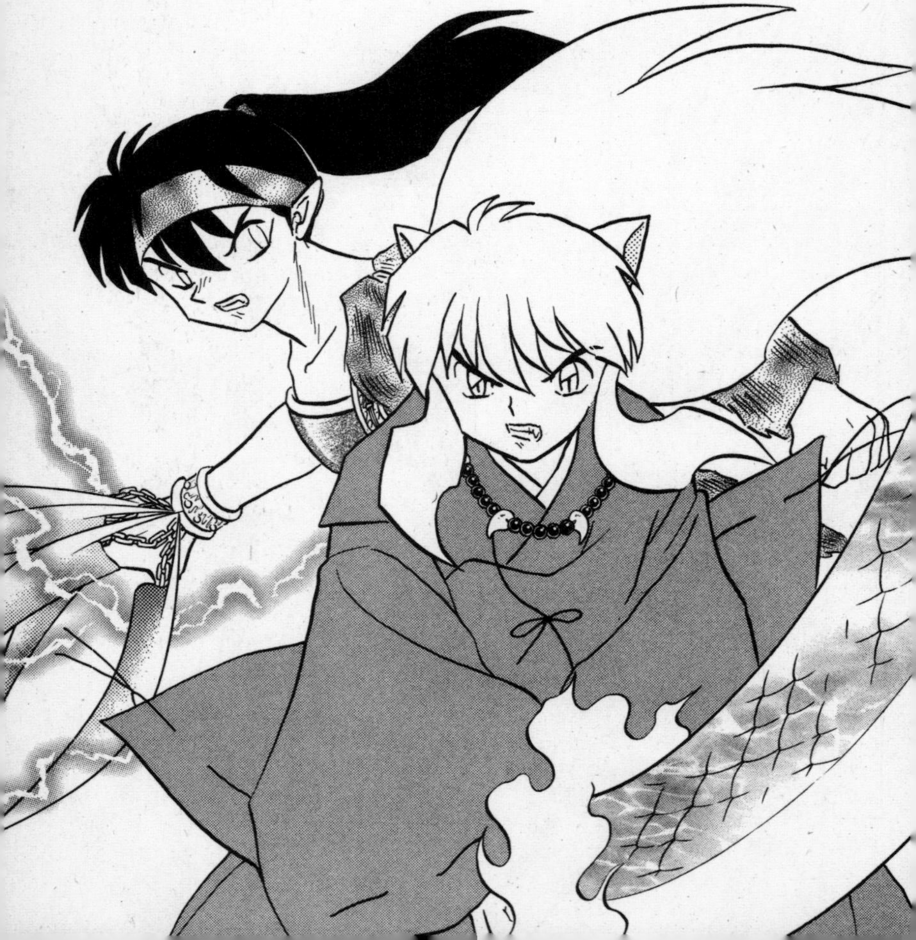

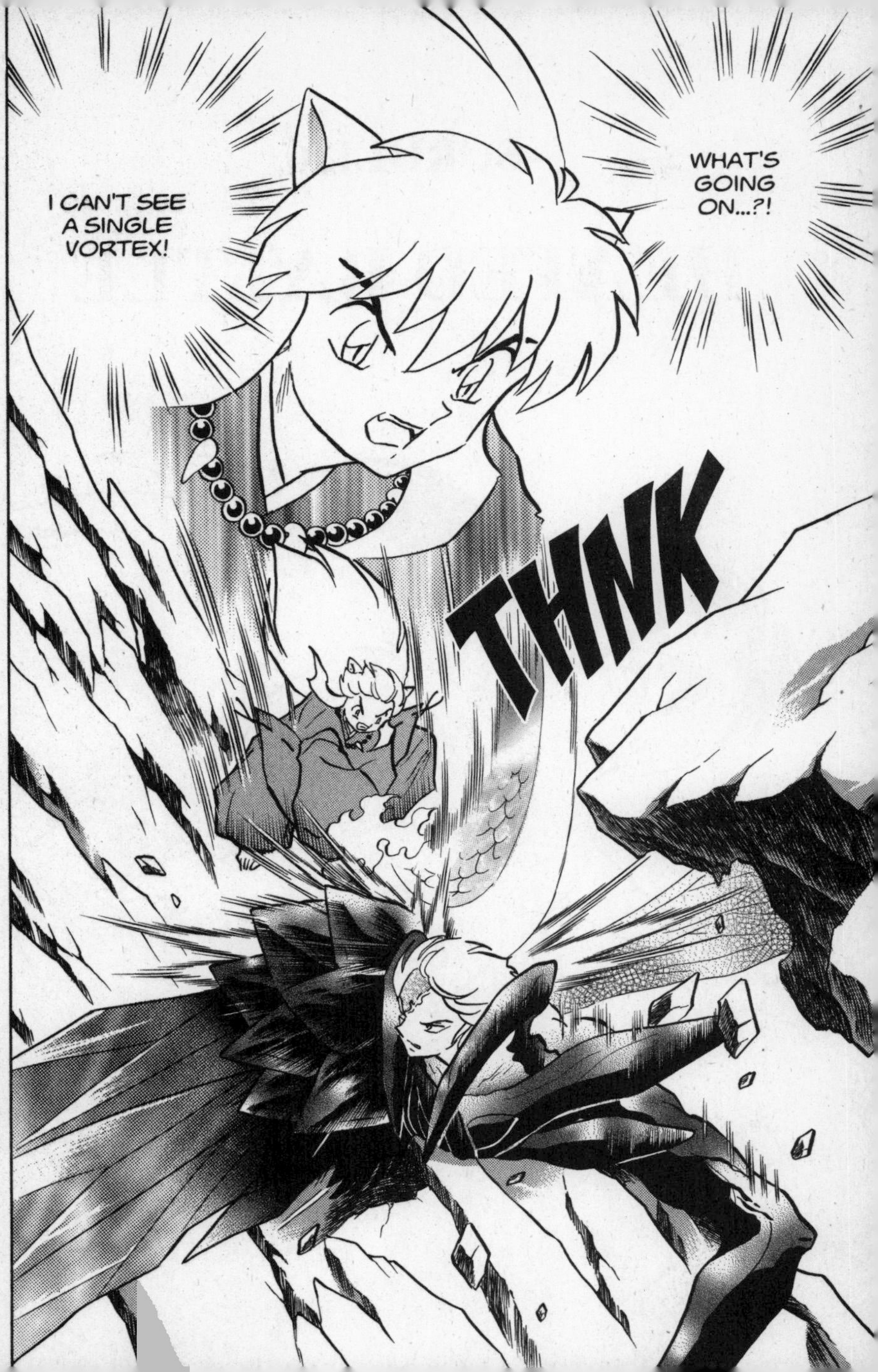
WHAT'S GOING ON...?!
I CAN'T SEE A SINGLE VORTEX!
THNK

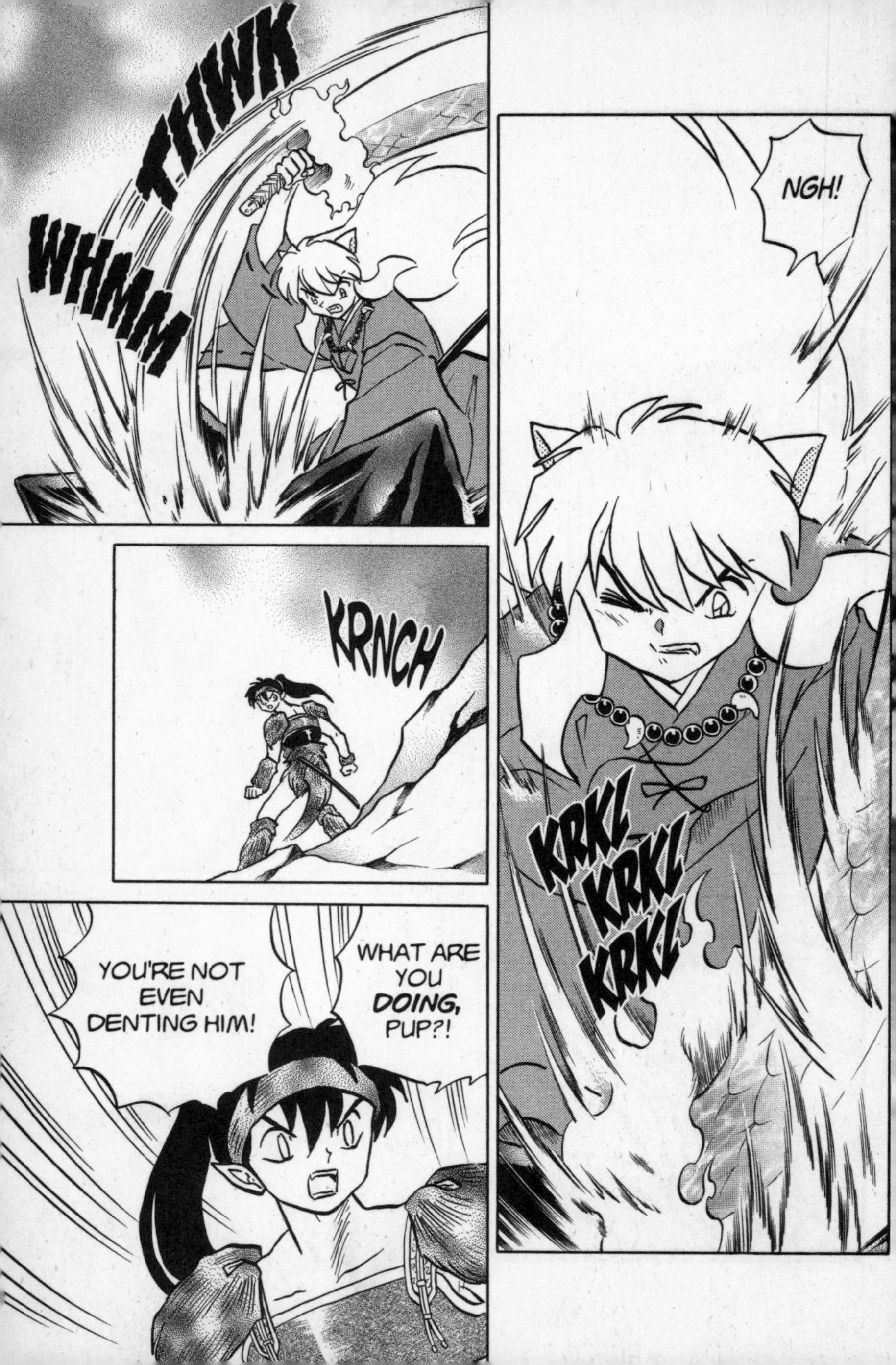
NGH!
KRKL KRKL KRKL
THWK
WHMM
KRNCH
WHAT ARE YOU DOING, PUP?!
YOU'RE NOT EVEN DENTING HIM!

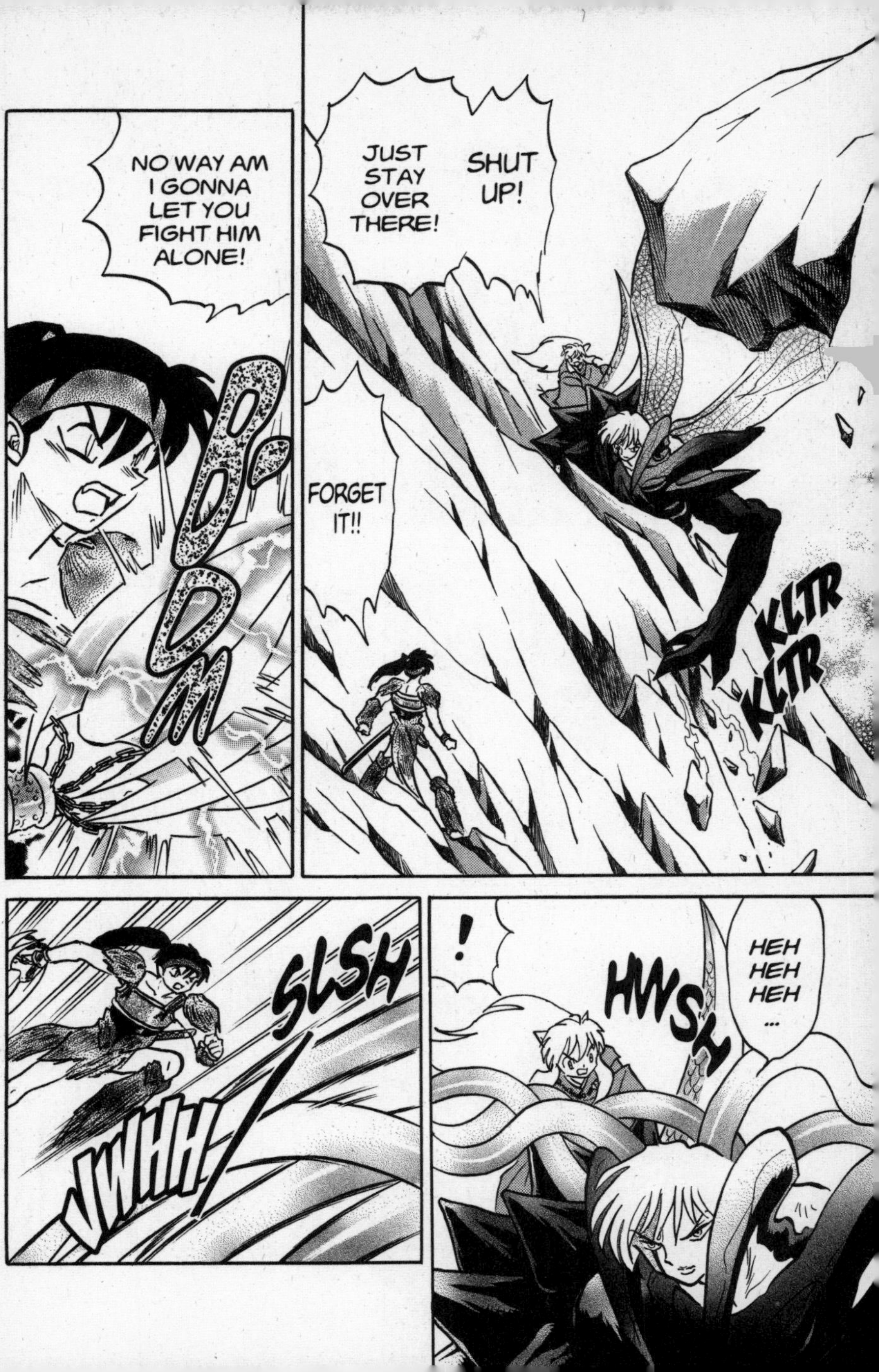
SHUT UP!
JUST STAY OVER THERE!
FORGET IT!!
KLTR KLTR
NO WAY AM I GONNA LET YOU FIGHT HIM ALONE!
BDDM
HEH HEH HEH ...
HWSH
!
SLSH
JWHH

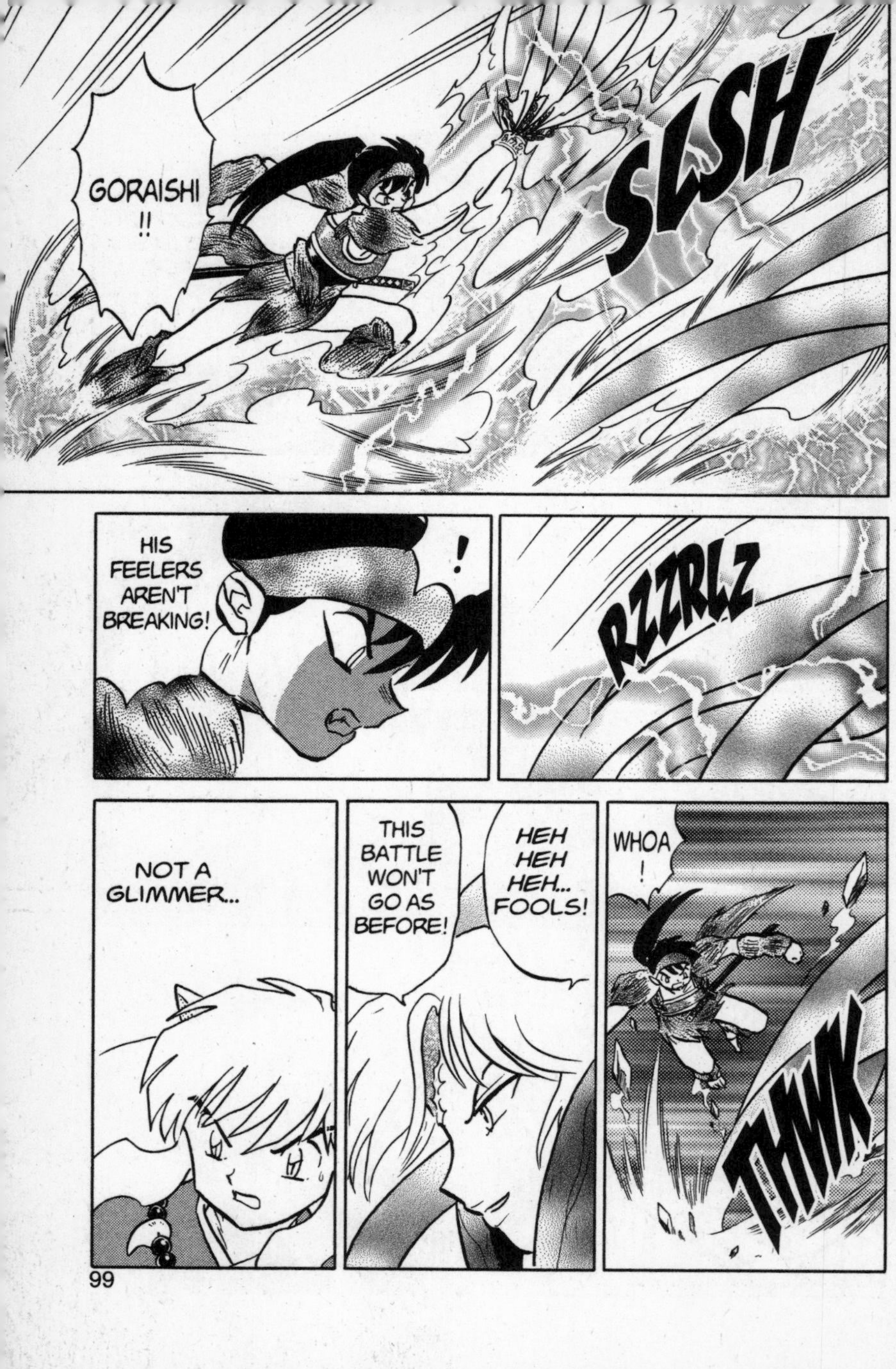
GORAISHI !!
SLSH
RZZRLZ
!
HIS FEELERS AREN'T BREAKING!
WHOA !
THNNK
HEH HEH HEH... FOOLS!
THIS BATTLE WON'T GO AS BEFORE!
NOT A GLIMMER...

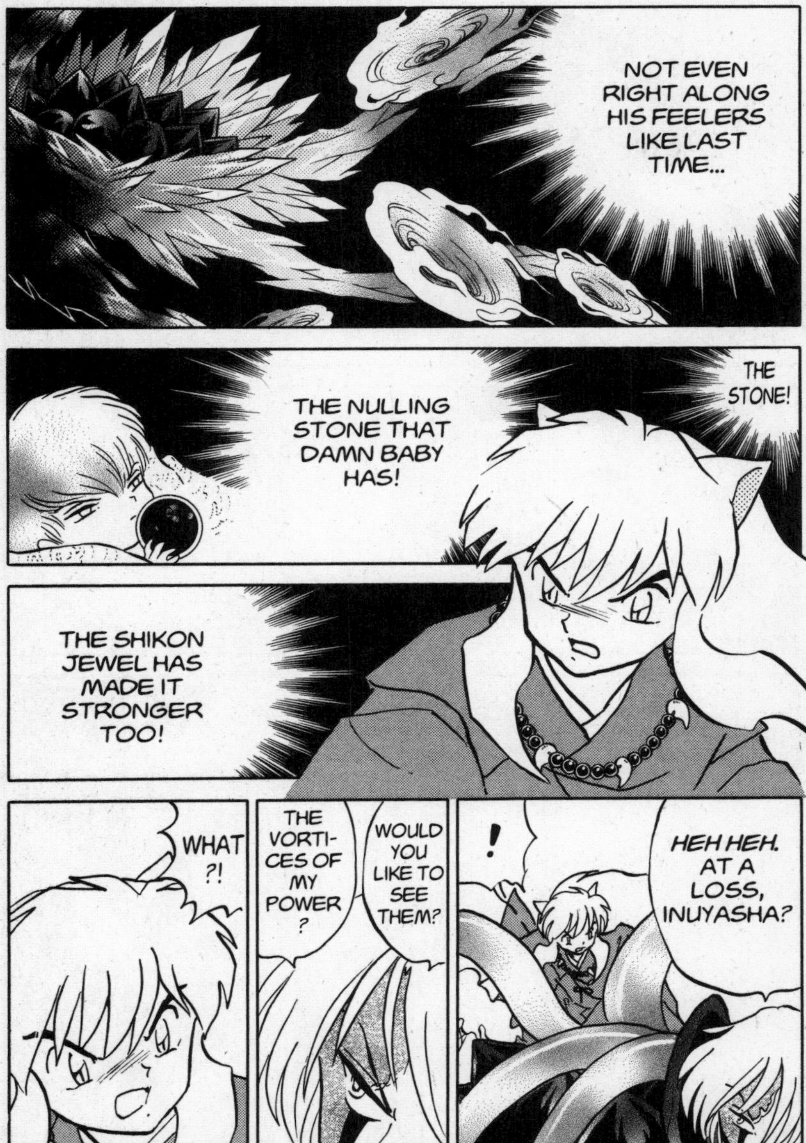
NOT EVEN RIGHT ALONG HIS FEELERS LIKE LAST TIME...
THE STONE!
THE NULLING STONE THAT DAMN BABY HAS!
THE SHIKON JEWEL HAS MADE IT STRONGER TOO!
HEH HEH. AT A LOSS, INUYASHA?
!
WOULD YOU LIKE TO SEE THEM?
THE VORTICES OF MY POWER?
WHAT?!

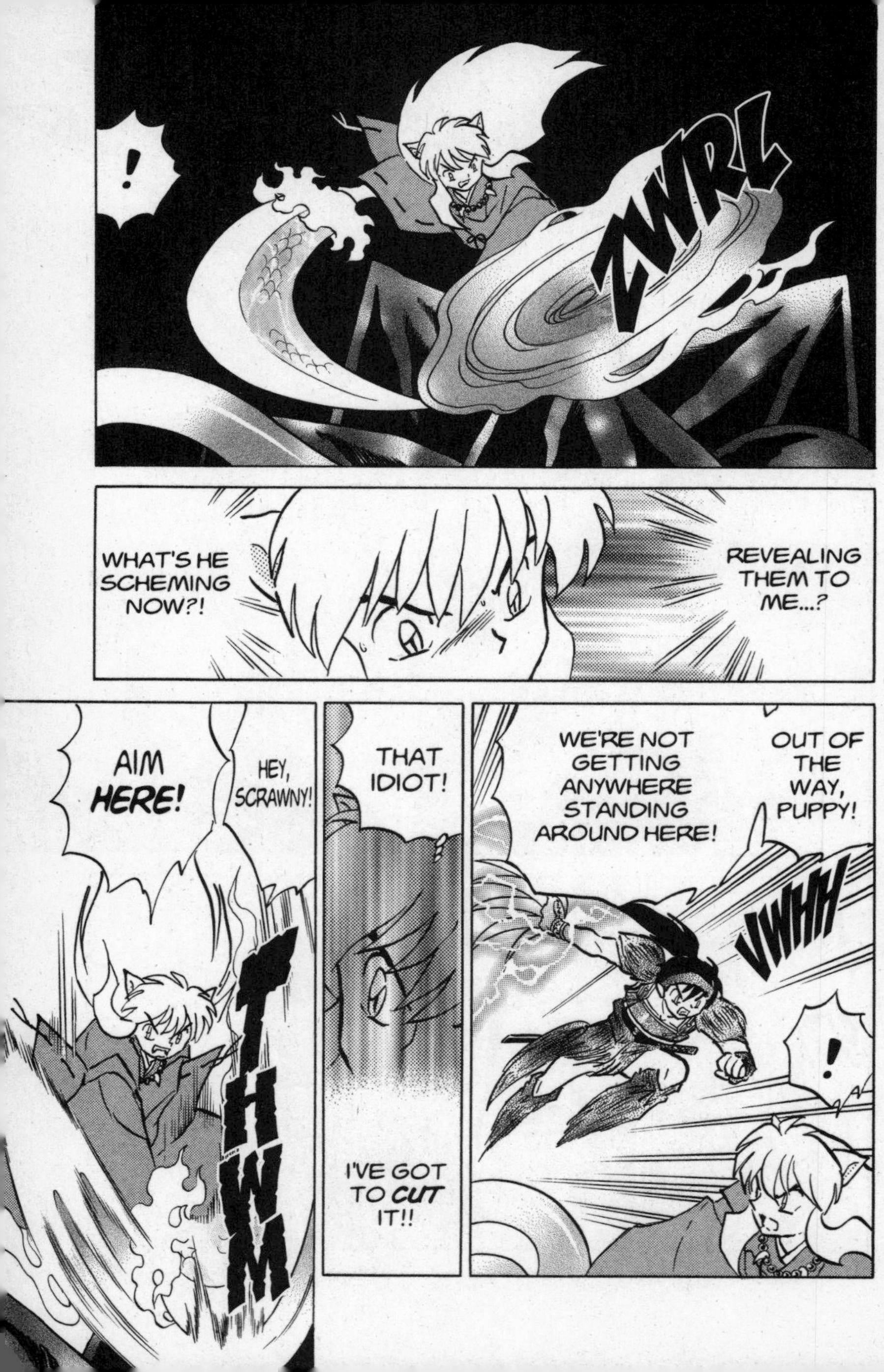
!
ZWRL
REVEALING THEM TO ME...?
WHAT'S HE SCHEMING NOW?!
OUT OF THE WAY, PUPPY!
WE'RE NOT GETTING ANYWHERE STANDING AROUND HERE!
VWHH
!
THAT IDIOT!
I'VE GOT TO *CUT* IT!!
HEY, SCRAWNY!
AIM **HERE!**
THWM

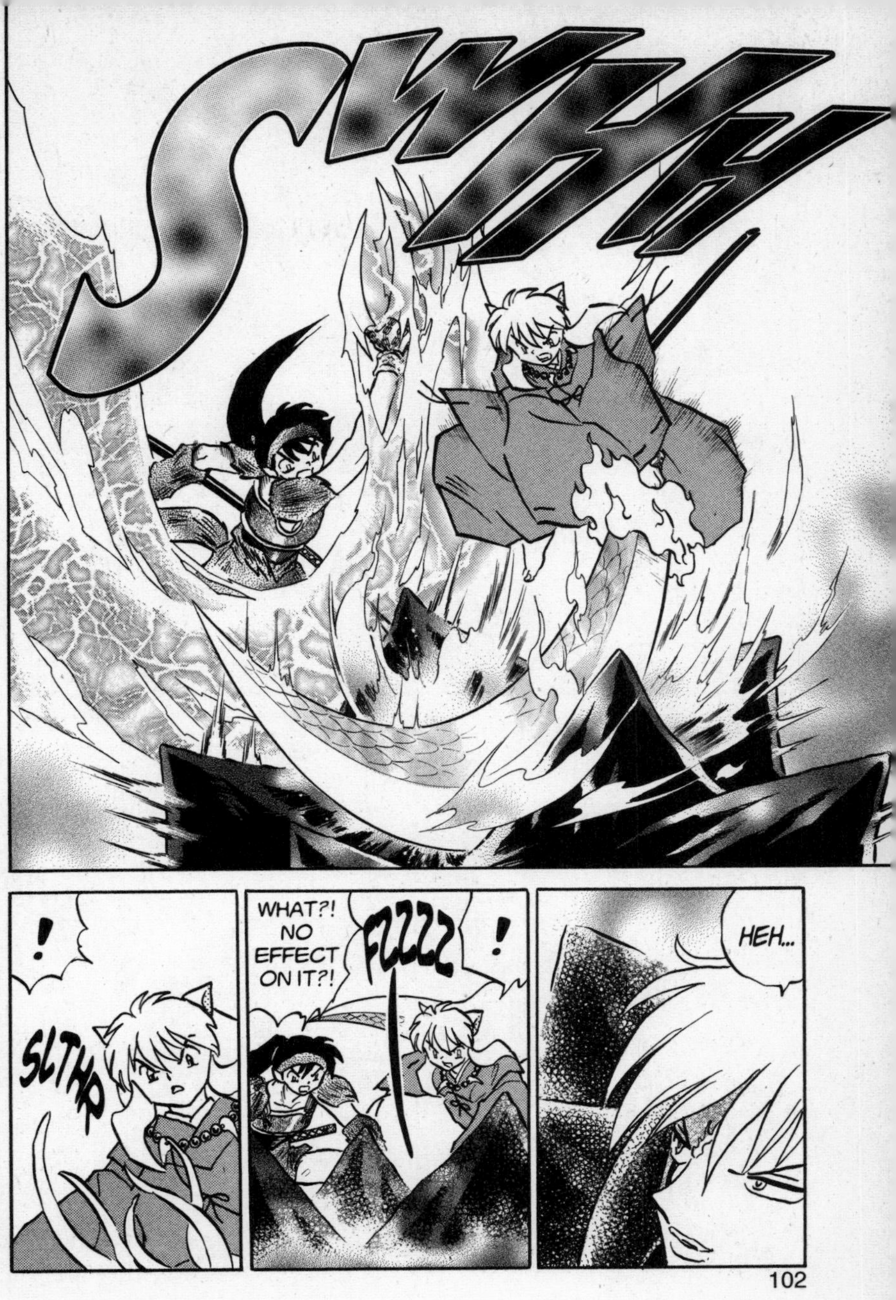
SWHH
HEH...
!
FZZZZ
WHAT?! NO EFFECT ON IT?!
!
SLTHR

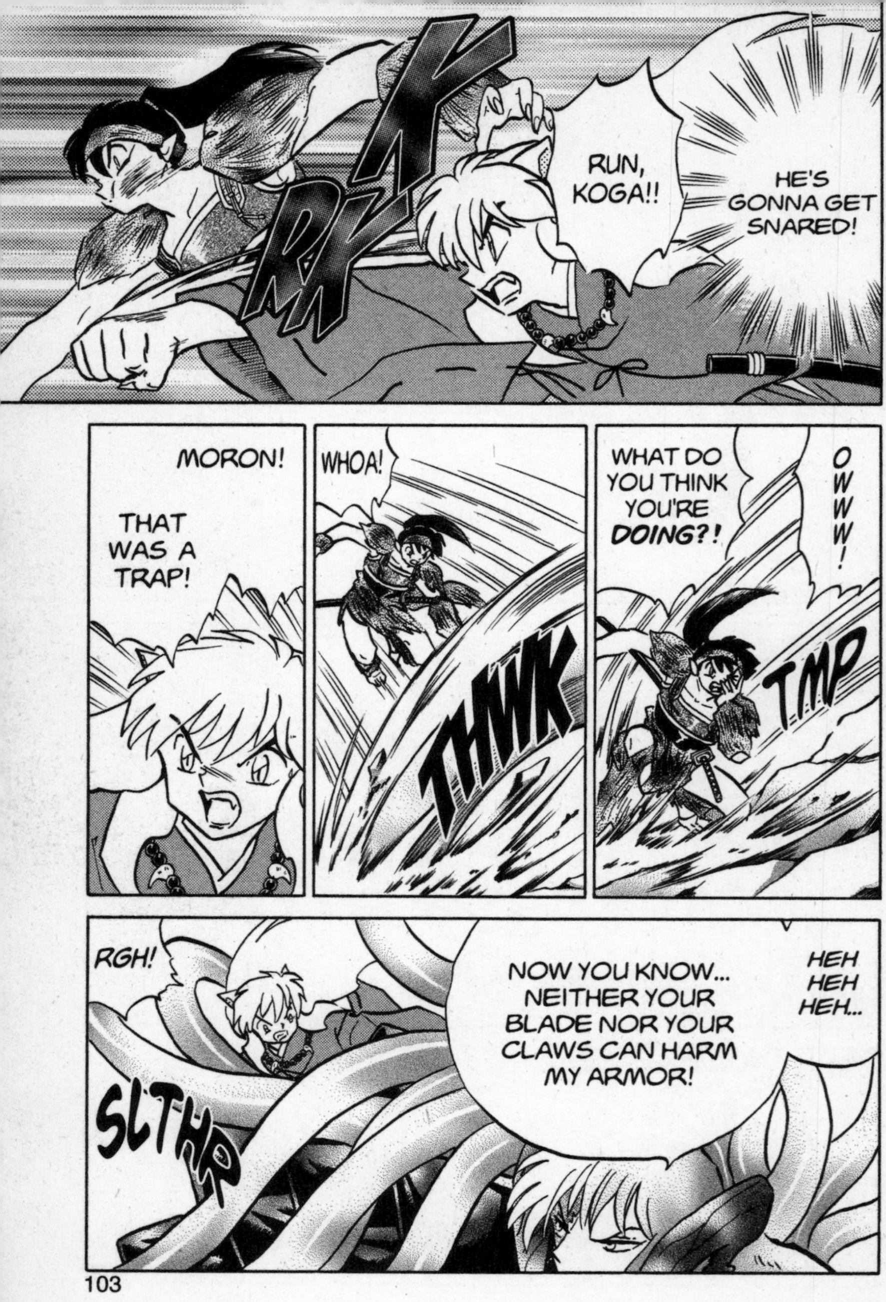
HE'S GONNA GET SNARED!
RUN, KOGA!!
OWWW!
WHAT DO YOU THINK YOU'RE DOING?!
TMP
WHOA!
THWK
MORON!
THAT WAS A TRAP!
HEH HEH HEH...
NOW YOU KNOW... NEITHER YOUR BLADE NOR YOUR CLAWS CAN HARM MY ARMOR!
RGH!
SLTHR

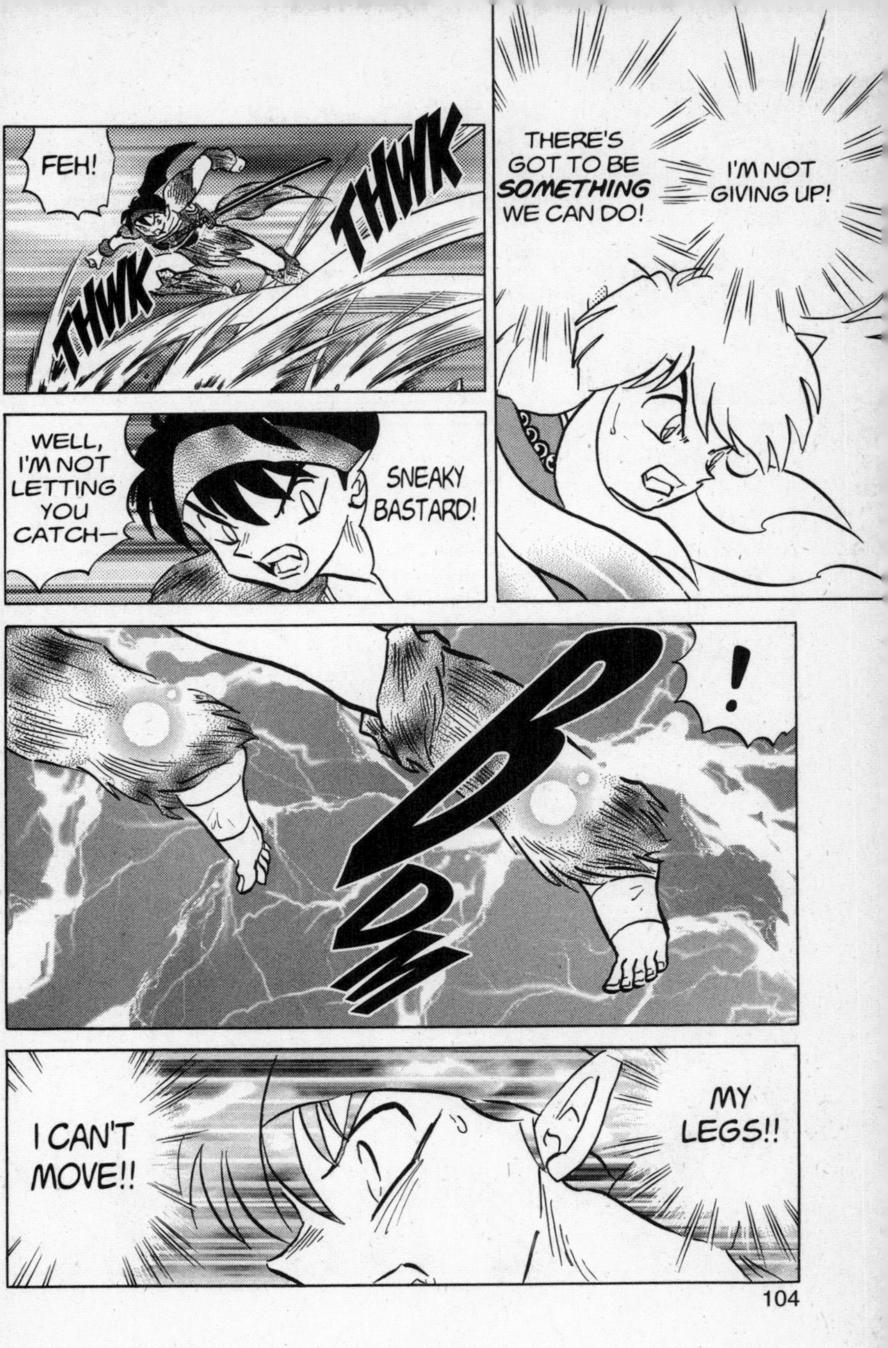
I'M NOT GIVING UP!
THERE'S GOT TO BE *SOMETHING* WE CAN DO!
FEH!
THWK
THWK
SNEAKY BASTARD!
WELL, I'M NOT LETTING YOU CATCH—
!
MY LEGS!!
I CAN'T MOVE!!

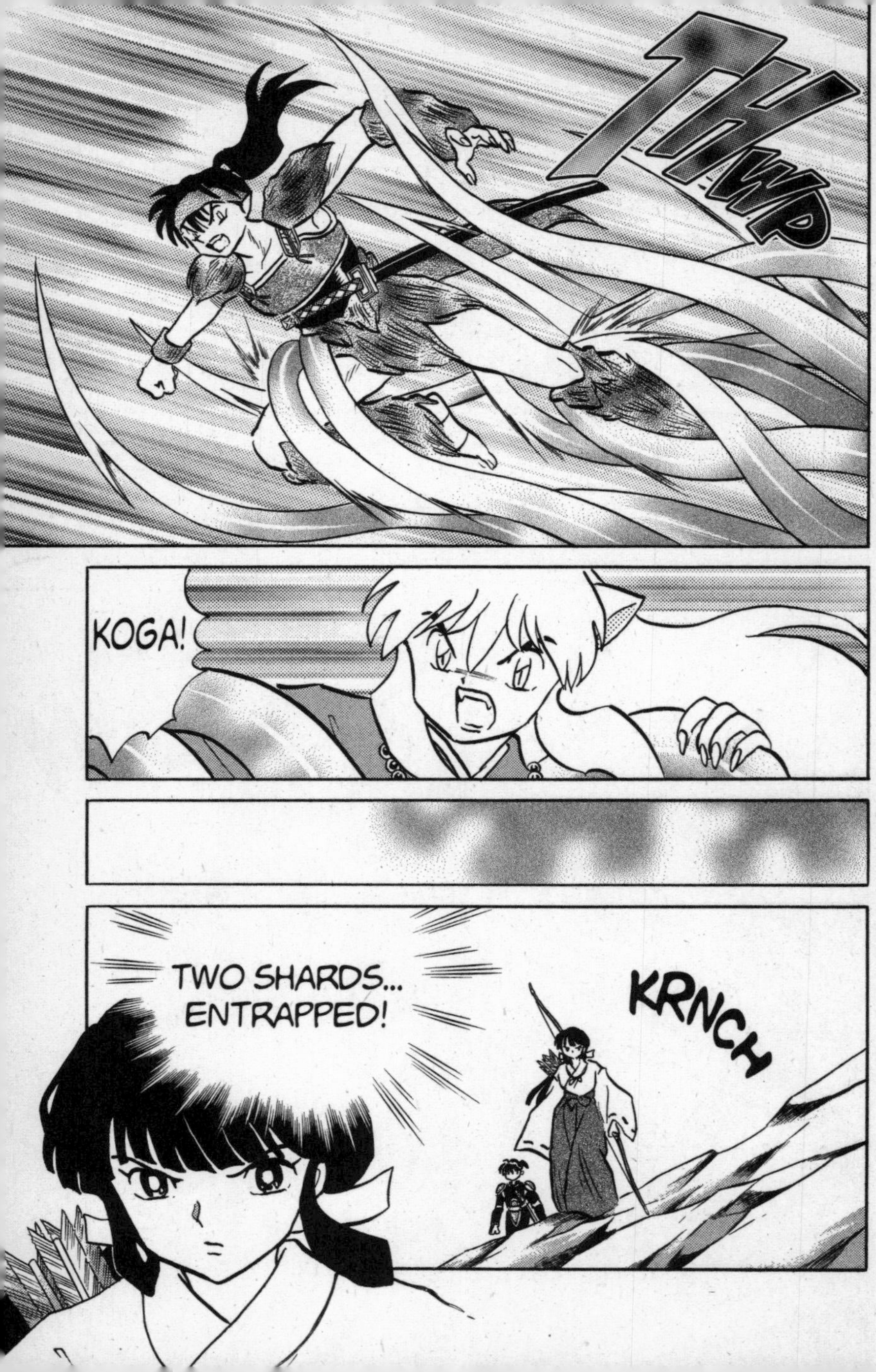
THWP
KOGA!
KRNCH
TWO SHARDS... ENTRAPPED!

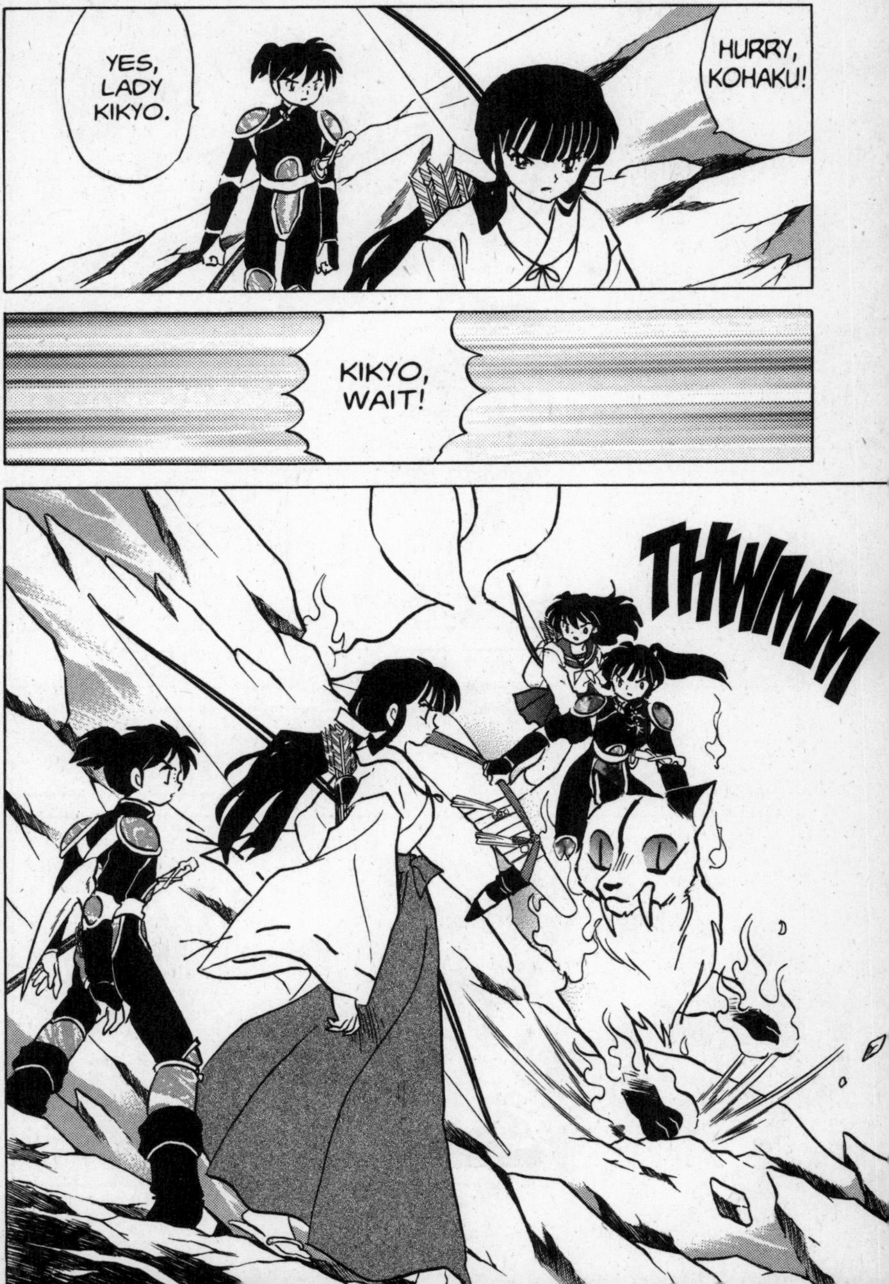
HURRY, KOHAKU!
YES, LADY KIKYO.
KIKYO, WAIT!
THWMMM

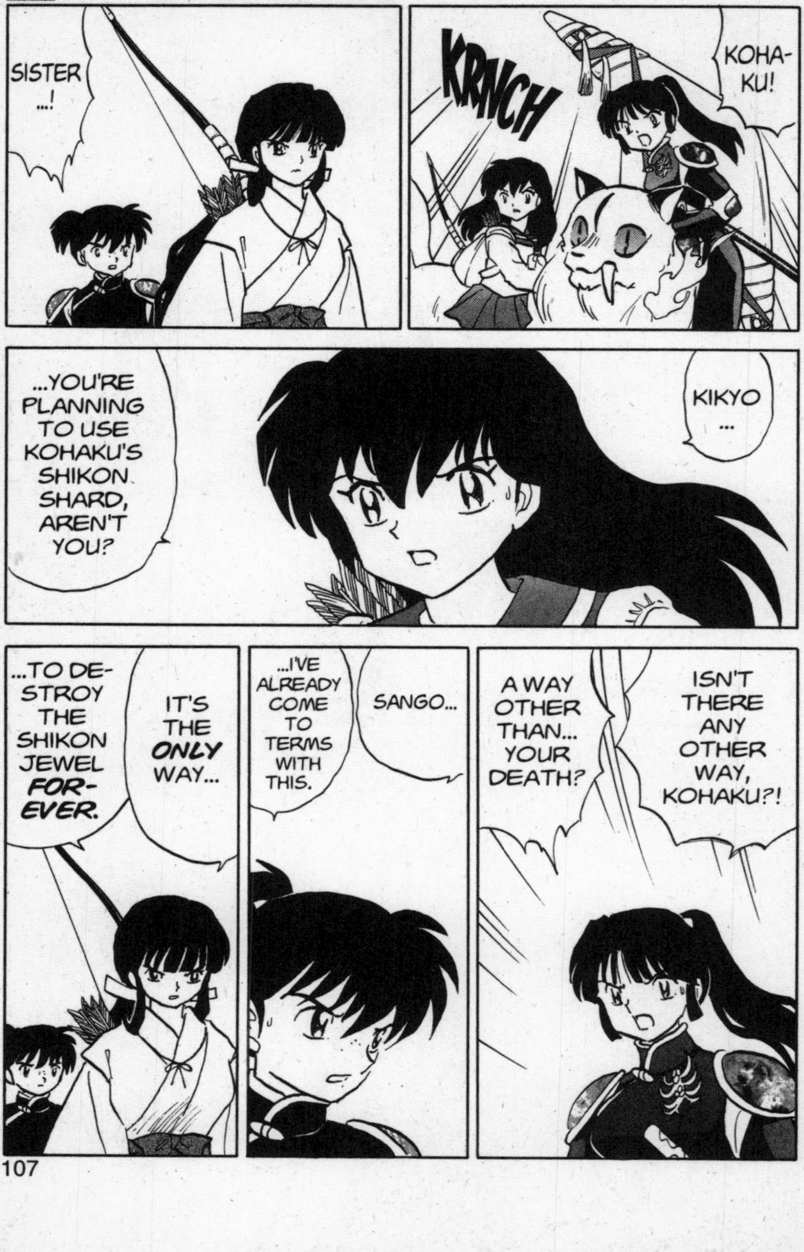
KRNCH
KOHA-KU!
SISTER ...!
KIKYO ...
...YOU'RE PLANNING TO USE KOHAKU'S SHIKON SHARD, AREN'T YOU?
ISN'T THERE ANY OTHER WAY, KOHAKU?!
A WAY OTHER THAN... YOUR DEATH?
SANGO...
...I'VE ALREADY COME TO TERMS WITH THIS.
IT'S THE ONLY WAY...
...TO DESTROY THE SHIKON JEWEL FOREVER.

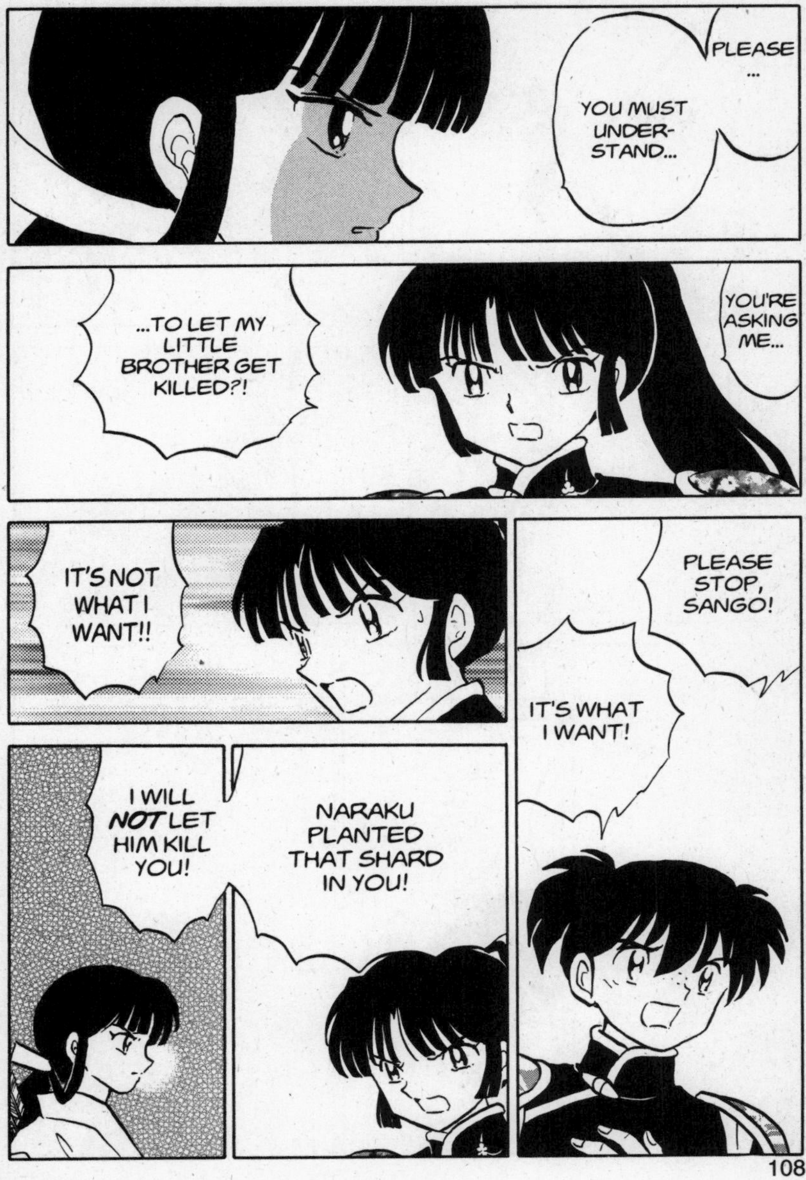
PLEASE ...
YOU MUST UNDER-STAND...
YOU'RE ASKING ME...
...TO LET MY LITTLE BROTHER GET KILLED?!
PLEASE STOP, SANGO!
IT'S WHAT I WANT!
IT'S NOT WHAT I WANT!!
NARAKU PLANTED THAT SHARD IN YOU!
I WILL ***NOT*** LET HIM KILL YOU!

...
SIS...
MOVE ASIDE.
THERE IS NO TIME.
NO!
SANGO...
KAGO-ME...
YOU SENSE IT TOO, DON'T YOU?
AT THIS VERY MOMENT, THE SHARDS IN THAT WOLF DEMON'S LEGS...

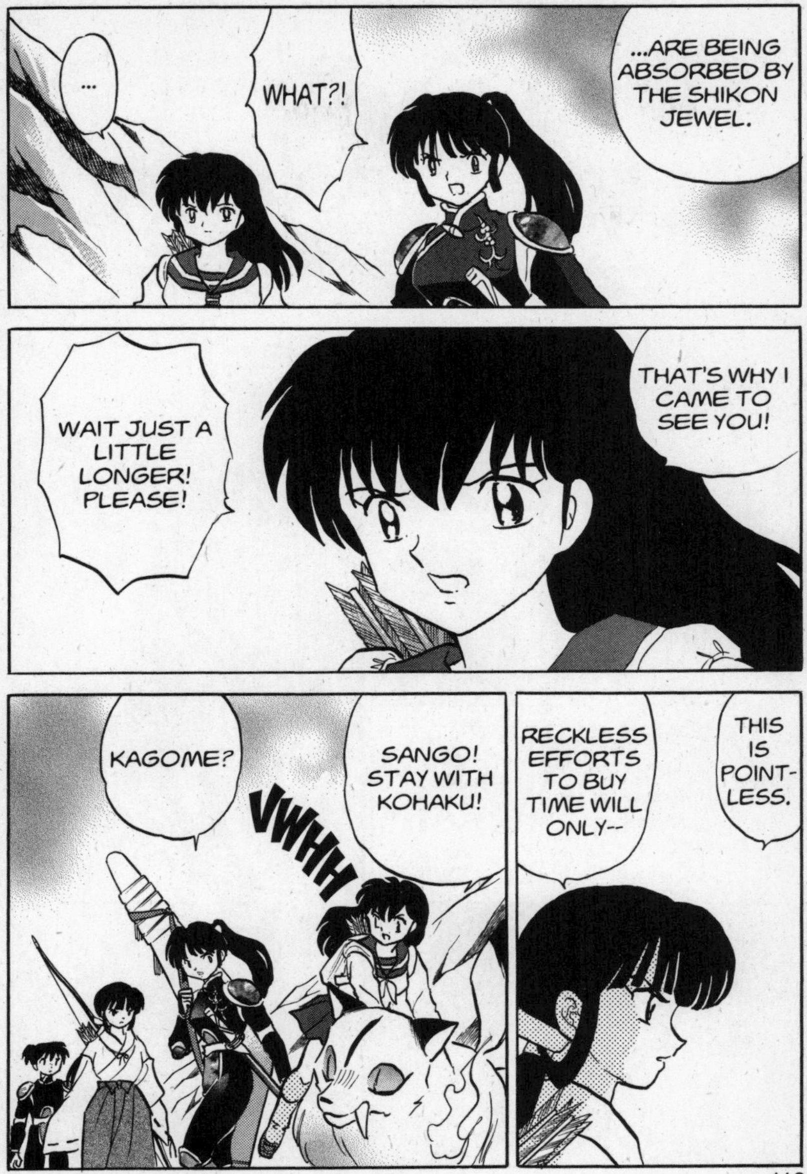
...ARE BEING ABSORBED BY THE SHIKON JEWEL.
WHAT?!
...
THAT'S WHY I CAME TO SEE YOU!
WAIT JUST A LITTLE LONGER! PLEASE!
THIS IS POINT-LESS.
RECKLESS EFFORTS TO BUY TIME WILL ONLY--
SANGO! STAY WITH KOHAKU!
VWHH
KAGOME?

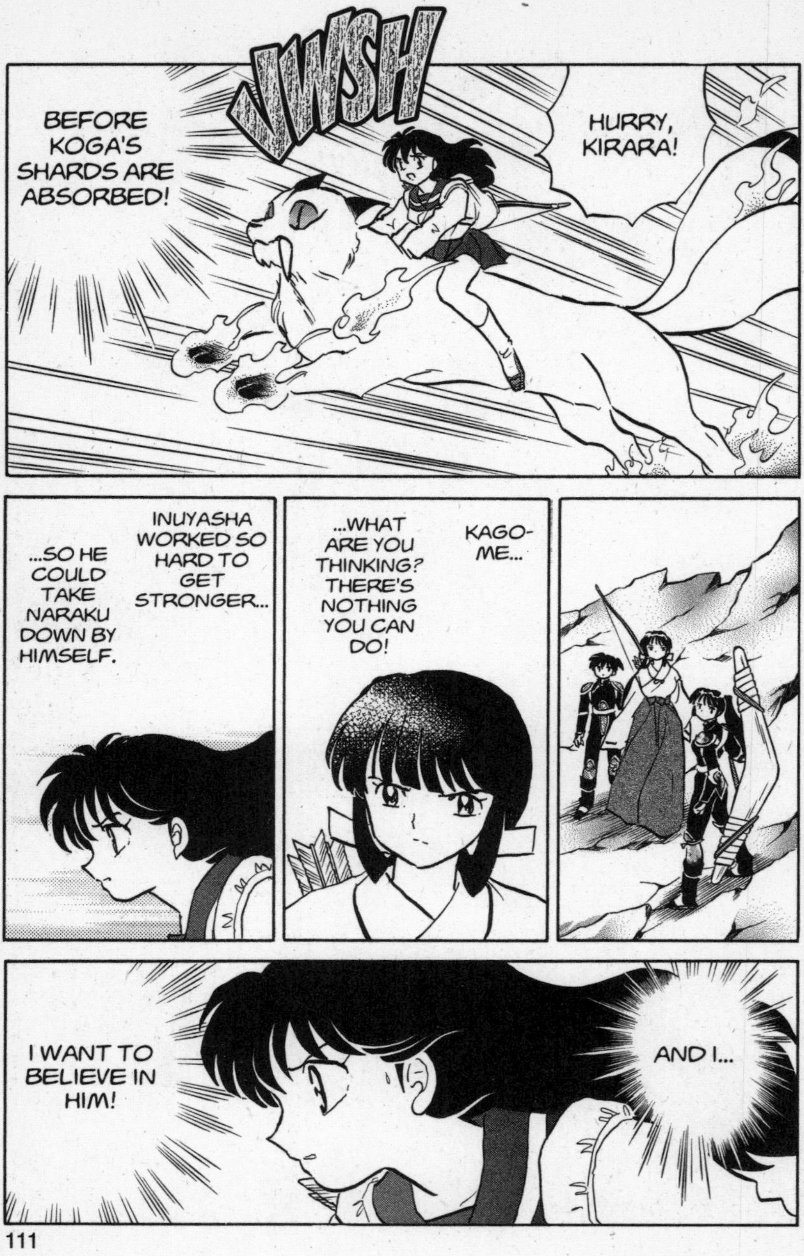
HURRY, KIRARA!
JWSH
BEFORE KOGA'S SHARDS ARE ABSORBED!
KAGO-ME...
...WHAT ARE YOU THINKING? THERE'S NOTHING YOU CAN DO!
INUYASHA WORKED SO HARD TO GET STRONGER...
...SO HE COULD TAKE NARAKU DOWN BY HIMSELF.
AND I...
I WANT TO BELIEVE IN HIM!

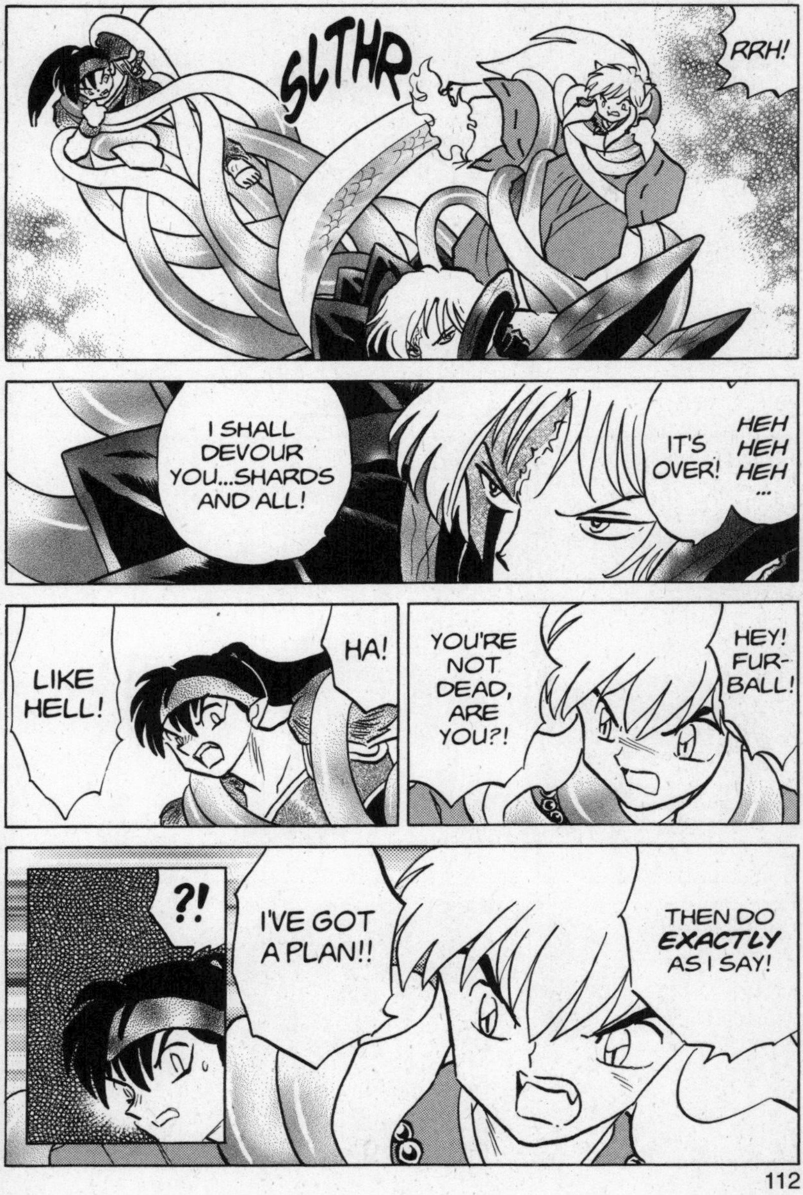
RRH!
SLTHR
HEH HEH HEH ...
IT'S OVER!
I SHALL DEVOUR YOU...SHARDS AND ALL!
HEY! FUR-BALL!
YOU'RE NOT DEAD, ARE YOU?!
HA!
LIKE HELL!
THEN DO *EXACTLY* AS I SAY!
I'VE GOT A PLAN!!
?!

SCROLL 7

THE INFANT'S MISTAKE

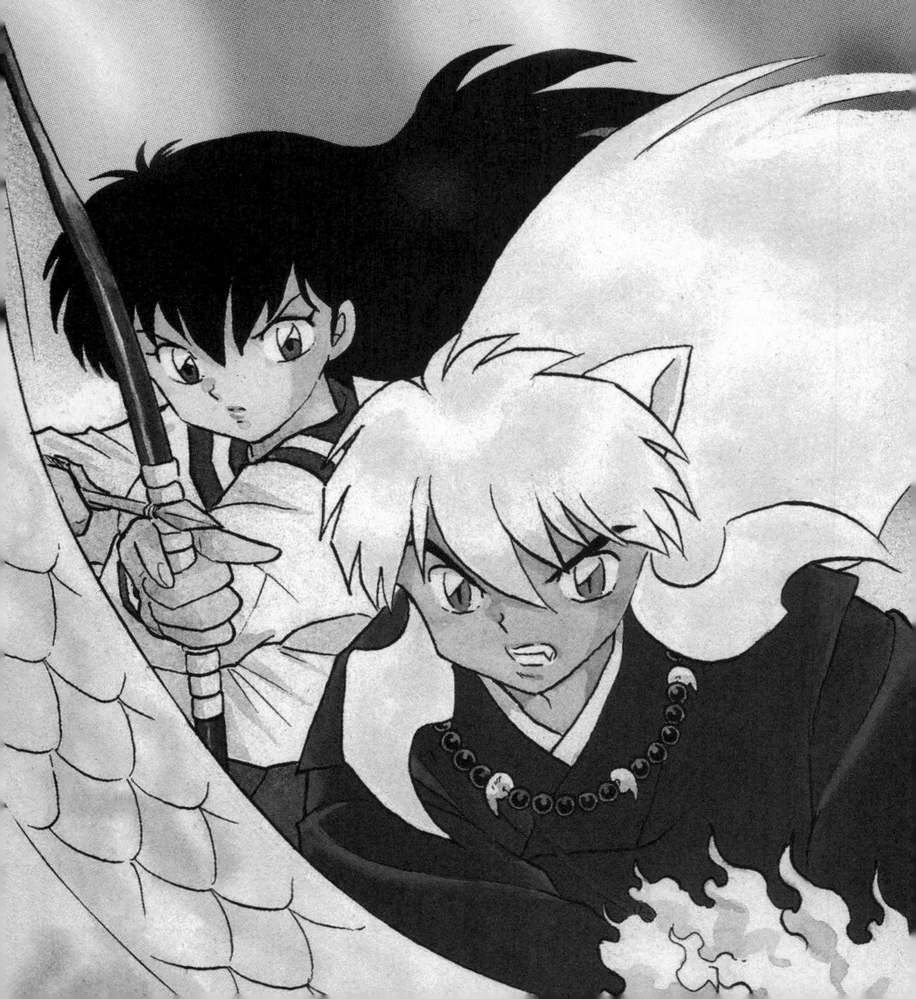

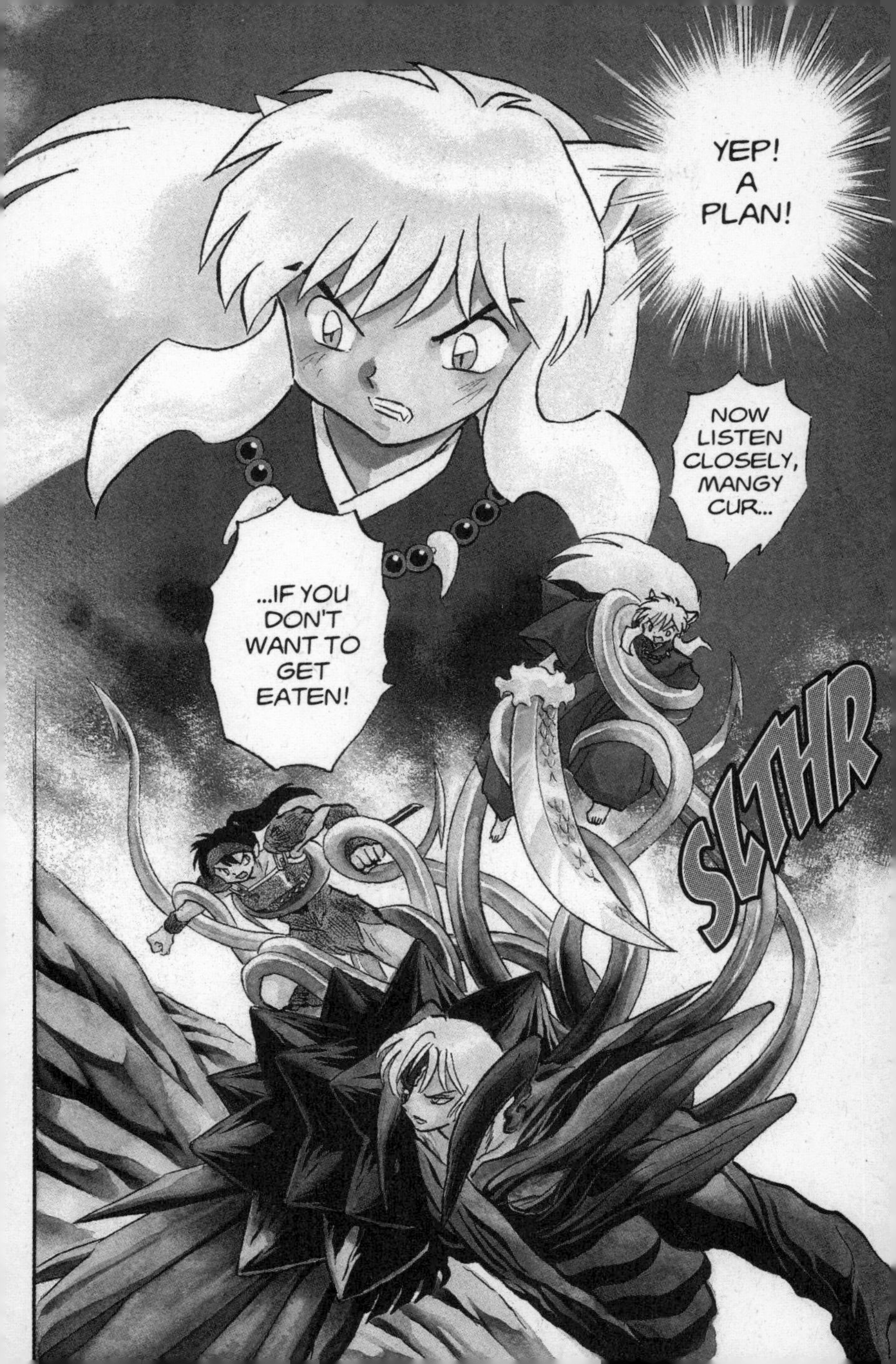
YEP! A PLAN!
NOW LISTEN CLOSELY, MANGY CUR...
...IF YOU DON'T WANT TO GET EATEN!
SLTHR

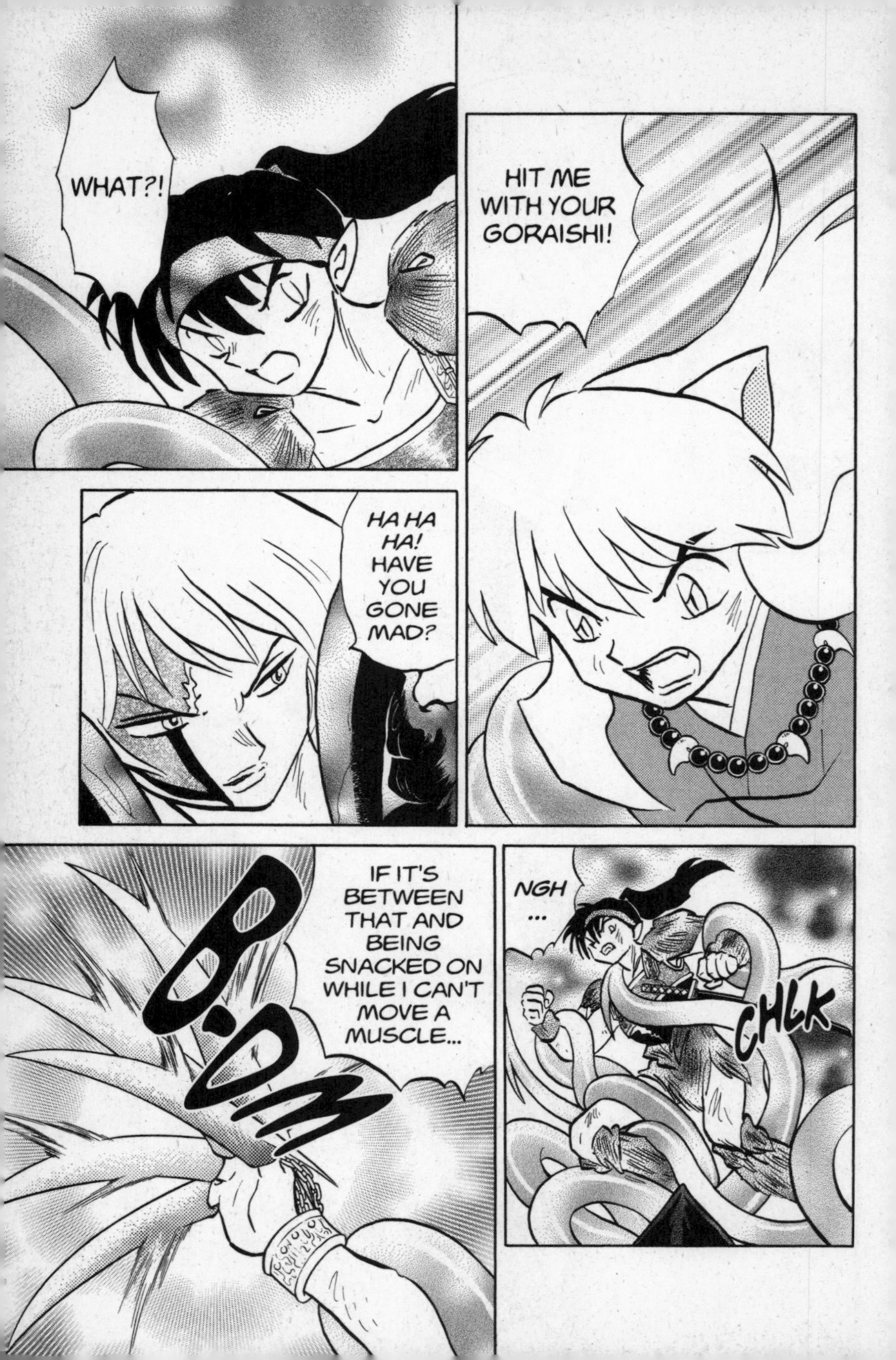

HIT ME WITH YOUR GORAISHI!
WHAT?!
HA HA HA! HAVE YOU GONE MAD?
NGH ...
CHLK
IF IT'S BETWEEN THAT AND BEING SNACKED ON WHILE I CAN'T MOVE A MUSCLE...
B-DM

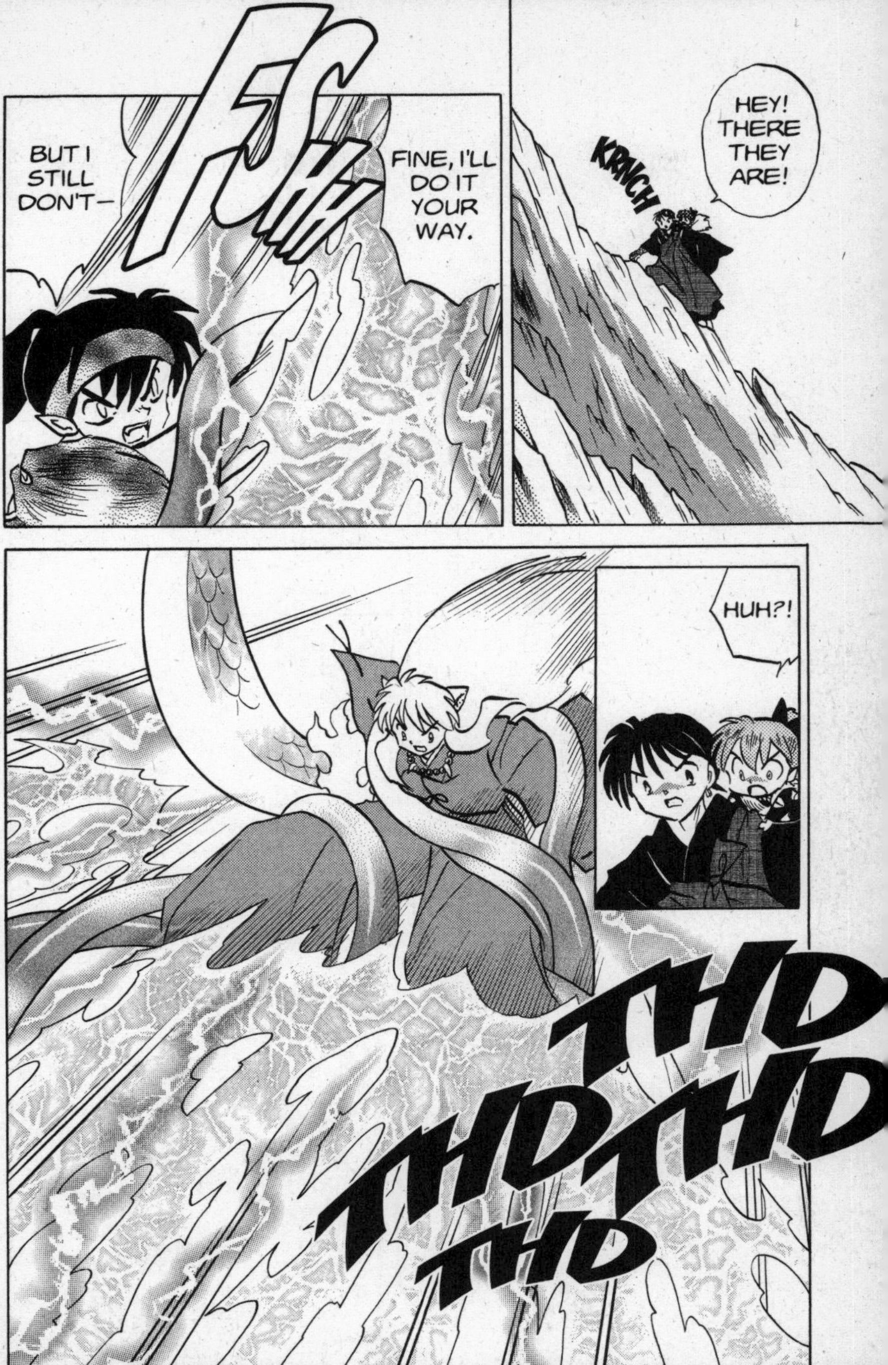
HEY! THERE THEY ARE!
KRNCH
FSHH
FINE, I'LL DO IT YOUR WAY.
BUT I STILL DON'T—
HUH?!
THD
THD THD
THD

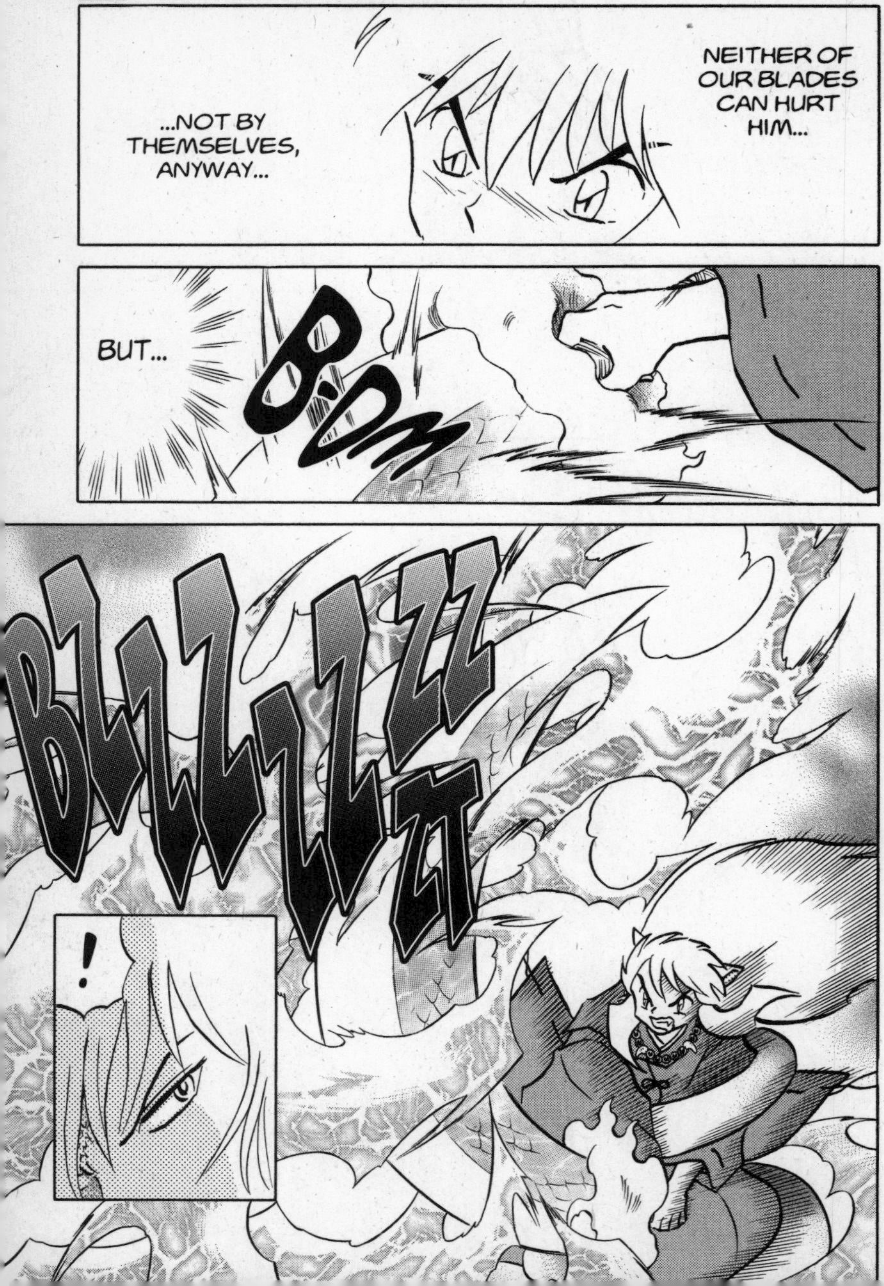
NEITHER OF OUR BLADES CAN HURT HIM...
...NOT BY THEMSELVES, ANYWAY...
BOOM
BUT...
BZZZZZZT
!

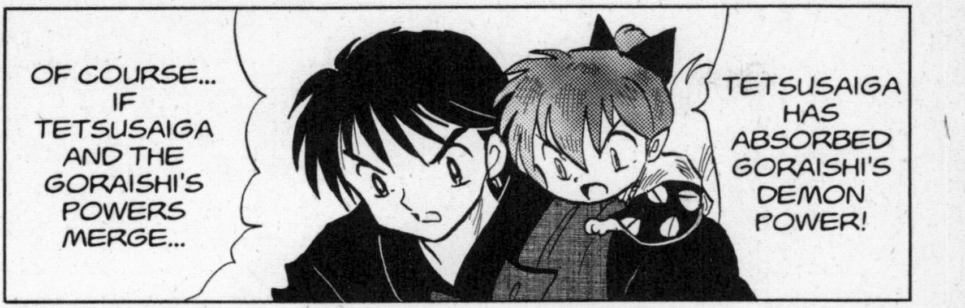
TETSUSAIGA HAS ABSORBED GORAISHI'S DEMON POWER!
OF COURSE... IF TETSUSAIGA AND THE GORAISHI'S POWERS MERGE...

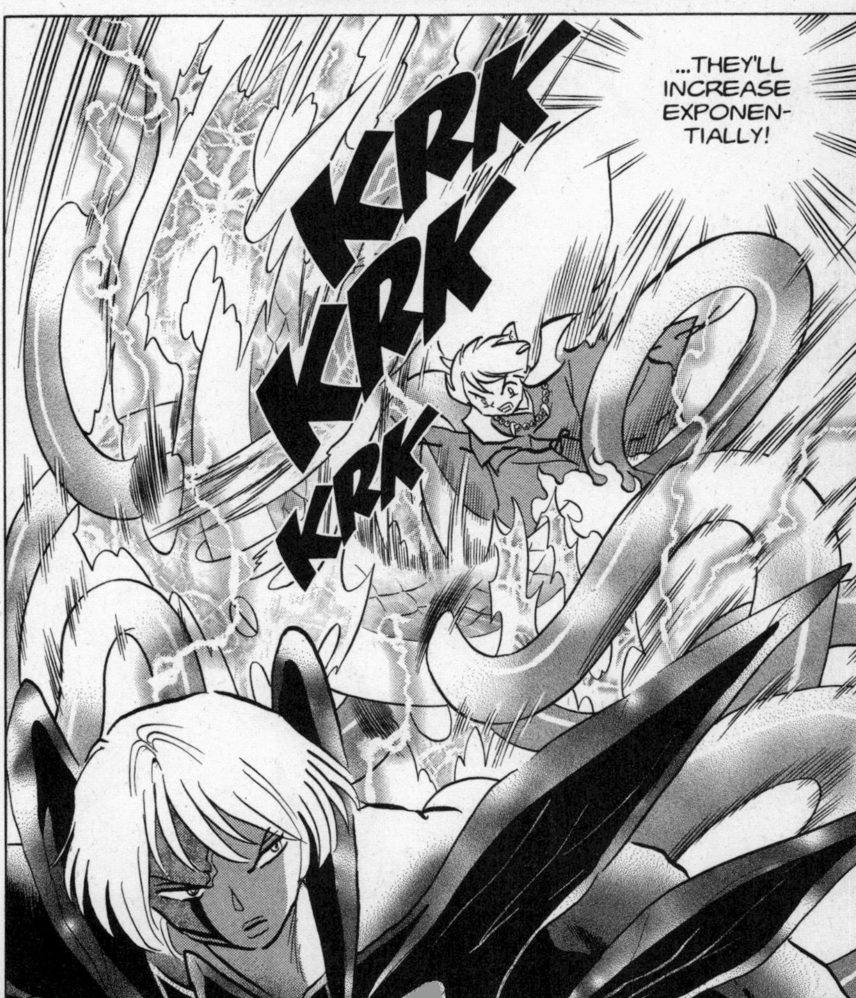
...THEY'LL INCREASE EXPONEN-TIALLY!
KRK KRK KRK

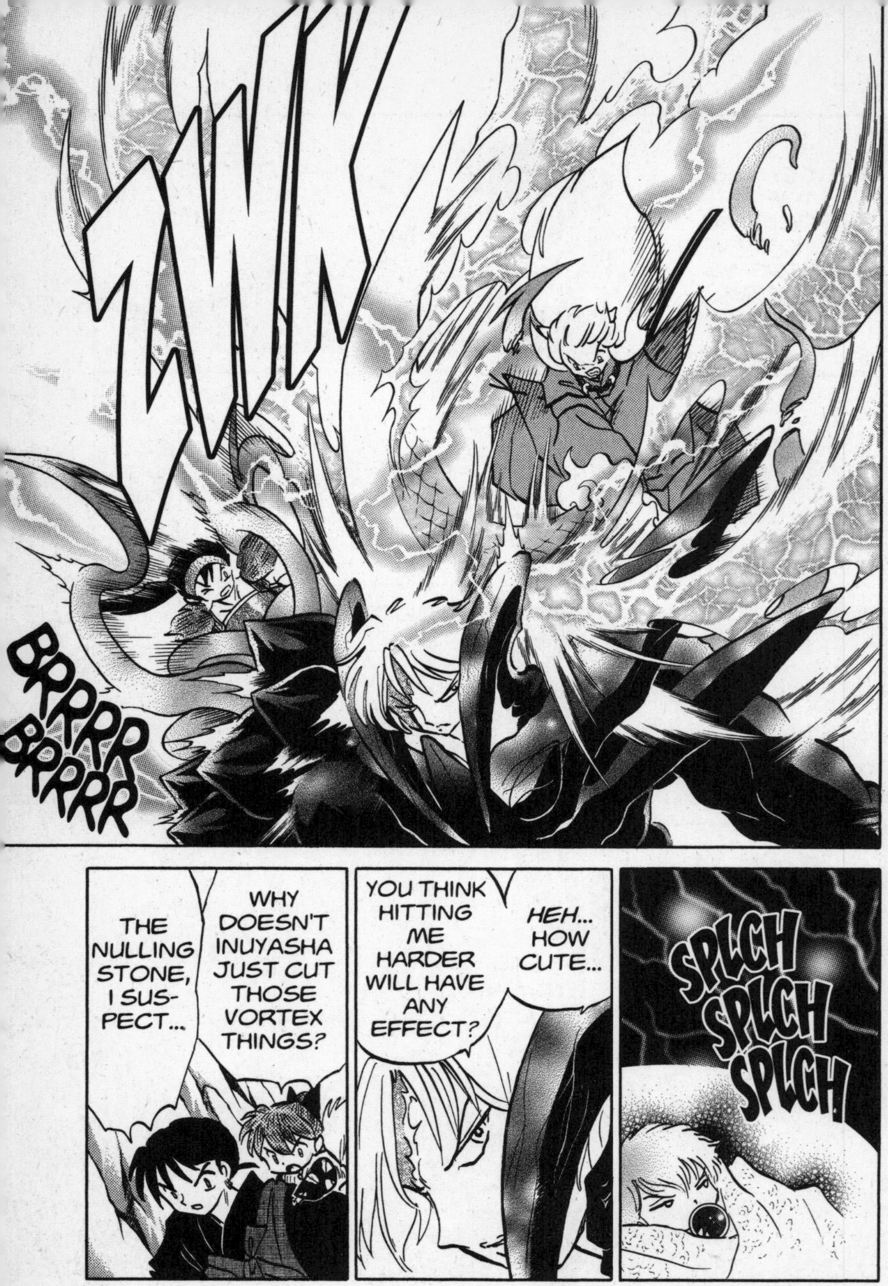
ZWIN
BRRRR
BRRRR
SPLCH
SPLCH
SPLCH
HEH... HOW CUTE...
YOU THINK HITTING ME HARDER WILL HAVE ANY EFFECT?
WHY DOESN'T INUYASHA JUST CUT THOSE VORTEX THINGS?
THE NULLING STONE, I SUSPECT...

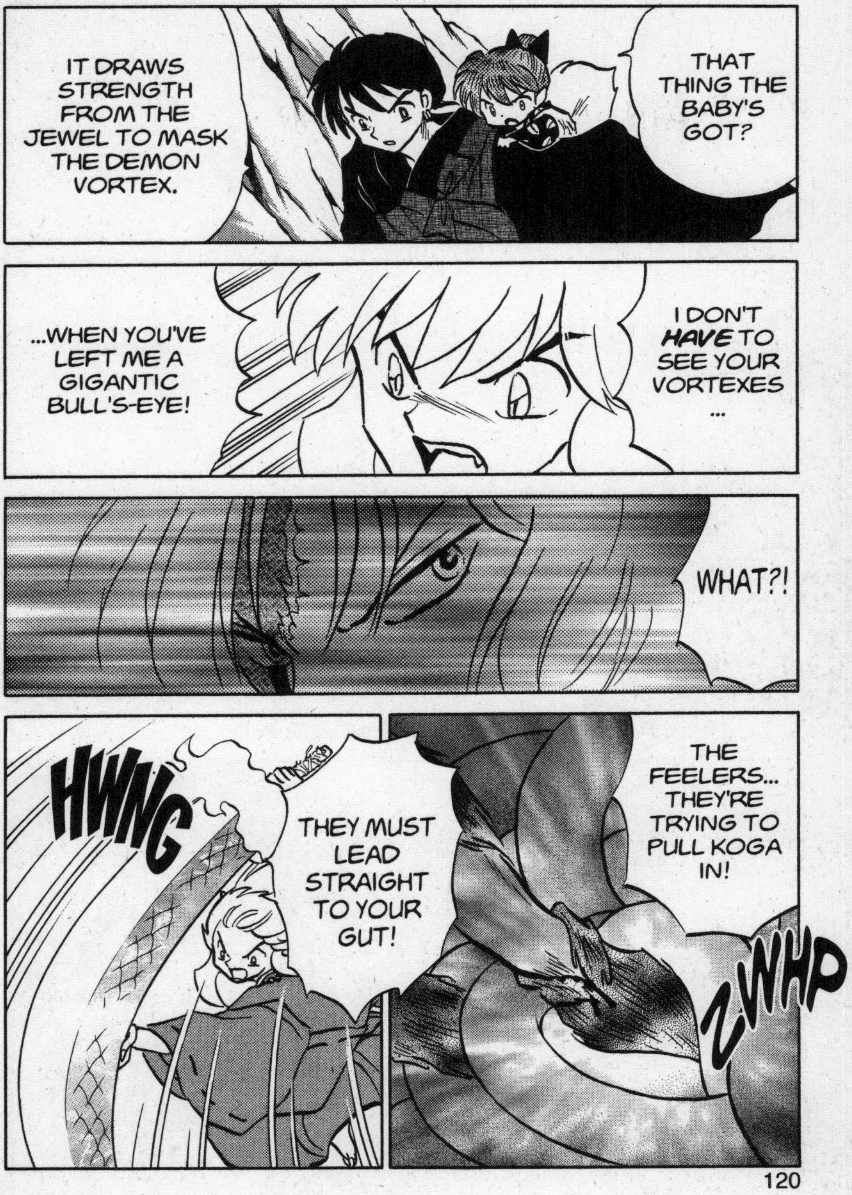
THAT THING THE BABY'S GOT?
IT DRAWS STRENGTH FROM THE JEWEL TO MASK THE DEMON VORTEX.
I DON'T *HAVE* TO SEE YOUR VORTEXES ...
...WHEN YOU'VE LEFT ME A GIGANTIC BULL'S-EYE!
WHAT?!
THE FEELERS... THEY'RE TRYING TO PULL KOGA IN!
ZWHP
THEY MUST LEAD STRAIGHT TO YOUR GUT!
HWNG

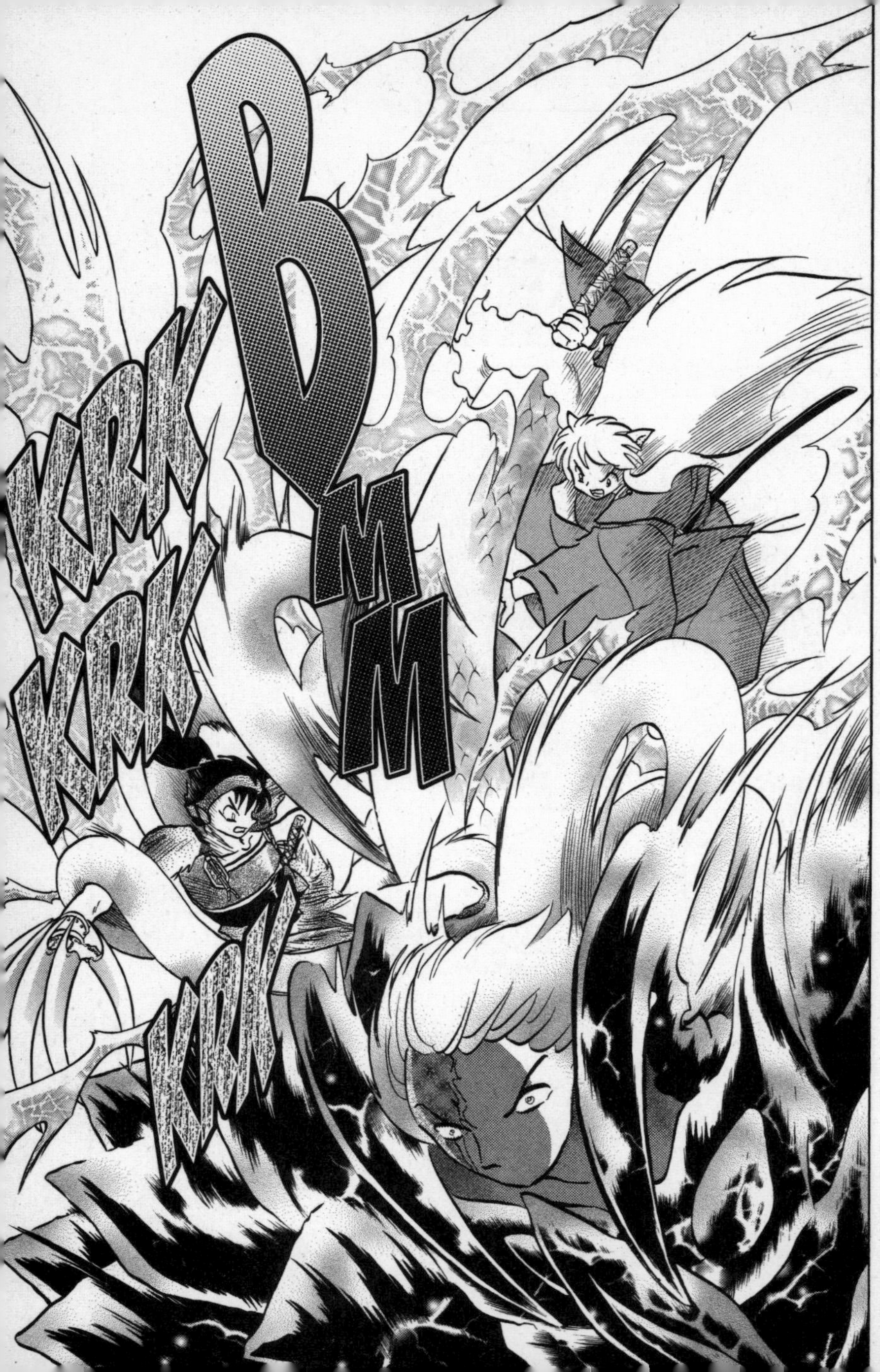
BMM
KRRK
KRRK
KRRK

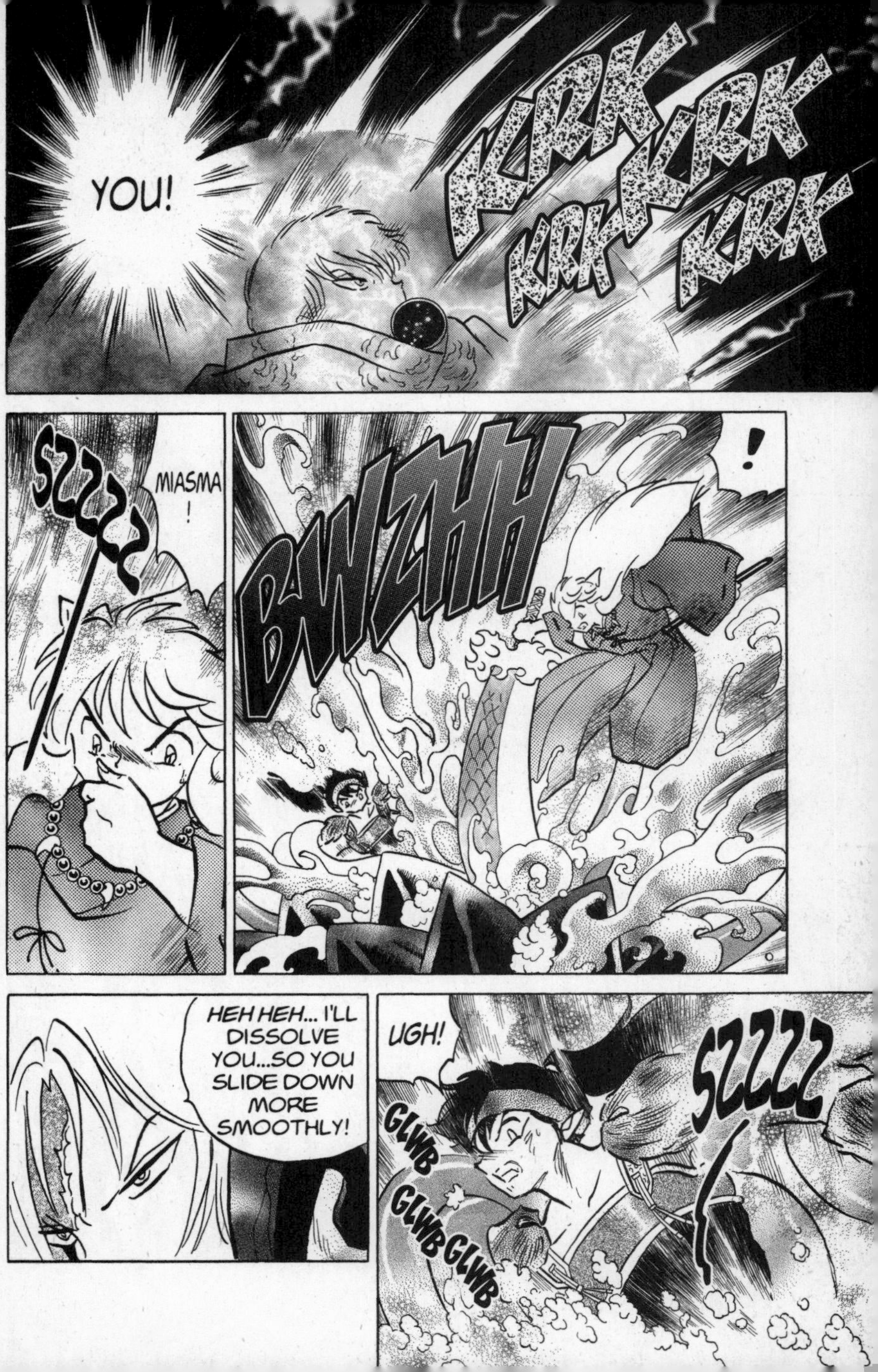
KRK KRK
KRK KRK
YOU!
!
BWZHH
MIASMA!
SZZZZ
SZZZZ
UGH!
GLWB
GLWB
GLWB
GLWB
HEH HEH... I'LL DISSOLVE YOU...SO YOU SLIDE DOWN MORE SMOOTHLY!

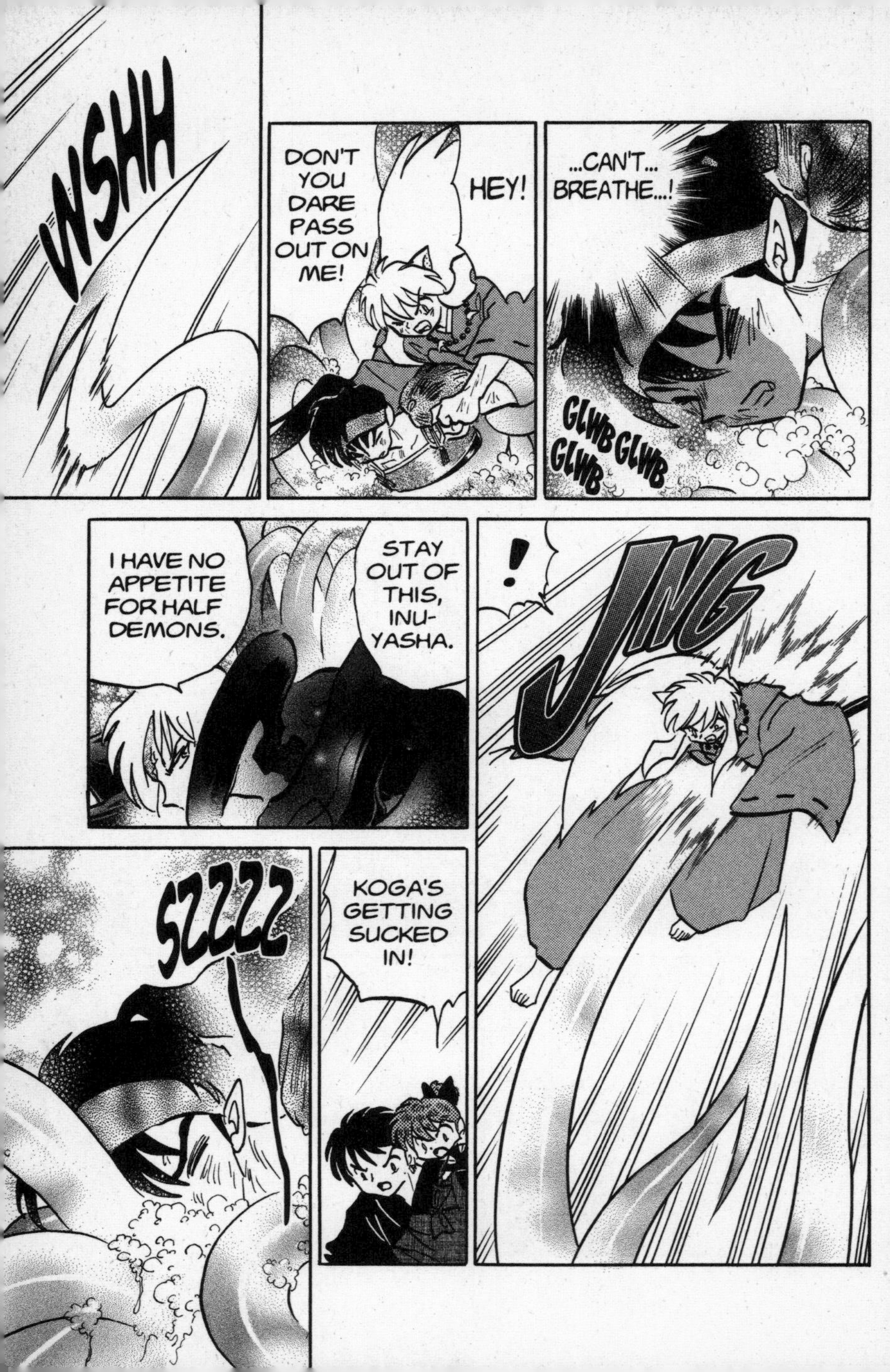
...CAN'T... BREATHE...!
GLWB GLWB GLWB
HEY!
DON'T YOU DARE PASS OUT ON ME!
WSHH
!
JING
STAY OUT OF THIS, INU-YASHA.
I HAVE NO APPETITE FOR HALF DEMONS.
KOGA'S GETTING SUCKED IN!
SZZZZ

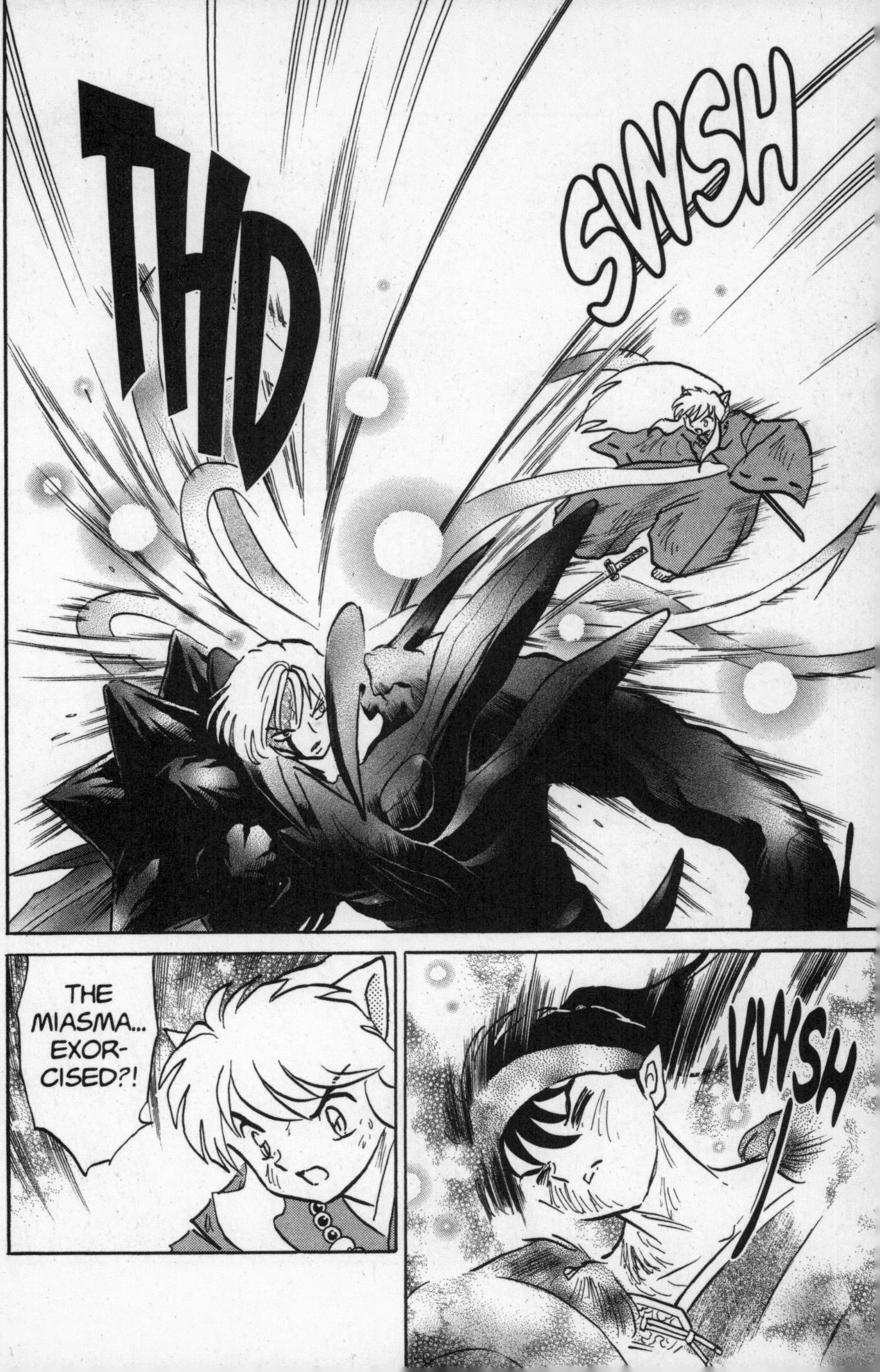
THD
SWSH
VWSH
THE MIASMA... EXOR-CISED?!

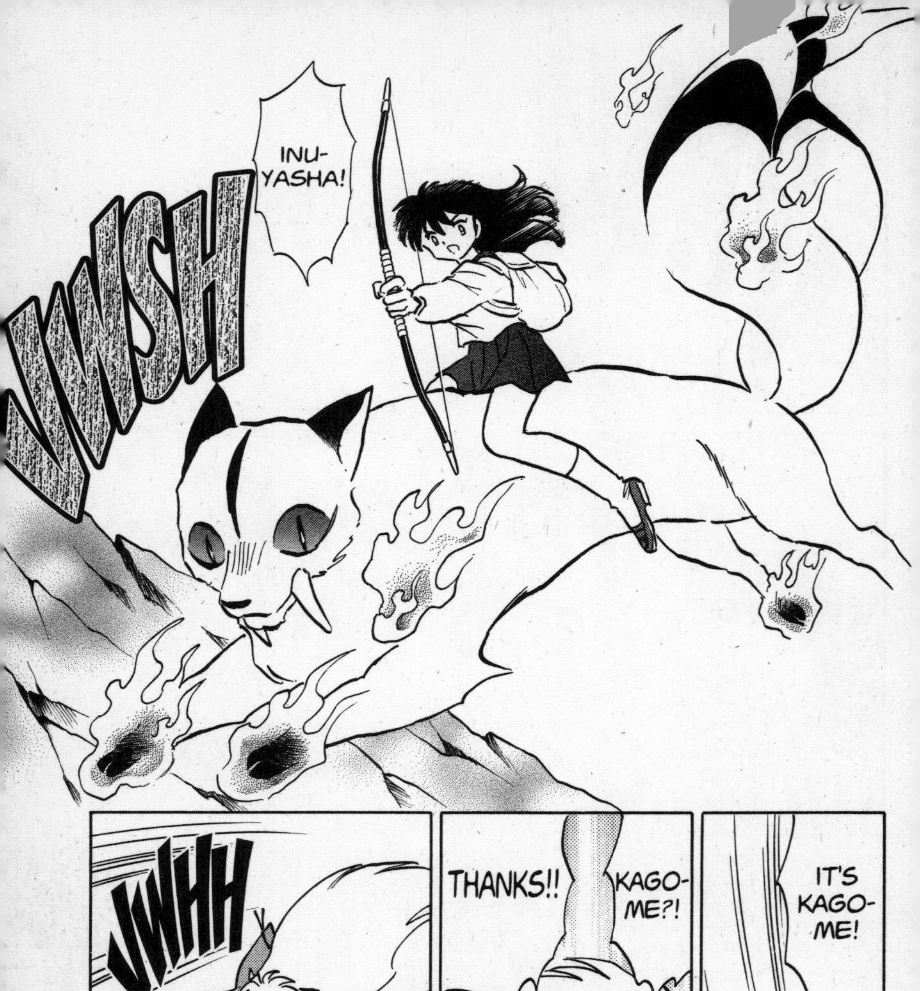
INU-
YASHA!
VWSH

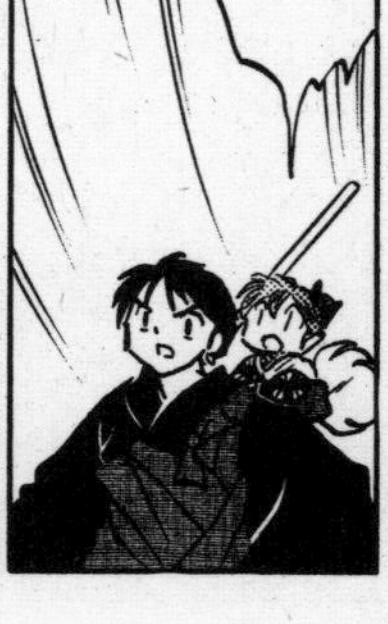
IT'S
KAGO-
ME!

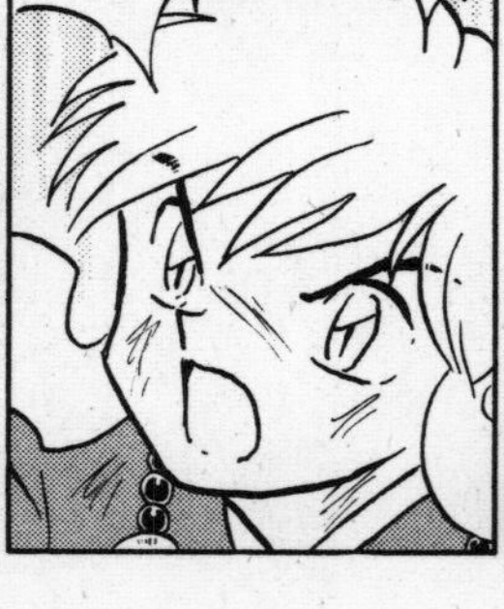
KAGO-
ME?!
THANKS!!

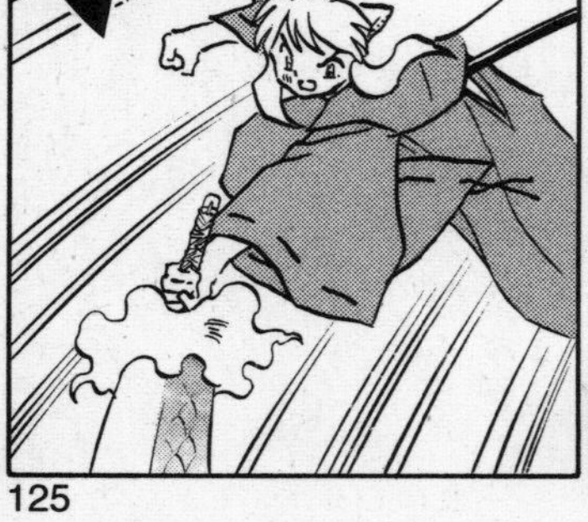
JWHH

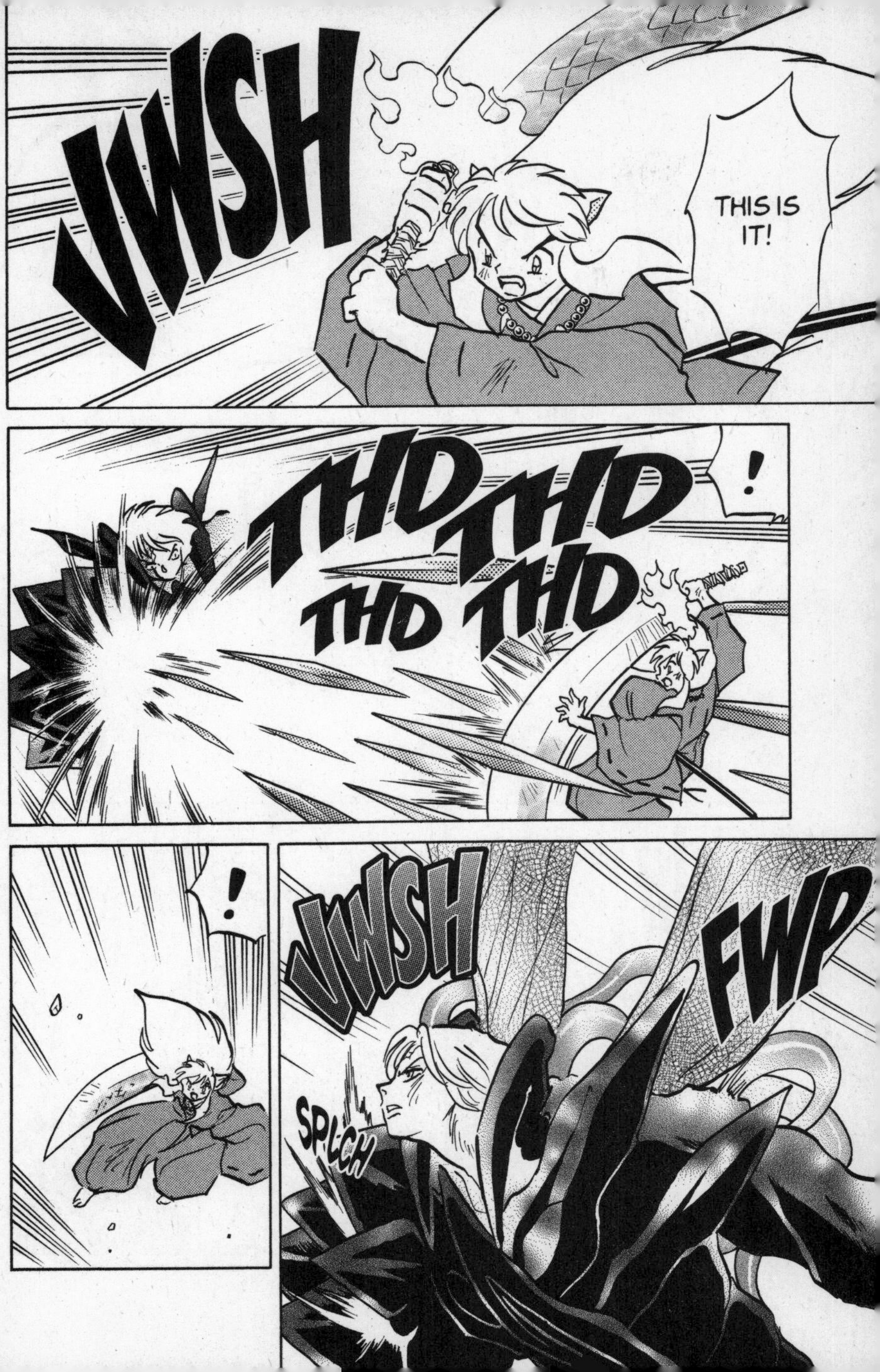
THIS IS IT!
JWSH
!
THD THD
THD THD
FWP
JWSH
SPLCH
!

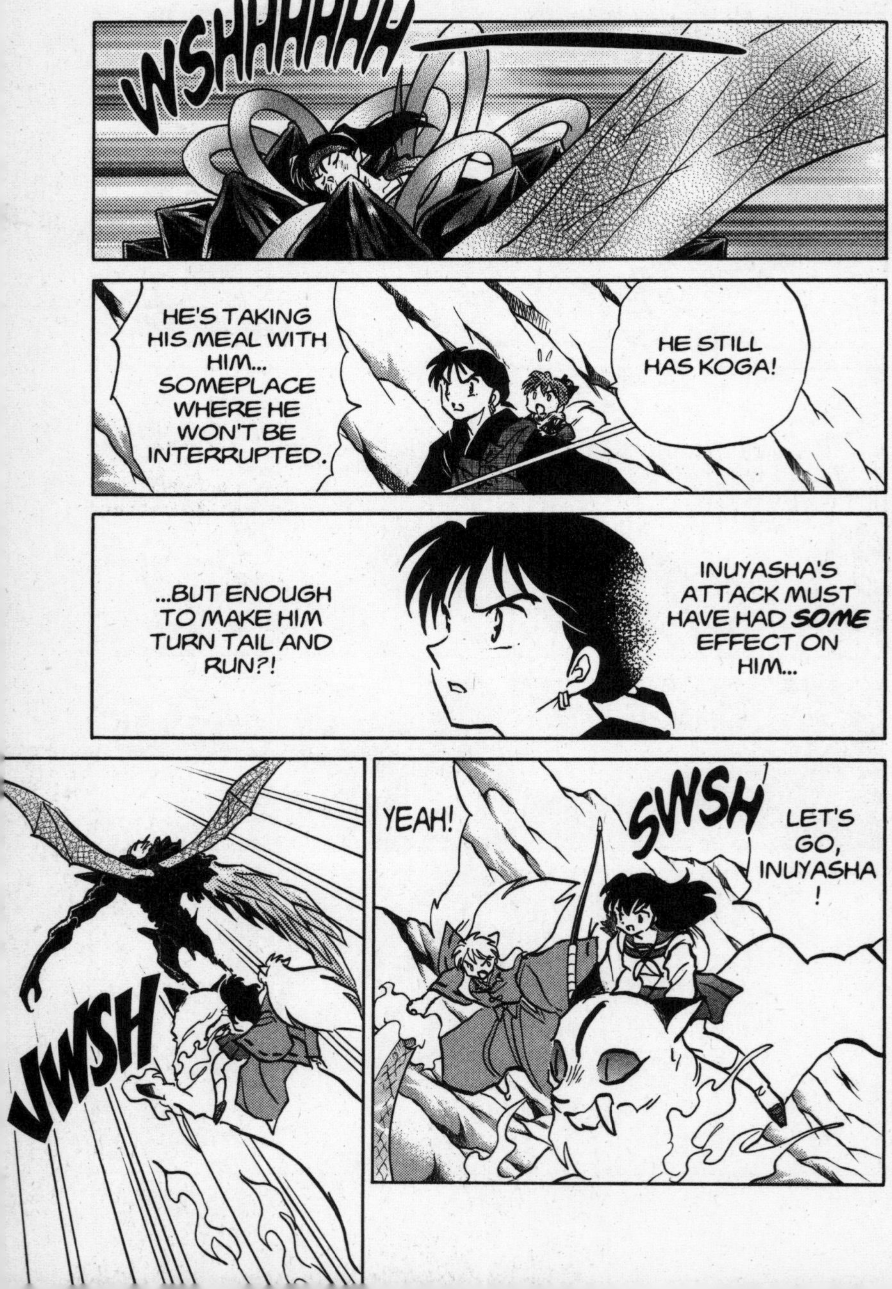
WSHHHHHH
HE STILL HAS KOGA!
HE'S TAKING HIS MEAL WITH HIM... SOMEPLACE WHERE HE WON'T BE INTERRUPTED.
INUYASHA'S ATTACK MUST HAVE HAD *SOME* EFFECT ON HIM...
...BUT ENOUGH TO MAKE HIM TURN TAIL AND RUN?!
LET'S GO, INUYASHA!
SWSH
YEAH!
VWSH

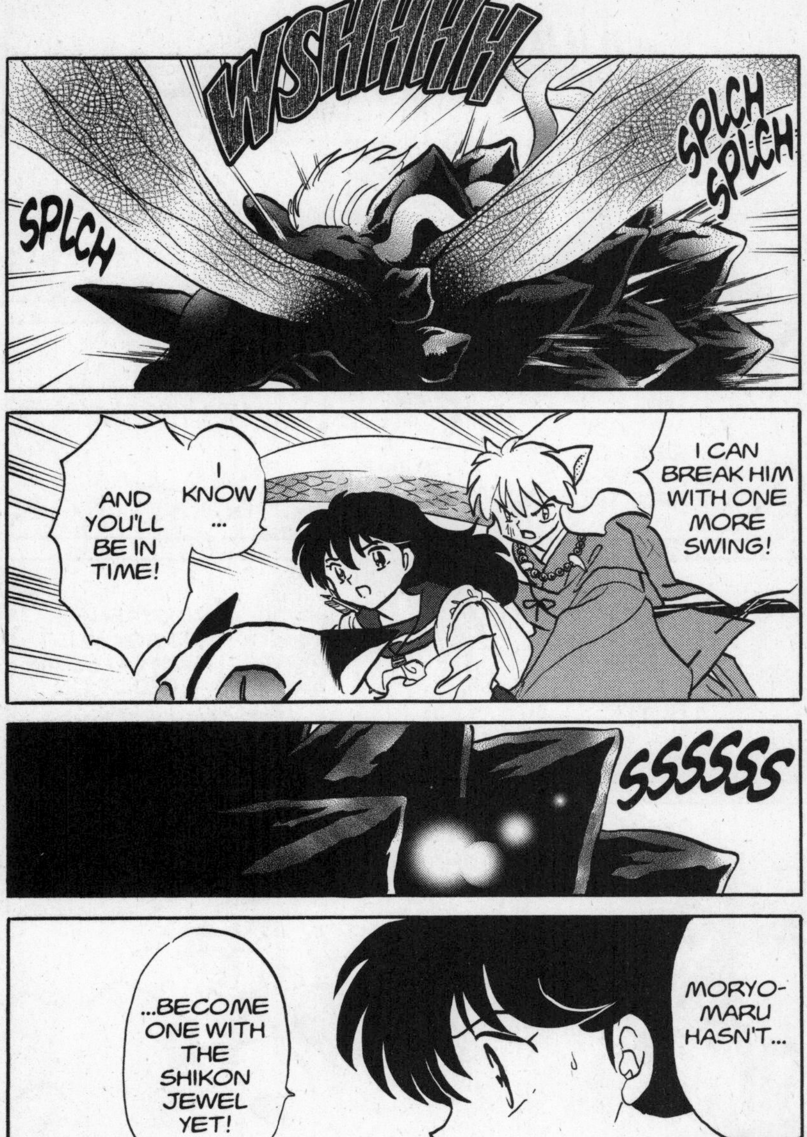

WSHHHH
SPLCH SPLCH
SPLCH
I CAN BREAK HIM WITH ONE MORE SWING!
I KNOW...
AND YOU'LL BE IN TIME!
SSSSSS
MORYO-MARU HASN'T...
...BECOME ONE WITH THE SHIKON JEWEL YET!

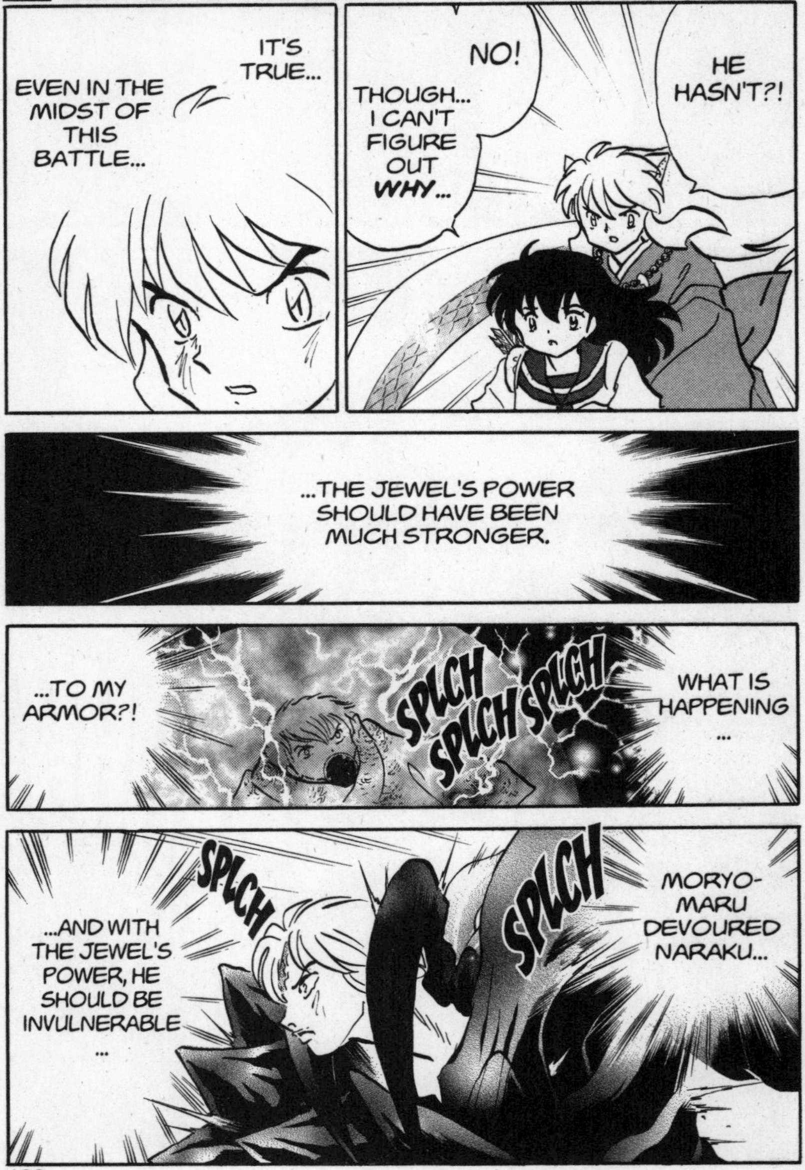
HE HASN'T?!
NO!
THOUGH... I CAN'T FIGURE OUT **WHY**...
IT'S TRUE...
EVEN IN THE MIDST OF THIS BATTLE...
...THE JEWEL'S POWER SHOULD HAVE BEEN MUCH STRONGER.
WHAT IS HAPPENING ...
SPLCH SPLCH SPLCH SPLCH
...TO MY ARMOR?!
MORYO-MARU DEVOURED NARAKU...
SPLCH
SPLCH
...AND WITH THE JEWEL'S POWER, HE SHOULD BE INVULNERABLE ...

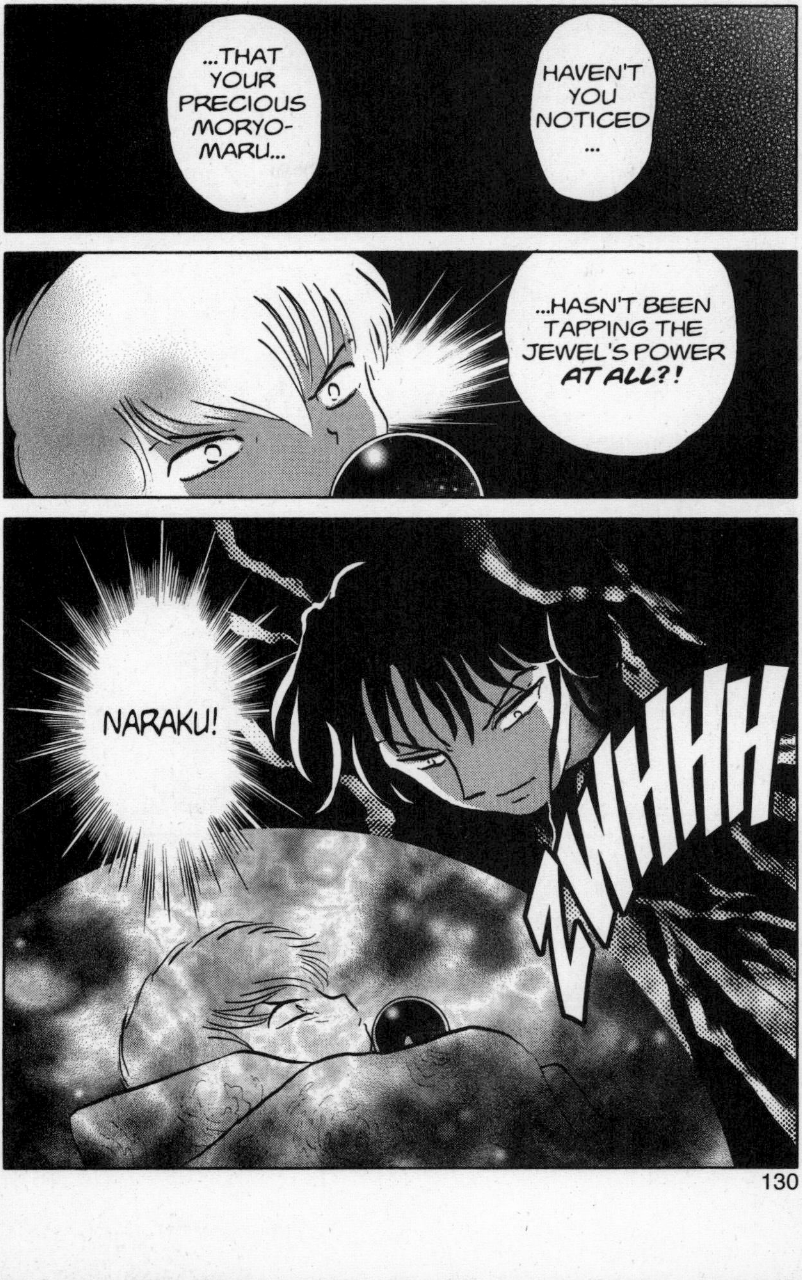

HAVEN'T YOU NOTICED ...
...THAT YOUR PRECIOUS MORYO-MARU...
...HASN'T BEEN TAPPING THE JEWEL'S POWER AT ALL?!
ZWHHHH
NARAKU!

SCROLL 8
EROSION

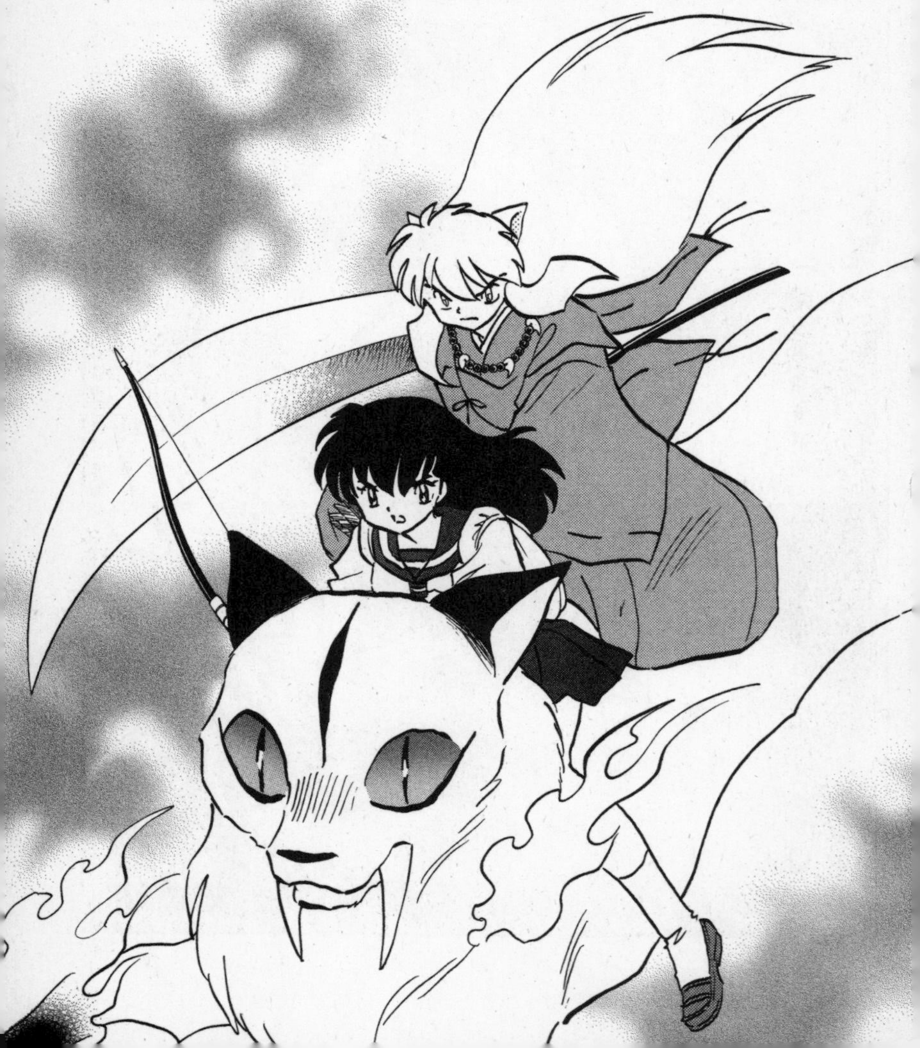

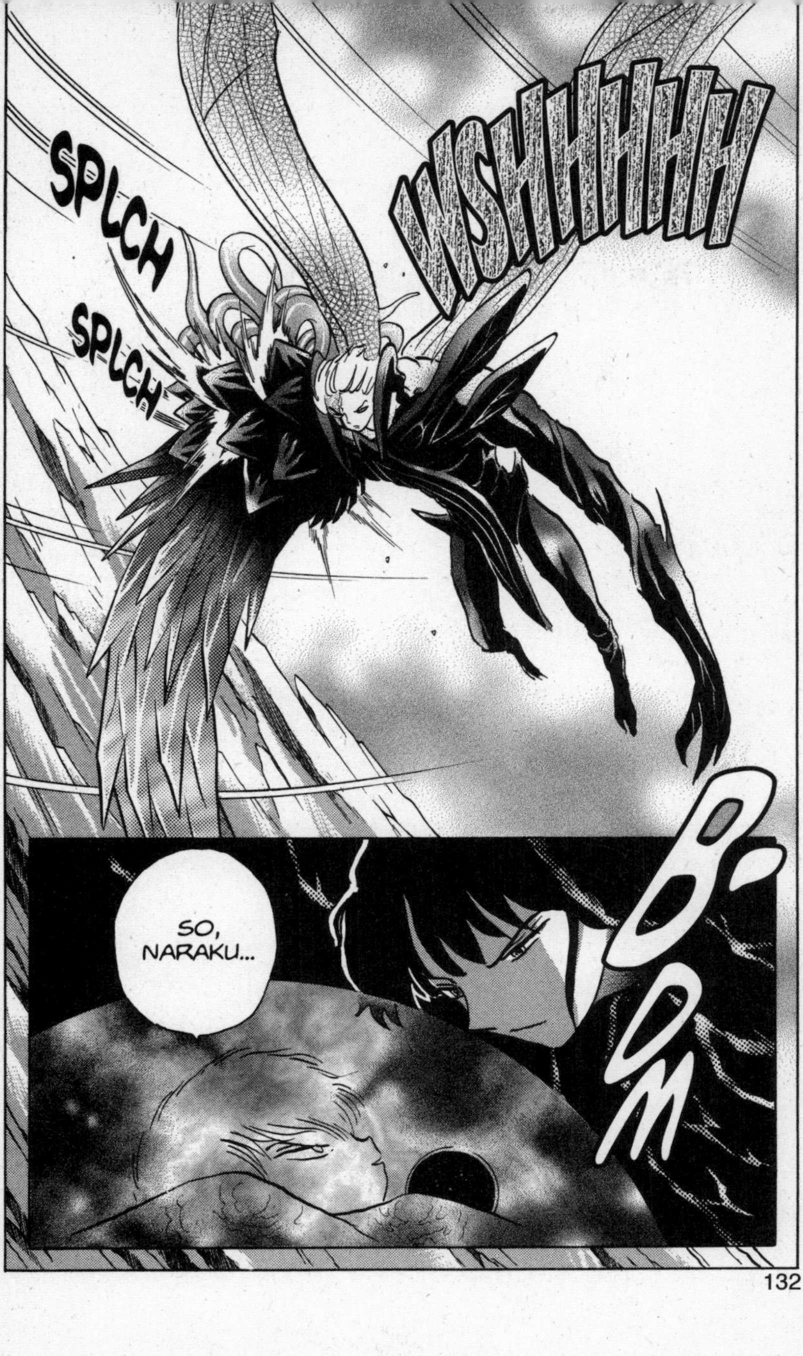
WSHHHHH
SPLCH
SPLCH
BOOM
SO, NARAKU...

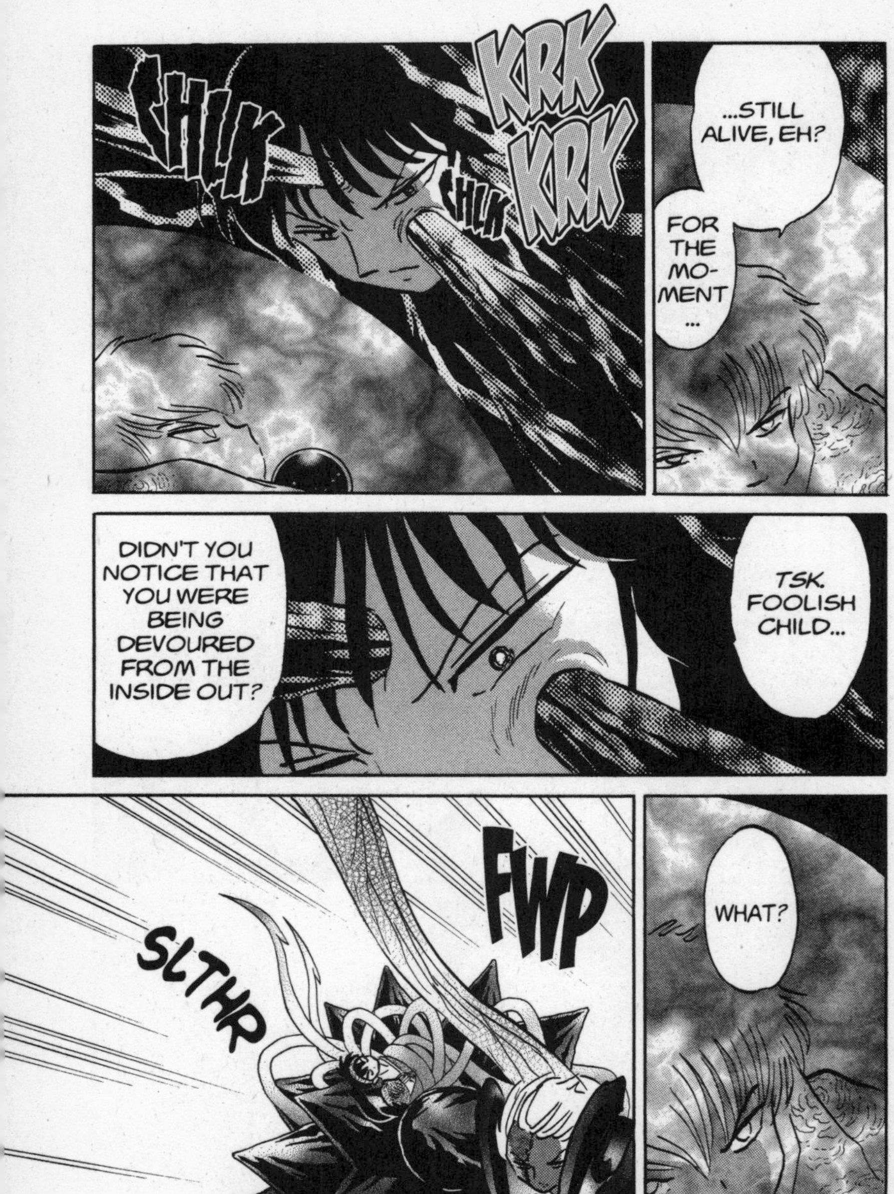
...STILL ALIVE, EH?
FOR THE MOMENT...
KRK KRK
CHLIK
CHLIK
TSK. FOOLISH CHILD...
DIDN'T YOU NOTICE THAT YOU WERE BEING DEVOURED FROM THE INSIDE OUT?
WHAT?
FWP
SLTHR

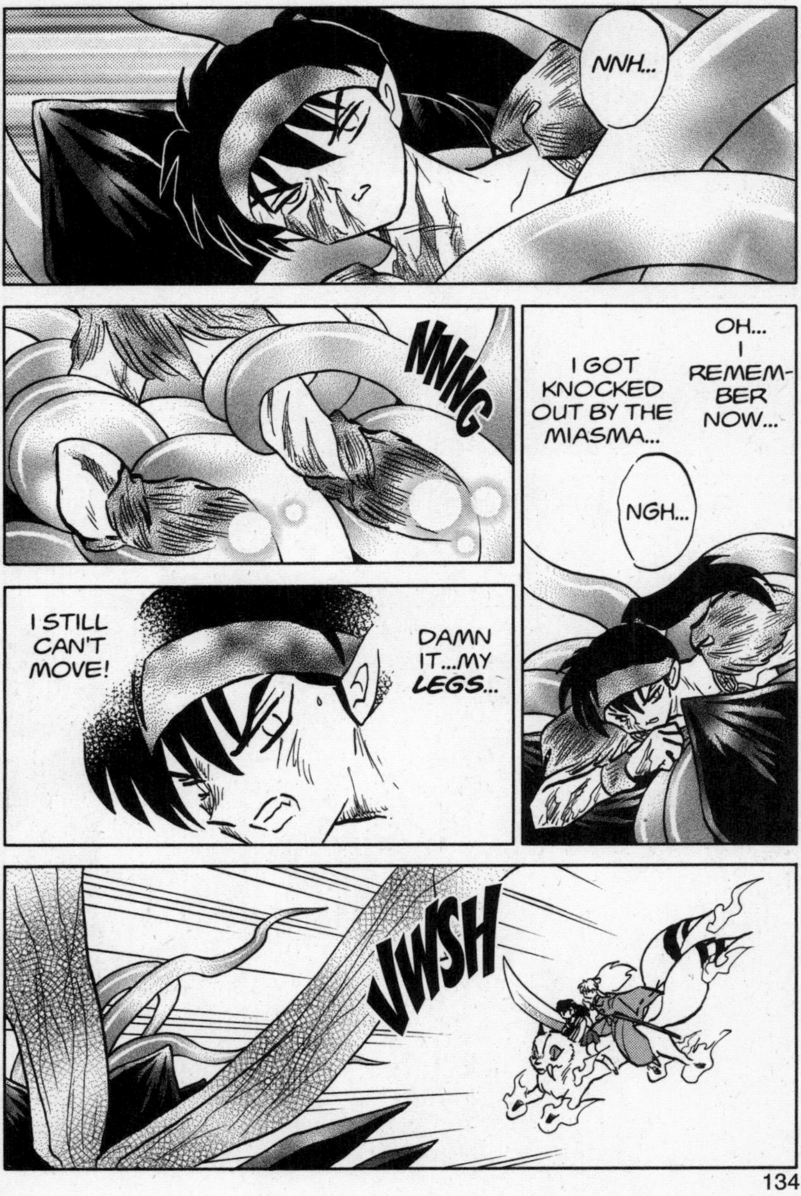
NNH...
OH... I REMEMBER NOW...
I GOT KNOCKED OUT BY THE MIASMA...
NGH...
NNNG
DAMN IT...MY *LEGS*...
I STILL CAN'T MOVE!
VWSH

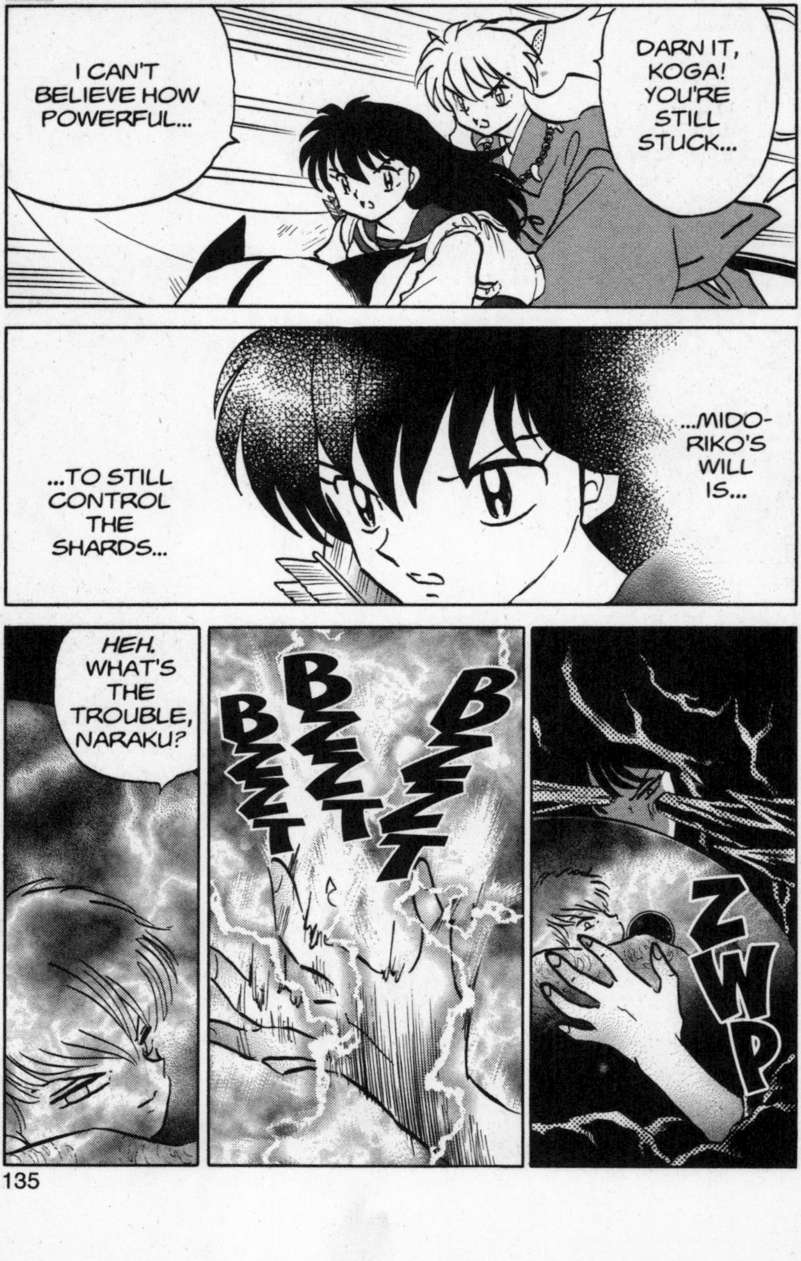
DARN IT, KOGA! YOU'RE STILL STUCK...
I CAN'T BELIEVE HOW POWERFUL...
...MIDO-RIKO'S WILL IS...
...TO STILL CONTROL THE SHARDS...
ZWP
BZZT
BZZT
BZZT
HEH. WHAT'S THE TROUBLE, NARAKU?

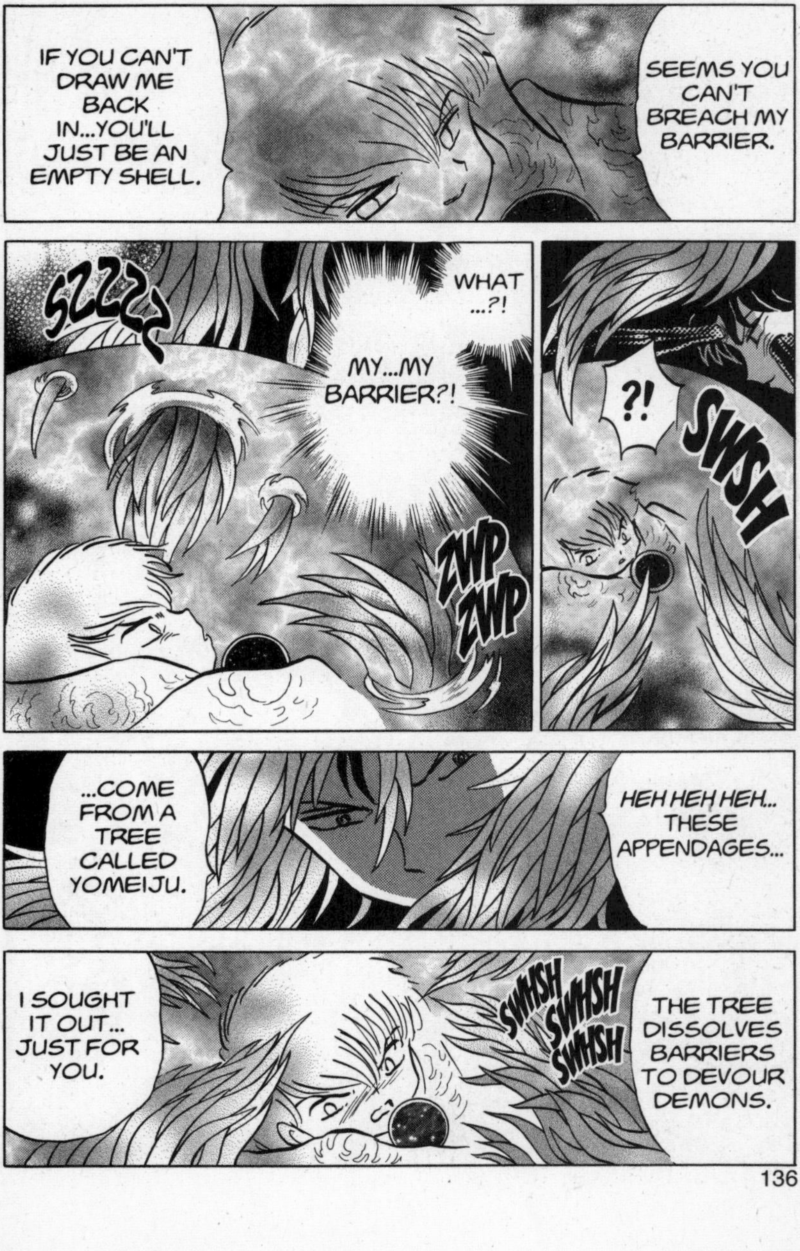
SEEMS YOU CAN'T BREACH MY BARRIER.
IF YOU CAN'T DRAW ME BACK IN...YOU'LL JUST BE AN EMPTY SHELL.
?!
SWSH
WHAT ...?!
MY...MY BARRIER?!
SZZZZ
ZWP ZWP
HEH HEH HEH... THESE APPENDAGES...
...COME FROM A TREE CALLED YOMEIJU.
THE TREE DISSOLVES BARRIERS TO DEVOUR DEMONS.
SWHSH SWHSH SWHSH
I SOUGHT IT OUT... JUST FOR YOU.

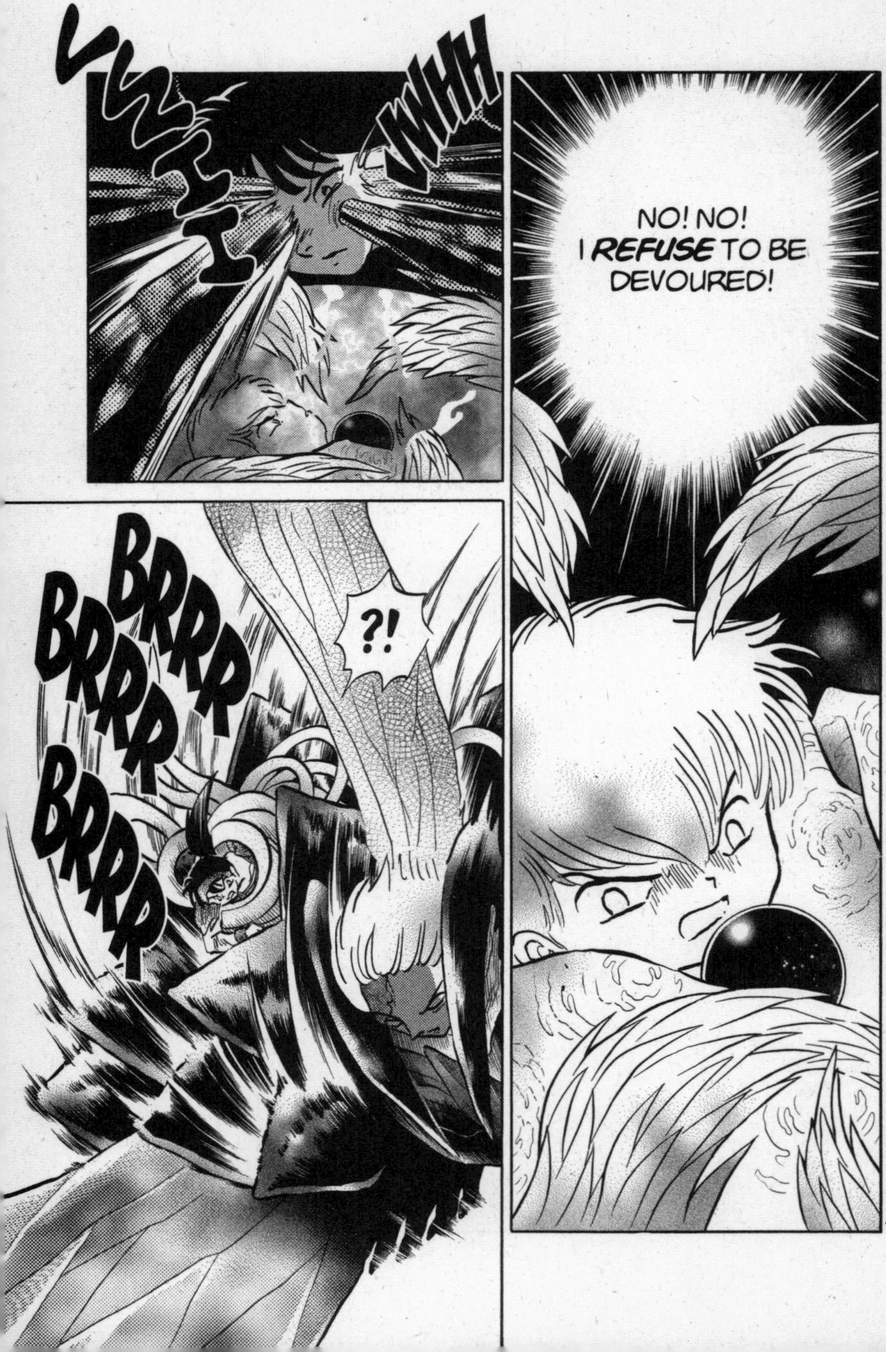
NO! NO! I **REFUSE** TO BE DEVOURED!
VWHH
?!
BRRR
BRRR
BRRR
BRRR

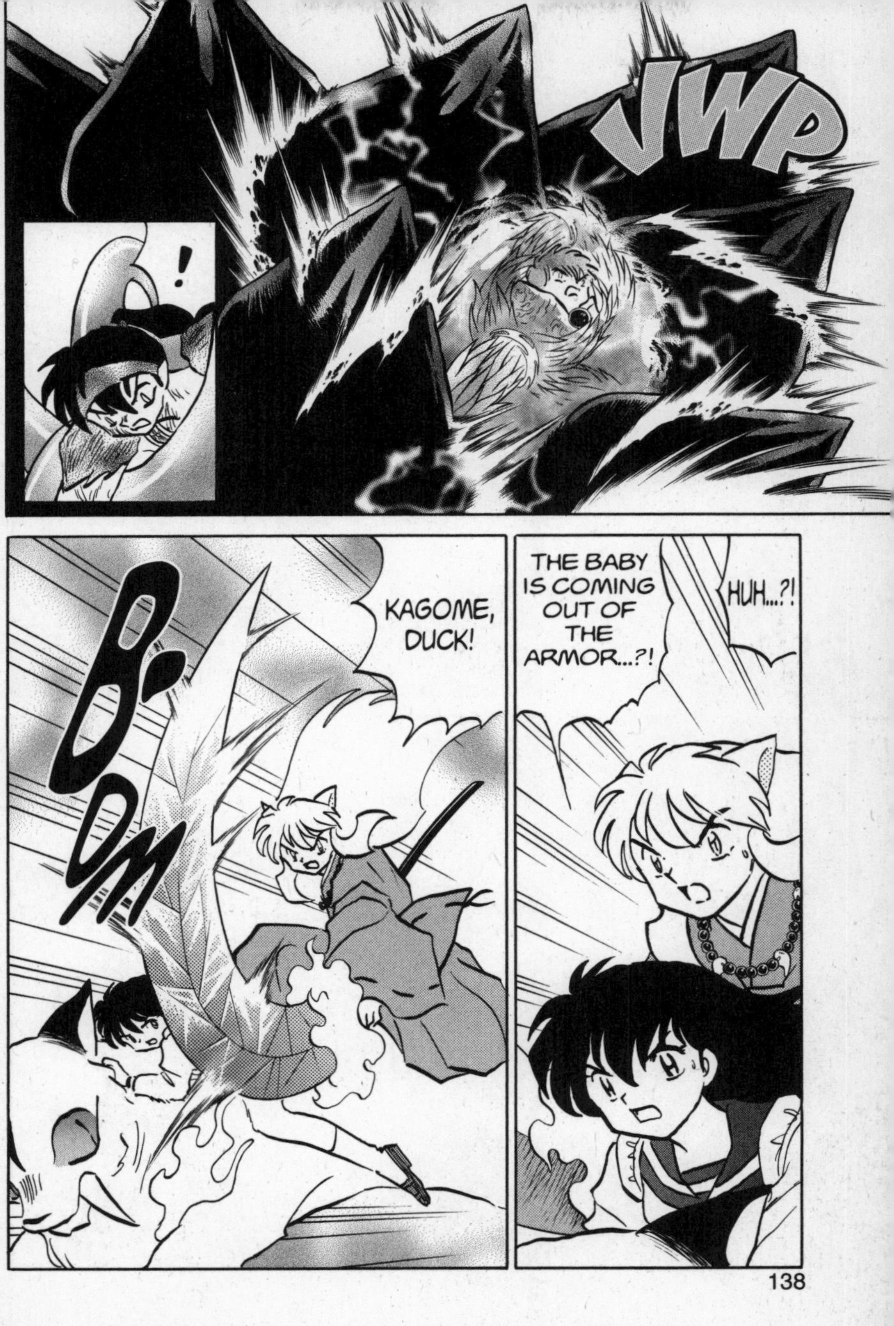
JWP
!
HUH...?!
THE BABY IS COMING OUT OF THE ARMOR...?!
KAGOME, DUCK!
BDOM!

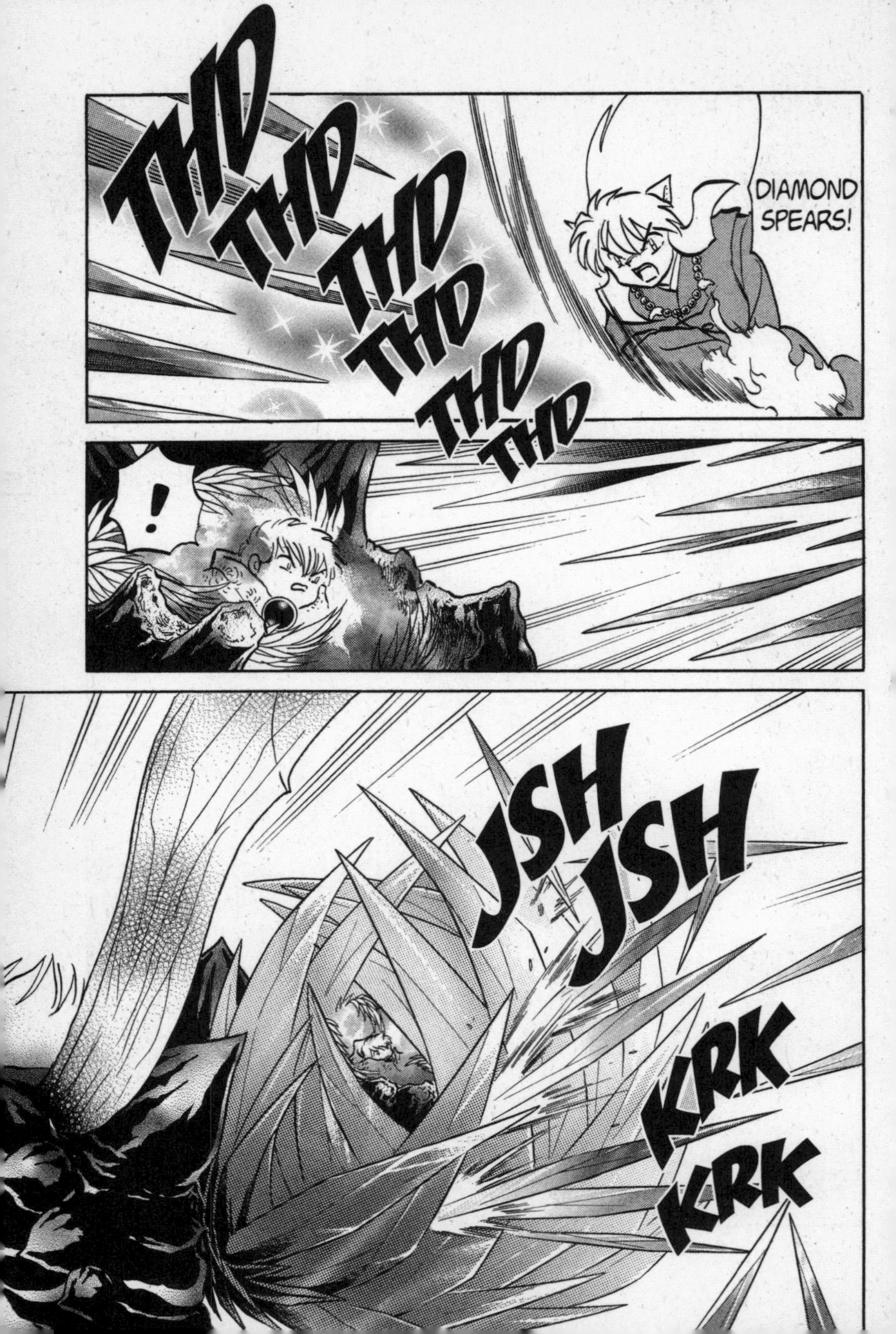
DIAMOND SPEARS!
THD THD THD THD THD THD THD
!
JSH JSH
KRK KRK

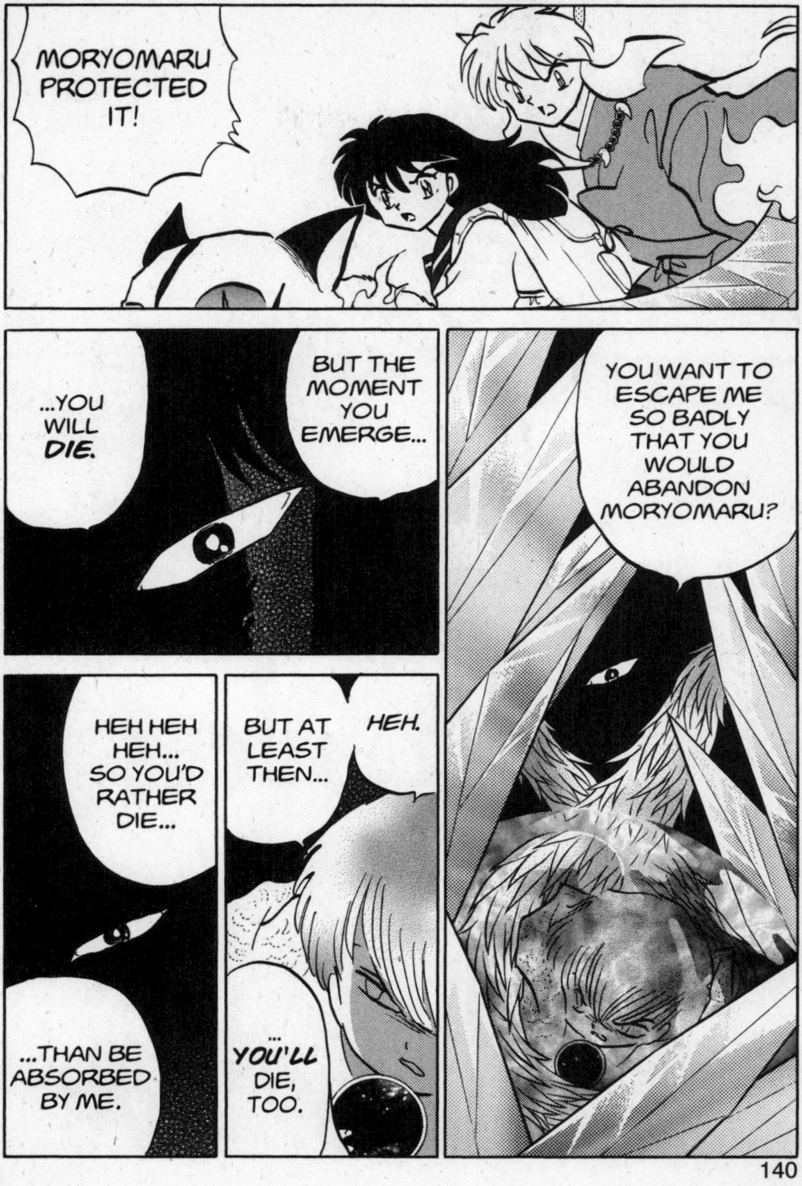
MORYOMARU PROTECTED IT!
YOU WANT TO ESCAPE ME SO BADLY THAT YOU WOULD ABANDON MORYOMARU?
BUT THE MOMENT YOU EMERGE...
...YOU WILL **DIE**.
HEH.
BUT AT LEAST THEN...
... ***YOU'LL*** DIE, TOO.
HEH HEH HEH... SO YOU'D RATHER DIE...
...THAN BE ABSORBED BY ME.

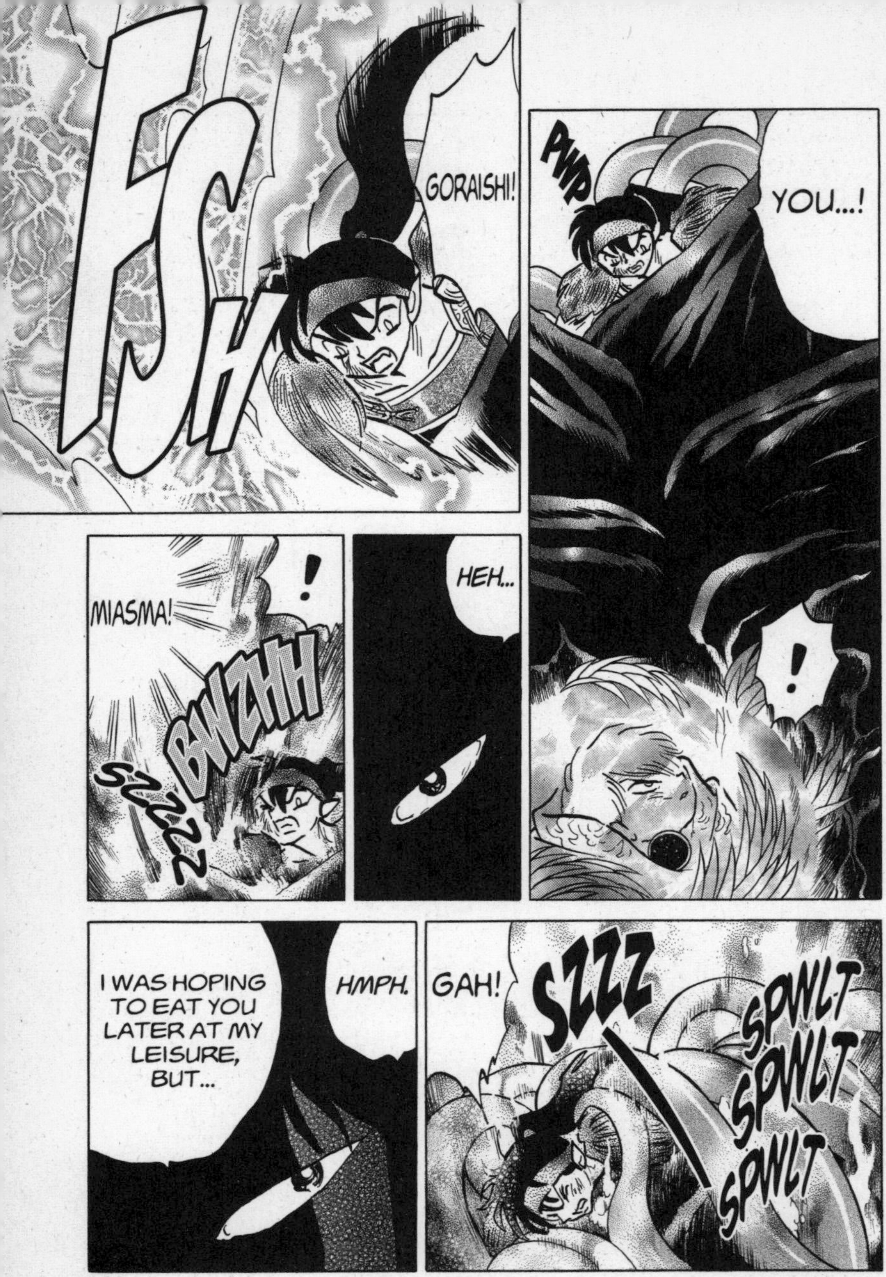
PWP
YOU...!
!
FSH
GORAISHI!
HEH...
!
MIASMA!
BWZHH
SZZZZ
GAH!
SZZZ
SPWLT-T
SPWLT
SPWLT
HMPH.
I WAS HOPING TO EAT YOU LATER AT MY LEISURE, BUT...

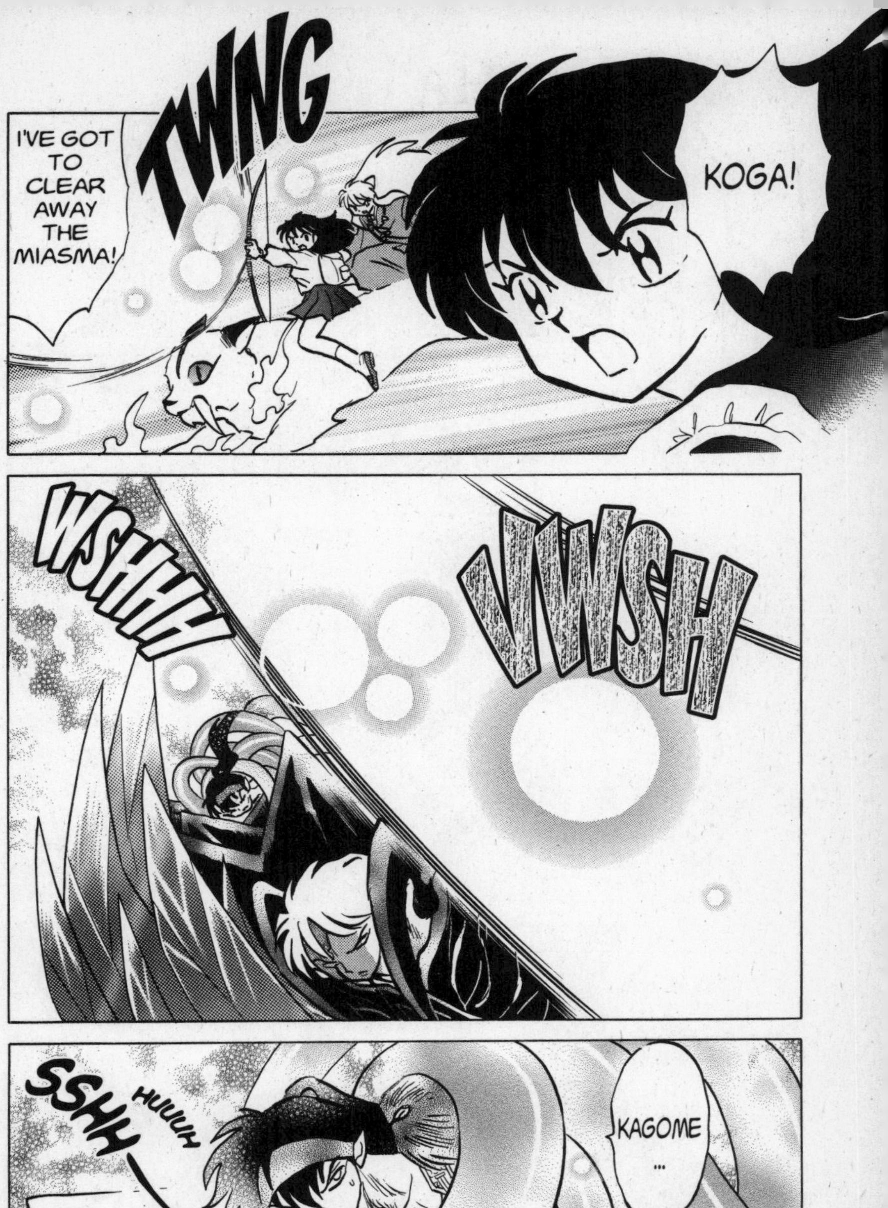
KOGA!
TWNG
I'VE GOT TO CLEAR AWAY THE MIASMA!
VWSH
WSHHH
KAGOME ...
HUUUH
SSHH—

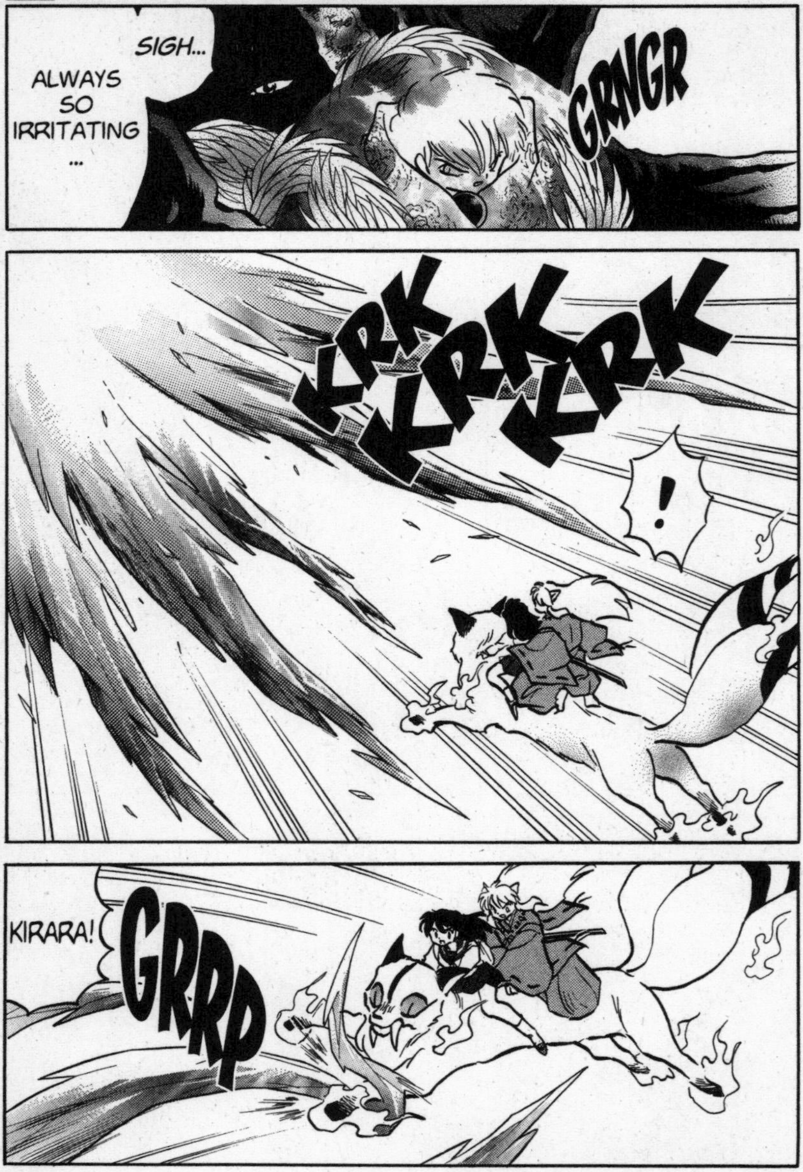
GRNGR
SIGH...
ALWAYS SO IRRITATING ...
KRK KRK KRK
!
GRRP
KIRARA!

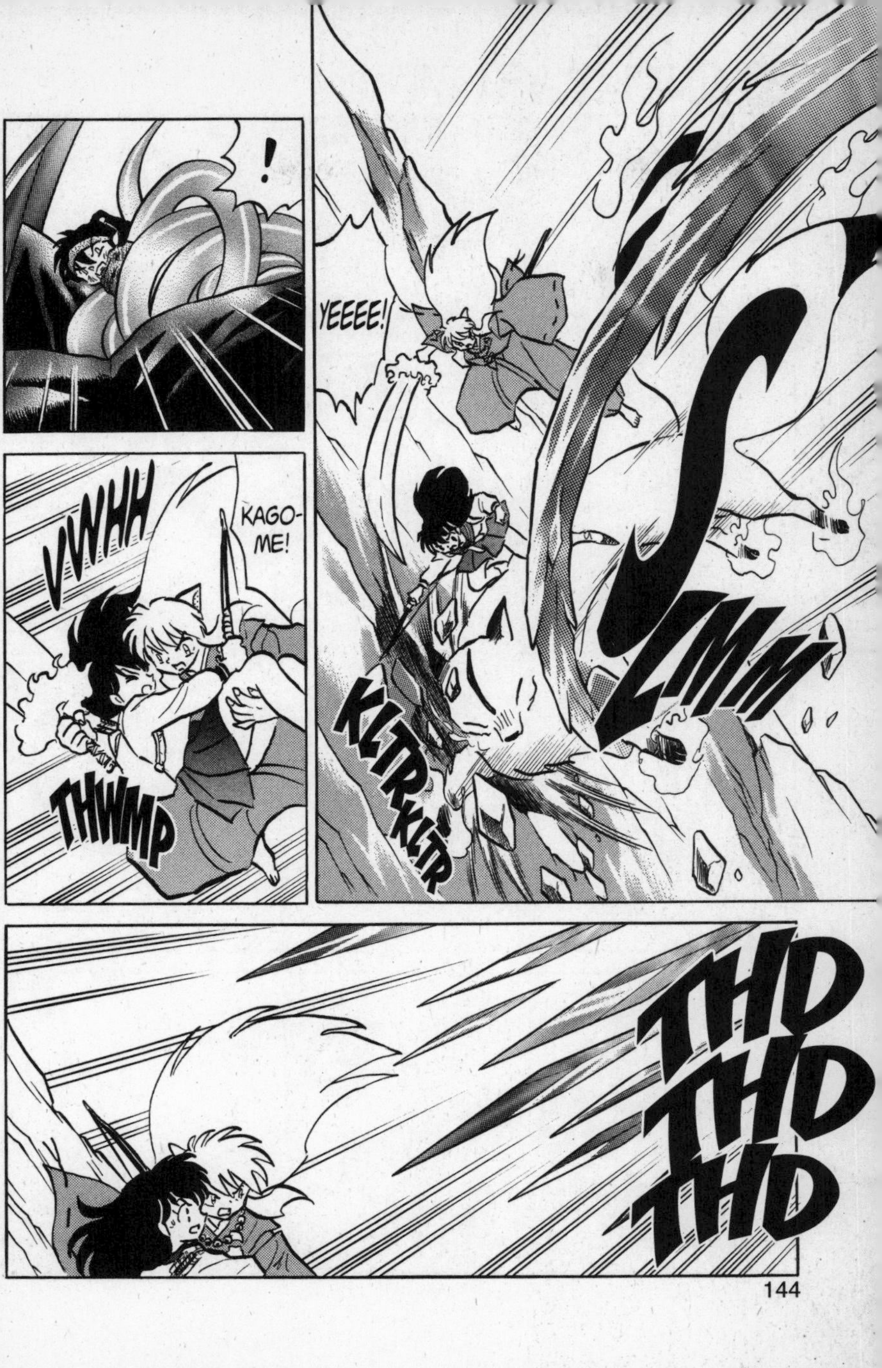
YEEEE!
KLTR KLTR
!
KAGO-ME!
VWHH
THWMP
THD THD THD

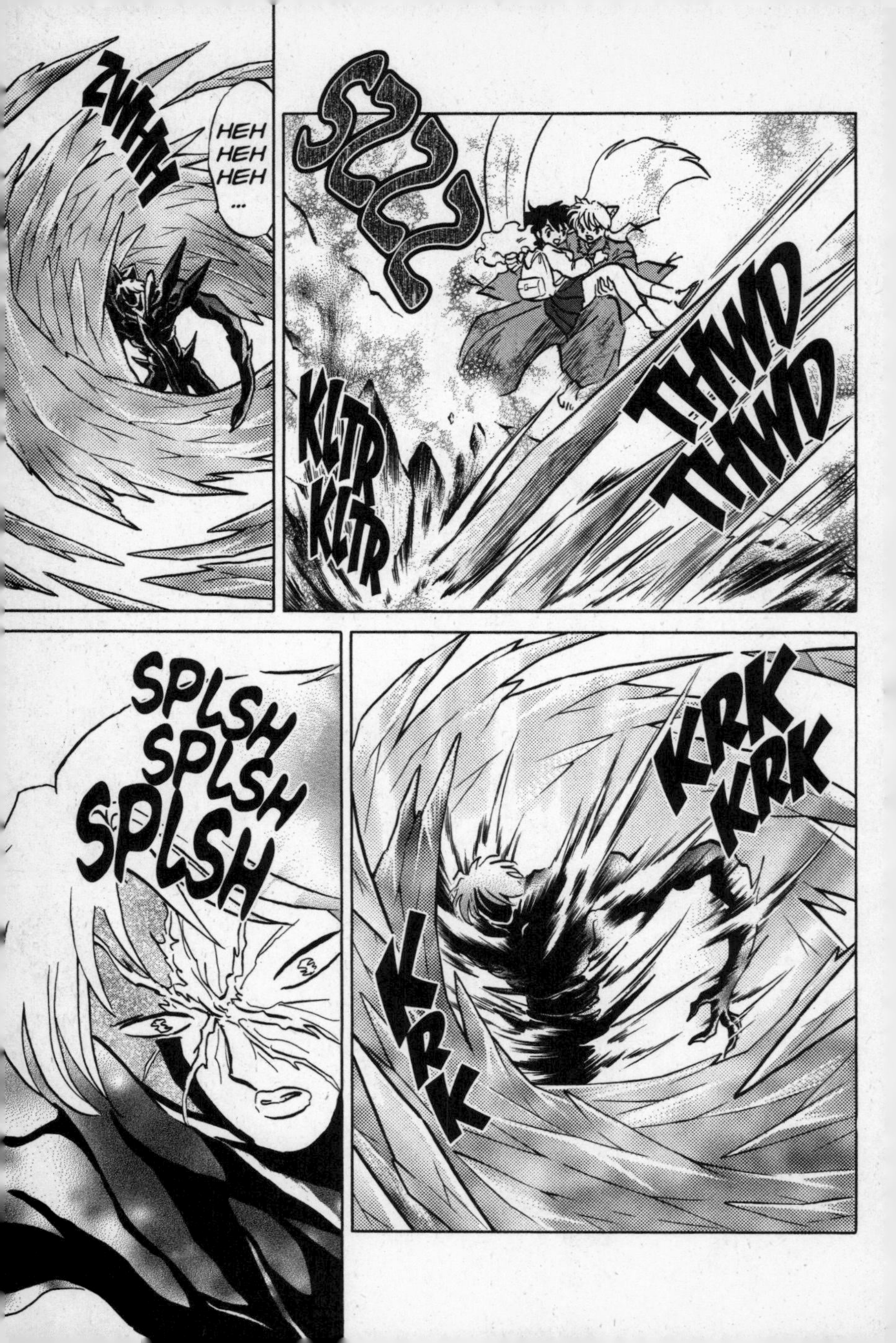
THWD THWD
SUUU
KLTR KLTR
ZWHH
HEH HEH HEH ...
KRK KRK
KRK
SPLSH SPLSH SPLSH

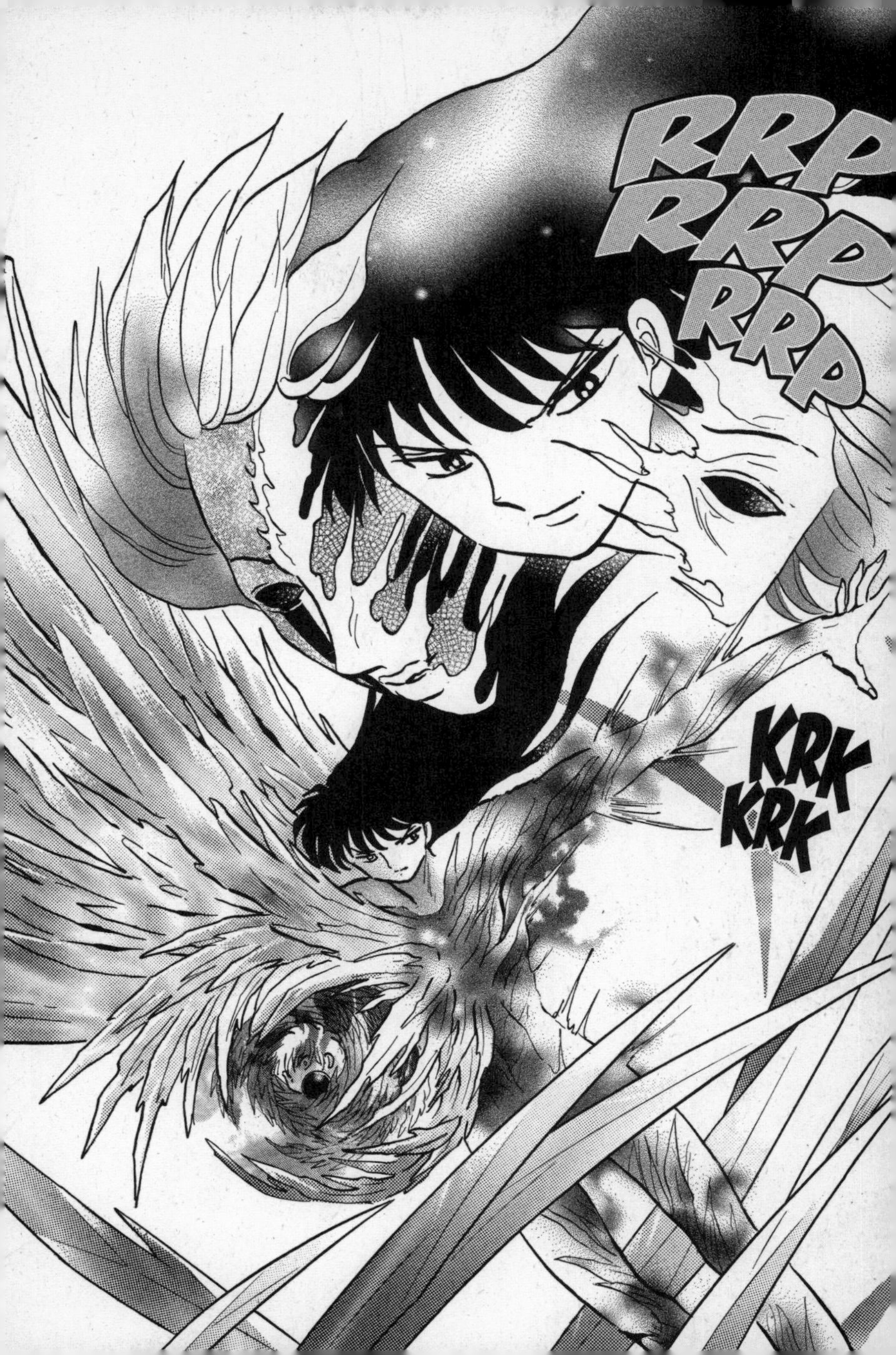
RRRP RRRP RRRP RRRP
KRK KRK

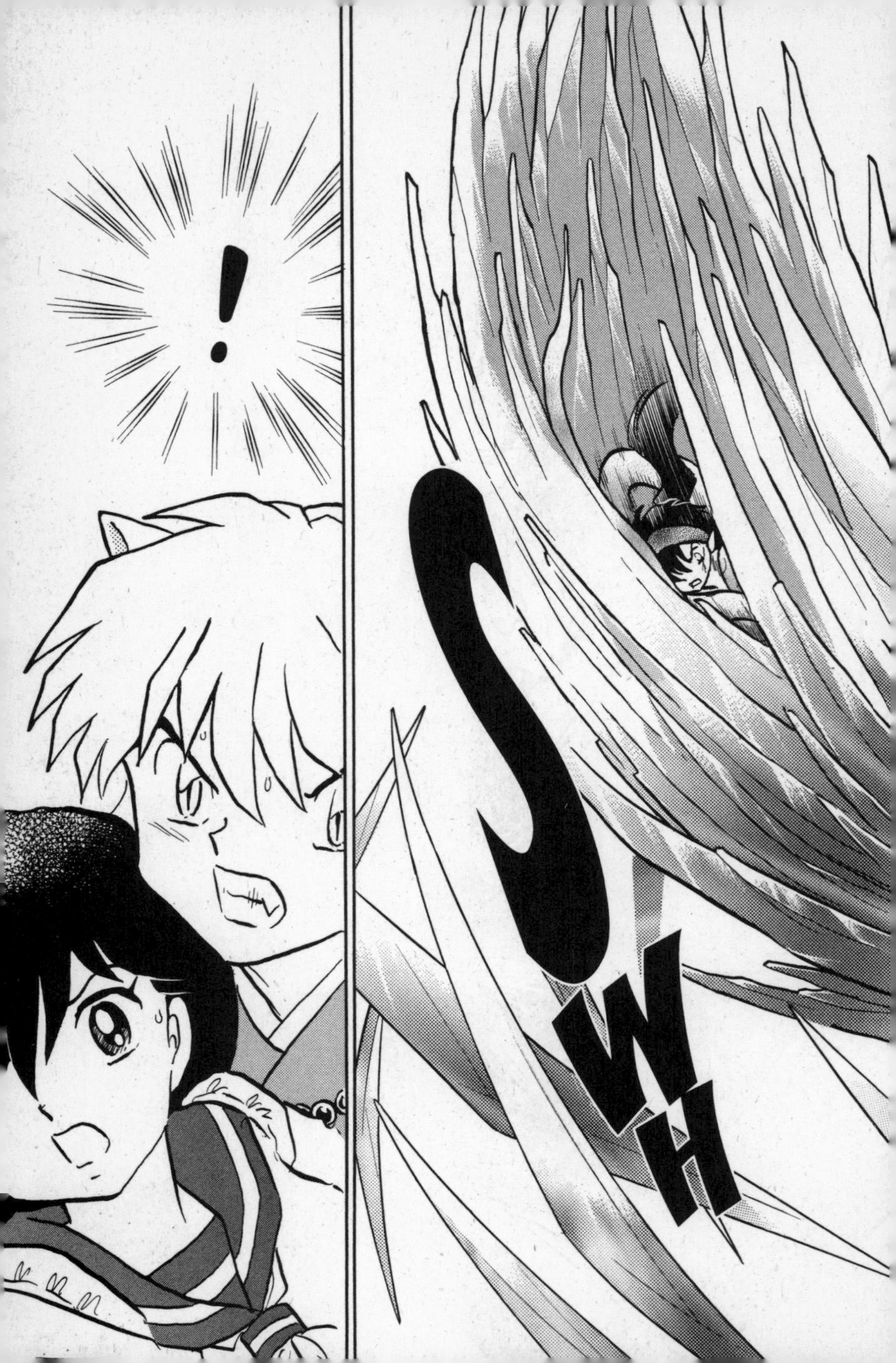
SWH
!

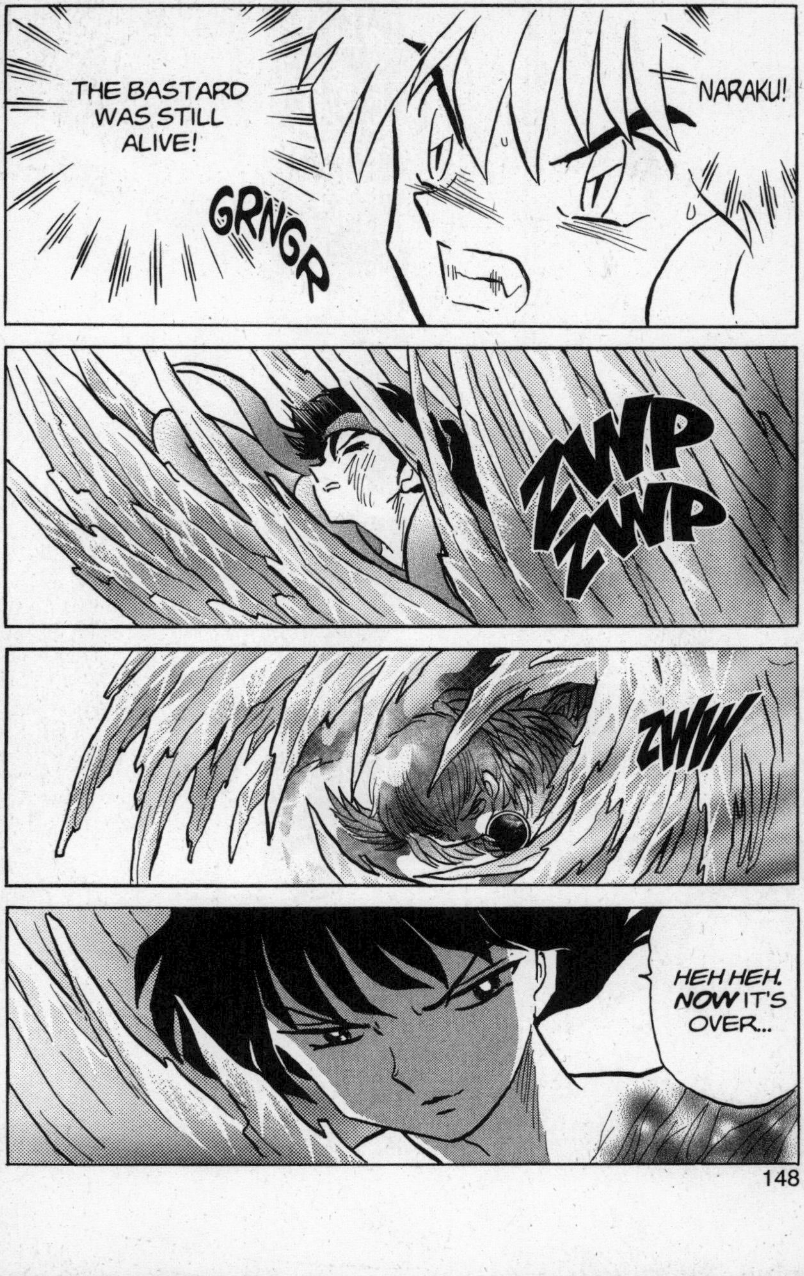
NARAKU!
THE BASTARD WAS STILL ALIVE!
GRNGR
ZWP ZWP
ZWW
HEH HEH. NOW IT'S OVER...

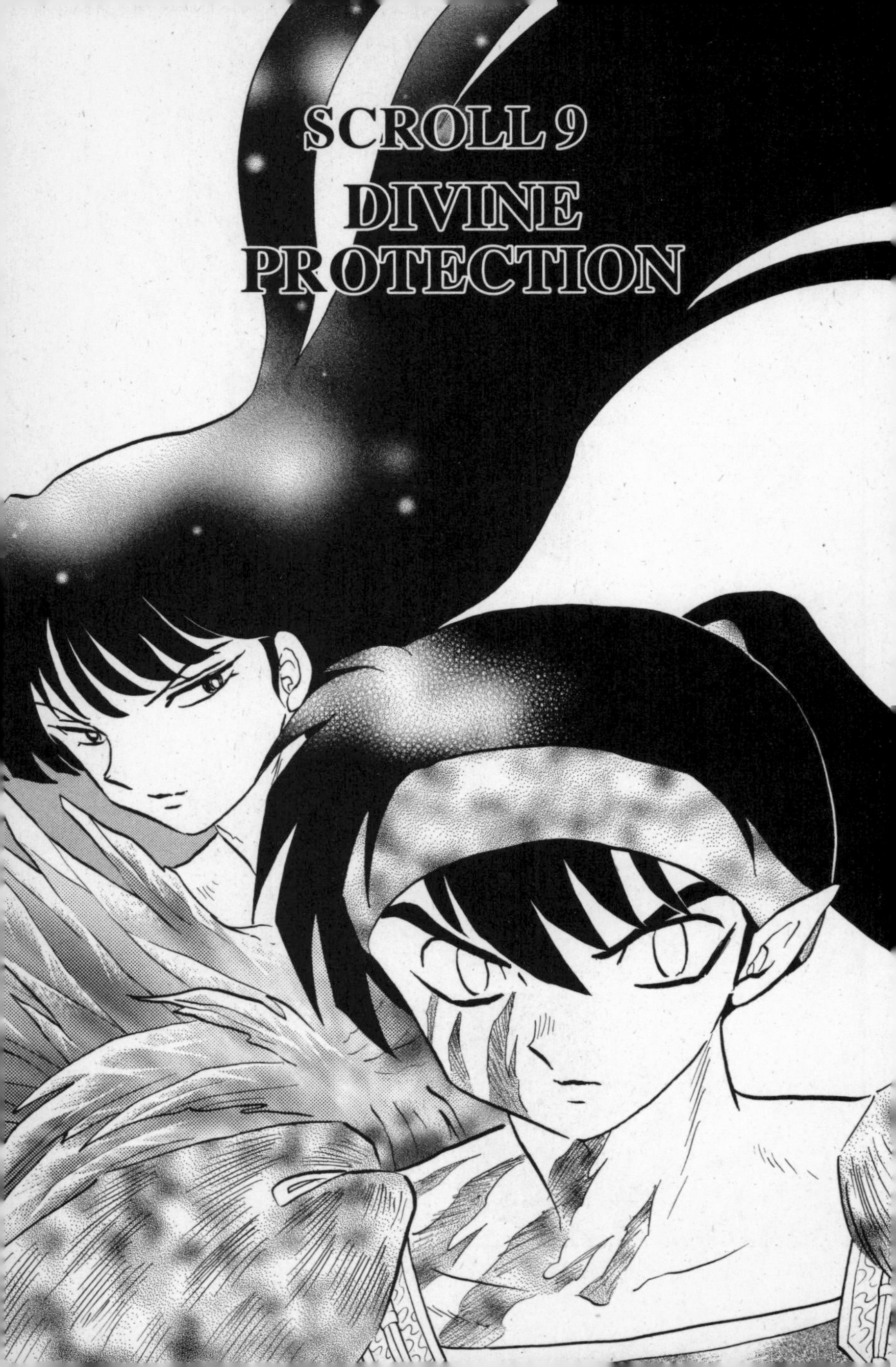
SCROLL 9
DIVINE
PROTECTION

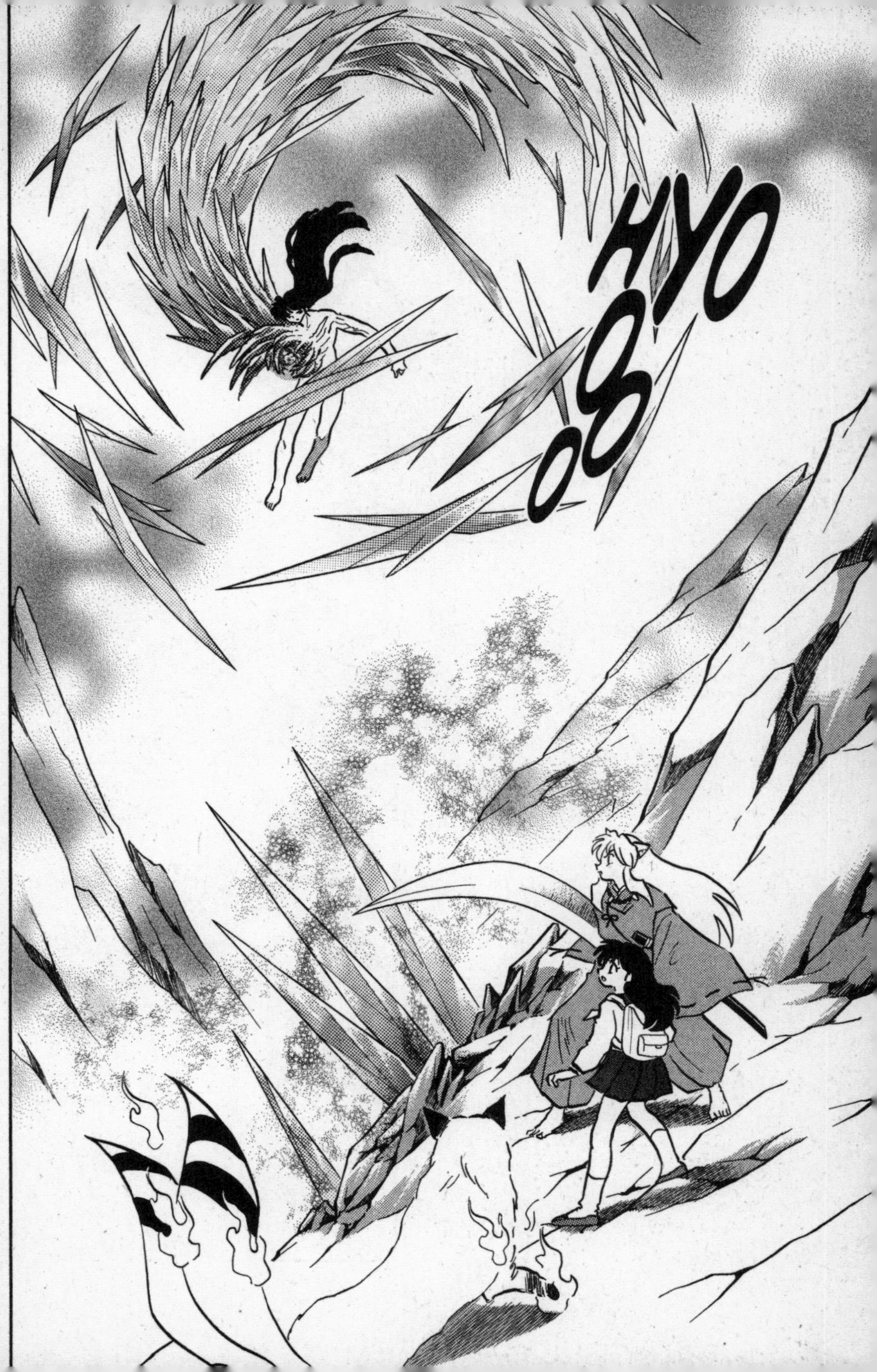
HYOOOO

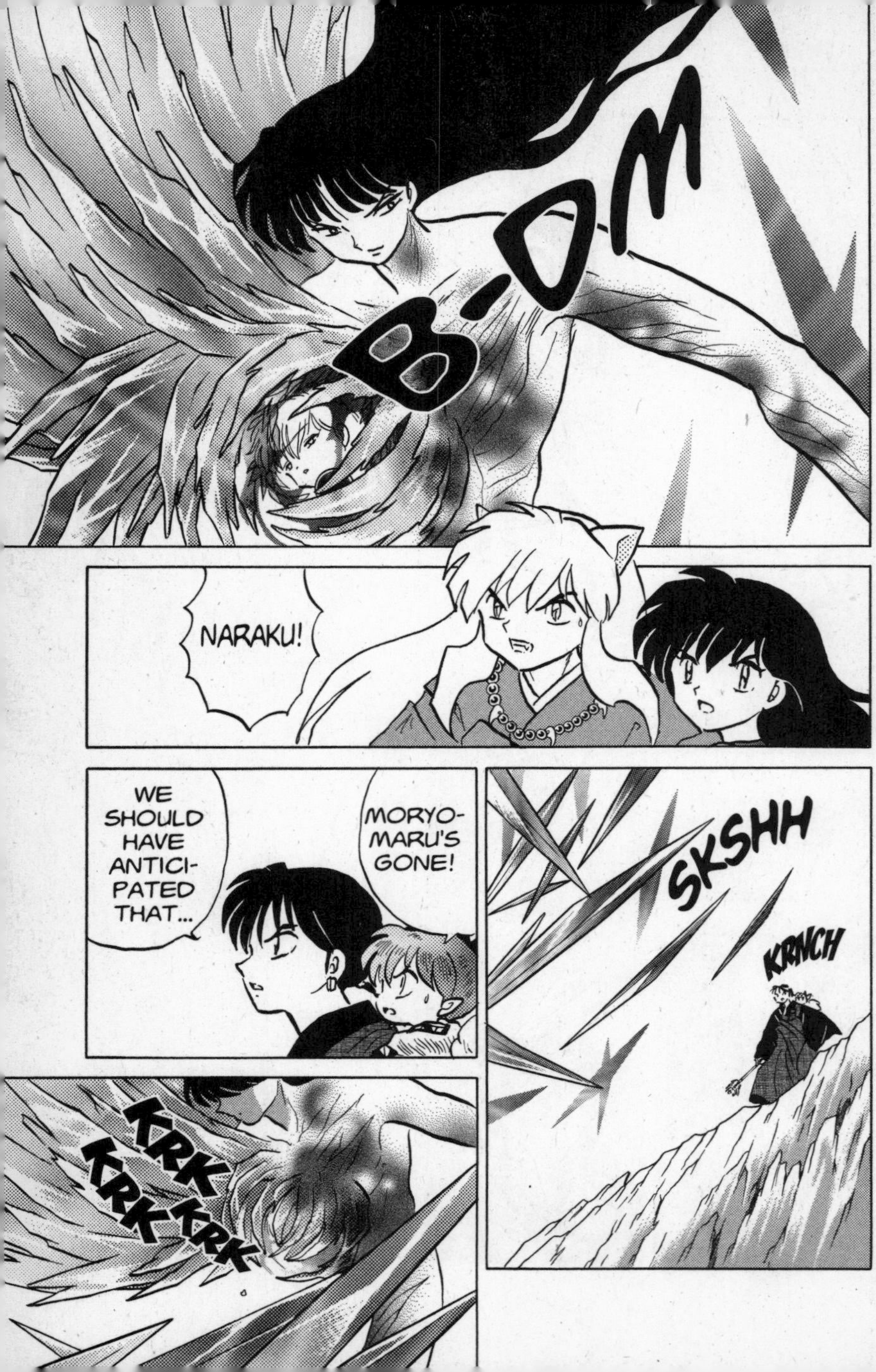
B-DM
NARAKU!
SKSHH
KRNCH
MORYO-MARU'S GONE!
WE SHOULD HAVE ANTICI-PATED THAT...
KRK KRK KRK KRK

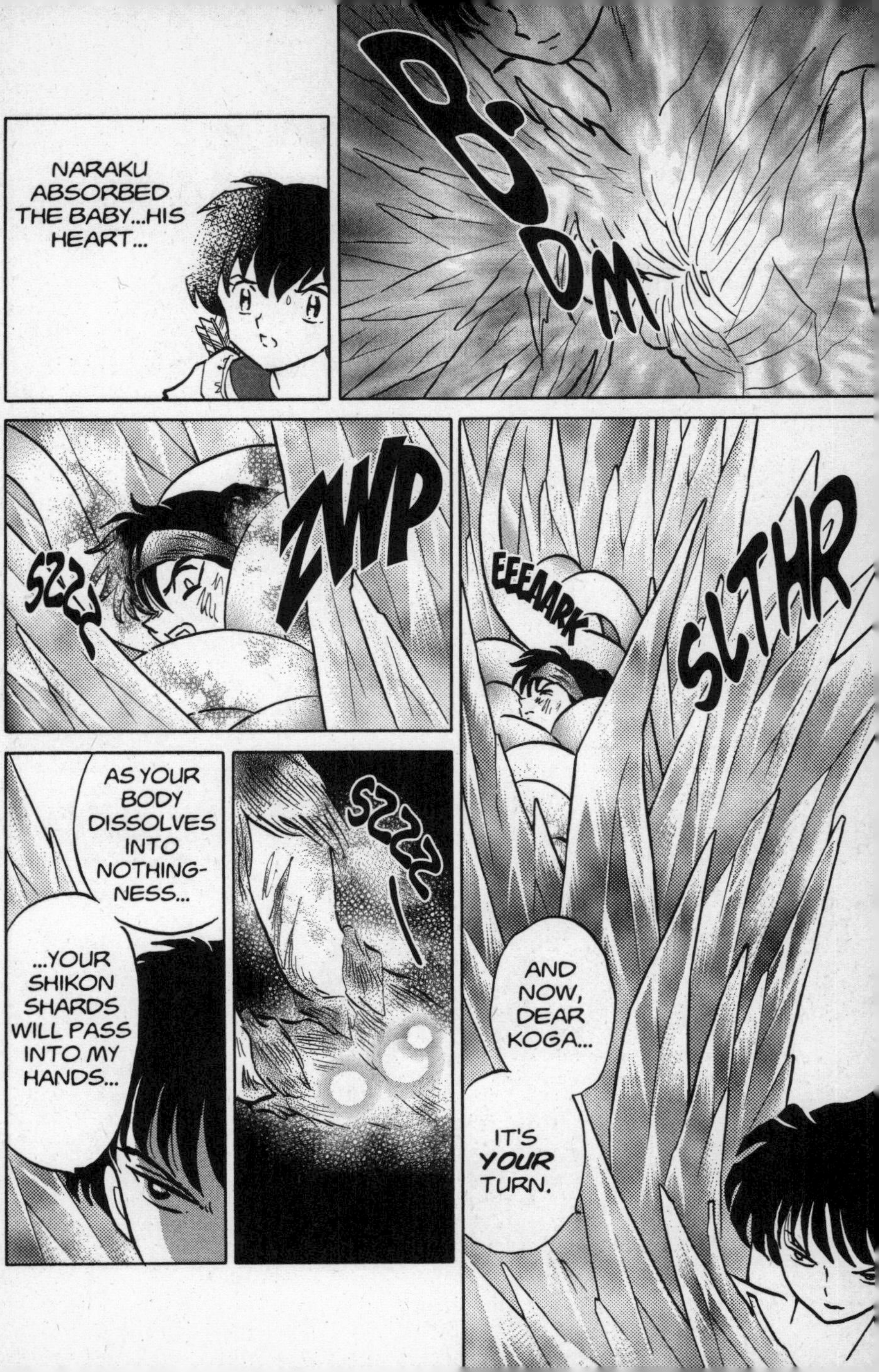

BUDM
NARAKU ABSORBED THE BABY...HIS HEART...
SLTHR
EEEAARK
AND NOW, DEAR KOGA...
IT'S ***YOUR*** TURN.
ZWP
SZZZ
SZZZ
AS YOUR BODY DISSOLVES INTO NOTHING-NESS...
...YOUR SHIKON SHARDS WILL PASS INTO MY HANDS...

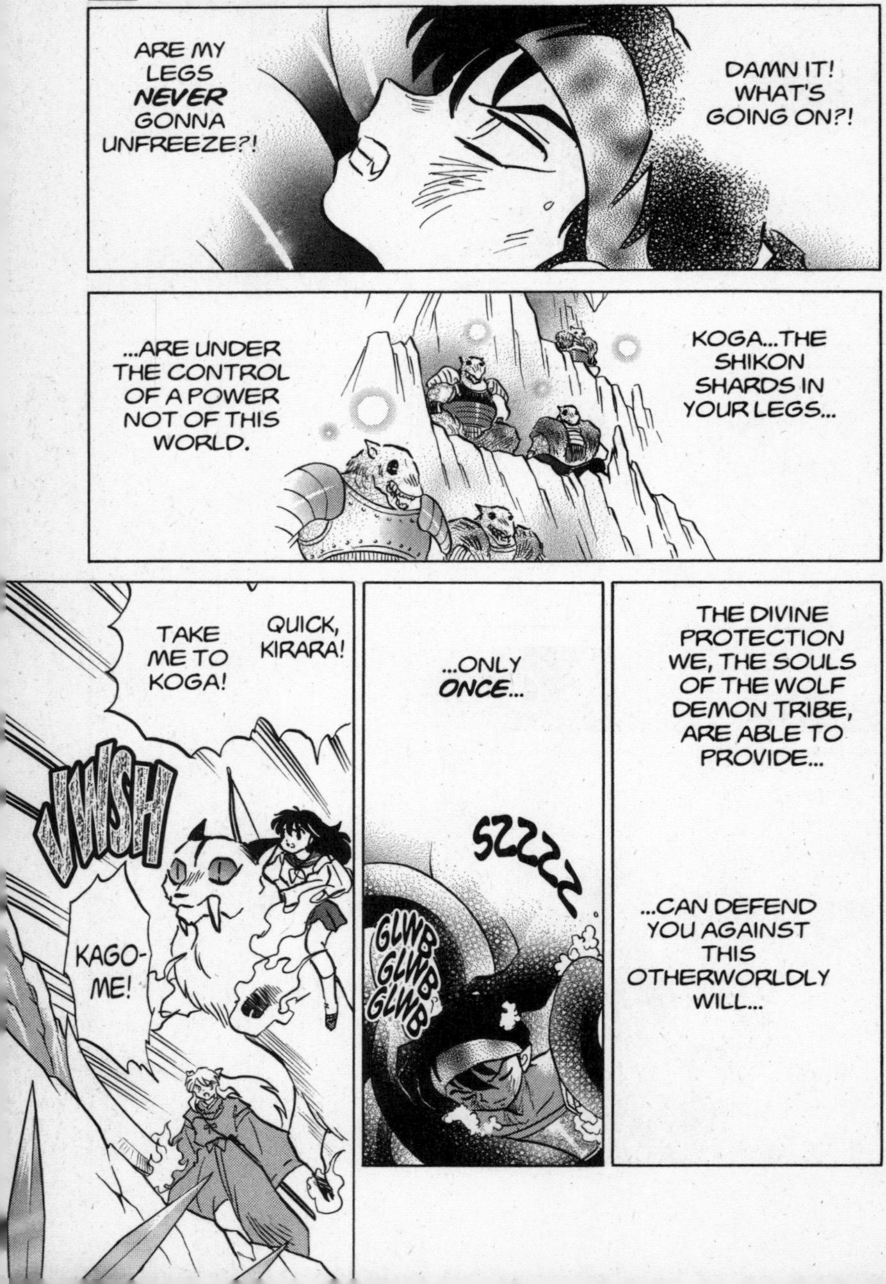
DAMN IT! WHAT'S GOING ON?!
ARE MY LEGS **NEVER** GONNA UNFREEZE?!
KOGA...THE SHIKON SHARDS IN YOUR LEGS...
...ARE UNDER THE CONTROL OF A POWER NOT OF THIS WORLD.
THE DIVINE PROTECTION WE, THE SOULS OF THE WOLF DEMON TRIBE, ARE ABLE TO PROVIDE...
...CAN DEFEND YOU AGAINST THIS OTHERWORLDLY WILL...
...ONLY **ONCE**...
SZZZZ
GLWB GLWB GLWB
QUICK, KIRARA!
TAKE ME TO KOGA!
JWSH
KAGO-ME!

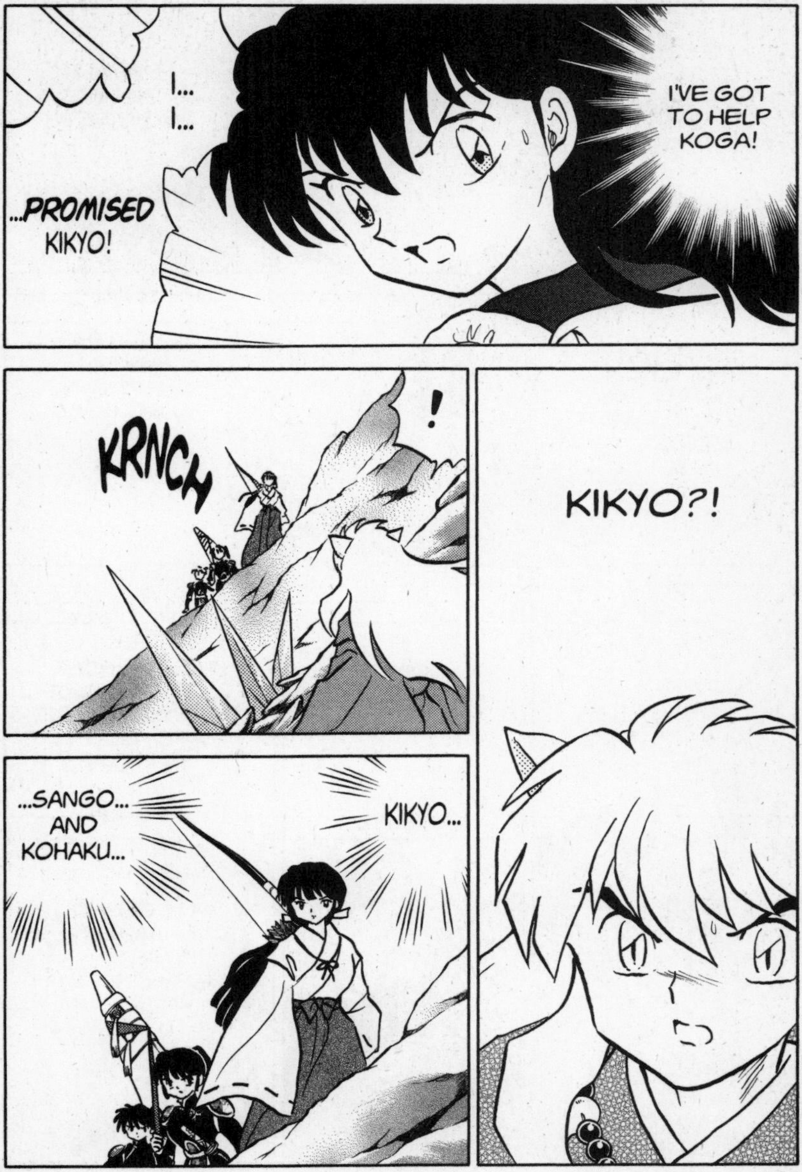
I'VE GOT TO HELP KOGA!
I... I...
...PROMISED KIKYO!
KIKYO?!
!
KRNCH
KIKYO...
...SANGO... AND KOHAKU...

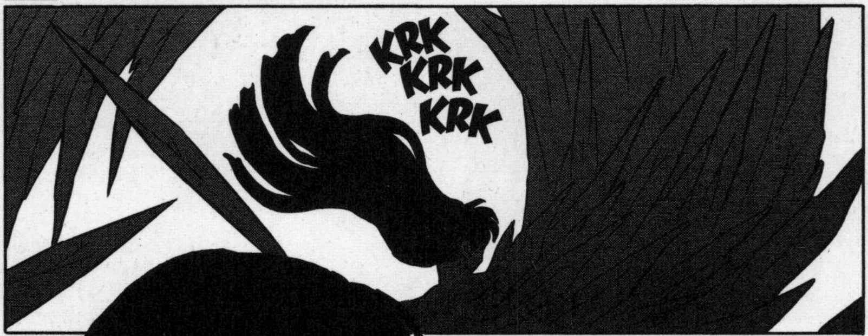
KRK
KRK
KRK

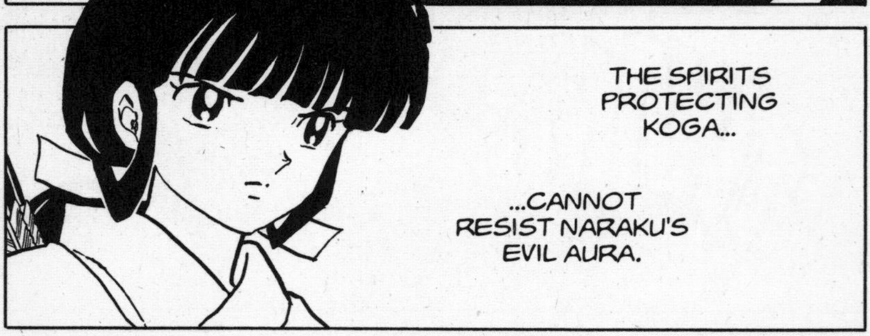
THE SPIRITS PROTECTING KOGA...
...CANNOT RESIST NARAKU'S EVIL AURA.

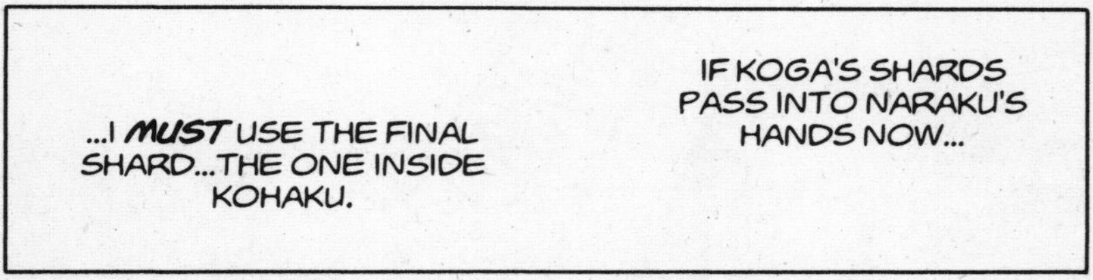
IF KOGA'S SHARDS PASS INTO NARAKU'S HANDS NOW...
...I MUST USE THE FINAL SHARD...THE ONE INSIDE KOHAKU.

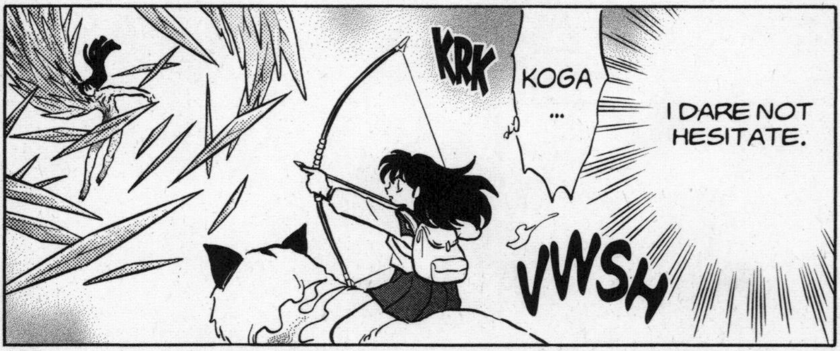
KOGA ...
I DARE NOT HESITATE.
KRK
VWSH

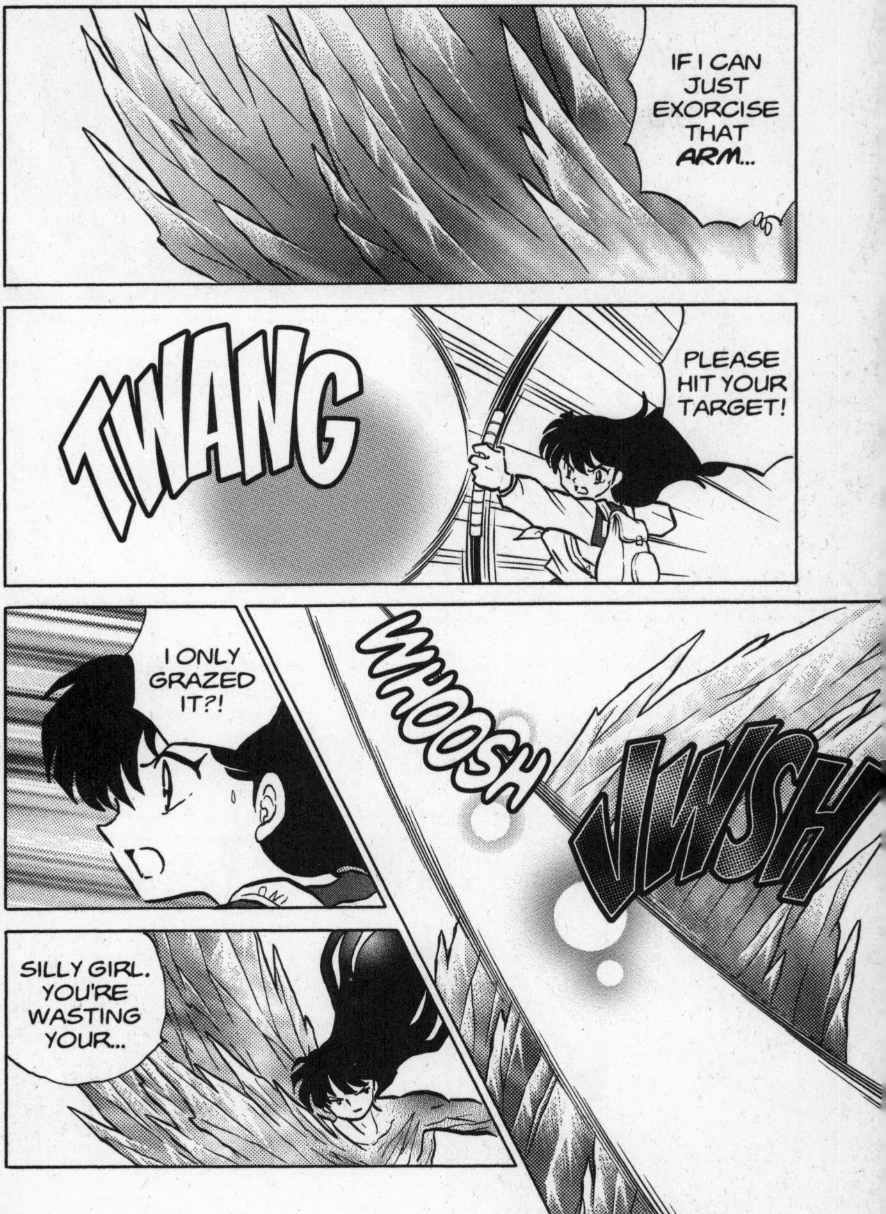
IF I CAN JUST EXORCISE THAT ARM...
PLEASE HIT YOUR TARGET!
TWANG
WHOOSH
JWISH
I ONLY GRAZED IT?!
SILLY GIRL. YOU'RE WASTING YOUR...

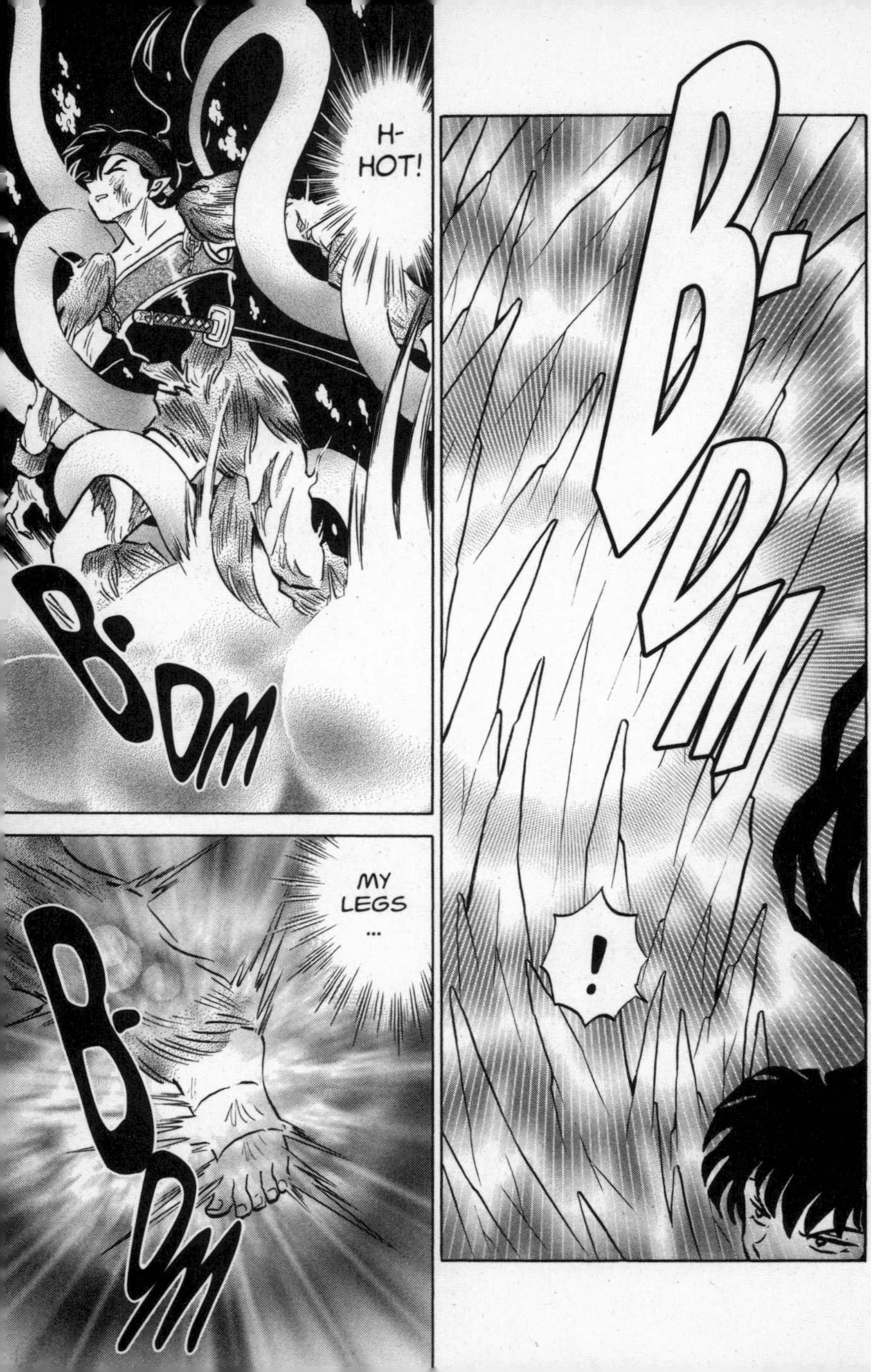
B-B-DM
!
H-HOT!
B-DOM
MY LEGS ...
B-DOM

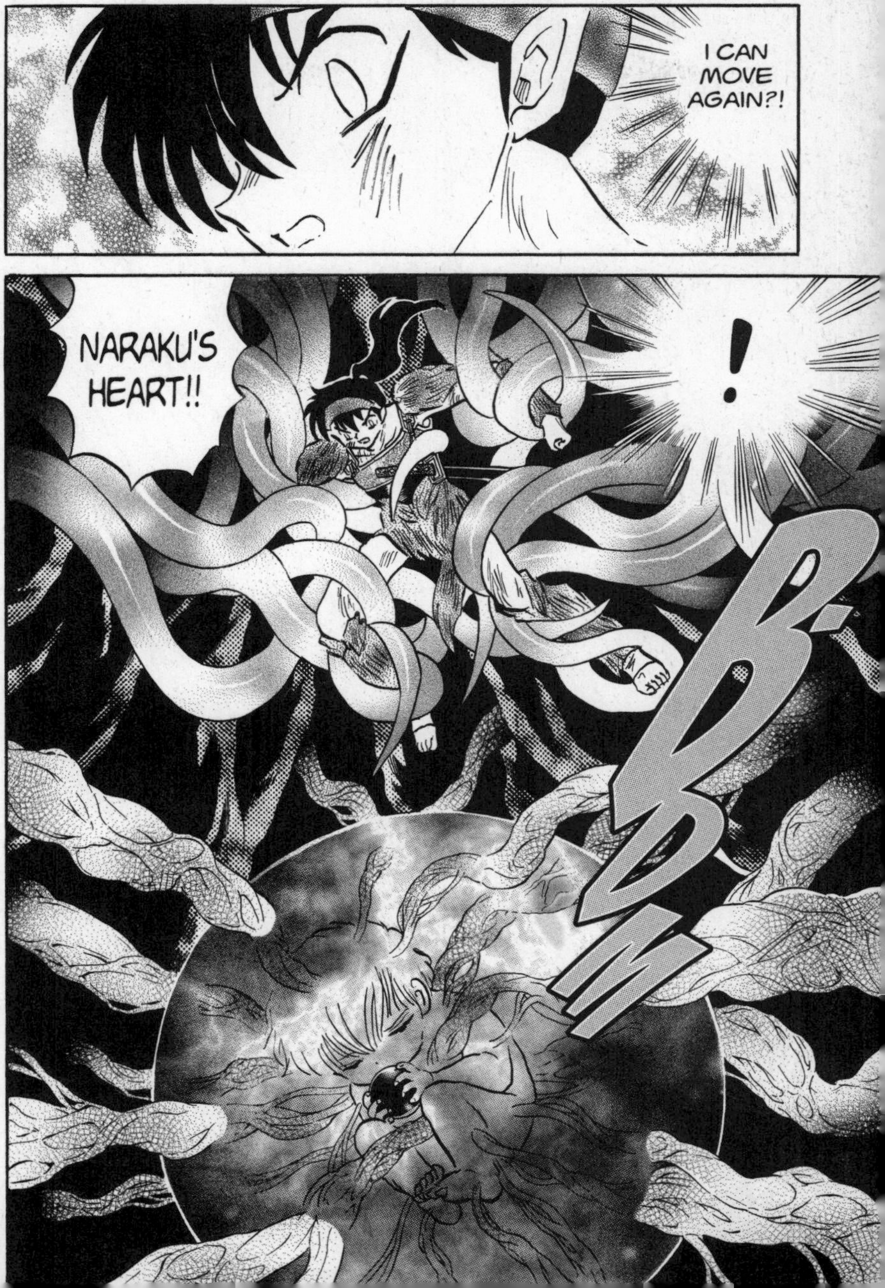
I CAN MOVE AGAIN?!
!
NARAKU'S HEART!!

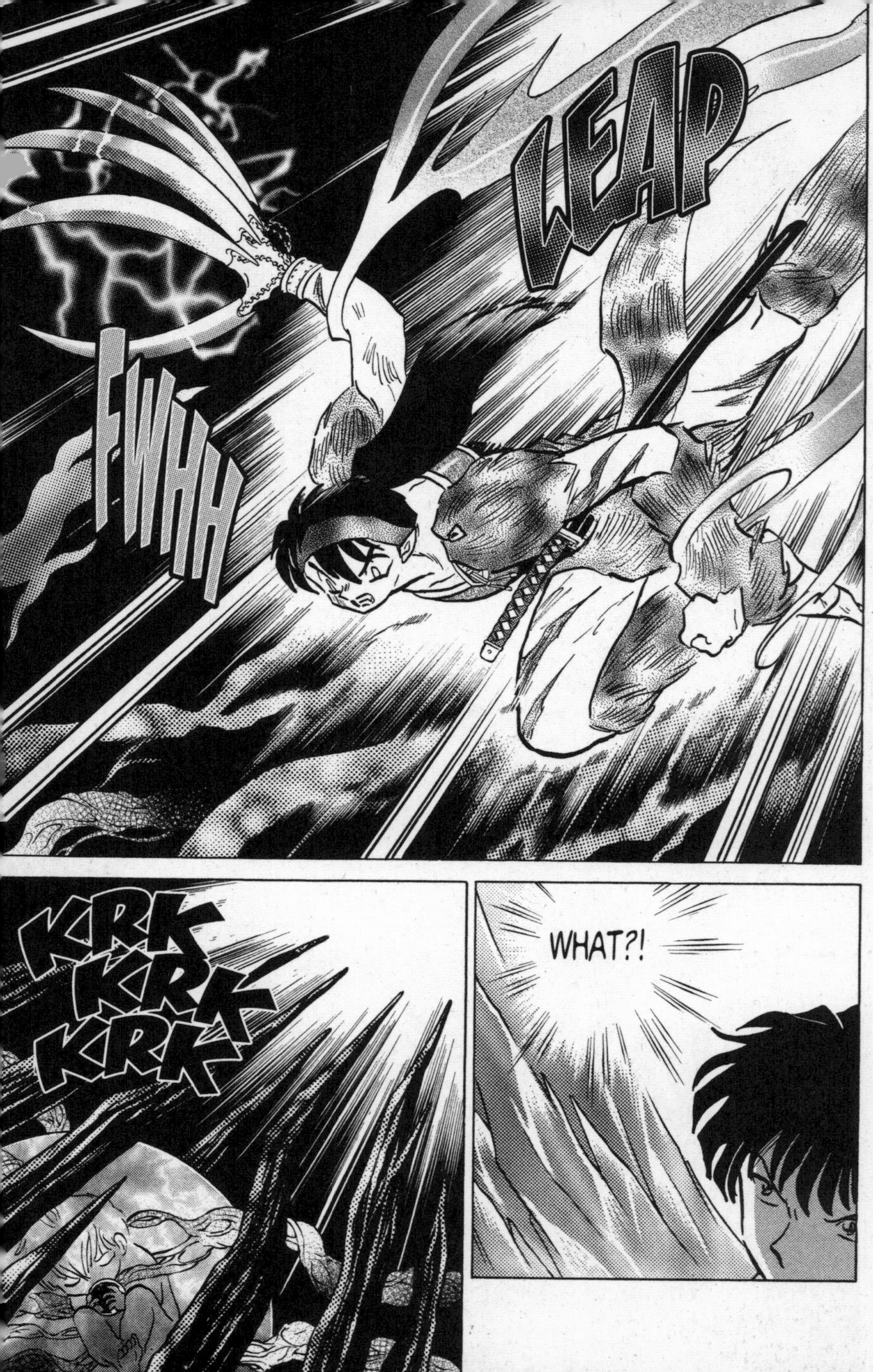
LEAP
FWHH
WHAT?!
KRK KRK KRK

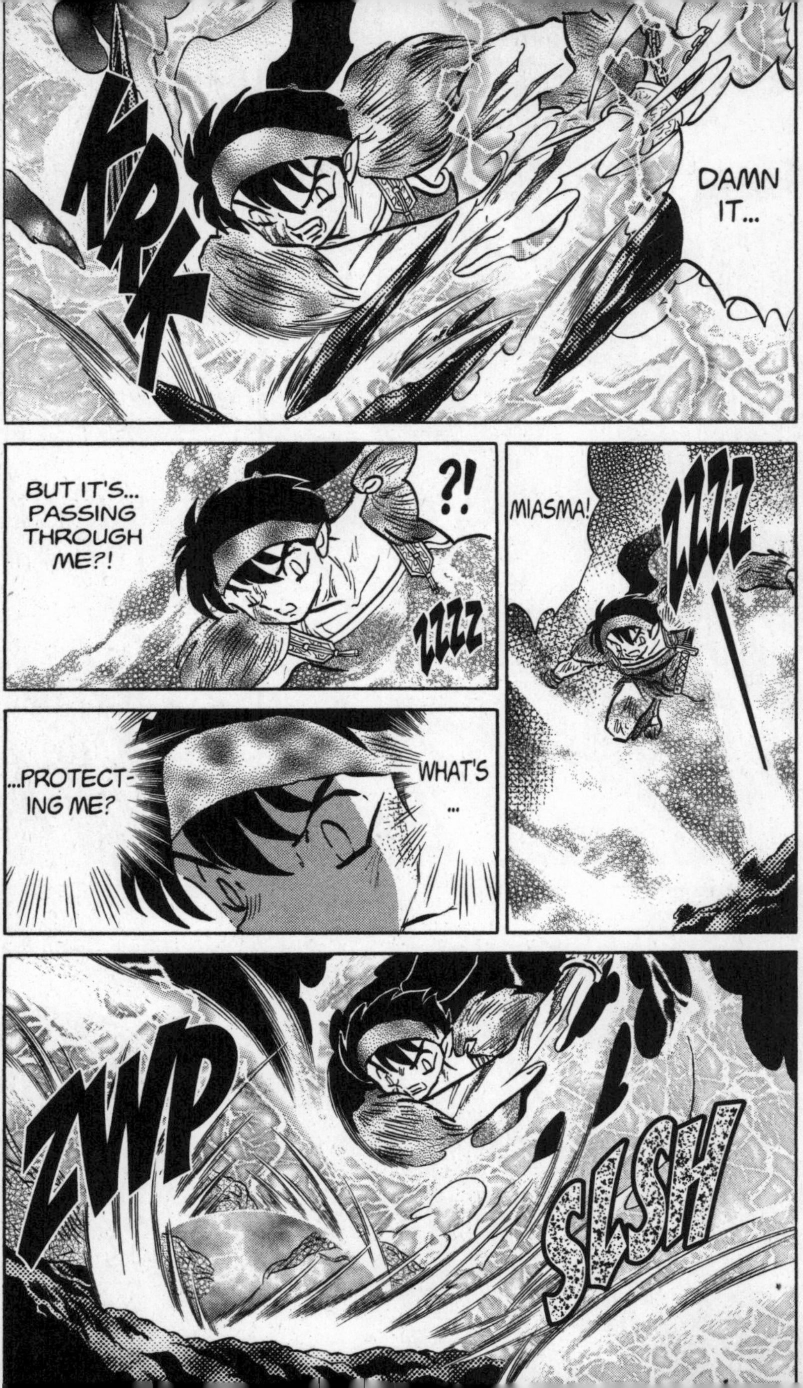
DAMN IT...
KRK
MIASMA!
ZZZZ
?!
BUT IT'S... PASSING THROUGH ME?!
ZZZZ
WHAT'S ...
...PROTECTING ME?
ZWP
SLSH

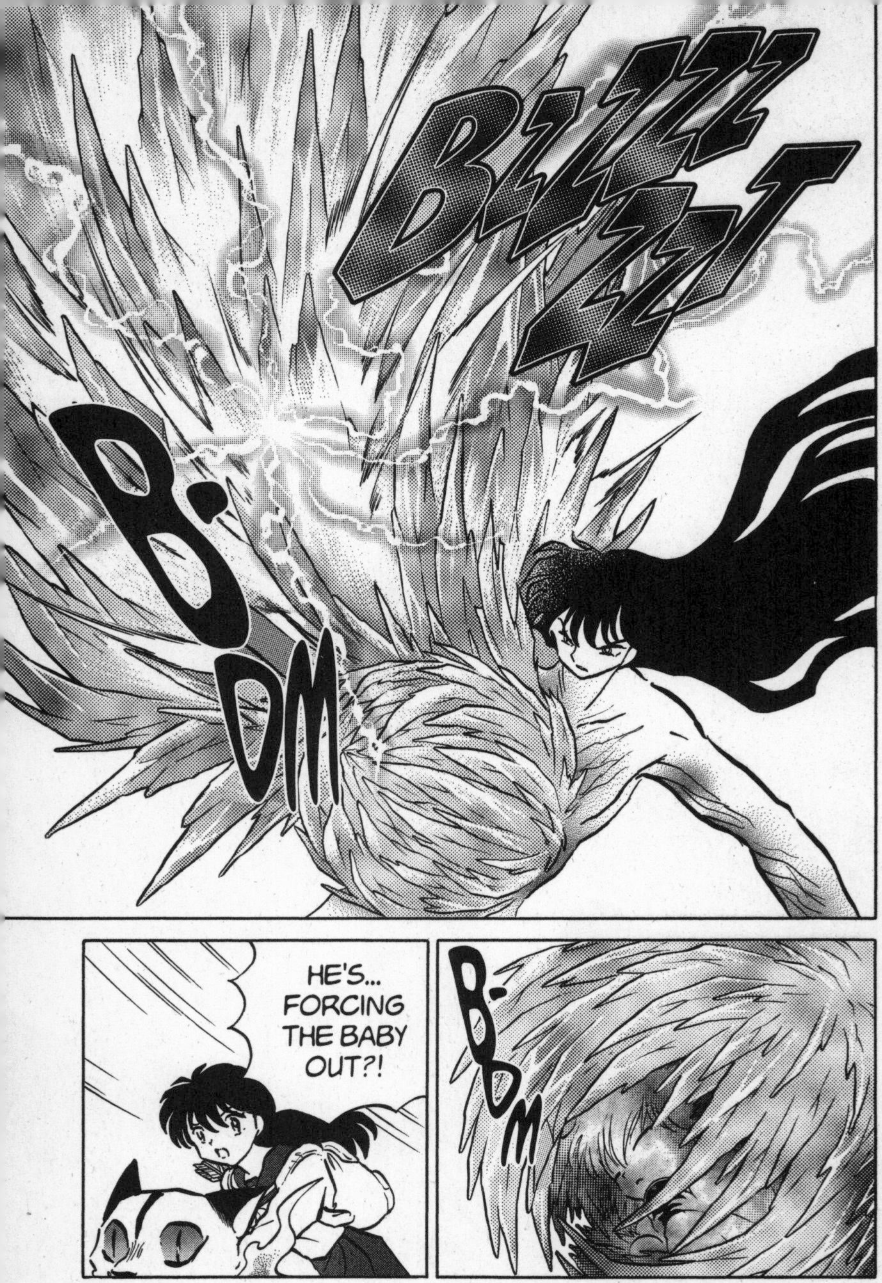
BZZZZT
B-DM
B-DM
HE'S... FORCING THE BABY OUT?!

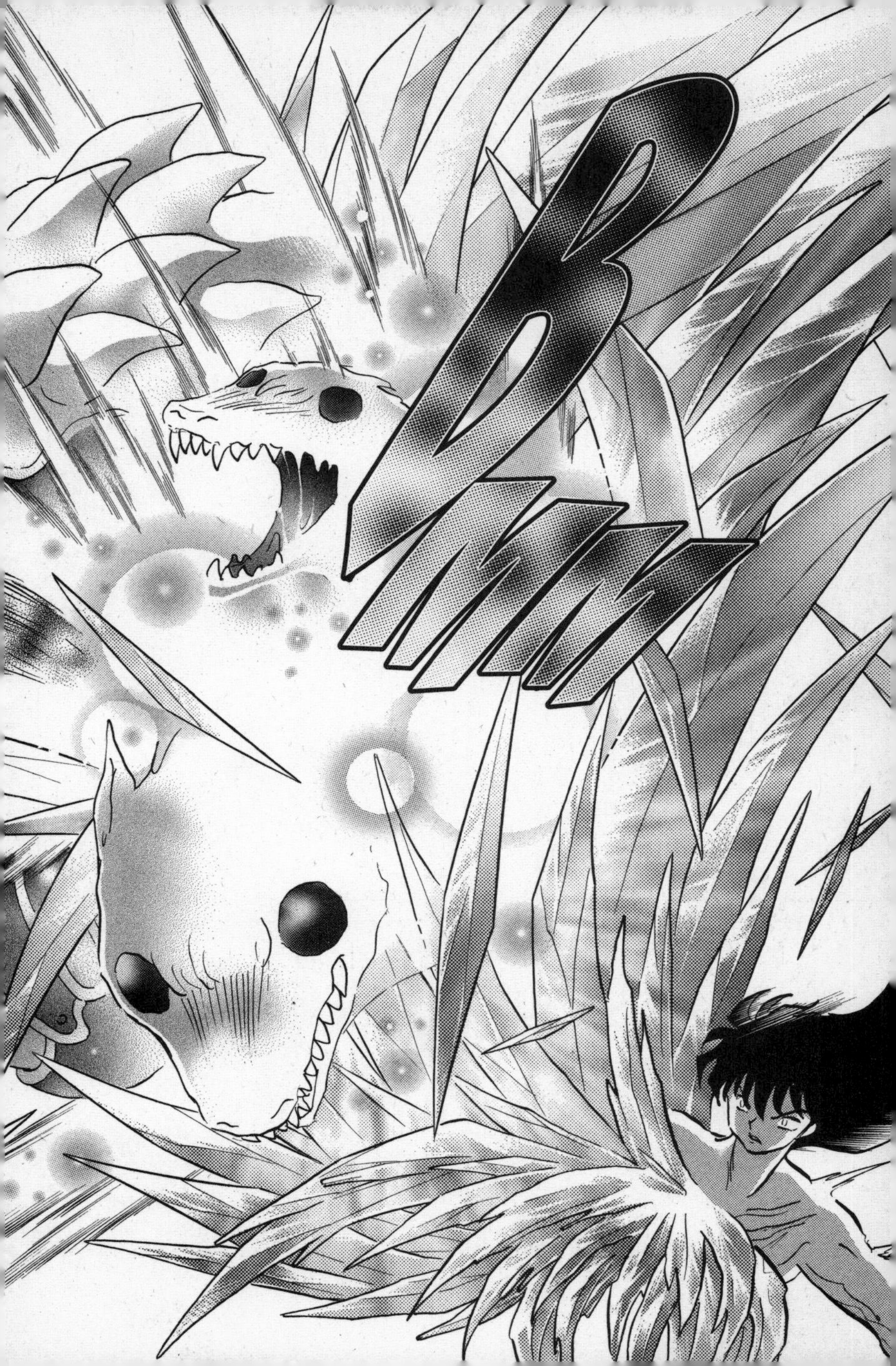

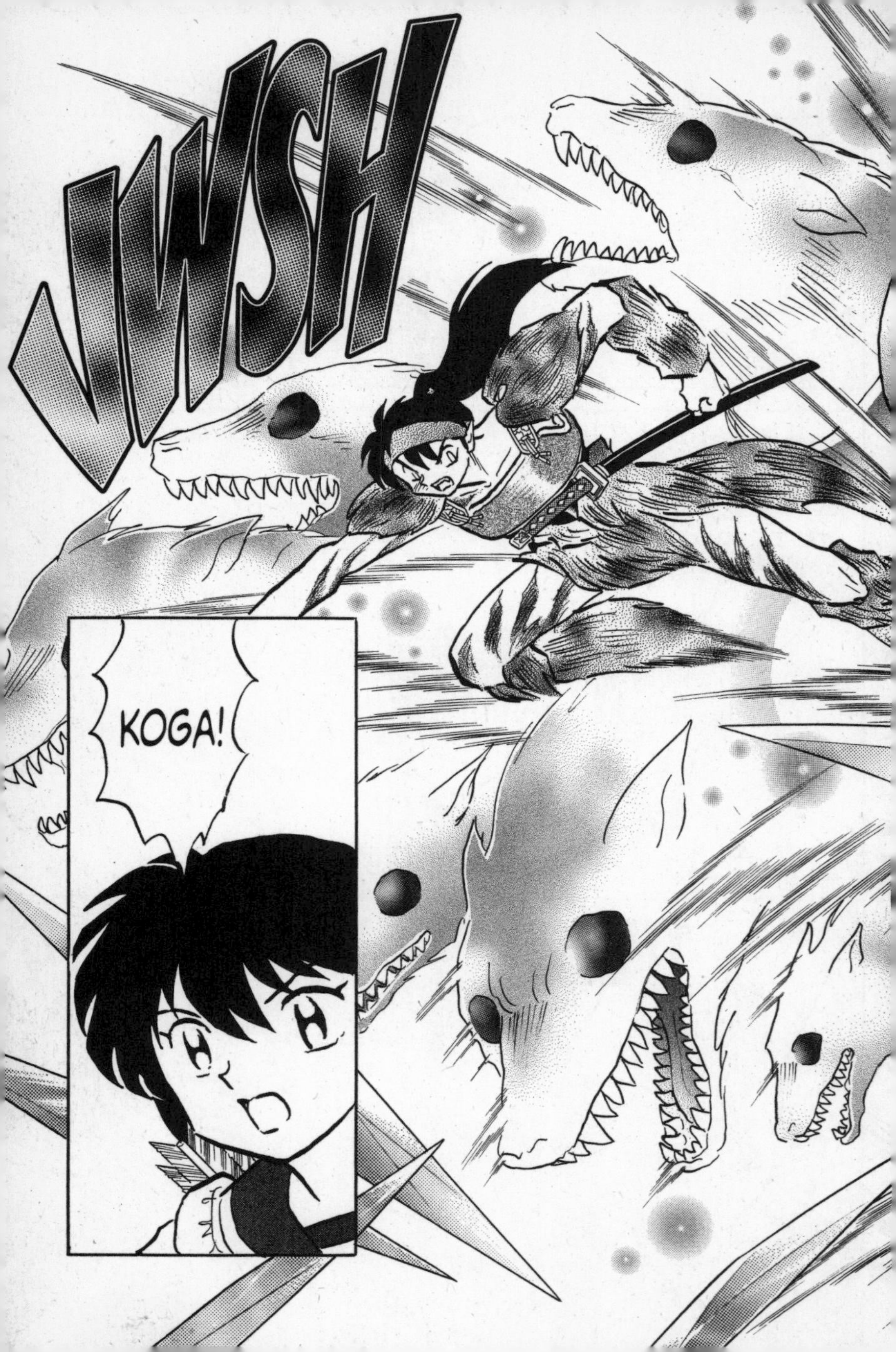
VWSH
KOGA!

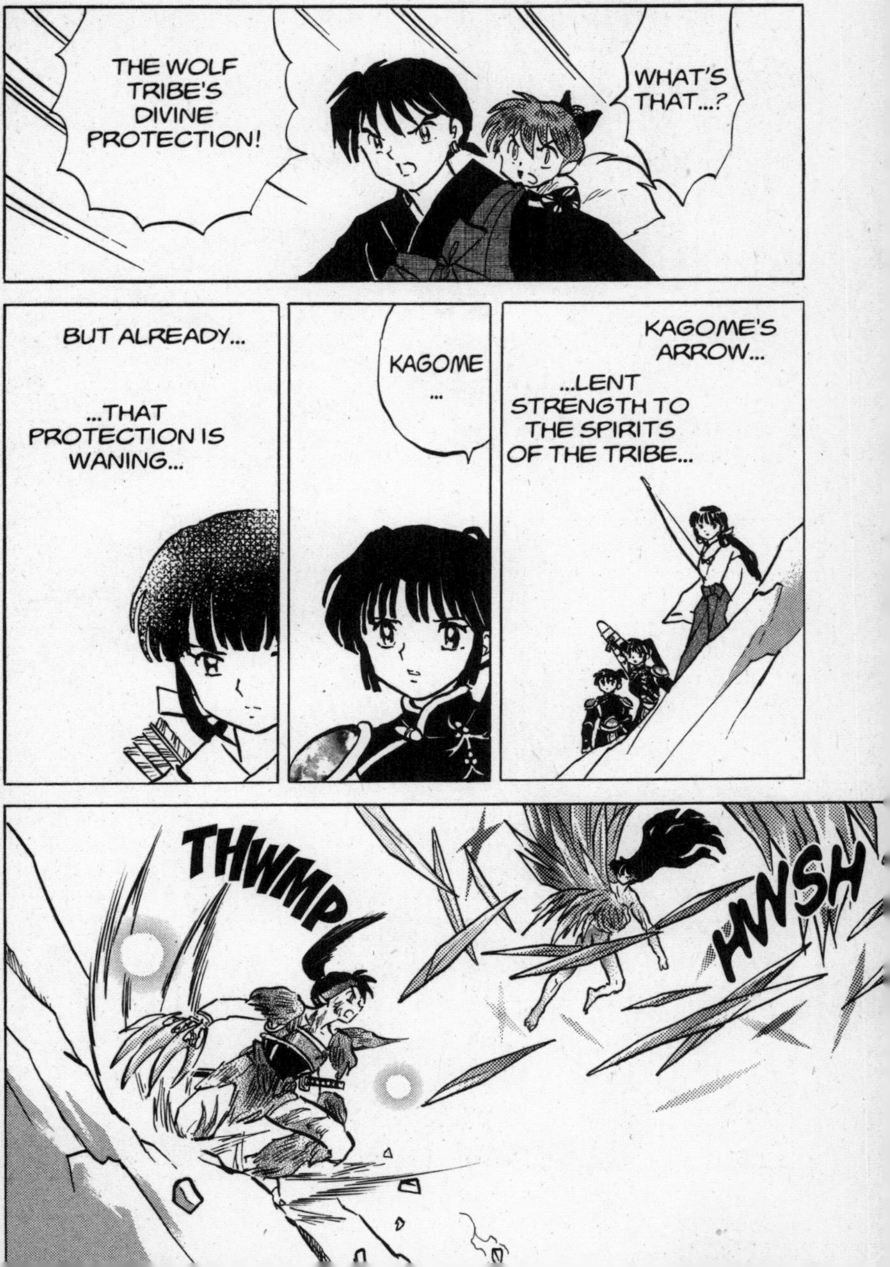
WHAT'S THAT...?
THE WOLF TRIBE'S DIVINE PROTECTION!
KAGOME'S ARROW...
...LENT STRENGTH TO THE SPIRITS OF THE TRIBE...
KAGOME...
BUT ALREADY...
...THAT PROTECTION IS WANING...
HWSH
THWMP

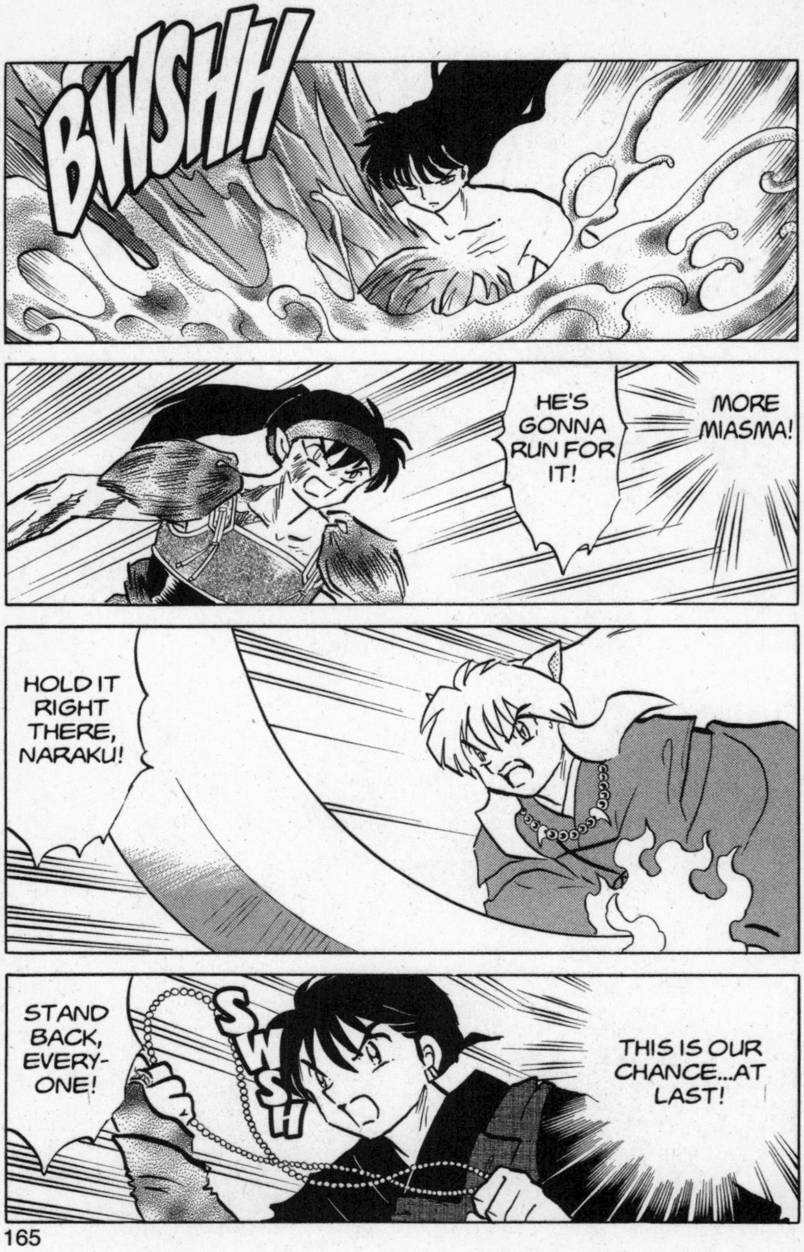
BWSHH
MORE MIASMA!
HE'S GONNA RUN FOR IT!
HOLD IT RIGHT THERE, NARAKU!
THIS IS OUR CHANCE...AT LAST!
SWSH
STAND BACK, EVERY-ONE!

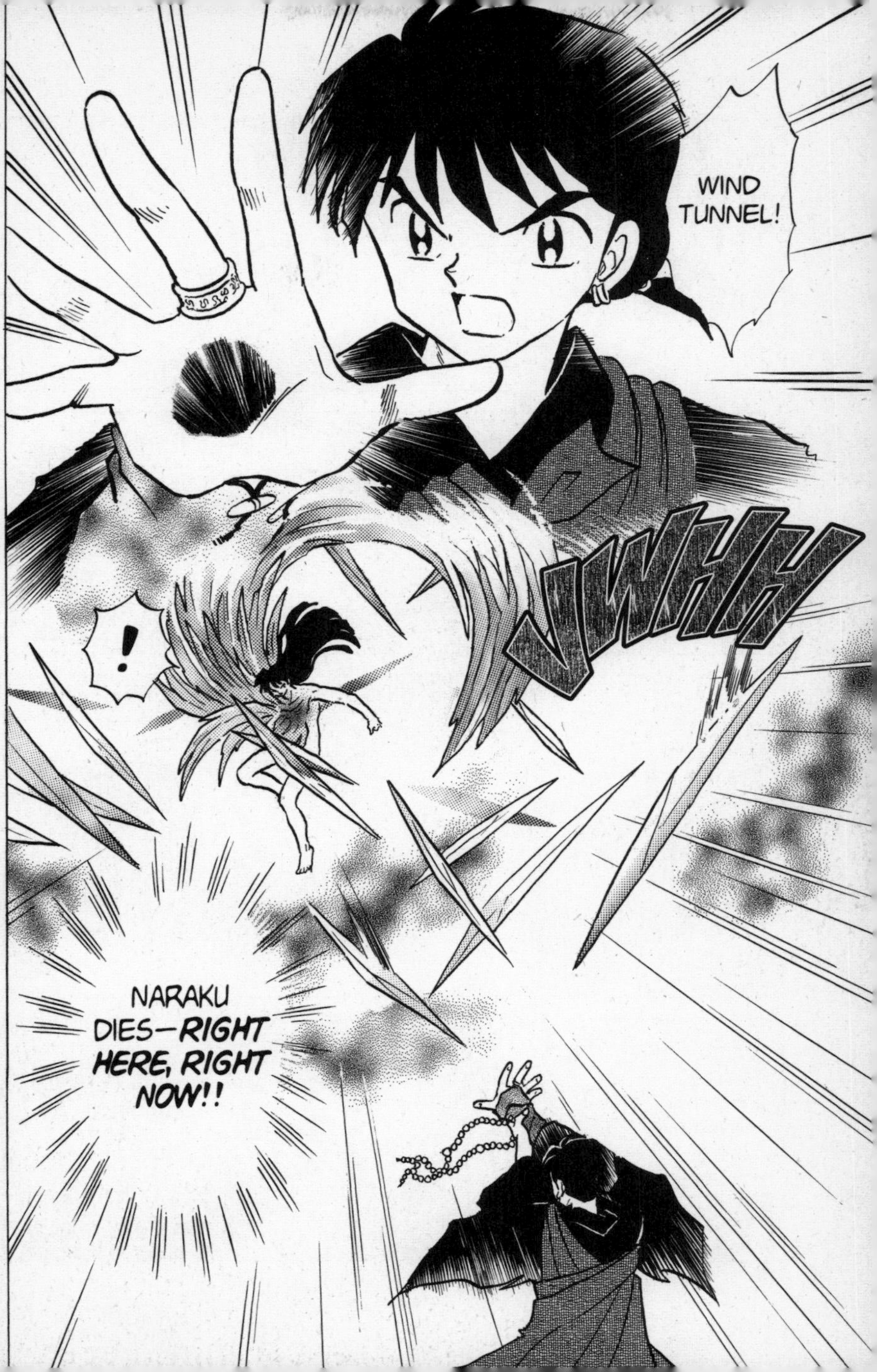
WIND TUNNEL!
JWHH
!
NARAKU DIES—RIGHT HERE, RIGHT NOW!!

SCROLL 10

THE POISON OF THE MIASMA

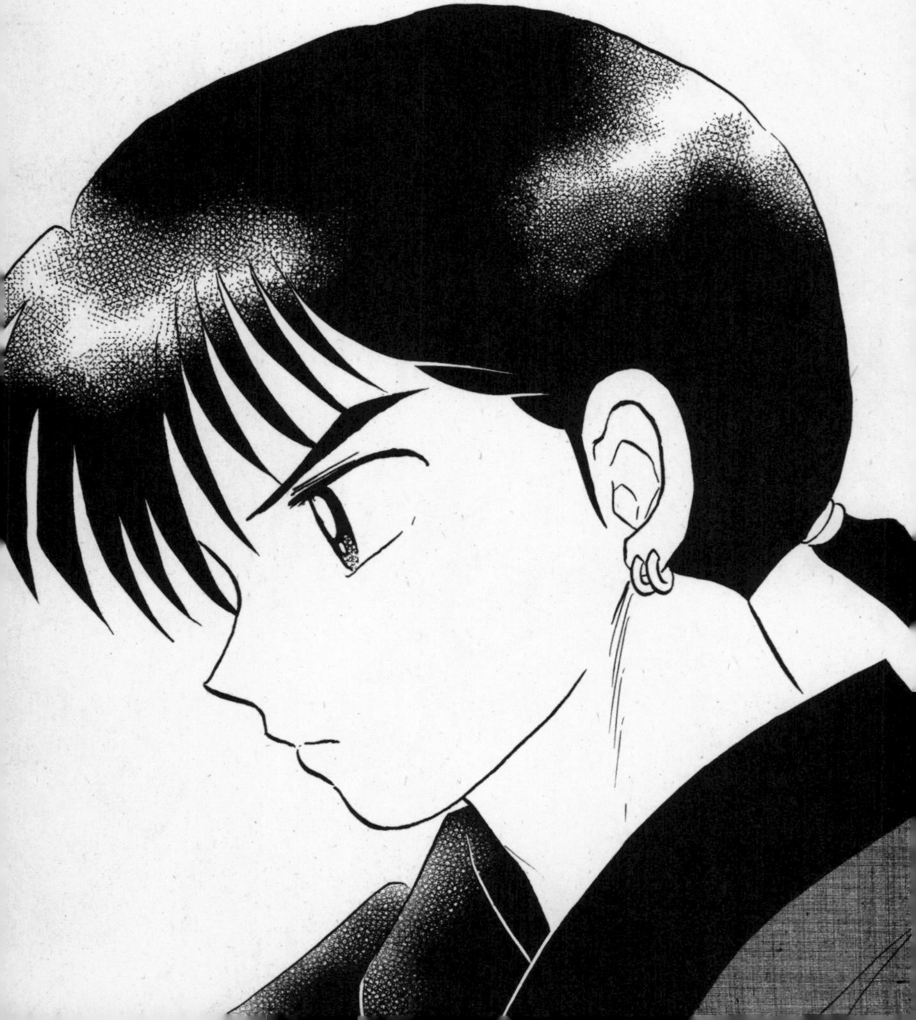

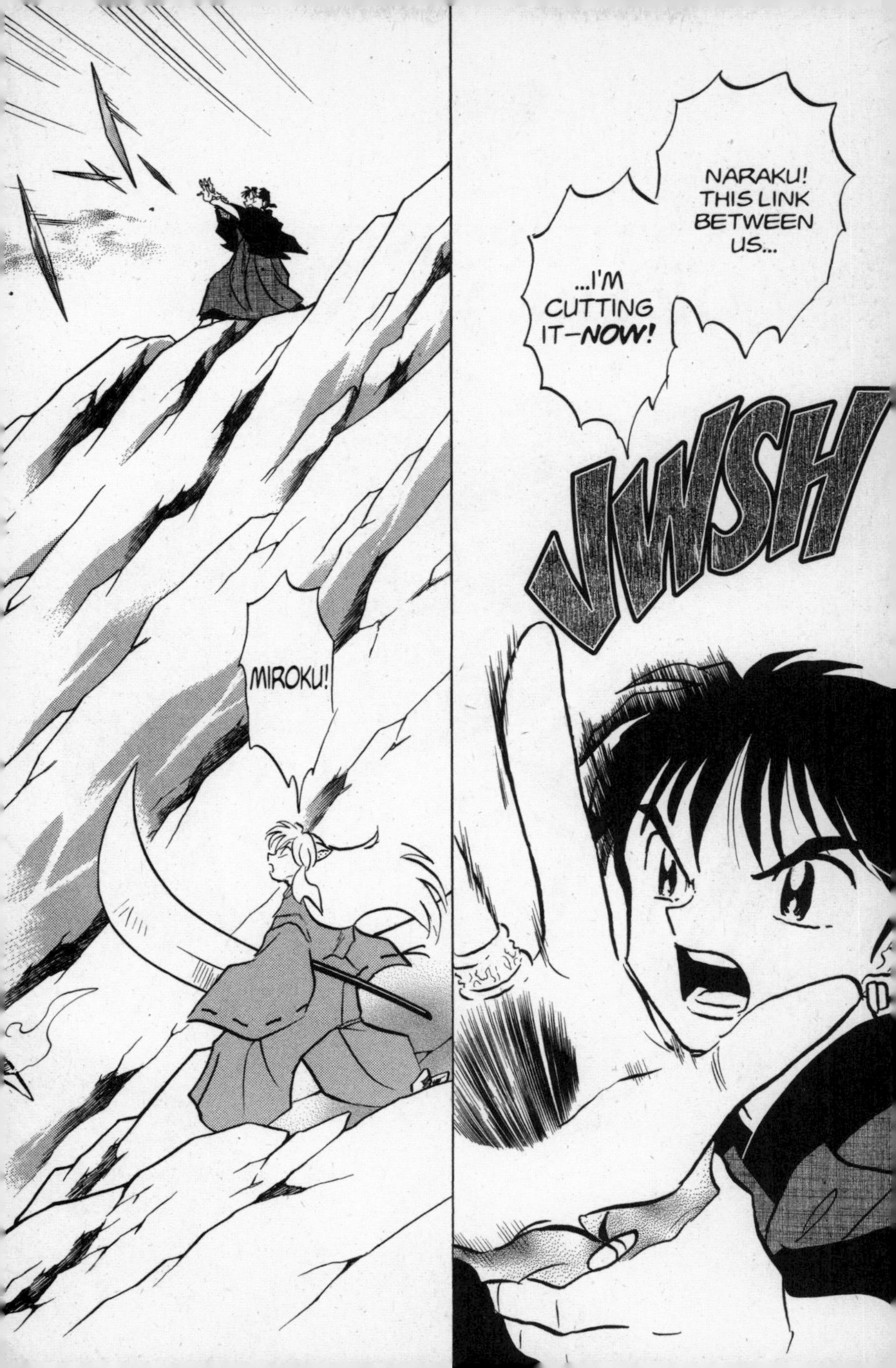
NARAKU! THIS LINK BETWEEN US...
...I'M CUTTING IT—*NOW!*
JWSH
MIROKU!

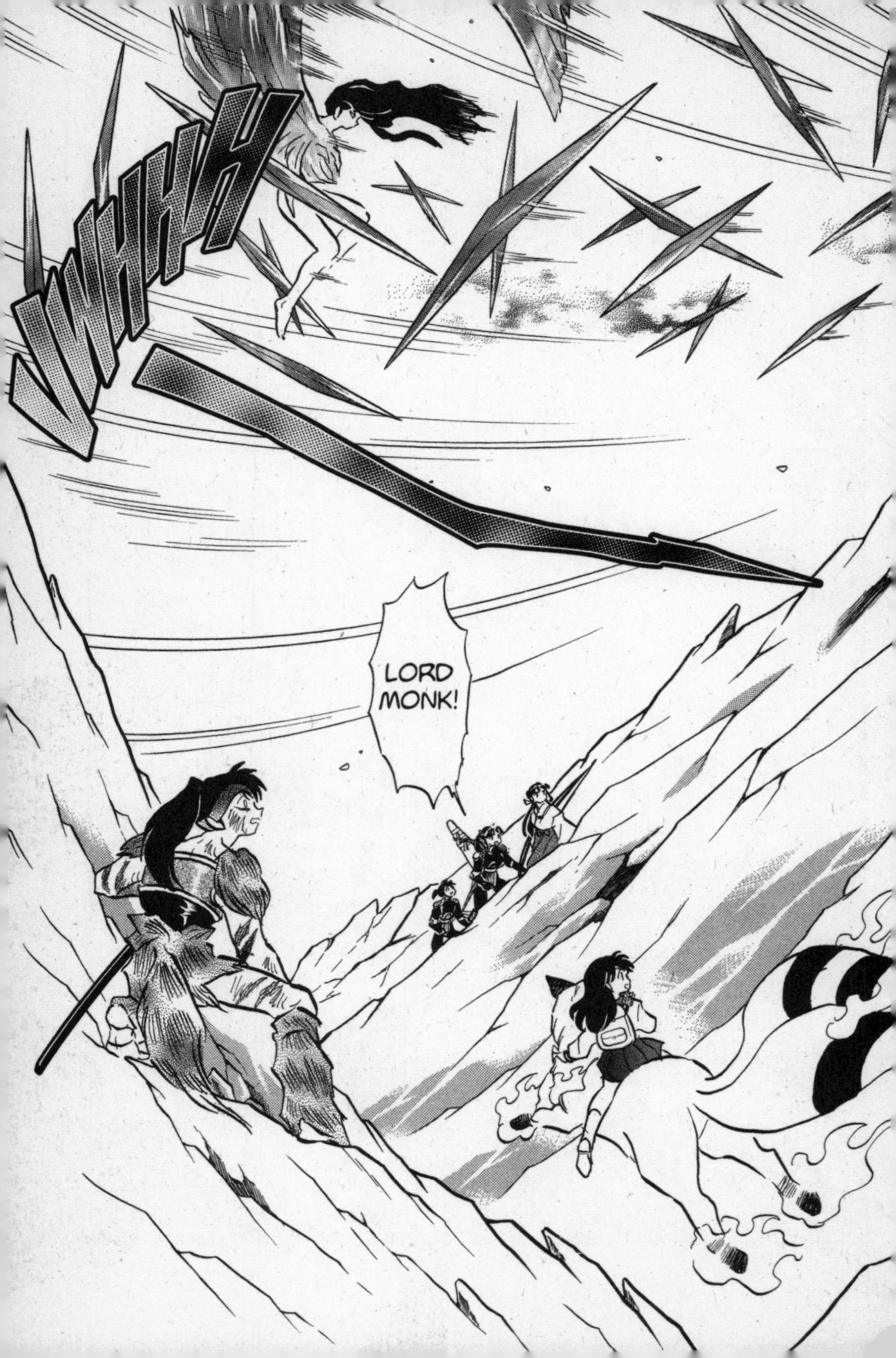
VWHHSH
LORD MONK!

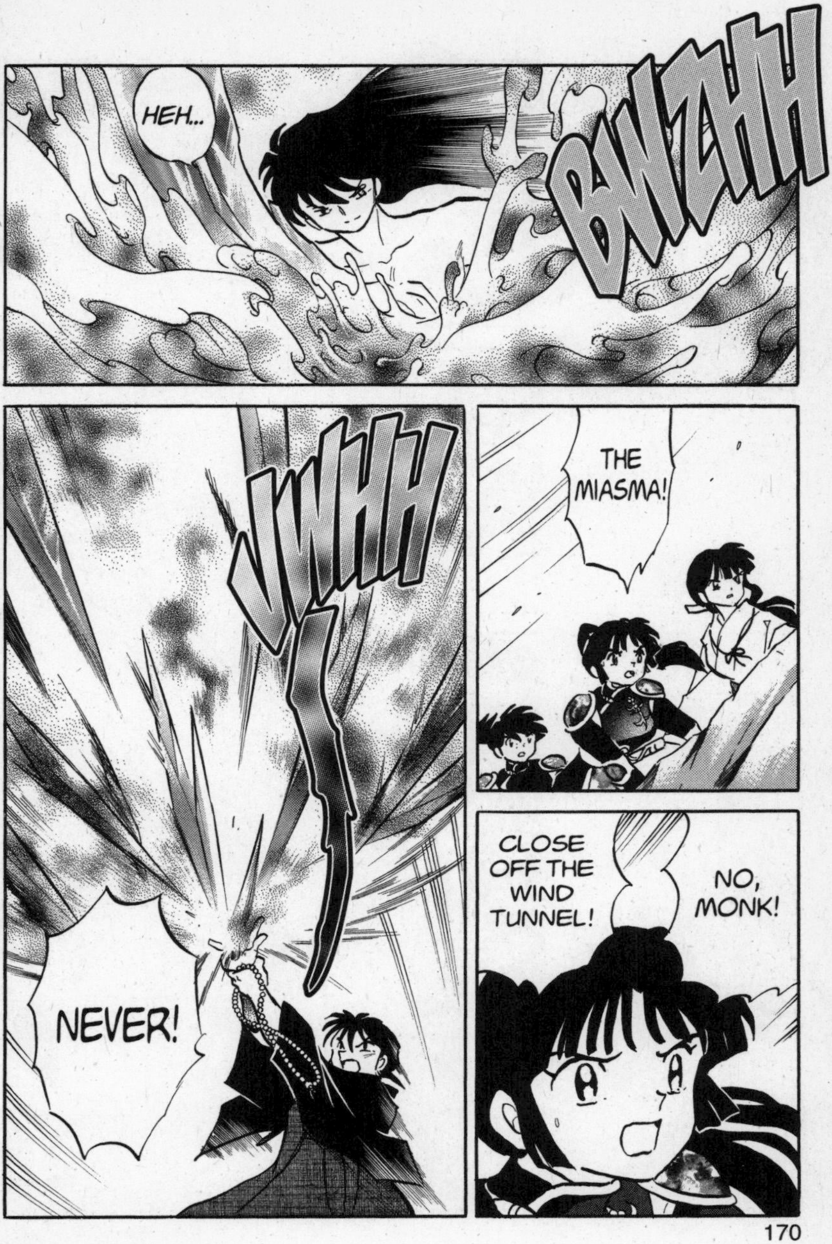
HEH...
BWZHH
THE MIASMA!
NO, MONK!
CLOSE OFF THE WIND TUNNEL!
JWHH
NEVER!

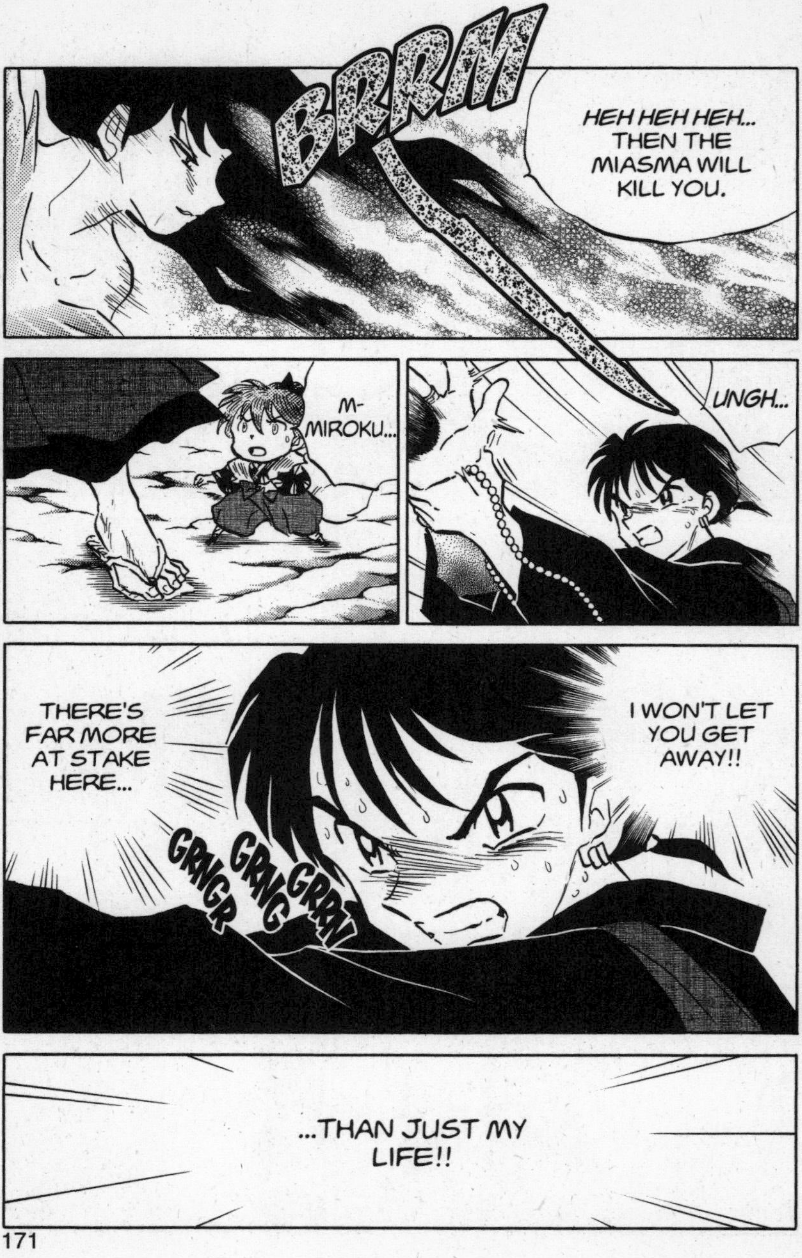
BRRM
HEH HEH HEH... THEN THE MIASMA WILL KILL YOU.
UNGH...
M- MIROKU...
I WON'T LET YOU GET AWAY!!
THERE'S FAR MORE AT STAKE HERE...
GRRN
GRNG
GRNGR
...THAN JUST MY LIFE!!

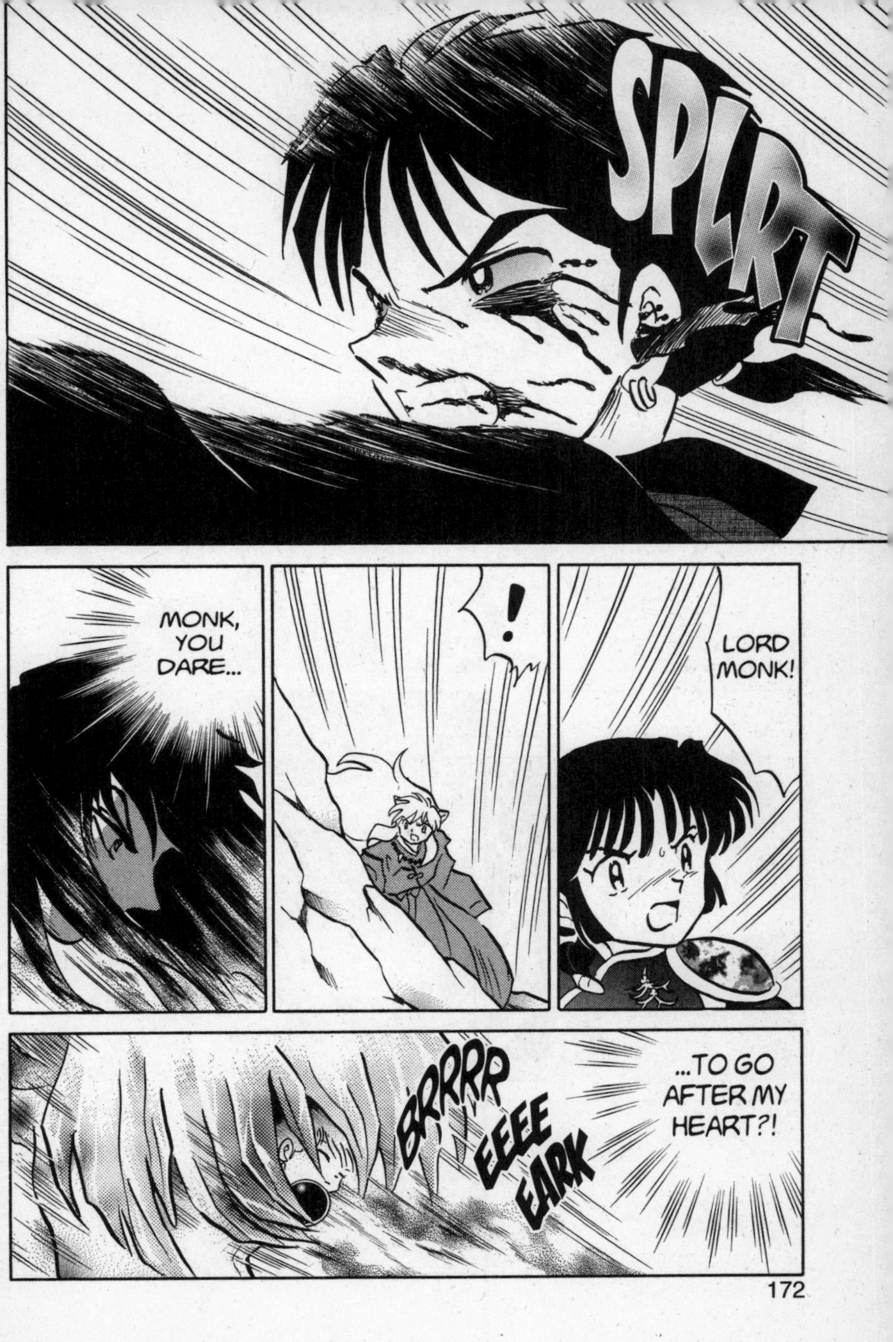
SPLRT
LORD MONK!
!
MONK, YOU DARE...
...TO GO AFTER MY HEART?!
BRRRR EEEE EARK

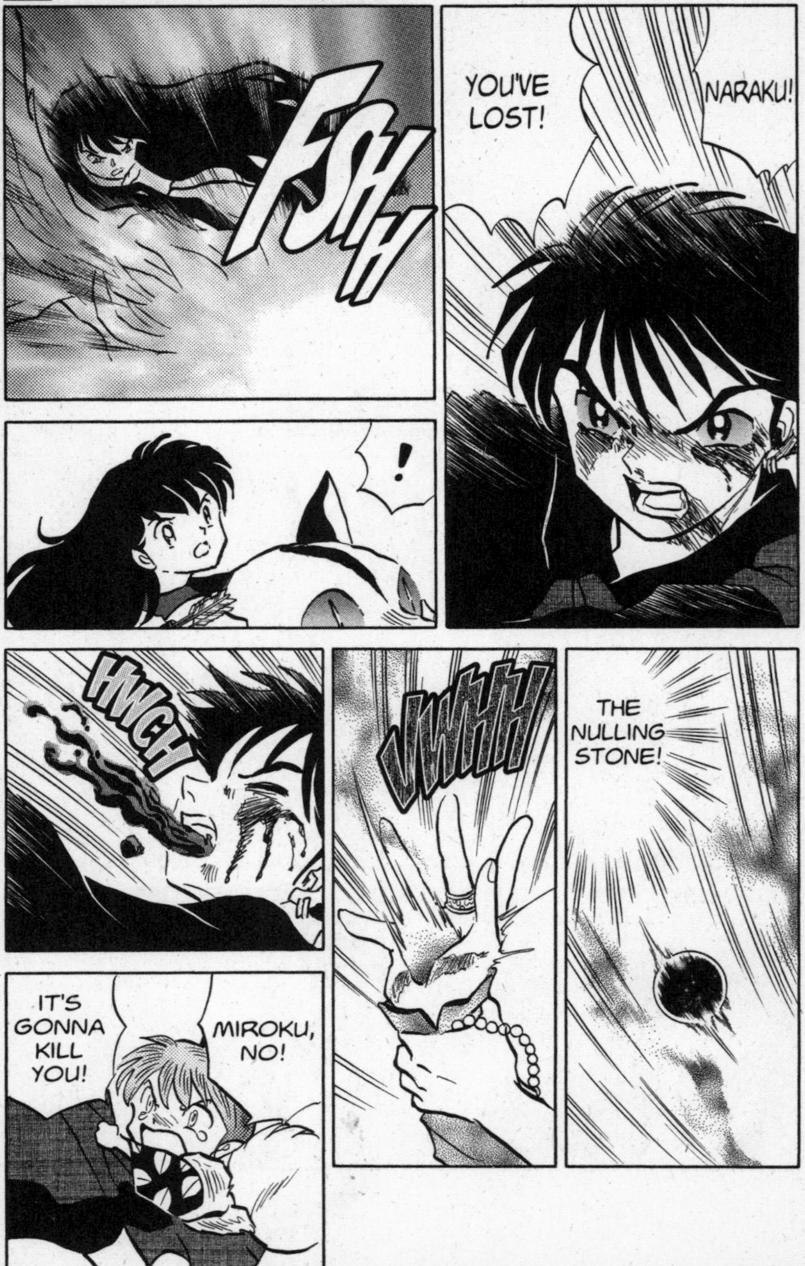
NARAKU!
YOU'VE LOST!
FSHH
!
THE NULLING STONE!
JWHH
HWCH!
MIROKU, NO!
IT'S GONNA KILL YOU!

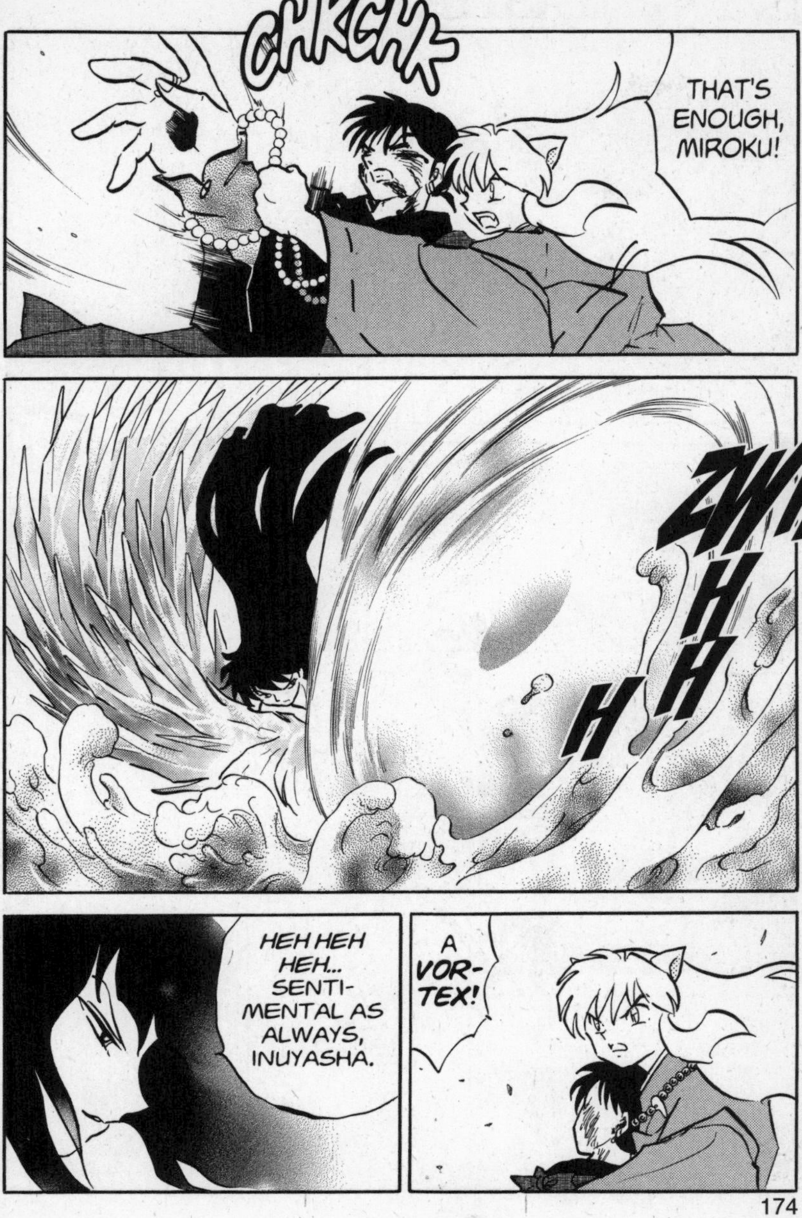
THAT'S ENOUGH, MIROKU!
CHKCHK
ZWHHHH
A VOR-TEX!
HEH HEH HEH... SENTI-MENTAL AS ALWAYS, INUYASHA.

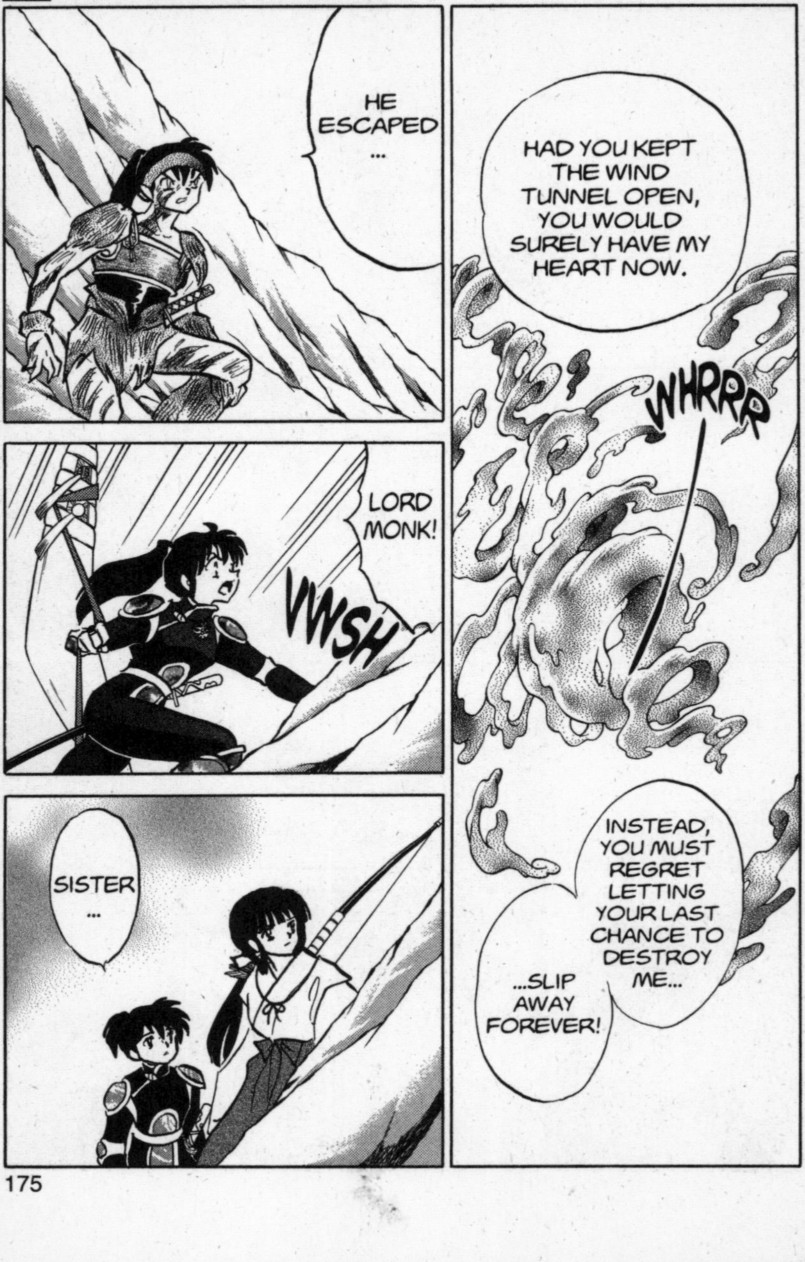
HAD YOU KEPT THE WIND TUNNEL OPEN, YOU WOULD SURELY HAVE MY HEART NOW.
WHRRR
INSTEAD, YOU MUST REGRET LETTING YOUR LAST CHANCE TO DESTROY ME...
...SLIP AWAY FOREVER!
HE ESCAPED ...
LORD MONK!
VWSH
SISTER ...

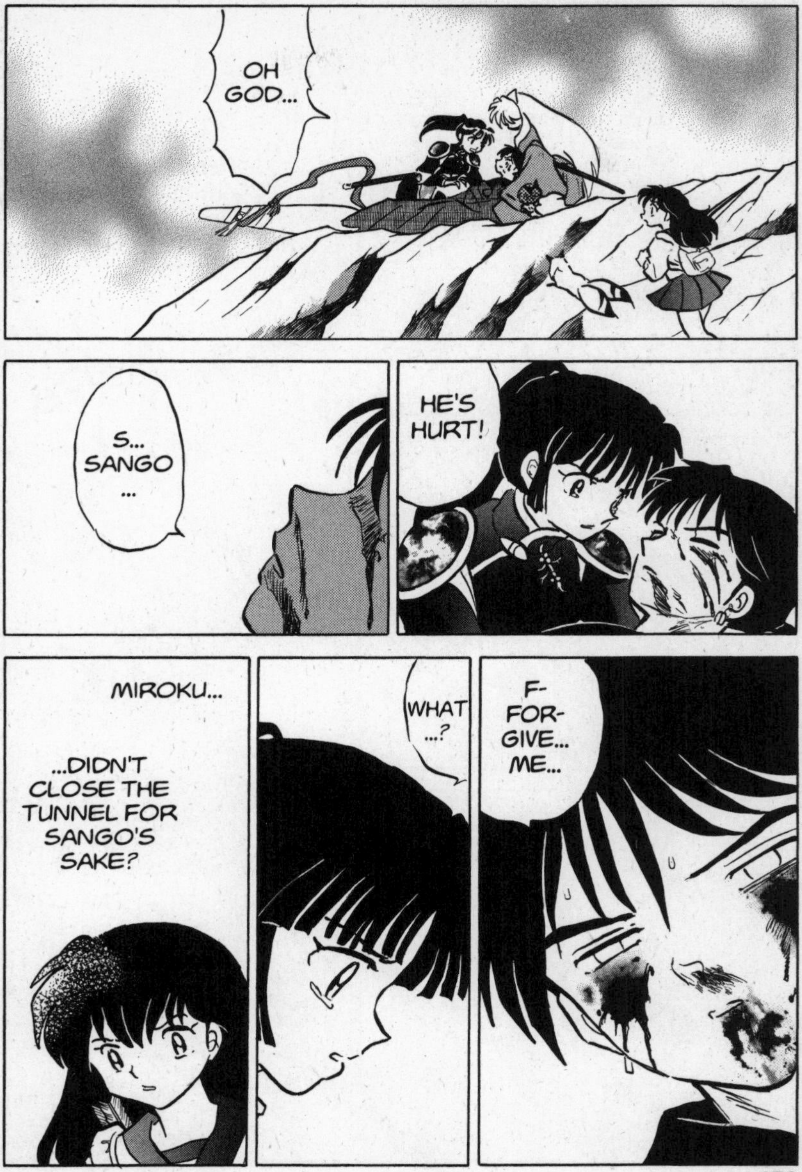
OH GOD...
HE'S HURT!
S... SANGO ...
F- FOR- GIVE... ME...
WHAT ...?
MIROKU...
...DIDN'T CLOSE THE TUNNEL FOR SANGO'S SAKE?

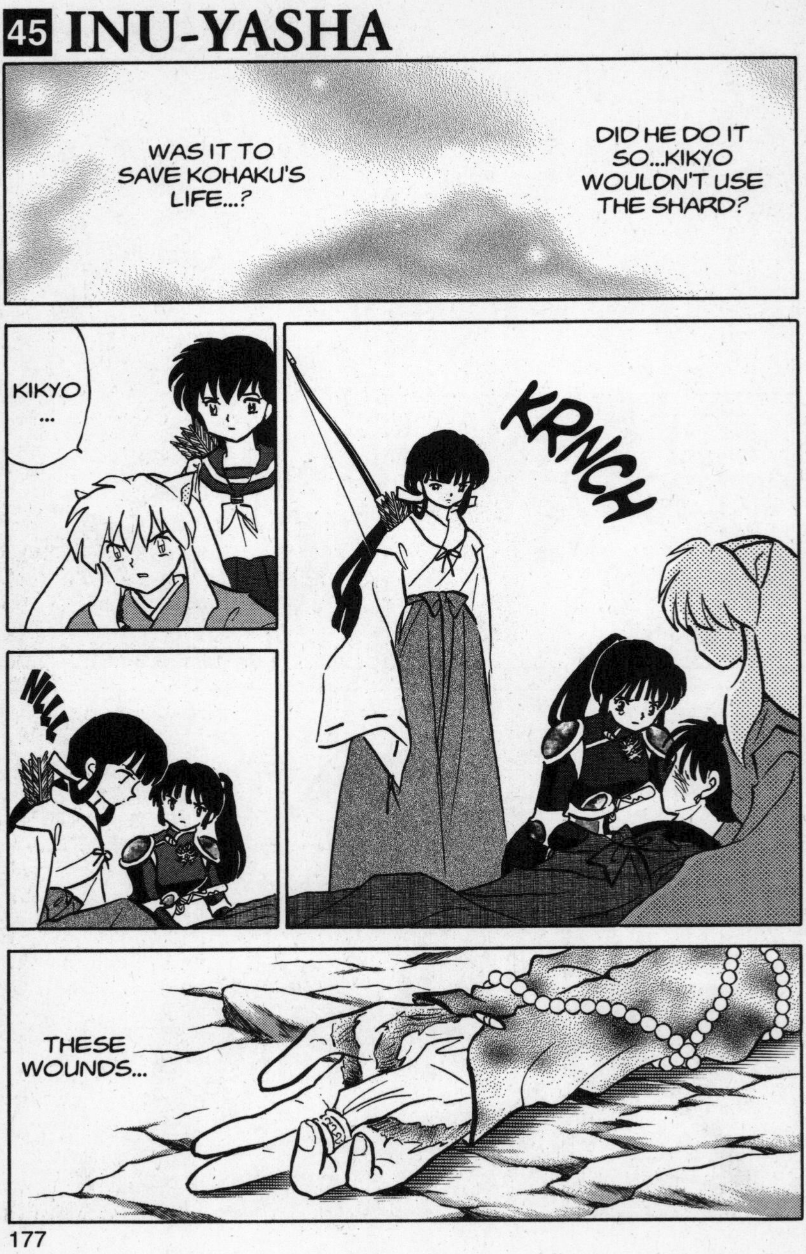
DID HE DO IT SO...KIKYO WOULDN'T USE THE SHARD?
WAS IT TO SAVE KOHAKU'S LIFE...?
KRNCH
KIKYO ...
NGLL
THESE WOUNDS...

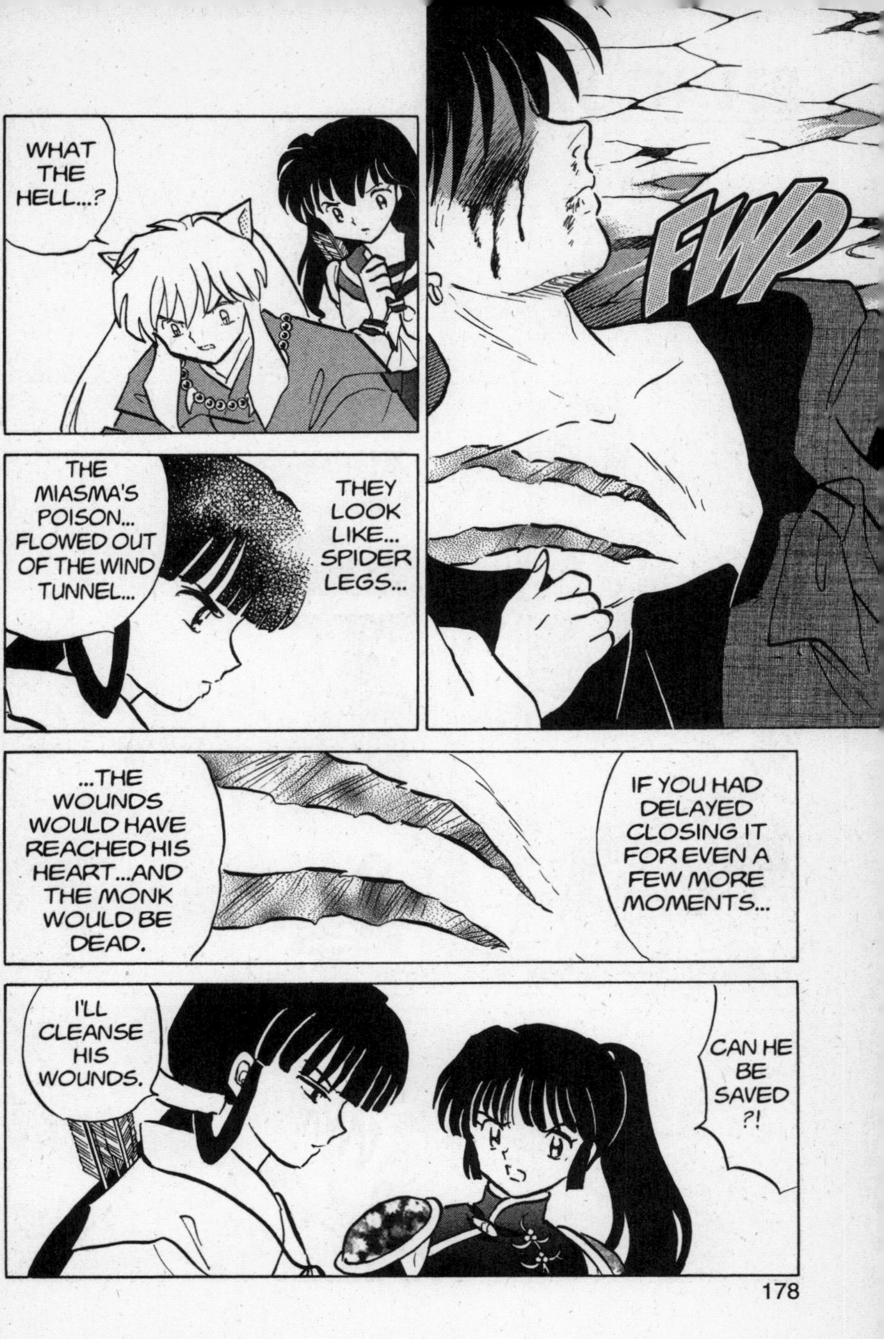
FWP
WHAT THE HELL...?
THEY LOOK LIKE... SPIDER LEGS...
THE MIASMA'S POISON... FLOWED OUT OF THE WIND TUNNEL...
IF YOU HAD DELAYED CLOSING IT FOR EVEN A FEW MORE MOMENTS...
...THE WOUNDS WOULD HAVE REACHED HIS HEART...AND THE MONK WOULD BE DEAD.
CAN HE BE SAVED?!
I'LL CLEANSE HIS WOUNDS.

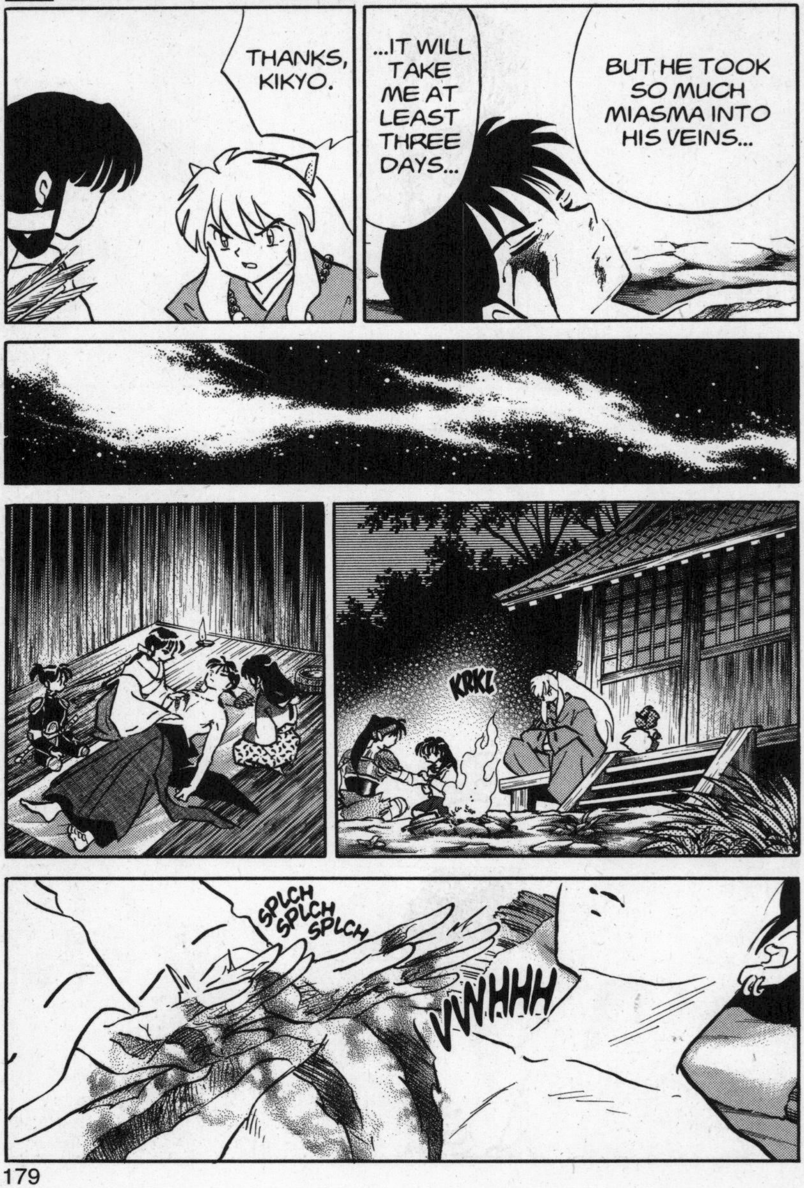
BUT HE TOOK SO MUCH MIASMA INTO HIS VEINS...
...IT WILL TAKE ME AT LEAST THREE DAYS...
THANKS, KIKYO.
KRKL
SPLCH SPLCH SPLCH
VWHHH

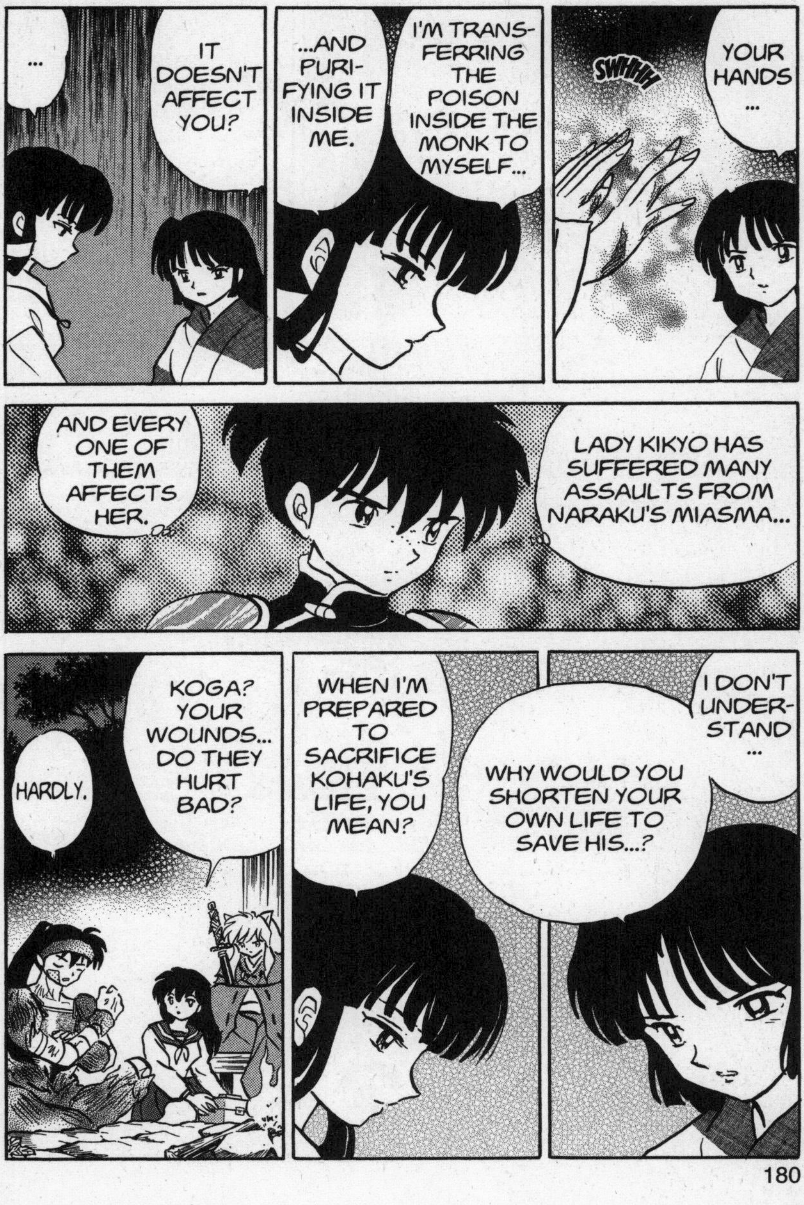
SWHHH
YOUR HANDS ...
I'M TRANSFERRING THE POISON INSIDE THE MONK TO MYSELF...
...AND PURIFYING IT INSIDE ME.
IT DOESN'T AFFECT YOU?
...
LADY KIKYO HAS SUFFERED MANY ASSAULTS FROM NARAKU'S MIASMA...
AND EVERY ONE OF THEM AFFECTS HER.
I DON'T UNDERSTAND ...
WHY WOULD YOU SHORTEN YOUR OWN LIFE TO SAVE HIS...?
WHEN I'M PREPARED TO SACRIFICE KOHAKU'S LIFE, YOU MEAN?
KOGA? YOUR WOUNDS... DO THEY HURT BAD?
HARDLY.

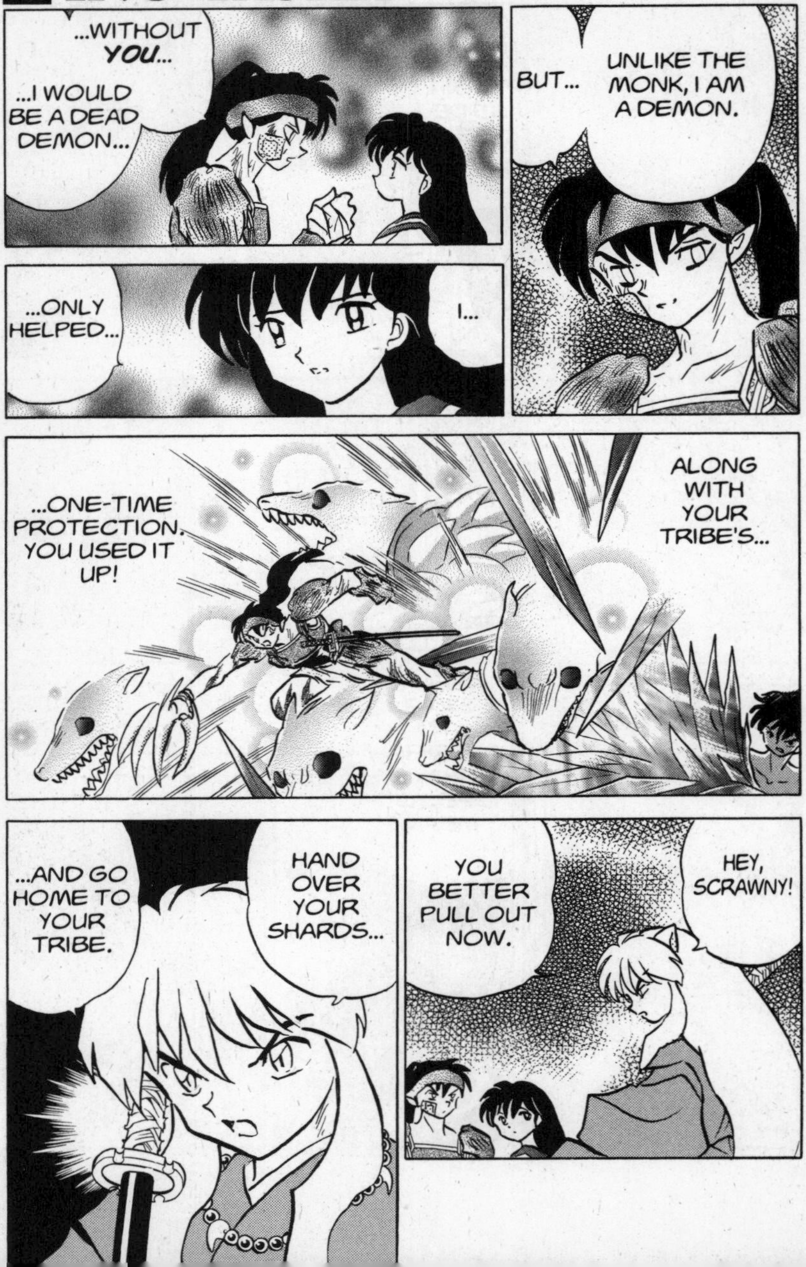
UNLIKE THE MONK, I AM A DEMON.
BUT...
...WITHOUT *YOU*...
...I WOULD BE A DEAD DEMON...
I...
...ONLY HELPED...
ALONG WITH YOUR TRIBE'S...
...ONE-TIME PROTECTION. YOU USED IT UP!
HEY, SCRAWNY!
YOU BETTER PULL OUT NOW.
HAND OVER YOUR SHARDS...
...AND GO HOME TO YOUR TRIBE.

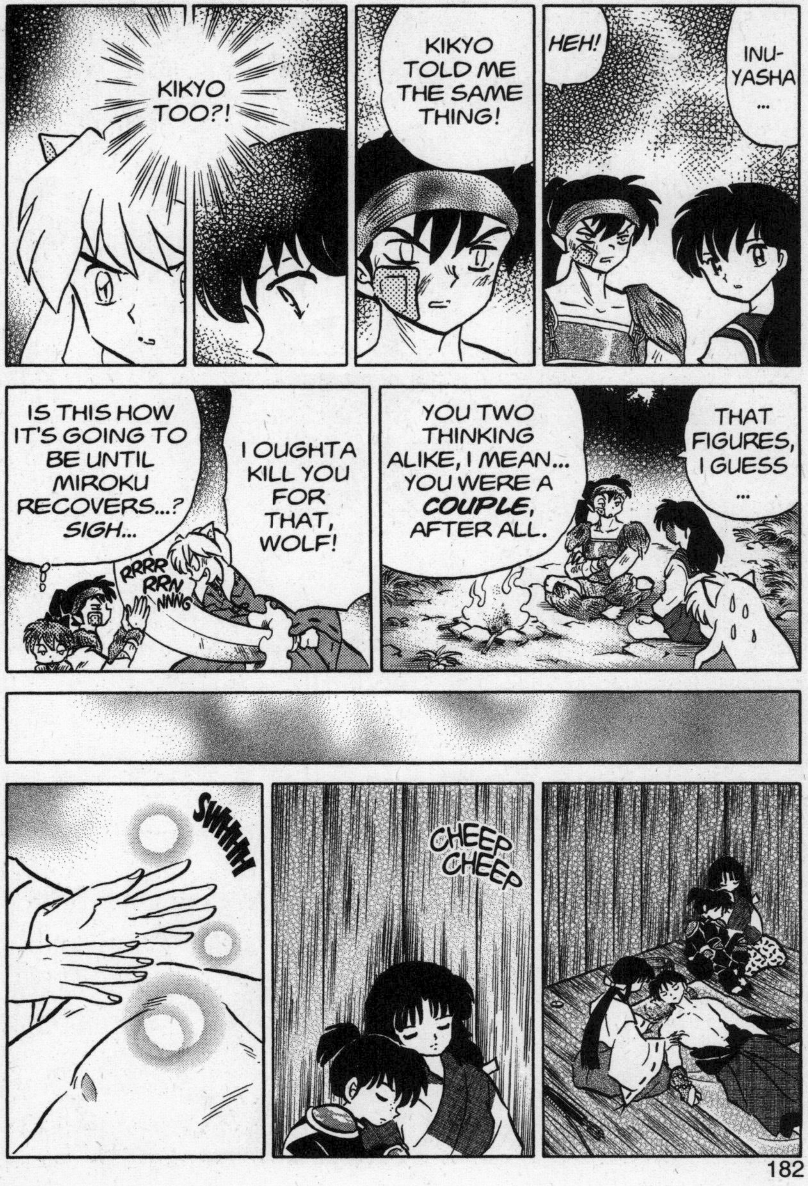
INU-YASHA ...
HEH!
KIKYO TOLD ME THE SAME THING!
KIKYO TOO?!
THAT FIGURES, I GUESS ...
YOU TWO THINKING ALIKE, I MEAN... YOU WERE A *COUPLE*, AFTER ALL.
I OUGHTA KILL YOU FOR THAT, WOLF!
IS THIS HOW IT'S GOING TO BE UNTIL MIROKU RECOVERS...? *SIGH...*
RRRR RRN NNNG
CHEEP CHEEP
SWHHHH

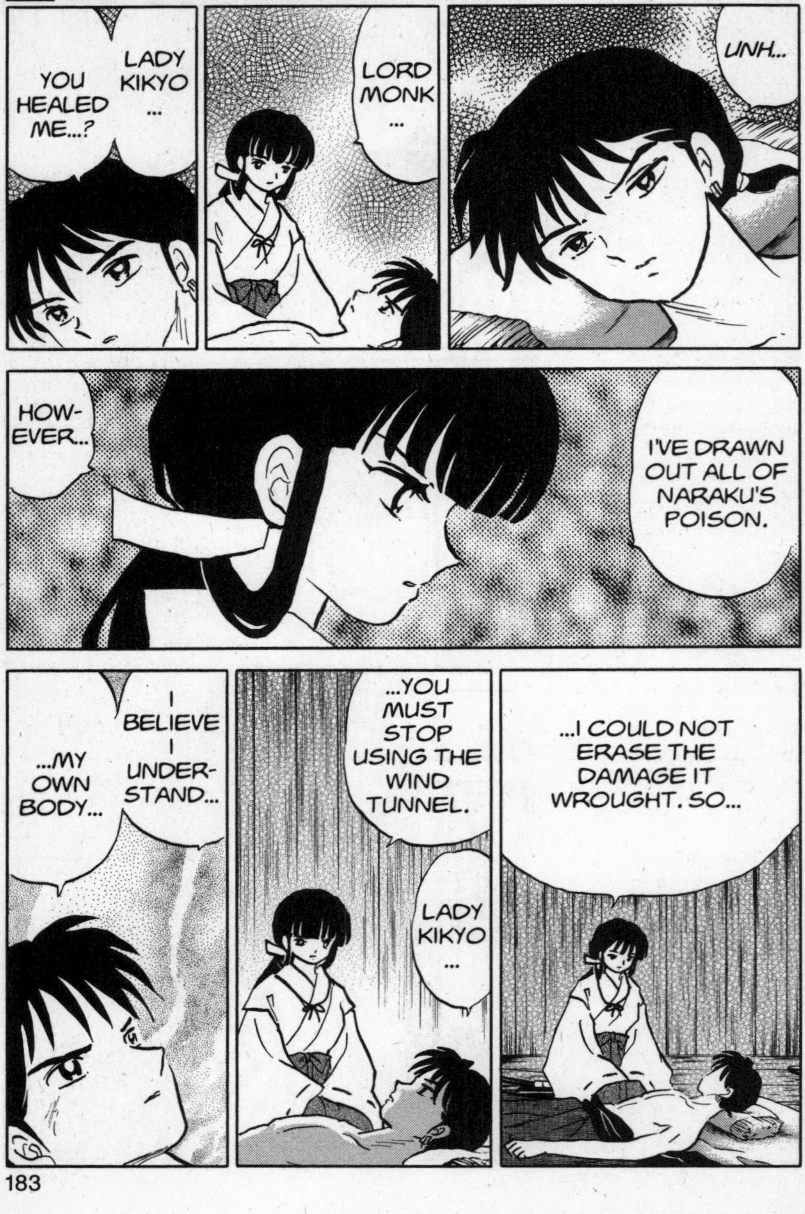
UNH...
LORD MONK ...
LADY KIKYO ...
YOU HEALED ME...?
I'VE DRAWN OUT ALL OF NARAKU'S POISON.
HOW-EVER...
...I COULD NOT ERASE THE DAMAGE IT WROUGHT. SO...
...YOU MUST STOP USING THE WIND TUNNEL.
LADY KIKYO ...
I BELIEVE I UNDER-STAND...
...MY OWN BODY...

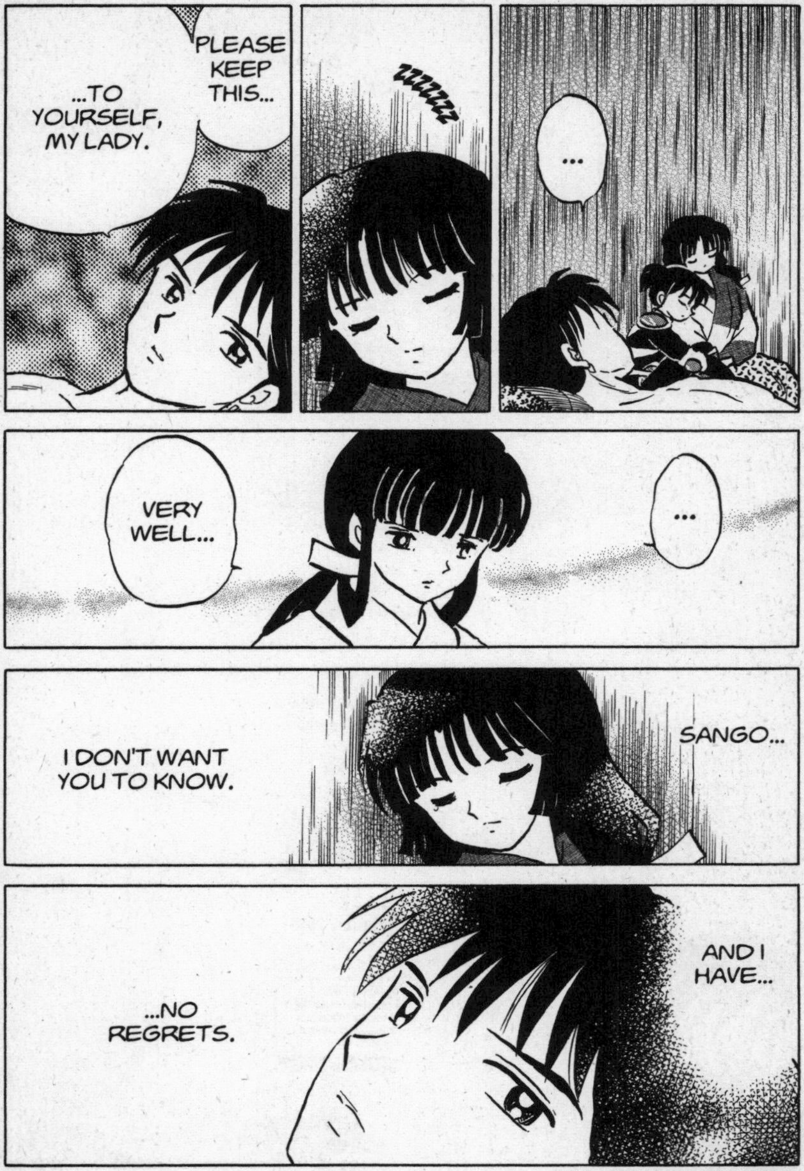
...
PLEASE KEEP THIS...
...TO YOURSELF, MY LADY.
...
VERY WELL...
SANGO...
I DON'T WANT YOU TO KNOW.
AND I HAVE...
...NO REGRETS.

TO BE CONTINUED...

INUYASHA

INUYASHA
VOL. 45
Shonen Sunday Edition

Story and Art by
RUMIKO TAKAHASHI

Original Japanese edition "INUYASHA"
published by SHOGAKUKAN Inc.

English Adaptation by Gerard Jones

Translation/Mari Morimoto
Touch-up Art & Lettering/Bill Schuch
Cover & Interior Graphic Design/Yuki Ameda
Editor/Annette Roman

VP, Production/Alvin Lu
VP, Sales & Product Marketing/Gonzalo Ferreyra
VP, Creative/Linda Espinosa
Publisher/Hyoe Narita

Printed in the U.S.A.

Published by VIZ Media, LLC
P.O. Box 77010
San Francisco, CA 94107

10 9 8 7 6 5 4 3 2 1
First printing, February 2010

RATED T+ FOR OLDER TEEN

PARENTAL ADVISORY
INUYASHA is rated T+ for Older Teen and is recommended for ages 16 and up. This volume contains violence.

ratings.viz.com

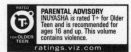

www.viz.com

WWW.SHONENSUNDAY.COM

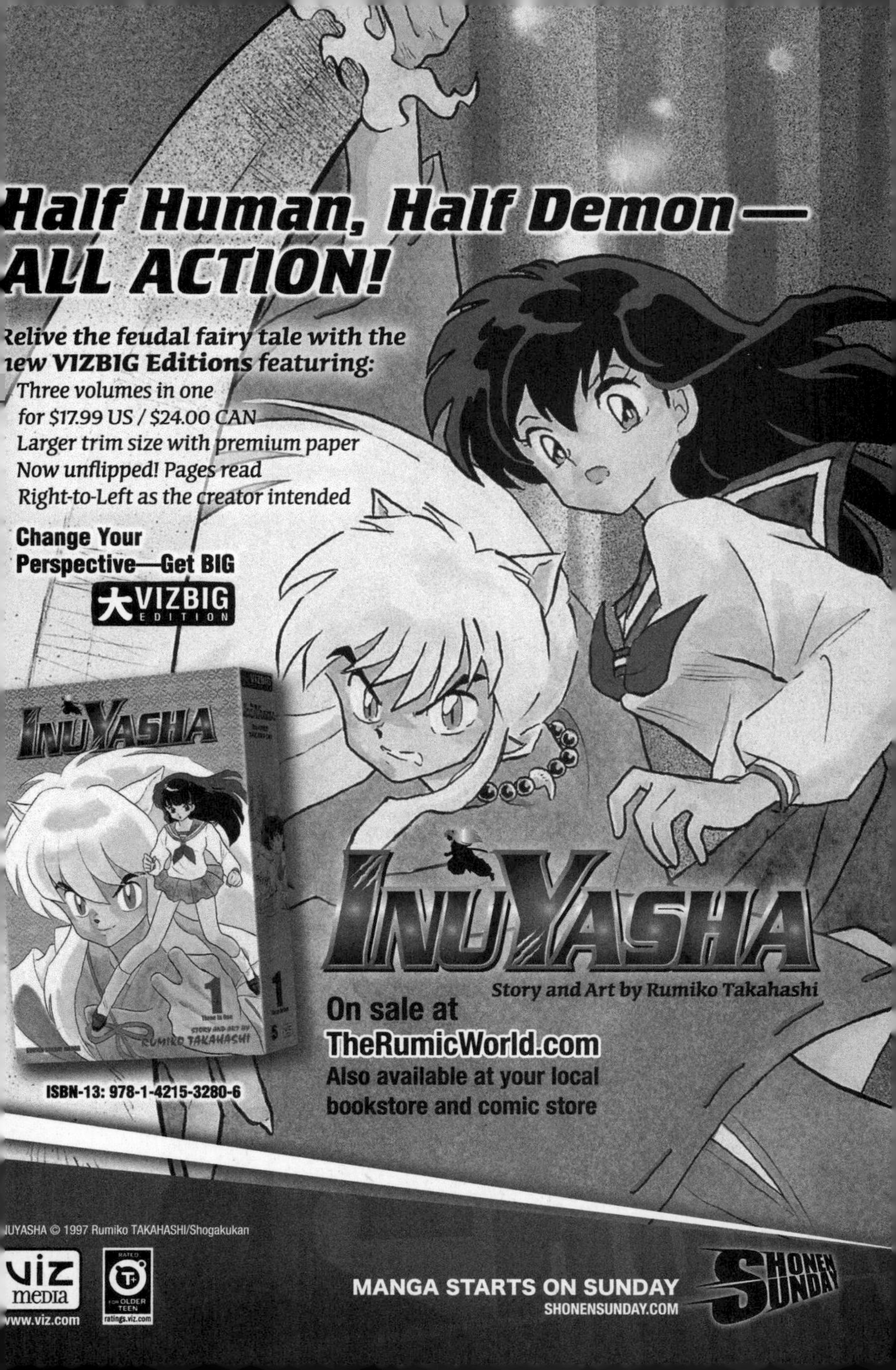

Half Human, Half Demon—
ALL ACTION!
Relive the feudal fairy tale with the new VIZBIG Editions featuring:
Three volumes in one for $17.99 US / $24.00 CAN
Larger trim size with premium paper
Now unflipped! Pages read Right-to-Left as the creator intended
Change Your Perspective—Get BIG
大 VIZBIG EDITION
INUYASHA
1
RUMIKO TAKAHASHI
ISBN-13: 978-1-4215-3280-6
INUYASHA
Story and Art by Rumiko Takahashi
On sale at
TheRumicWorld.com
Also available at your local bookstore and comic store
INUYASHA © 1997 Rumiko TAKAHASHI/Shogakukan
viz media
www.viz.com
RATED T+ FOR OLDER TEEN
ratings.viz.com
MANGA STARTS ON SUNDAY
SHONENSUNDAY.COM
SHONEN SUNDAY

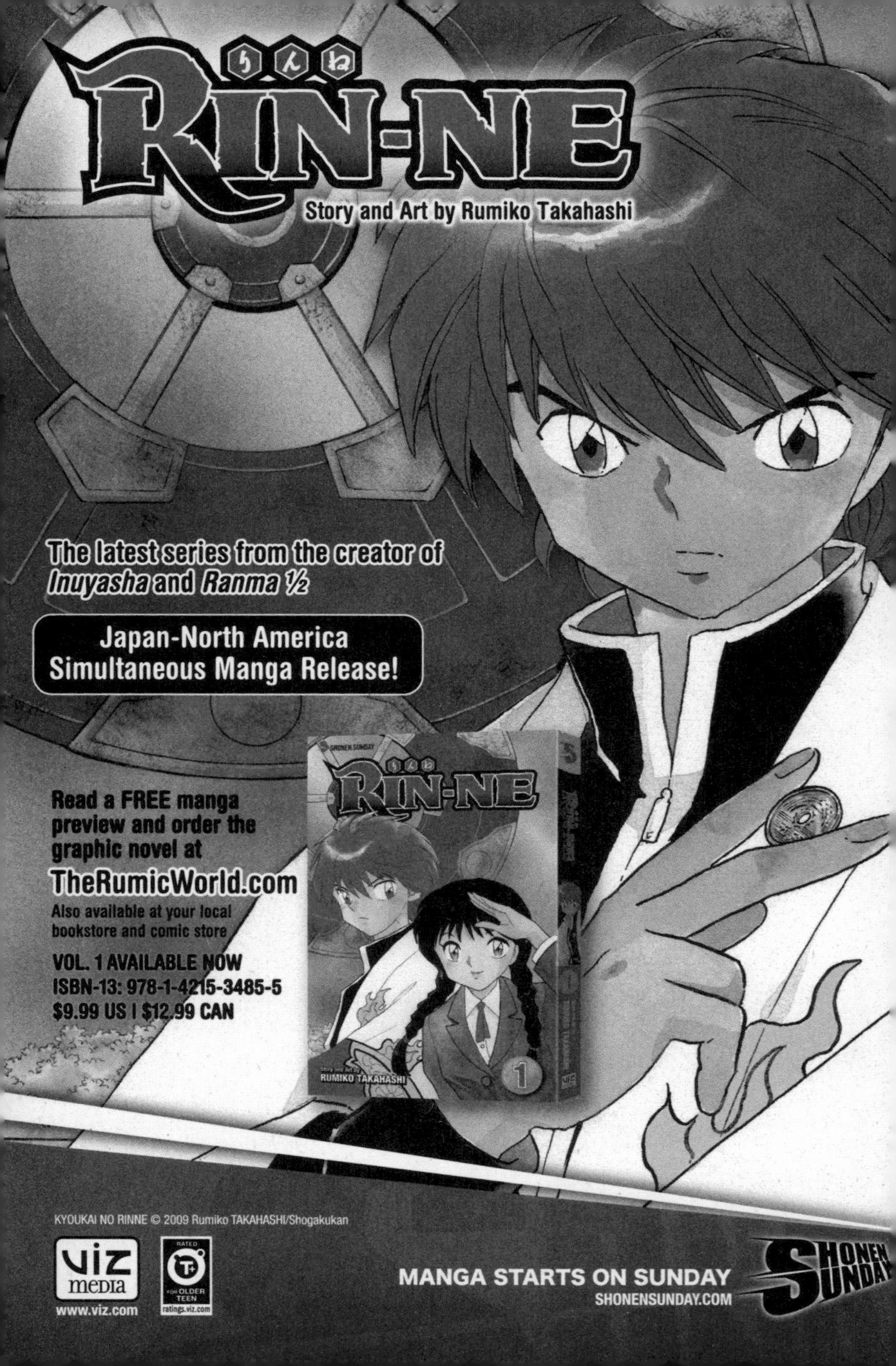

りんね
RIN-NE
Story and Art by Rumiko Takahashi
The latest series from the creator of
Inuyasha and Ranma ½
Japan-North America Simultaneous Manga Release!
Read a FREE manga preview and order the graphic novel at
TheRumicWorld.com
Also available at your local bookstore and comic store
VOL. 1 AVAILABLE NOW
ISBN-13: 978-1-4215-3485-5
$9.99 US | $12.99 CAN
SHONEN SUNDAY
RIN-NE
Story and Art by RUMIKO TAKAHASHI
1
KYOUKAI NO RINNE © 2009 Rumiko TAKAHASHI/Shogakukan
viz media
www.viz.com
RATED T+ FOR OLDER TEEN
ratings.viz.com
MANGA STARTS ON SUNDAY
SHONENSUNDAY.COM
SHONEN SUNDAY

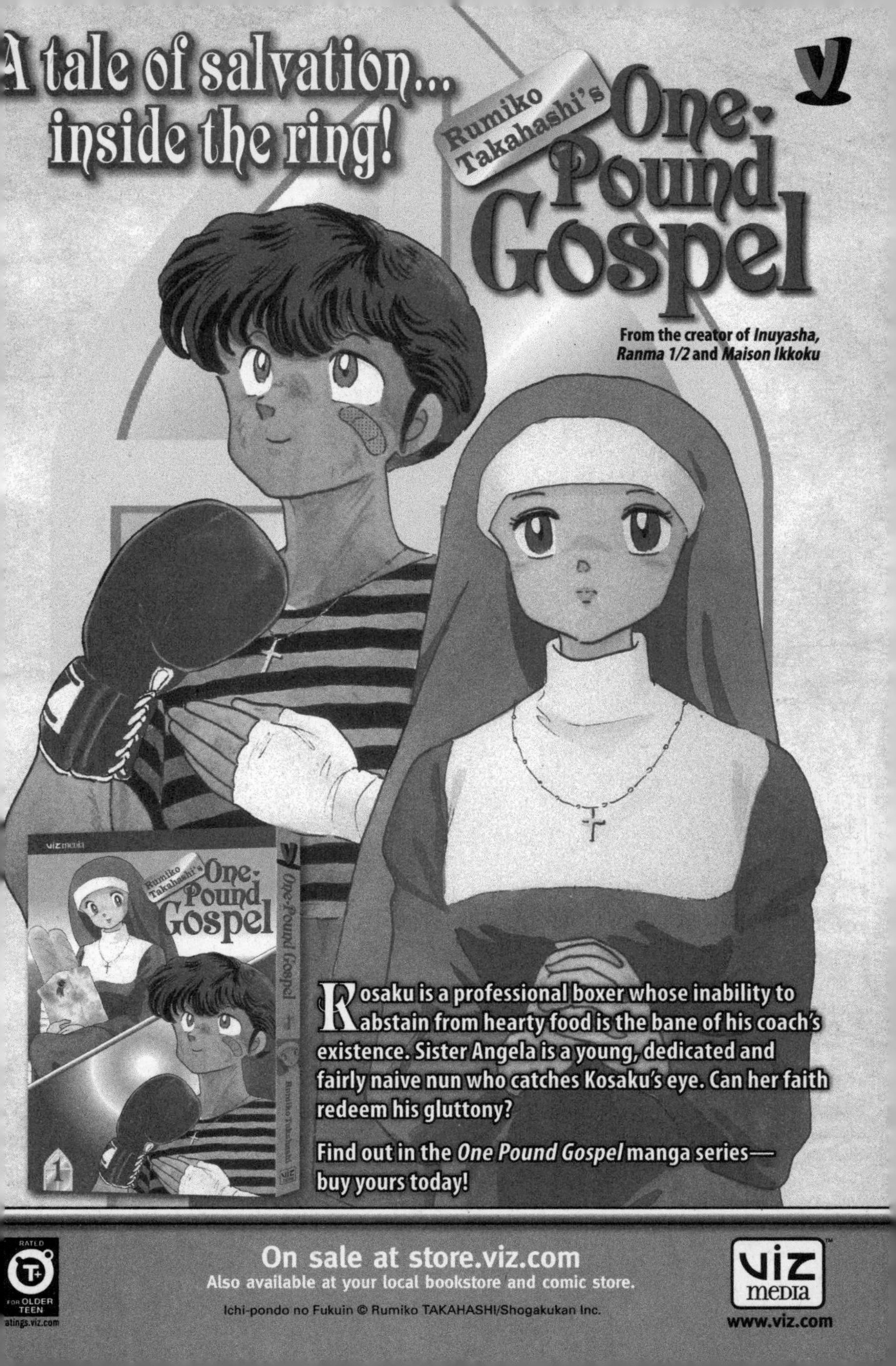
A tale of salvation...
inside the ring!
Rumiko Takahashi's One-Pound Gospel
From the creator of Inuyasha, Ranma 1/2 and Maison Ikkoku
viz media
Rumiko Takahashi's One-Pound Gospel
One-Pound Gospel 1
Rumiko Takahashi
Kosaku is a professional boxer whose inability to abstain from hearty food is the bane of his coach's existence. Sister Angela is a young, dedicated and fairly naive nun who catches Kosaku's eye. Can her faith redeem his gluttony?
Find out in the One Pound Gospel manga series— buy yours today!
RATED T+ FOR OLDER TEEN
atings.viz.com
On sale at store.viz.com
Also available at your local bookstore and comic store.
Ichi-pondo no Fukuin © Rumiko TAKAHASHI/Shogakukan Inc.
viz media
www.viz.com

A Comedy that Redefines a

Due to an unfortunate accident, when martial artist Ranma gets splashed with cold water, he becomes a buxom young girl! Hot water reverses the effect, but when blamed for offenses both real and imagined, and pursued by lovesick suitors of both genders, what's a half-boy, half-girl to do?

Ranma ½

A full TV season in each DVD box set

Only $119.98 each!

THE DIGITAL DOJO

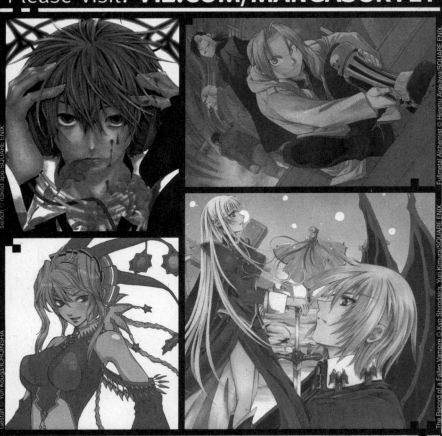

At Your Indentured Service

Hayate's parents are bad with money, so they sell his organs to pay their debts. Hayate doesn't like this plan, so he comes up with a new one—kidnap and ransom a girl from a wealthy family. Solid plan... so how did he end up as her butler?

Find out in *Hayate the Combat Butler*— buy the manga at store.viz.com!

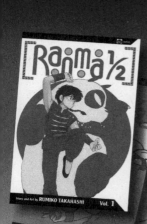